Modernism and Theory

Modernism and Theory boldly asks what role—if any—theory has to play in the new modernist studies. Separated into three sections, each with a clear introduction, this collection of new essays from leading critics outlines ongoing debates on the nature of modernist culture.

This collection

- examines aesthetic and methodological links between modernist literature and theory;
- addresses questions of the importance of theory to our understanding of 'modernism' and of modernism as a literary category;
- considers intersections of modernism and theory within ethics, ecocriticism and the avant-garde.

Concluding with an afterword from Fredric Jameson, the book makes use of an innovative dialogic format, offering a direct and engaging experience of the current debates in modernist studies.

Stephen Ross is Associate Professor of English and Cultural, Social, and Political Thought at the University of Victoria, where he teaches courses in modernism and theory. He is author of *Conrad and Empire* (University of Missouri Press, 2004), as well as numerous articles on modernism.

Modernism and Theory

A critical debate

Edited by
Stephen Ross

Routledge
Taylor & Francis Group

LONDON AND NEW YORK

First edition published 2009
by Routledge
2 Park Square, Milton Park, Abingdon, OX14 4RN

Simultaneously published in the USA and Canada
by Routledge
270 Madison Ave, New York, NY 10016

Routledge is an imprint of the Taylor & Francis Group, an informa business

Typeset in Baskerville by
Taylor & Francis Books
Printed and bound in Great Britain by
TJ International Ltd, Padstow, Cornwall

British Library Cataloguing in Publication Data
A catalogue record for this book is available from the British Library

Library of Congress Cataloging in Publication Data
Modernism and theory : a critical debate / edited by Stephen Ross. –
1st ed.
    p. cm.
  Includes bibliographical references and index.
  1. Modernism (Literature) 2. Modernism (Aesthetics) I. Ross,
  Stephen, 1970–
  PN56.M54M613 2008
700′.4112–
dc22   2008011223

ISBN 978-0-415-46156-6 (hbk)
ISBN 978-0-415-46157-3 (pbk)
ISBN 978-0-203-09110-4 (ebk)

Contents

Notes on contributors   viii
Acknowledgments   xi

Introduction: The missing link   1
STEPHEN ROSS

PART I
Theory's modernism: concrete connections   19

1   Rip the veil of the old vision across, and walk through the
    rent: thinking through affect in D. H. Lawrence and Deleuze
    and Guattari   23
    ANNELEEN MASSCHELEIN

    Deleuze and his sources
    Response to Anneleen Masschelein   40
    IAN BUCHANAN

2   Modernism, postmodernism, and the two sublimes of
    surrealism   49
    ROGER ROTHMAN

    The two sublimes, fourth time around
    Response to Roger Rothman   60
    ALLAN STOEKL

3   "What true project has been lost?" Modern art and Henri
    Lefebvre's *Critique of Everyday Life*   65
    THOMAS S. DAVIS

    Disdained everyday fields
    Response to Thomas S. Davis   80
    BEN HIGHMORE

4 Time and its countermeasures: modern messianisms in
   Woolf, Benjamin, and Agamben   86
   HILARY THOMPSON

   Time's exception
   Response to Hilary Thompson   99
   PAMELA CAUGHIE

PART II
Modernism's theory: abstract affiliations   113

5 The persistence of the old regime: late modernist form in the
   postmodern period   117
   NEIL LEVI

   In the time of theory, the timeliness of modernism
   Response to Neil Levi   127
   GLENN WILLMOTT

6 Invisible times: modernism as ruptural unity   137
   C. D. BLANTON

   More than a hint of desperation – historicizing modernism
   Response to C. D. Blanton   153
   MORAG SHIACH

7 "This new evolution of art": Adorno's modernism as a
   re-orientation of aesthetics   156
   OLEG GELIKMAN

   What's new? On Adorno and the modernist aesthetics of
   novelty
   Response to Oleg Gelikman   171
   MARTIN JAY

8 Fables of progression: modernism, modernity, narrative   176
   ANDREW JOHN MILLER

   Modernism and the moment of defeat
   Response to Andrew John Miller   190
   SCOTT MCCRACKEN

PART III
Forum   195

9   Aesthetics   197
     CHARLES F. LTIERI

10   Ethics   208
     MELBA CUDDY-KEANE

11   Green   219
     BONNIE KIME SCOTT

12   Avant-garde   225
     JANE GOLDMAN

13   Theory   237
     SUSAN STANFORD FRIEDMAN

     Afterword   247
     FREDRIC JAMESON

     Index   253

Contributors

Charles F. Altieri is Stageberg Professor of English at the University of California, Berkeley. He has published a number of books, including *Postmodernism Now: Essays on Contemporaneity in the Arts* (1998) and *The Particulars of Rapture: An Aesthetic of Affects* (2003).

C. D. Blanton is Assistant Professor of English at the University of California, Berkeley. He writes on modernism and modern poetry generally, and has co-edited *Pocket Epics: British Poetry after Modernism* and *A Blackwell Companion to Post-War British and Irish Poetry*. He is currently working on late modernist long forms.

Ian Buchanan is Professor of Critical and Cultural Theory at Cardiff University. His books include *Fredric Jameson: Live Theory* (2007), and *Deleuzism* (2000). He has published widely on the work of Deleuze, de Certeau and Jameson, and is founding editor of *Deleuze Studies*.

Pamela Caughie is Professor of English at Loyola University, Chicago. Her published books include *Passing and Pedagogy* (1999), *Virginia Woolf and Postmodernism* (1991), and, as editor, *Virginia Woolf in the Age of Mechanical Reproductions*. Her articles have appeared in *PMLA*, *Differences*, and *Modernism/ Modernity*, among others.

Melba Cuddy-Keane is Professor of English and a Northrop Frye Scholar at the University of Toronto. She has published widely on modernism, globalism, narrative, and culture, including the acclaimed volume *Virginia Woolf, the Intellectual and the Public Sphere* (2003) and the Harcourt annotated edition of *Between the Acts* (2008).

Thomas S. Davis is an Assistant Professor of English at the Ohio State University. His research interests include literary modernism, philosophical aesthetics, and political theory. He is currently working on a book project entitled "Distressed Histories: Late Modernism and Everyday Life, 1929–1945."

Susan Stanford Friedman is Virginia Woolf Professor of English and Women's Studies at the University of Wisconsin-Madison, co-editor of the journal *Contemporary Women's Writing*, and author of *Mappings: Feminism and the*

Cultural Geographies of Encounter (1998), books on H. D. and Joyce, and articles on modernism, diaspora, feminism, and world literature.

Oleg Gelikman is Assistant Professor of Comparative Literature at the Soka University of America. He has published articles and reviews in journals such as *Angelaki*, *boundary2*, *PMLA*, and *Modern Language Notes*.

Jane Goldman is Reader in English Literature at the University of Glasgow, and General Editor of the Cambridge University Press Edition of *The Writings of Virginia Woolf*. She has published a number of works on Woolf and on modernism, including *Modernism, 1910–1945: Image to Apocalypse* (2004) and *Modernism: An Anthology of Sources and Documents* (1998).

Ben Highmore is Reader in Media Studies at the University of Sussex. His research concerns the culture of daily life, and his published books include *Cityscapes* (2005), *Michel de Certeau* (2002), and *Everyday Life and Cultural Theory: An Introduction* (2002). He is presently at work on a project entitled *A Passion for Cultural Studies*.

Fredric Jameson is the William A. Lane Jr. Professor of Comparative Literature and Romance Studies at Duke University, where he directs the Institute for Critical Theory. Author of *Postmodernism, or, The Cultural Logic of Late Capitalism* (Duke University Press, 1991) and *A Singular Modernity* (Verso, 2002), his most recent works include *Archeologies of the Future* (Verso, 2005) and *The Modernist Papers* (Verso, 2007).

Martin Jay is the Sidney Hellman Ehrman Professor of History at the University of California, Berkeley. His published works include *Cultural Semantics* (1998), *Refractions of Violence* (2003), and *Songs of Experience* (2004). Professor Jay's books have been widely translated, appearing in over fourteen languages worldwide.

Neil Levi is Associate Professor of English at Drew University. He is co-editor (with Michael Rothberg) of *The Holocaust: Theoretical Readings* (2003) and has published articles in such journals in *October*, *New German Critique*, and *History & Memory*. His book *Modernism, Dirt, and the Jews* is forthcoming from Fordham University Press.

Scott McCracken is Professor of English at Keele University in Staffordshire. His main research areas are literature and culture 1880–1920, modernism, gender, critical theory, and popular fiction. His most recent publication is *Masculinities, Modernist Fiction and the Urban Public Sphere* (Manchester University Press, 2007).

Anneleen Masschelein is Professor of Literary Theory at K. U. Leuven and Postdoctoral Fellow at FWO-Vlaanderen, both in Belgium. She is author of *The Unconcept* (2008) and co-editor for the journal *Image and Narrative*.

Andrew John Miller is Associate Professor of English Studies at the Université de Montréal. He is author of *Modernism and the Crisis of Sovereignty* (2008), and also of numerous articles on modernism and theory. He is currently completing a book on the geopolitics of late modernist exile.

Stephen Ross is Associate Professor of English and Cultural, Social, and Political Thought at the University of Victoria, where he teaches courses in modernism and theory. He is author of *Conrad and Empire* (2004), as well as numerous articles on modernism.

Roger Rothman is the Samuel H. Kress Chair and Assistant Professor of Art History at Bucknell University, Pennsylvania. He has published articles on Cubism, Dada, and Surrealism and is currently completing a book on the paintings and writings of Salvador Dalí entitled *Little Things Prick: Salvador Dalí, 1927–1940*.

Bonnie Kime Scott is Chair of Women's Studies at San Diego State University. She has published widely on gender in modernist literature and culture. Recent books include *Selected Letters of Rebecca West* (2000), *Gender in Modernism: New Geographies, Complex Intersections* (2007), and *Gender and Modernism*, 4 volumes (Routledge, 2008).

Morag Shiach is Professor of Cultural History and Vice-Principal of Teaching and Learning at Queen Mary, University of London. Her research interests are in the cultural history of the late nineteenth and early twentieth centuries. She is editor of *The Cambridge Companion to the Modernist Novel* (2007).

Allan Stoekl is Professor of French and Comparative Literature at Penn State University. He is the author of numerous books and essays on French literary theory and intellectual history, focusing on Georges Bataille, Maurice Blanchot, and Jean-Paul Sartre. His most recent book is *Bataille's Peak* (2007).

Hilary Thompson is Visiting Assistant Professor of English at Bowdoin College in Brunswick, Maine. She has published articles in the *Virginia Woolf Miscellany* and the anthology *The Asian Gothic: A Critical Reader* (2007).

Glenn Willmott is Professor of English at Queen's University in Canada. He has published widely on Canadian and modernist literatures; his books include *Modernist Goods: Primitivism, the Market, and the Gift* (2008), *Unreal Country* (2002), and *McLuhan, or Modernism in Reverse* (1996).

Acknowledgments

From its inception, this project has benefited from generous intellectual and material support from a wide range of people. First, I'd like to thank the University of Victoria for the study leave that gave me the time to formulate the project, and my colleagues in the English department for their support, especially G. Kim Blank, Christopher Douglas, Cheryl Suzack, Allan Mitchell, and Robert Miles. For their early encouragement, Stephen Scobie, Marjorie Perloff, Jean-Michel Rabaté, and Andreas Huyssen, as well as all those who responded to the initial call for papers, deserve thanks. Thomas Saverance Davis, James Gifford, Rahul Sapra, and David Cecchetto provided stimulating conversation about the project throughout; and Emily Blacker, Tara Thomson, and particularly Sarah Mead-Willis provided essential research assistance. I'd especially like to thank the contributors, whose stimulating essays have made the volume all I could have hoped for. The respondents to the eight papers in the first two sections of the book, and the contributors to the Forum in Part III in particular merit thanks; their presence here speaks of the generosity and devotion to critical dialogue that are essential to scholarly inquiry. Especially helpful in this regard have been Susan Stanford Friedman, Charles Altieri, Glenn Willmott, and Melba Cuddy-Keane, without whose timely encouragement and suggestions the introduction may still be languishing on my desktop. Thanks also to Vasiliki Koloctroni and the other, anonymous, reader for Routledge; and to Polly Dodson and Emma Nugent, who have been unfailingly gracious and efficient in guiding the volume through to completion. Finally, I'd like to thank my wife and daughter, Stephanie and Kathleen, for putting up with my obsession with this book for the last three years.

Introduction

The missing link

Stephen Ross

The advent of the new modernist studies has been a boon for scholars of twentieth-century literature and culture. Any consensus about modernism in the singular has given way to numerous and disparate understandings of modernisms in the plural, as the old geographical, temporal, and material limits on what qualified as modernism have been determinedly dismantled. Scholars now work with new materials, new regions, and new questions, recognizing that all cultural production, and not just the monuments of Pound, Eliot, Woolf, Lawrence, Joyce, *et al.*, must be taken into account. This energizing turn has reopened modernism to a more comprehensive gaze, taking in the full range of culture from roughly 1890 to 1950: journals and magazines, manifestoes, Canadian modernism, transnational modernism, realist writing, contemporary science and philosophy, writing by women and people of color, vaudeville shows, postcards, advertising, radio shows, commercial films, spiritualism, sports, toys, cookbooks, etc. Behind all of this is a renewed vision of modernism as a variegated response to a manifold modernity. Modernism is thus recast by the new modernist studies as a cultural formation occurring in different forms, in different times, and in different places, as a particular instantiation of "intelligence, complexity, and curiosity" (Mao and Walkowitz 2006: 16) that recognizes its own historicity and challenges prevailing pieties. The interactions charted in such work have transformed our understanding of modernism, and rejuvenated a field that had become moribund by the end of the twentieth century.

This diversification of modernist studies has produced an interesting elision, however: theory has been forgotten. Perhaps because it belongs to the same realm of the "high" as did canonical modernism, perhaps because it is seen as an outdated instrument whose usefulness has been superseded by a return to the archive and historicism,[1] theory has been marginalized in the new modernist studies. The ironies attending this elision verge on modernist absurdity: theory's challenge to predominant notions of the literary, canon formation, disciplinary formations, high and low culture, progress, civilization, and imperialism helped make the new modernist studies possible. Also, theory's concern with globalization, imperialism, gender and sex roles, race and racism, reason and superstition, enlightenment and benightedness, sovereignty and slavery, margins and peripheries, and ethical complexity continues, albeit in a different register, modernism's already articulated concerns. Modernism's critique of modernity animated theory's invention of postmodernity, while theory's anti-foundational stance extended modernism's indeterminacy, linguistic complexity, and reflexivity. The relationship between them is unique; though certain specific theories no doubt have particular relevance for other literary movements or eras (e.g. the New Historicism and the renaissance), theory *per se*—that massive influx of challenges to conventions of form, aesthetics, ideology, race, class, sex, gender, institutions, and subjectivity dating from the mid-1960s to the 1990s—is integrally bound to modernism. Theory directly follows, shares a vast range of concerns with, and develops the aesthetics of modernism. Its philosophical roots are either modernist (e.g. Heidegger, Husserl, Sartre, Wittgenstein) or shared by modernism (e.g. Kant, Hegel, Schopenhauer, Nietzsche, Kierkegaard). Modernist writing thinks theoretically and theory writes modernistically; they are not simply interestingly coincidental phenomena, but mutually sustaining aspects of the same project. This does not only mean that psychoanalysis is a quintessentially modernist theory, or that formalism (Russian and New Critical alike) emerges alongside modernist art's emphasis on technique and significant form; that Bakhtin, Benjamin, Adorno, Bergson, William James, and Wittgenstein are all modernists. It also means that phenomenology, existentialism, third-wave feminism, queer studies, postcolonial theory, Lacanian psychoanalysis, structuralist Marxism and neo- or post-Marxism, structuralism and post-structuralism do not merely parallel the development of modernism, but partake of it. Theory continues modernism's concerns, aesthetics, and critical energies. The same cannot be said of any other literary movement: the affinities between modernism and theory are wide, deep, and pervasive—and they demand exploration. There is a massive amount of work to be done here, extending the boundaries of modernism even further, and enhancing our understanding of the unique affinity between modernism and theory. If we are truly to understand either of them, modernism and theory simply must be thought together.

In this vein, *Modernism and Theory* has three objectives: (1) to continue the new modernist revolution by showing that theory is modernism's key continuation, (2) to redress the misperceptions of modernism installed by theory, and by the same token (3) to redress theory's marginalization within the new modernist studies. These objectives necessitate dealing with the "intelligence, complexity, and curiosity" modernism and theory hold in common, as well as confronting the problems created by theory's dismissal of modernism, if we are to retain significant elements of both that we risk losing in the rush to bring low all that was once "high." In this light, the literary component in *Modernism and Theory* focuses predominantly on canonical and recognized authors, since their work has been the primary target of theory's reductive characterization of modernism. This collection similarly focuses for the most part on prominent Western theorists, since it was in their name that theory built its reputation, in large part by recasting high modernism in a negative mould. The following essays thus concern such familiar names as Eliot, Stevens, Lawrence, Woolf, Bataille, Breton, Derrida, Deleuze, Agamben, Foucault, Adorno, and Benjamin, but their implications are incredibly far-reaching. Modernist modes of thought run throughout experimental and traditional forms, canonical and uncanonical works, and are dispersed variously throughout the world. Our project begins with the work of undoing established and rigidified assumptions to open the whole to new speculative inquiry. *Modernism and Theory* accordingly participates in the new modernist project of expanding modernist studies not only by engaging further materials but also by returning to and rereading the old. This double movement allows us to discover new dimensions in modernism and also to recover dimensions lost in the late twentieth-century turn away from modernism. To understand the twists and turns by which the current state of play has been arrived at, we need first to review the complicated history of modernism and theory, a narrative of repeated attempts to break with the past that nonetheless depends upon a profound, if occulted, continuity.

At the heart of the affinity between modernism and theory is a peculiar narrative strategy, a repeated story of critique that modernism and theory tell themselves to legitimize their difference from their predecessors. Paul de Man maintains that this move is in fact the essence of modernity:

> Although it is in the nature of modernity to be without precedent, the phenomenon of modernity itself is by no means unique: "modern" movements, each with a distinctive content of their own, occur again and again, and become the very articulations of history. It is characteristic of periods that live off the capital accumulated by their predecessors, so to speak, that they would think of their era as the only one worthy of being called truly modern.
>
> (de Man 1989 [1965]: 137)

Jameson builds on this to claim both that "modernity is not a concept, philosophical or otherwise, but a narrative category" and that "we cannot not periodize" (Jameson 2002: 40, 29). That is, although modernity and its attendants (Enlightenment, modernism, postmodernism, theory) are narrative categories, and thus interchangeable with other narrative categories, narrative itself is the inevitable means by which we attempt to make sense of the Real of history: we don't have to narrate the way we do, but we do have to narrate. For our purposes here, perhaps the most important way we narrate history through periodization is the modern. Like modernity, the modern is not a concept, but a trope that names a break with the past and establishes the current moment as qualitatively distinct and new: it is a fundamental means by which cultural moments narrate their own sense of singularity.

For modernism and theory both, this narrative technique depends upon reinventing/reviving a spirit of critique, particularly the critique of modernity (though modernity itself is differently construed by modernism and theory, and indeed by specific modernists and theorists). Modernism and theory's appropriations of the power of critique both emerge from and orient themselves in relation to the Enlightenment, and follow a logic of misprision. This logic, traced by Harold Bloom in *The Anxiety of Influence*, describes how poets willfully

misinterpret their predecessors to open space for their own creations. The better
the poet, the stronger the misreading, the more he or she supersedes his or her
predecessor (or appears to), and the more original he or she seems. Each misreading becomes the necessary condition for producing a new narrative, one that
will include the previous narrative in a distorted form that validates the progression to the new. Distortion is not fabrication, though: each misreading can
only function as it does because it is partly true; were it wholly false, the misreading would be glaring and the narrative built on it would lack validity.
Importantly, each such transition constitutes a shift in narrative perspective
within a common story and not the inauguration of a new story with each
chapter break; each repetition of misprisial logic takes us from one version of
events to another as each subsequent narrator wrests control of the narrative
from her predecessor and recasts the story to validate what comes next. This
cycle of narrative production/misreading/narrative production circumscribes a
line of intellectual development from the Enlightenment to the present, a line
persuasively linked to the form of the manifesto by Janet Lyon, and which I outline
in a somewhat different vein below. And what follows is undeniably an outline; my objective is not by any means to be exhaustive but to contextualize the
present volume's critical intervention and situate its essays in a genealogy of
critique. Doing so in the space I have necessitates broad strokes and almost
guarantees additional misprisions, but these are necessary if not wholly accep-
table risks for clarifying the nature of *Modernism and Theory*'s intervention into
contemporary modernist studies.

The first stop in this genealogy is the Enlightenment. Originating in the late
seventeenth and early eighteenth centuries with the rise of empiricism and a
reinvigorated humanism, the Enlightenment produced massive discontent with
the social, political, and cultural order of the *ancien régime*. Popular frustration at the
slowness with which social change followed economic change (generated by
the explosion of imperialism and the first full manifestations of capitalism),
coupled with an intellectual context that privileged human reason's capacity to
understand the world, set the stage for a qualitative shift in history. The result
was an explosively diverse set of energies, including a series of scientific and
political revolutions extending from the late seventeenth to the late nineteenth
centuries; utopian experiments in America (Brook Farm, Walden) and elsewhere;
declarations of the universal rights of man and woman; challenges to slavery
from both slaves (e.g. Toussaint L'Ouverture) and Europeans; a rash of new laws
broadly extending rights of property ownership and franchise; populist leaders
and egomaniacal dictators (e.g. for both, Napoleon Bonaparte); horrifying brutality in the midst of celebrations of reason and humanity (the Terror following
the 1789 revolution, imperialist exploitation and cruelty); vociferous critiques of the
prevailing social order such as those of Marxism, anarchism, feminism, and
abolitionism; angry retrenchments by dominant social groups; massive industrialization; the "permanent revolution" of capitalism gone metastatic; and even
the persistence of the *ancien régime* to which the revolution of 1789 was meant to
put an end. It provoked William Wordsworth into a transport of joy—"Bliss was

it in that dawn to be alive, / But to be young was very heaven!" (1979 [1805]: ll. 692–3)—but it also drove Karl Marx to call for "the ruthless criticism of everything existing" (1978 [1843]: 13). Nor is this disparity just a matter of historical progression. While it is true that Wordsworth's early enthusiasm for the 1789 revolution gave way to disappointment and Marx's critique appears after two failed revolutions (1789 and 1832), G. W. F. Hegel's epic *Phenomenology of Spirit* (1807) charts both sides of the equation as it tries to bring the force of negation together with a progressivist model of human consciousness and history in the name of a utopian outcome. The authoritarian tenor of that outcome, however, with its claim to "absolute knowing" (the title of Hegel's last chapter); its identification of the utopian end of history with the totalization of the German state; and its collapsing of all meaningful difference among particular individuals—and among individuals, the state, and world-spirit—articulates yet another aspect of the nineteenth century's complicated and variegated engagement with the Enlightenment.[2] Everything seemed up for grabs with the elevation of human agency to the driving force of history and the celebration of what seemed to be an infinite potential for improvement. But the tensions among the competing versions of what counted as improvement and how it could best be achieved also produced massive conflict. They led at once to the horrifying excesses of industrial labor and imperialist exploitation, and to the human triumphs of abolition and a scientific worldview that would ease untold human misery.

Modernism announced its difference from the Enlightenment through a misreading that reduced its messy complexity to an image of complacency, decadence, and corruption. Originating the very narrative category of "the Enlightenment,"[3] modernism portrayed the Enlightenment as coextensive with the mortifying aspects of a modernity that had become an "iron cage" (Weber 1958 [1904]: 181), and the challenge to "make it new" a promise to break out of it. It was cast as privileging nationalism over cosmopolitanism, corporatism over individualism, uncritical loyalty over critical affiliation, and social hierarchy over egalitarianism, at once barrenly superstitious in its mania for spiritualism and too rational in its treatment of human beings. This latter element in particular cemented the association of the Enlightenment with the bad elements of modernity, totemized by men like Frederick Winslow Taylor and Henry Ford, who refined the treatment of human beings as machines (memorably depicted in Charlie Chaplin's *Modern Times*). In Max Horkheimer and Theodor Adorno's terms, the Enlightenment had ceased any longer to critique myth, and had become a myth itself, "the scientific ethos of the philosophes [was] dramatized as a misguided will to power and domination over nature, and their desacralizing program as the first stage in the development of a sheerly instrumentalizing world-view which will lead straight to Auschwitz" (Jameson 1998b: 25). The application of reason had become an *a priori* good, serving rather than critiquing the ideology of progress and human perfectibility, even when it resulted in human misery. Perhaps because they had the benefit of historical distance to temper their account, Horkheimer and Adorno realized that the legacy with which they contended was that of the failed or perverted Enlightenment, and not its essence. But as they articulated modernism's anti-Enlightenment stance in the midst of World War II and the horrifyingly rationalized effort to exterminate Jews, homosexuals, gypsies, communists, and other "degenerates," they also recognized the ethical imperative of the modernist critique of modernity. When the Nazis condemned and burnt modernist works of art as degenerate (as did, also, the Americans), Horkheimer and Adorno's intuitions in *Dialectic of Enlightenment* seemed to be absolutely correct and the modernist antipathy for the Enlightenment to have been right on the mark. The progression from the Boer war to the Holocaust, from Joseph Conrad's bleak vision of the product of "all Europe" indulging in "unspeakable rites" in the colonial Congo (Conrad 1924 [1899]: 117, 118) to Beckett's nightmare visions of people whose sole purpose seems to be to suffer, had made it clear that the instrumentalist, technologically rationalist, and utilitarian strain of the Enlightenment harbored an unfathomable potential for barbarism. As Walter Benjamin put it, modernism had discovered that "there is no document of civilization which is not at the same time a document of barbarism" (1968 [1955]: 256). To all appearances in the first half of the twentieth century, what had originated as "ruthless" critique one hundred years before had not only bred its own antithesis, but also succumbed to it, becoming a parody of itself that stood desperately in need of critique. And whatever their generation or political orientation, the modernists answered that need.

Doing so meant, first and foremost, following up the strong misreading of the Enlightenment with a new narrative. This depended heavily upon the misreading of the Enlightenment outlined above. At the same time, modernism did not simply deny that the Enlightenment had produced a strong tradition of critique—rather, it claimed that Enlightenment critique had failed to develop into a viable challenge to Enlightenment modernity because it had been a critique *in modernity's name* rather than a critique *of* it. Staking out the latter position for itself, modernism produced the first full critique of modernity *that saw itself as a critique of modernity*. This differentiation allowed modernism to imagine itself as radically distinct from the Enlightenment legacy, and to situate itself as a necessary corrective to it: witness Horkheimer's massively influential articulation of "critical theory" as an alternative to "traditional theory" in 1937 (Horkheimer 1986 [1968]: 198–9). In the process, what had been positive about the Enlightenment—its youthful energy, its challenge to prevailing norms, its unconventionality, its utopian drive—was made over as the key elements of modernism. In effect, modernism recast the tradition of Enlightenment critique as reformist rather than revolutionary, as an opposition internal to modernity, rather than a radical critique of its very basis.

In response, modernism produced a massive outpouring of works that challenged the Enlightenment legacy (differently understood by different modernists). If the need for critique was evident, the diagnosis of what needed critique varied almost from individual to individual, and from season to season. Thus we find Virginia Woolf deploring the pervasive casual brutality at the roots of modern war, while F. T. Marinetti endorses its potential to cure the epidemic of degeneration he sees as characteristic of the same moment. Ezra Pound celebrates the "conspiracy of intelligence" (cited in Surette 1993: 23) behind the apparent chaos of the modern world, while Djuna Barnes ridicules the heterosexist and patriarchal assumptions that sustain oppressive power structures in the midst of that chaos. D. H. Lawrence urges an ethic of land, blood, and heterosexual sex, while Gertrude Stein seeks to abolish the fixity of gender and sex identities. Depending on which one you read, and which of their works you read, you can find Woolf, Lawrence, Ford Madox Ford, E. M. Forster, Conrad, Pound, W. B. Yeats, T. S. Eliot, Dorothy Richardson, *et al.* critiquing imperialism, capitalism, socialism, progressivism, liberalism, fascism, sexism, hetero-normativity, racism, Euro-centrism, reason, superstition, religion, and industrialization. Pick up Wyndham Lewis and you can find the modernists themselves critiqued. The differences are enormous, but they share an underlying consistency in their intention to critique modernity. Indeed, though it is very much out of fashion today to attempt to find a characteristic or set of characteristics that defines modernism, I would join an attitude of critique to formal experimentation as the defining nexus of modernism, a nexus that persists among all modernists regardless of their ideological commitments and degrees of complicity with the mass-market culture they often claimed to—and did—deplore.

As was the case with the Enlightenment, modernism's capacity for critique carried with it—in fact entailed—a counter-movement of regression and dogmatism.[4] This capacity is evident from the start in various characteristic elements of modernism: Pound's dicta, Lewis's screeds, Marinetti's manifestoes, Lawrence's imperatives, Breton's excommunications, even Woolf's semi-facetious proclamation that human nature changed "on or about December 1910" (1988 [1924]: 421). Interestingly, this aspect of modernism does not start out as a regressive or conservative feature but as a key mode of critique. Such pronouncements emphasize critique as a positive practice that generates alternatives, not a negative one that only clears space for alternatives. Perhaps impatient with the negative mode of critique (of which Marxism is perhaps the most prominent example), many modernists put forward concrete alternatives to the status quo; they told their contemporaries not only that the present state of affairs was corrupt and unacceptable, but also what the world should be like. Key to such pronouncements' function as critique are their affective and intellectual contexts, and—perhaps most importantly of all—the lack of authority of the pronouncers. Only if one has no power to change the world can one's pronouncement function as critique; if it immediately becomes the law—if the critique is a performative—then it is not critique but establishment. At the outset, these conditions held for modernism, and its pronouncements could function as critiques.

As modernism gained cultural currency, and particularly as it became part of the academic institution through the tireless efforts of T. S. Eliot, F. R. Leavis, and the New Critics, modernists' pronouncements took on an authoritative hue and became doctrines rather than objections to be heard and responded to. A radical separation took place between modernism's capacity to disrupt conventions, and its increasing ability to set them. "Modernism," which like the Enlightenment was only ever named as such retroactively, emerged as the reified counterpart to the disruptive energies of the avant-garde. The particular affective and intellectual contexts that made its pronouncements so challenging were stripped as modernism gained the cultural clout that hardened its claims into inviolable rules. The more respectable "Modernism" became, the more its powers of critique seemed to be the purview of the avant-garde to which it stood, as often as not, in opposition.[5] The transformation of T. S. Eliot's brief for the impersonality of the poet, uttered in 1919, three years before *The Waste Land* appeared, into W. K. Wimsatt's and Monroe C. Beardsley's "Intentional Fallacy" is a case in point. Eliot's claim that "the suffering man and the poet should be kept distinct" (1969: 54) comes from a position of little authority, and is made in an effort to shift conceptions of the relationship between writers and their work: it functions as critique. By 1945, when Wimsatt and Beardsley rephrase the notion, it has become a fallacy not to follow Eliot's pronouncement: it stands in need of critique.

The cultural and institutional pressures that saw modernism rise to prominence in the middle of the century thus transformed its fiery, subversive, avant-garde pronouncements into hardened dogma; that is, into precisely the kind of conventional wisdom they were initially articulated to disrupt. Just as the Enlightenment celebration of reason ultimately produced the counter-Enlightenment and its ideology (against which modernism reacted in the first place), so modernism's dogmatism produced counter-modernism and gave rise to the putative ideology of modernism against which theory reacted. In remarkably short order, avant-garde modernism became "late" modernism. But, as with the Enlightenment, this is not to say that modernism was totally bereft of its capacity for critique. Many of the conditions it challenged persisted even as modernism was canonized, and its texts continued—and continue today—to confront them eloquently. Likewise, its avant-garde dimension continued to produce new challenges to accepted orthodoxies, including institutional modernism, long after Eliot and Pound had become *éminences grises*. Like the Enlightenment, modernism presented a contradictory, complex, and chaotic range that had to be boiled down if a new movement were to displace it and reactivate the power of critique it had apparently forfeited. Neither the avant-garde experiments of late modernism nor the disdain for mass culture and bourgeois philistinism that represented the two most prominent aspects of modernist critique by the end of the 1960s did justice any longer to the force of critique necessary to sustain a narrative of transgression.

The Bloomian logic of misprision reappears at this juncture, as theory repeats the narrative logic of misreading to produce a new narrative of critique. Just as modernism had mistaken the counter-Enlightenment for the essence of the Enlightenment, so theory mistakes the official version of modernism for the whole. The elements of modernist critique that persisted through its institutionalization became so clichéd, insular, and weakened as to be easily ignored, and the official version of modernism furnished an ideal corpse upon which to feed. Providing an intellectually rigorous validation of postmodernism's rejection of narrative unity, hidden order, deep significance, hierarchy, meaning, and identity, theory made postmodernism *post*modernism by replaying a fundamentally modernist trope:

the clean break with the past. Identifying these values with modernist dogmatism and retrogression, theory fuelled postmodernism's identification of the effort to shore Eliot's "fragments" "against … ruins" (1963 [1922]: l. 430) as totalizing and tendentially fascist. Where postmodernism parodied modernism with a playful extension of modernist aesthetics that strenuously refused to be serious, theory took the official story of modernism produced by modernism itself through its institutionalization and canonization, further reduced it, and subjected it to a sustained and vociferous critique.

In the hands of this new narrator, the story of modernism was retold through rigorous and closely argued challenges to the pieties that had produced the bloodiest century in human memory (and still wasn't over), and sustained global inequalities in an age of unprecedented wealth. Reading modernism as continuous with modernity rather than a critique of it, and focusing on the separation of aesthetics from politics and ethics upon which modernist doctrine was putatively based, theory completed the transformation of Conrad, Lawrence, Woolf, Forster, Ford, Pound, Yeats, Eliot, Joyce, James from vocal critics of modernity's dehumanizing excesses to its official spokespersons. As the century neared its end, critiques of modernism driven by theoretical challenges to its philosophical, metaphysical, epistemological, and ontological underpinnings proliferated in all quarters. First feminist, then African-American and postcolonial critics attacked: critiques of modernism as sexist, racist, homophobic, hetero-normative, misogynist, anti-Semitic, imperialist, and fascist became conventional. Theoretical challenges to categories like taste, culture (of the high variety), and civilization, along with resurgent debates over the ideological significance of form, style, and technique cleared the way to reading the very categories of aesthetic value on which modernism staked its reputation as themselves ideological. The difficulty by which much of modernism had sought to shake its audience out of complacency could now be read as indicative of elitism, snobbery, dour self-seriousness, and even crypto-aristocratic or crypto-fascist tendencies. Modernism's at times dubious politics were given centre-stage and its revolutionary aesthetic force—and the critique it sought thereby to articulate—was unceremoniously shown the door. By the 1980s, modernism had become, in the words of Andrew John Miller, "a target-rich environment for ideology critique" (p. 180), appearing to all savvy critics a "doddering old paranoiac" (North 1999: 10) who deserved everything he got as he was marched to the curb.

By contrast, theory absorbed the energies of critique with which modernism had begun and articulated a dizzying—often contradictory—array of challenges not just to modernity, but to the whole of Western intellectual history. Identifying strongly with critique *per se*, theory took the Enlightenment promise of reason's potential for disrupting accepted pieties and norms as an ethical imperative, and positioned itself as its latest and best incarnation. In 1978, de Man asserted that "our own literary modernity has reestablished contact with a 'true' Enlightenment that remained hidden from us by a nineteenth-century Romantic and realist epistemology that asserted a reliable rhetoric of the subject or of representation" (29); and eleven years later Slavoj Žižek announced that

"Lacanian theory is perhaps the most radical contemporary version of the Enlightenment" (7). Many structuralist, Marxist, feminist, postcolonial, queer, and semiotic approaches strenuously reasoned out the irrational bases for much of what had been accepted as given or natural. Gender identity, sexuality, race, and class difference were systematically taken apart as ideologies rather than concrete truths. Aspects of other approaches like deconstruction, third-wave feminism, post-Marxism, queer theory, and Lacanian psychoanalysis in particular homed in on what Georg Lukács called the *hiatus irrationalis*: the point at which reason subverts itself and exposes its irrational underpinnings (Lukács 1997 [1968]: 122). The scandalous exception to a given epistemological ordering was sought with inquisitorial fervor, celebrated when found, and given pride of place in the conversion of certainty to doubt. Without abandoning the power of reasoned argument for critique, theory often rejected its capacity to reveal the truth about anything. Attention to silences, gaps, incongruities, undecidability, *mises en abyme*, and *aporiae* became de rigueur as theorists sought to think and say not only what had not yet been thought and said, but what was by definition—at least within the epistemological and ontological traditions of philosophy—unthinkable and unsayable. Louis Althusser's and Slavoj Žižek's claims that subjectivity and ideology are coeval—that one cannot occupy a non-ideological position and that reality itself is an ideological fantasy—transformed virtually all inquiry (with the possible exception of Marxist critiques that held out for the possibility of objective knowledge of historical material conditions) into ideology critique. Following Foucault, theorists no longer asked what was the truth hidden behind the ideological mask. Instead, they asked how power was being configured in a given situation and whom it served. The notion of regimes of truth displaced knowledge of the world, and the hybrid term power/knowledge entered the lexicon as the marker of sophisticated inquiry.

Theory's recognition and embrace of critique as a fundamentally negative energy, a process of incessant disruption and challenge rather than synthesis, allowed it to avoid for the most part the modernist mistake of proffering concrete alternatives to what was being critiqued. Abstract calls for greater equality, for the annihilation of "man" and "woman" as classes (Wittig 2001 [1981]), for an unimaginable "democracy-to-come" (Derrida 1994), for a post-national world, for sexual and gender politics based upon fluid conceptions of "bodies and pleasures" (Foucault 1990 [1976]), for the transformation of the liberal humanist subject into a plateau of "intensity" (Deleuze and Guattari 1987 [1980]), and so on. Not all theory took this path—Jean Baudrillard lamented the loss of the real in the "precession of simulacra" (1988 [1967]: 167); N. Katherine Hayles (1999) objected to the presumption that subjectivity is merely an informational pattern; and many feminist, queer, and postcolonial or race theorists insisted upon the continuing relevance of the body, or at least of embodied experience, if the nature of the body itself could not be safely determined (e.g. Judith Butler [1993; 1999], Frantz Fanon [2005 (1961); 1967 (1952)], Hélène Cixous [2001 (1975)], Julia Kristeva [1980; 1984], Luce Irigaray [1985 (1974); 1985], bell hooks [1981 (1999); 1990]). Even with this difference among theoretical prescriptions, though, the metaphor of Heisenberg's uncertainty principle hovered over all inquiry, and relativism seemed at times to be an inevitable—if not positively desired—outcome. Critique seemed to have reached an apotheosis, to have become an unassailable means of being, if not absolutely right, then less wrong than one's predecessor. The logic of misprision and seizing narrative control I've outlined so far had become a rule: all reading was by definition misreading, and she who controlled the narrative could enable certain outcomes and prevent others.

As with the Enlightenment and modernism, however, theory's appropriation of critique also yielded distinctly negative, i.e. dogmatic and authoritarian, results. First, theory's challenge to what had been considered thus far "the best that has been thought and said" (Arnold 1993 [1869]: 190) gave rise to what is now known as political correctness. Driven largely by identity politics—the notion that who one is licenses one to speak about certain issues and not others (only women can write about women's issues, etc.)—political correctness often produced an atmosphere of antagonism that could close rather than open the kinds of dialogue essential to critique. In these instances, the force of critique itself hardened into a sense of moral superiority that failed to see its own blind spots, acting as though what it thought was true, rather than just a different interpretation. One of the more painful ironies of political correctness is that its insistence that we must accommodate multiple competing narratives rather than decide on which is right has opened the way for the infiltration of politically and intellectually regressive agendas into academia. Its intention to open space for previously silenced accounts by women, people of color, homosexuals, and other traditionally oppressed groups has also enabled Christian fundamentalists to demand that the creationist theory of intelligent design be taught alongside the theory of evolution, and theological understandings of the world be taught alongside secular humanism. In this respect, theory's challenge to the privilege accorded reason has succeeded all too well, even as its inclusive agenda remains incomplete (women, people of color, homosexuals, and indigenous people remain marginalized in contemporary culture).

Nor is this problem likely to go away soon, since theory has, like modernism before it, been institutionalized into a set of propositions, "schools," and perspectives that bear little resemblance to the vibrant spirit of critique that drove it. We are awash in handbooks, guide books, and introductions to theory that lay out the primary tenets, methods, and assumptions of each approach. There's even a *Norton Anthology of Theory and Criticism*—one of many such collections; theory has not just arrived in the academy but been given official sanction. Such systematization threatens to transform theory from a fully committed mode of critique into a set of stable entities that can be subjected to a standard set of approved critiques. The names of erstwhile intellectually dangerous subversives like Derrida, Lacan, Barthes, Kristeva, Butler, Cixous, Irigaray, and Sedgwick have become institutional authorities and their writings authoritative—in spite of all the ink they spilled challenging the very concept of authority. An ideology, or myth, of theory has thus been forged, which at last, in its reductive oversimplification, gives purchase to the various efforts that have been made to critique it.[6] As it was with the Enlightenment and modernism, so has it been with theory.

We might expect that the next step would be a critique of theory, a challenge to its authority by a reinvigorated spirit of critique, at least from scholars of modernism who would seem to have the most to gain from restoring the critical impulse to their field. Indeed, given the recent revival of modernist studies and the emphasis in it on recovering a fuller, more inclusive and thus authentic understanding of modernism, we might well expect to discover a whole sub-genre of modernist critiques of theory aimed at redeeming modernism from the more egregious misrepresentations it has suffered. But while some work has been done to recuperate modernism from challenges of regressiveness, it has been largely defensive rather than critical. There has been little effort by scholars of modernism to advance a critique of theory as modernism did to the Enlightenment and theory to modernism. Instead, modernist studies have continued theory's project of tearing down the fantasy of high modernism. In its place, scholars have begun to construct an alternative set of modernisms that are much more clearly *of* the world they were in. Such work continues the critique of modernism set in motion by theory, but it also tends to minimize modernism's critical energies, characterizing it instead as thoroughly continuous with modernity.

The occlusion of theory from this new project, as has overwhelmingly been the case, is the key symptom; it is the missing link between modernism old and modernisms new. At risk in forgetting this link is the force of critique, the energy with which modernism differentiated itself from the Enlightenment, and with which theory began the challenge to modernism. Though the ecumenical reconstruction of modernism certainly continues the critique of modernism initiated by theory, it also risks suppressing the consciousness of that energy that is so central to avoiding a repetition of the narrative logic I have charted above. Remembering Derrida's discussion of the origin of the word *archive* in *Archive Fever*, we must be vigilantly self-conscious *archons*, powerful interpreters of the documents we discover as well as their guardians (Derrida 1995: 1–4). We must also remain highly self-conscious about our own activities—our investments in them, the assumptions behind them, and the contradictions embedded in them. In this light, we might even suggest that *Modernism and Theory* is itself an archivalist enterprise aimed at recuperating a lost set of links among documents, figures, and traditions. It is an effort to recapture the continuities among modernism and theory, continuities that are crucial to an adequate understanding of modernism and theory, both individually and in relation to each other.

As I have argued above, critique—particularly the critique of modernity—is essential to those continuities, and remains the core of the affinities between modernism and theory. It is the key reason why Edward Said refers continually to the work of Conrad, why Lefebvre relies upon Woolf and Beckett, why Kristeva turns to Gide and Joyce, why Derrida writes of Bataille, Deleuze of Lawrence and Kafka, Lacan of Joyce, Jameson of Conrad and Lewis, Foucault of Borges, Žižek of Kafka and Henry James, and so on. It is also why theorists of globalization and its impact upon subject formation turn to Pound and Eliot;

why theorists of nation and sovereignty turn to Yeats, Beckett, and Joyce; why theorists of postcoloniality turn to Joyce, Conrad, Woolf, Forster, and Lawrence; why theorists of race and ethnicity turn to William Faulkner, Jean Toomer, Langston Hughes, James Baldwin, Claude MacKay, and James Weldon Johnson. These affiliations are not accidental; they point toward a common critical orientation to modernity, an unwillingness to accept what is, and always to challenge what is in the name of something better. Such a proposition is risky, as is claiming the kind of lineage I am asserting here, but it is also the essence of critical practice. In this regard, it is an ethical imperative to which the critical thinkers of the Enlightenment, modernism, and theory were all keenly alive, and to which we owe the best of those traditions. To abandon modernism as critique, or to scant it in favor of less contentious characterizations in our zeal to critique it in turn, is to accept a strong misreading of it that threatens to strip away the real core power of modernism and theory both.

* * *

The essays in this volume were selected to open up discussion about the relationship between modernism and theory. To facilitate those goals, they have also been organized in a rather unusual manner. The essays are grouped in three sections, the first two with eight articles each, and the last with five. In each of the first two sections, initial contributions by emerging scholars have been paired with responses by established scholars. The mandate for all these exchanges was to maintain an atmosphere of cooperation and mutually beneficial inquiry. The nature of the relationships between the papers varies somewhat, so that some of the responses pick up and comment directly upon the points made in the initial contributions while others take the initial contributions and develop their insights more fully or in slightly different directions. Ideally, each such pairing will provoke in readers the desire to contribute further, to carry the discussion beyond the covers of the book.

The three sections of *Modernism and Theory* progress roughly from the particular to the general. The essays in the first part, "Theory's modernism: concrete connections," focus closely on direct links between modernist cultural producers and their theoretical heirs. The aim in these papers and their responses is to show that there are, in fact, traceable lines of flight from modernism to theory. In a sense, they provide the most concrete and conclusive evidence of the link I've been arguing in this introduction. More importantly, they show that theory's clear affinity for modernist concepts is not simply a matter of those concepts having been "in the air" as the various theorists who used them wrote. Rather, they demonstrate that many of the most important theoretical figures of the last half of the twentieth century were reading and thinking about modernism directly. Their ideas have been influenced by modernist ideas, and they even borrow them outright.

In the second section, "Modernism's theory: abstract affiliations," *Modernism and Theory* moves in a more abstract direction, taking up issues of form, time, art-as-theory, and narrative. Modernism and theory are fluid and often at odds with themselves, their self-conceptions, and others' conceptions of them. But as contradictory and highly complex phenomena, one key approach to their affinities is through complexity and contradiction themselves. The papers in this section thus move away from direct influence and onto the variegated relations that obtain when we begin to think of theory as modernist and modernism as theoretical. Asking at their core how modernism and its study can go forward, all four of the papers here insist—at times aggressively—upon a theoretical perspective that is also deeply modernist.

The third section of the volume is its "Forum," in which Charles Altieri, Melba Cuddy-Keane, Bonnie Kime Scott, Jane Goldman, and Susan Stanford Friedman interrogate the relationship between modernism and theory. All of the contributors in this section are prominent critics of modernism whose work will have a profound impact on the future direction of modernist studies. They represent a range of theoretical and methodological orientations, as well as positions regarding the value of theory itself. In this Forum, they engage with such timely and complex notions as ethics, aesthetics, eco-criticism, the avant-garde, and theory itself. Their engagement with the question of how modernism relates to theory is energetic, feisty, and at times contentious. Their essays pose a range of arguments that all verge on the *raison d'être* of *Modernism and Theory*, and insist upon the necessity of integrating theory into the study of modernism, no matter what one's critical orientation.

The chief objective of this volume is to revive theory in modernist studies, not in any dogmatic way but as a point of discussion that can no longer be avoided. The question of how modernism and theory interrelate has been taken up ably in the past by the likes of Andreas Huyssen and Fredric Jameson; and the question of modernism and/or theory as critique or even the critique of critique (Horkheimer) has equally been raised. But since the end of the twentieth century the interrelationship between modernism and theory has been downplayed in favor of materialist, archivalist, and reconstructivist approaches. Clearly, methodologies change with the times, but separating modernism from theory actually deforms the object of study itself in a way that separating the New Historicism from early modern studies does not. Ignoring theory in the effort to reconstruct a more authentic or accurate picture of modernism ironically produces a distorted understanding just when a richer account is sought. This is because theory is not merely a methodology for studying modernism but an integral part of its formation, flourishing, and afterlife. Nor is modernism merely an object on which theory can be exercised, providing brilliant examples—but still just examples—of theoretical insights. Modernism and theory are trying to articulate, to gesture towards, insights and problems that remain beyond the purview of accepted aesthetics, lexicons, and paradigms. Revolutions of form are as integral to thinking the unthought—at times the unthinkable—as is the thinking itself. Indeed, it is hard to see how they can possibly be separated, as, I contend, is also the case with modernism and theory themselves. But the aim here is not by any means to provide the last word. *Modernism and Theory*, with its dialogic framework and open-ended forum, is designed to provoke countless more discussions of such points. It is clearly anything but comprehensive—witness the absence, perhaps glaring and outrageous to some but no doubt welcome to many more, of any essays on James Joyce and Jacques Lacan. Rather, *Modernism and Theory* is partial, incomplete, suggestive, and—I hope—provocative. Not everyone will like everything they find here, and most everyone will find something to disagree with.

One thing, however, is clear: the relationship between modernism and theory can no longer be ignored or sidelined in the new modernist revolution of modernist studies. Nor can we stop at reintegrating theory into modernist studies in a purely instrumental fashion. Rather, our task now is to explore the occulted relationship between modernism and theory as aspects of the twentieth century's massive cultural upheavals. We must approach the problematic of modernism/theory from a range of perspectives, including the institutional, historical, and discursive constructions of them as distinct fields. Additionally, we must push beyond disciplinary squabbles to ask not just what modernism can tell us about theory and what theory can tell us about modernism, but also what the nexus modernism/theory can tell us about the twentieth century's preoccupations, tendencies, triumphs, and failures. Modernist studies have been changing radically in the new century, as have studies of theory, though in very different directions. Healthy, open debate about the continuity between these two major intellectual currents has the potential to reorient the critical conversation and provoke scholars on all sides of it to rethink their understanding of the last century.

Notes

1 Though turns to the archive and historicism are not necessarily untheoretical, this has frequently been the case; witness North and Rainey as vivid examples.
2 The question of whether Hegel ultimately comes down on the side of authoritarianism or critique remains open, though many assume that because his work was absorbed by national socialism in Germany it must be inherently authoritarian. For an alternative viewpoint, see Žižek 1993.
3 See Schmidt 2006: 651 and 655.
4 See Jameson 1998a: 18, 19.
5 Andreas Huyssen advances this reading in *After the Great Divide*, though he has been roundly criticized for it by critics who wish to challenge the story of modernism that it tells (i.e. the story of modernism produced by postmodernism). For more on the avant-garde, see Poggioli 2003 [1968] and Burger 1984.
6 For a collection of such critiques—virtually all of them excellent examples of strong misreading—see Patai and Corral 2005.

Bibliography

Arnold, M. (1993 [1869]) "Culture and Anarchy," in *Culture and Anarchy and Other Writings*, ed. S. Collini, Cambridge Texts in the History of Political Thought, New York: Cambridge University Press.

Baudrillard, J. (1988 [1967]) "Simulacra and Simulations," in *Selected Writings*, ed. M. Poster, Stanford, CA: Stanford University Press.

Benjamin, W. (1968 [1955]) "Theses on the Philosophy of History," in *Illuminations: Essays and Reflections*, ed. H. Arendt and trans. H. Zohn, New York: Schocken Books, 253–64.

Bloom, H. (1997) *The Anxiety of Influence: A Theory of Poetry*, New York: Oxford University Press.

Burger, P. (1984) *Theory of the Avant-Garde*, Theory and History of Literature, Minneapolis: University of Minnesota Press.

Butler, J. (1993) *Bodies that Matter: On the Discursive Limits of Sex*, New York: Routledge.

—— (1999) *Gender Trouble: Feminism and the Subversion of Identity*, New York: Routledge.

Cixous, H. (2001) "The Laugh of the Medusa," trans. K. Cohen and P. Cohen, in V. B. Leitch, W. Cain, L. Finke, and B. Johnson (eds) *The Norton Anthology of Theory and Criticism*, New York: W. W. Norton, 2039–56.

Conrad, J. (1924) "Heart of Darkness," in *Youth and Two Other Stories*, London: J. M. Dent and Sons, 45–162.

Deleuze, G. and Guattari, F. (1987 [1980]) *A Thousand Plateaus: Capitalism and Schizophrenia*, trans. B. Massumi, Minneapolis: University of Minnesota Press.

de Man, P. (1978) "The Epistemology of Metaphor", *Critical Inquiry* 5(1): 13–30.

—— (1989 [1965]) "What is Modern?" in Lindsay Waters (ed.) *Critical Writings 1953–1978*, Theory and History of Literature Volume 66, Minneapolis: University of Minnesota Press, 137–44.

Derrida, J. (1994) *Specters of Marx: The State of the Debt, The Work of Mourning, and The New International*, trans. P. Kamuf, New York: Routledge.

—— (1995) *Archive Fever: A Freudian Impression*, ed. E. Prenowitz, Chicago: University of Chicago Press.

Eliot, T. S. (1963 [1922]) "The Waste Land," *Collected Poems 1909–1962*, London: Faber and Faber, 61–86.

—— (1969 [1920]) "Tradition and the Individual Talent," *The Sacred Wood: Essays on Poetry and Criticism*, London: Methuen, 47–59.

Fanon, F. (1967 [1952]) *Black Skin, White Masks*, trans. C. L. Markmann, New York: Grove Press.

—— (2005 [1961]) *The Wretched of the Earth*, trans. R. Philcox, New York: Grove Press.

Foucault, M. (1990 [1976]) *The History of Sexuality, Vol. I: An Introduction*, trans. R. Hurley, New York: Vintage (Random House).

Hayles, N. K. (1999) *How We Became Posthuman: Virtual Bodies in Cybernetics, Literature, and Informatics*, Chicago: University of Chicago Press.

Hegel, G. W. F. (1977) *Phenomenology of Spirit*, trans. A. V. Miller, New York: Oxford University Press.

hooks, b. (1990) *Yearning: Race, Gender, and Cultural Politics*, Cambridge, MA: South End Press.

—— (1999) *Ain't I a Woman: Black Women and Feminism*, Cambridge, MA: South End Press.

Horkheimer, M. (1986 [1968]) "Critical and Traditional Theory", in *Critical Theory: Selected Essays*, trans. M. J. O'Connell *et al.*, New York: Continuum, 188–252.

Horkheimer, M. and Adorno, T. (2002) *Dialectic of Enlightenment: Philosophical Fragments*, in G. S. Noerr (ed.) and E. Jephcott (trans.), *Cultural Memory in the Present*, Stanford: Stanford University Press.

Huyssen, A. (1986) *After the Great Divide: Modernism, Mass Culture, Postmodernism*, Bloomington and Indianapolis: Indiana University Press.

Irigaray, L. (1985 [1974]) *Speculum of the Other Woman*, trans. G. C. Gill, Ithaca: Cornell University Press.

—— (1985) *This Sex Which is Not One*, trans. C. Porter and C. Burke, Ithaca: Cornell University Press.

Jameson, F. (1998a) "Postmodernism and Consumer Society," in *The Cultural Turn: Selected Writings on the Postmodern 1983–1998*, New York: Verso, 1–20.

—— (1998b) "Theories of the Postmodern," in *The Cultural Turn: Selected Writings on the Postmodern 1983–1998*, New York: Verso. 21–32.

—— (2002) *A Singular Modernity: Essay on the Ontology of the Present*, New York: Verso.

Kristeva, J. (1980) *Desire in Language*, ed. L. S. Roudiez and trans. T. Gora, A. Jardine, and L. S. Roudiez, New York: Columbia University Press.

—— (1984). *Revolution in Poetic Language*, ed. L. S. Roudiez and trans. M. Waller, New York: Columbia University Press.

Leitch, V. B., Cain, W. Finke, L. and Johnson, B. (eds) (2001) *The Norton Anthology of Theory and Criticism*, New York: W. W. Norton.

Lukács, G. (1997 [1968]) *History and Class Consciousness: Studies in Marxist Dialectics*, trans. R. Livingstone, Cambridge, MA: MIT Press.

Lyon, J. (1999) *Manifestoes: Provocations of the Modern*, Ithaca, NY: Cornell University Press.

Mao, D. and Walkowitz, R. L. (eds) (2006) *Bad Modernisms*, Durham: Duke University Press.

Marx, K. (1978) "Letter to Arnold Ruge, September 1843," in *The Marx–Engels Reader*, second edn, ed. R. C. Tucker, New York: W. W. Norton, 12–15.

North, M. (1999) *Reading 1922: A Return to the Scene of the Modern*, New York: Oxford University Press.

Patai, D. and Corral, W. H. (eds) (2005) *Theory's Empire: An Anthology of Dissent*, New York: Columbia University Press.

Poggioli, R. (2003 [1968]) *The Theory of the Avant-Garde*, trans. G. Fitzgerald, Cambridge, MA: Belknap Press.

Rainey, L. (2007) *Revisiting "The Waste Land"*, New Haven: Yale University Press.

Schmidt, J. (2006) "What Enlightenment Was, What It Still Might Be, and Why Kant May Have Been Right After All," *American Behavioral Scientist* 49(5): 647–63.

Surette, L. (1993) *The Birth of Modernism: Ezra Pound, T. S. Eliot, W. B. Yeats and the Occult*, Montreal and Kingston: McGill-Queen's University Press.

Weber, M. (1958 [1904]) *The Protestant Ethic and the Spirit of Capitalism*, New York: Charles Scribner's Sons.

Wimsatt, W. K. and Beardsley, M. C. (2001) "The Intentional Fallacy," in V. B. Leitch, W. Cain, L. Finke, and B. Johnson (eds) *The Norton Anthology of Criticism and Theory*, New York: W. W. Norton, 1387–1403.

Wittig, M. (2001) "One is Not Born a Woman," in V. B. Leitch, W. Cain, L. Finke, and B. Johnson (eds) *The Norton Anthology of Criticism and Theory*, New York: W. W. Norton, 2014–21.

Woolf, V. (1988 [1924]) "Character in Fiction," *The Essays of Virginia Woolf, Vol. III 1919–1924*, ed. A. McNeillie, London: The Hogarth Press. 420–38.

Wordsworth, W. (1979) *The Prelude 1799, 1805, 1850*, ed. J. Wordsworth, M. H. Abrams, and S. Gill, New York: W. W. Norton.

Žižek, S. (1989) *The Sublime Object of Ideology*, New York: Verso.

—— (1993) *Tarrying with the Negative: Kant, Hegel, and the Critique of Ideology*, Durham: Duke University Press.

Part I

Theory's modernism

Concrete connections

Introduction

The essays and responses in this section focus on demonstrable links between theory and modernism. They show how concepts today associated chiefly with Gilles Deleuze and Felix Guattari, Jacques Derrida, Henri Lefebvre, and Giorgio Agamben derive in many cases directly from encounters with D. H. Lawrence, Georges Bataille, André Breton, Virginia Woolf, and Walter Benjamin. These essays demonstrate how modernism had already begun to think about how art, philosophy, and science think; the postmodern sublime; the everyday; and messianic time well before their contemporary theoretical articulations. Their revelations are startling, and provide a strong basis for further inquiries into the linkages between modernism and theory that follow.

Though the essays in this section focus on relationships between specific modernists and theories, they are criss-crossed with common concerns and terms that need elaboration. First, there is the relationship between philosophy and literature. For Deleuze and Guattari, as discussed by Masschelein and Buchanan, philosophy and literature occupy distinct planes of immanence: each has a particular sphere in which it operates best and to which it relates most clearly. When we take a concept from one such plane and transfer it to another, it takes on a new meaning. Though both literature and philosophy think, they think differently, and cannot be transposed upon one another. One key difference between them is the status of affect and the body in relation to thought. For Deleuze and Guattari, as for Lawrence before them, philosophy loses the body in its cerebral focus, reducing even sex to a function of the mind. By contrast, they endorse the notions of vitalism and the body without organs (BwO). These notions conceive of the body as dominated by flows, energies, and intensities, rather than broken up into particular zones (erogenous, oral, anal, etc.) and organs with discrete tasks. The turn to vitalism and the BwO is also political, in its break with what Deleuze and Guattari saw as psychoanalysis' attempt to naturalize capitalism: by breaking the body down into component parts with discrete functions and conceiving of desire as a lack that must constantly be redressed, psychoanalysis portrayed capitalism's division of labor and consumerist ethos as fundamental elements of human nature.

Consistent with Lawrence's, Deleuze's, and Guattari's vitalist focus on the body is the study of the everyday inaugurated by Henri Lefebvre and elaborated by Michel de Certeau, Guy Debord, Rita Felski, and Ben Highmore. For these thinkers, the everyday refers to the mundane realities that make up most human experience; it merits study for precisely this reason. Its study counters analyses that focus on great events, instead asking about the material realities and underlying ideas about the world encoded in the repetitive, semi-conscious actions of everyday life. This exploration is closely tied to artistic practice. Lefebvre's first forays into the everyday originate, as Tommy Davis shows here, in his encounter with Surrealism's effort to bring art and the everyday together. By focusing on "disdained everyday fields"—the banal realities often overlooked by both art and philosophy—both modernism and studies of the everyday sought to restore a vast realm of human experience to consciousness, taking on the artistic impera- tive voiced by Viktor Shklovsky in 1921, "Habitualization devours works, clothes, furniture, one's wife, and the fear of war ... And art exists that one may recover the sensation of life: it exists to make one feel things, to make the stone *stony*" (Shklovsky 2007: 778). Close attention to the ephemera of everyday life strives to defamiliarize the mundane, laying bare its beauty, complexity, and significance (even when it is neither beautiful nor complex) in ways that break decisively with traditional conceptions of art and philosophy.

The tensions between the body and the mind, between literature and philo- sophy, also feed into the concern with the sublime that animates Roger Rothman's account of the splits between André Breton and Georges Bataille, and between Deleuze and Jacques Derrida. Dating back to at least pseudo- Longinus (first century CE), the notion of the sublime is most influentially treated by Immanuel Kant and Edmund Burke.[1] Distinct from the beautiful, which the mind can comprehend, the sublime is the "sense of overwhelming grandeur or irresistible power ... calculated to inspire awe, deep reverence, or lofty emotion, by reason of its beauty, vastness, or grandeur" (*Oxford English Dictionary*). Kant subdivides the sublime into mathematical and dynamic varieties. The mathe- matical sublime results from an encounter with an incomprehensibly large whole, e.g. the universe; the dynamic sublime results from an encounter with the unimaginable. In both cases, the sublime is reflexive; it issues not from the entity encountered, but from the mind's encounter with its own limits. We experience it when reason's capacity is surpassed and the mind comprehends incomprehensibility as such.

As Hilary Thompson shows, Virginia Woolf, Walter Benjamin, and Giorgio Agamben similarly approach the limits of rationality in their understanding of time and temporality. There are two key concepts at work in their thought: the state of exception and messianic time. Though it has been most fully worked out by Agamben, the notion of the state of exception comes from Carl Schmitt's 1922 *Political Theology*. The state of exception occurs when the sovereign ruler suspends the laws of a given state due to an extraordinary threat; the very social order itself is suspended and the laws that sustain it replaced by the determina- tions of the sovereign. Agamben has argued that much of the history of the twentieth century is characterized by the state of exception, and that it provides a key to understanding the political and social realities of today. Similarly, messianic time refers to Benjamin's notion of a quality of time that can blast "open the continuum of history" (1968: 262) and give meaning to the whole. In this, Benjamin rejects the progressivist model of history that sees human society as continually improving. Instead, Benjamin sees the Utopian future as a constellation where moments of messianic time coalesce in a fully dialectical leap out of ordinary time to the end of history. Thompson credits Agamben with separating the notion of messianism from this eschatological dimension, allowing us to conceive of messianic time in terms of the lag between our representations of time and the time it takes us to make those representations: the gap between saying "now" and the *now* that saying was meant to describe.

The question of ethics emerges when the state of exception and messianic time encounter the problem of justice. Thompson approaches this aspect of their relationship through Benjamin's distinction between mythic and divine violence. Mythic violence makes and sustains laws, where divine violence wipes the slate clean and begins again. Mythic violence refers to an abstract basis of authority upon which laws are grounded; divine violence sweeps all such appeals away in its massive force. It's the difference between punishing someone for violating the laws of a given system and destroying the system itself. Divine violence thus steps outside of time (like messianic time) and the given order (like the state of exception) to posit a radical alternative to the status quo. Taking its lead from the connections among these ideas, Thompson's essay performs the mode of reading implied by them. It attends to resonances among disparate figures regardless of influence, historical continuity, or precedence. She cites Woolf as an example of how such a reading practice opens up new vistas for understanding the particular ways in which literature thinks (in its specific plane of immanence) these same issues, though at times in different—perhaps even "disdained"—fields: the psychological as well as the political, the interpersonal as well as the theological.

Common concerns with the relationship between literature and philosophy, body and mind, the sublime and the mundane, ethics and time run through this group of essays. Though they approach the question of how modernism and theory relate concretely from different perspectives, they reveal telling linkages and pose provocative new ways of reading.

Note

1 Kant and Burke differ importantly on the sublime, but I lack the space to elaborate. See Ferguson (1992) and Shaw (2006).

Bibliography

Benjamin, W. (1968) "Theses on the Philosophy of History," in *Illuminations: Essays and Reflections*, trans. Harry Zohn, New York: Schocken Books.

—— (1996 [1921]) "Critique of Violence," in *Selected Writings Vol. 1 1913–1926*, ed. Marcus Bullock and Michael W. Jennings, trans. Edmund Jephcott, Cambridge, MA: Belknap Press, 236–52.

Ferguson, F. (1992) *Solitude and the Sublime: Romanticism and the Aesthetics of Individuation*, New York and London: Routledge.

Kant, I. (1952) *The Critique of Judgment*, trans. James Creed Meredith, Oxford: Clarendon Press.

Pseudo-Longinus (2001) "On Sublimity," in V. B. Leitch, W. Cain, L. Finke, and B. Johnson (eds) *The Norton Anthology of Theory and Criticism*, New York: W. W. Norton, 135–54.

Schmitt, C. (1985 [1922]) *Political Theology: Four Chapters on the Concept of Sovereignty*, trans. George Schwab, Chicago: University of Chicago Press.

Shaw, P. (2006) *The Sublime*, London and New York: Routledge.

Shklovsky, V. (2007) "Art as Technique," trans. Lee T. Lemon and Marion Reis, in David H. Richter (ed.) *The Critical Tradition: Classic Texts and Contemporary Trends*, New York: Bedford/St Martin's Press, 775–84.

1   Rip the veil of the old vision across, and walk through the rent

Reading D. H. Lawrence with Deleuze and Guattari

Anneleen Masschelein

And finally it seems to me that even art is utterly dependent on philosophy: or if you prefer it, on a metaphysic. The metaphysic or philosophy may not be anywhere very accurately stated, and may be quite unconscious in the artist, yet is a metaphysic that governs men at the time, and is by all men more or less comprehended, and lived ... Our vision, our metaphysics is wearing woefully thin, and the art is wearing absolutely threadbare. We have no future: neither for our hopes nor our aims nor our art. It has all gone grey and opaque. We've got to rip the old veil of a vision across, and find what our heart really believes in, after all: and what the heart really wants for the next future ... Rip the veil of the old vision across, and walk through the rent.

(Lawrence 1932: 65)

Although D. H. Lawrence does not appear to be a key influence on Gilles Deleuze and Félix Guattari like Marcel Proust, Antonin Artaud or Franz Kafka, he is a consistent reference in their work from the 1970s onwards.[1] One cannot help being struck by similarities in vocabulary (polarities, planes, intensities, vibrations, singleness) and modernist imagery (machines, wireless communication, oddly mixed with natural and cosmological metaphors) in Lawrence and Deleuze and Guattari. The curious way Deleuze and Guattari paraphrase Lawrence's minor texts, especially the essays, betray a great familiarity.[2] In this light, it is surprising so little critical attention has been devoted to Lawrence–Deleuze and Guattari.[3] Examining the extent to which preconceptual images such as the impersonal unconscious, sexuality and the unconscious as flow, the line of flight, the writer as athlete of becoming have been directly borrowed from Lawrence and modified may illuminate how Deleuze and Guattari deal with sources (assemblage) as well as their conception of art and philosophy.

Deleuze and Guattari's involvement with D. H. Lawrence can roughly be organized around interrelated moments and themes.[4] First, Lawrence's idiosyncratic critique of psychoanalysis is a model for Deleuze and Guattari in *Anti-Oedipus*. Second, Lawrence's criticism of literature influenced Deleuze and Guattari. In the dialogue with Claire Parnet on "The Superiority of Anglo-American Literature" (1977) and in *A Thousand Plateaus* (1978), they remain very close to Lawrence's *Studies of Classical American Literature* (1923).[5] (Third, Deleuze casts Lawrence as a direct heir of Nietzsche and Spinoza in the preface to Fanny Deleuze's translation of Lawrence's *Apocalypse*, "Nietzsche and Saint-Paul, Lawrence and John of Patmos" [Deleuze 1992], and in his essay "To Have Done with Judgment" [Deleuze 1992].[6] Finally, the figure of Lawrence reappears once more in *What is Philosophy?* [1996].) Unexpectedly, Lawrence's essay "Chaos in Poetry" (1928) figures quite extensively in the concluding chapter of their attempt to distinguish between three domains of thinking: philosophy, science, and art.

Deleuze and Guattari's frequent returns to Lawrence illuminate their distinction and interference between philosophy and art.

> These thinkers are "half"-philosophers but also much more than philosophers. But they are not sages. There is such force in those unhinged works of Hölderlin, Kleist, Rimbaud, Mallarmé, Kafka, and many English and American novelists, from Melville to Lawrence or Miller, in which the reader discovers admiringly that they have written the novel of Spinozism. To be sure, they do not produce a synthesis of art and philosophy. They branch out and do not stop branching out. They are hybrid geniuses who neither erase nor cover over differences in kind but, on the contrary, use all the resources of their "athleticism" to install themselves within this very difference, like acrobats torn apart in a show of strength.
>
> (Deleuze and Guattari 1996: 67)

Lawrence's branching, rhizomatic, anarchic, iconoclast style of thinking moves to and fro between the domains of literature and philosophy, his metaphysic permeating his art and vice versa.[7] However, in spite of his passionate pleas for reuniting literature and philosophy, Lawrence rarely produces a successful synthesis.[8] Torn between the two, Lawrence is not so much a mediator as an outsider: his failure to achieve a "perfect" dialectic between literature and philosophy demonstrates how the outside of philosophy, science and art—nonphilosophy, nonart and nonscience—are constitutive to thinking. I propose to reread Lawrence *with* Deleuze and Guattari[9] to grasp the substance of this passionate, eccentric thinker who fascinated them for so many years.

The Lawrentian unconscious

The first traces of Deleuze and Guattari's involvement with Lawrence are in *Anti-Oedipus*.[10] Much like Freud, who repeatedly claimed poets intuited the truths of psychoanalysis, Deleuze and Guattari cast literary authors like Artaud, Beckett, Proust, Kafka, Miller, Burroughs, Lawrence, etc. as the main precursors of their criticism of Freud and the Oedipus complex, alongside dissident psychoanalysts like Wilhelm Reich or the anti-psychiatrists David Cooper and Robert D. Laing. Literary authors offer images and a language for a positive conception of schizo-analysis, the most well-known example of Artaud's "body without organs." Deleuze and Guattari appreciate Lawrence's and Miller's alternative models: "We think that Lawrence and Miller have a more accurate view of sexuality than Freud, even from the viewpoint of the famous scientificity"

(Deleuze and Guattari 1982 [1977]: 292), which leads us back to Lawrence's essays on the unconscious.

Psychoanalysis and the Unconscious and *Fantasia of the Unconscious* are Lawrence's iconoclast answers to the popularity of Freudian and Jungian psychoanalysis in literary circles (and part of a curious attempt to target the American market). *Psychoanalysis and the Unconscious* begins with an ironic polemic against the Freudian conception of the unconscious, based on incest (Lawrence rarely if ever uses the term "Oedipus complex"), sexuality, and repression. According to Lawrence, repression and inhibitions stop the glorious stream of consciousness discovered by William James, and the contemporary attention to (diseased) sexuality has turned sex into "sex in the head," a pure idea. Instead,

> We have actually to go back to our own unconscious. But not the unconscious which is the inverted reflection of our own ideal consciousness. We must discover, if we can, the true unconscious, where our life bubbles up in us, prior to any mentality.
>
> (Lawrence 2004: 15)

For Lawrence, the unconscious is a force of life, dynamic and causeless, a flow or current that gradually activates different zones in the body. The model he develops is an idiosyncratic combination of philosophical references (Heracleitos, Nietzsche, Bergson, and James), biological terminology (ganglion and plexus) and physics (electricity, wireless communication) as well as esoteric Eastern philosophy (chakras and kundalini), and occultism (Mme Blavatsky and Pryse).

Lawrence's dynamic consciousness is based on a double polarity. A sympathetic energy between mother and child flows from the solar plexus, the centre of the consciousness. This energy is negatively polarized with another source of energy, flowing from the voluntary lumbar ganglion (the spine), which works towards isolation. Two fluxes of energy are directed outwards towards contact, and inwards towards singleness. This polar model does not seem that far removed from Freud's dual model of the drives, but Lawrence multiplies this diagram of the body into different energy centers that dynamically interact. Vibrations run through various planes of the body, below and above the diaphragm, circulating between the upper and lower consciousness. In *Fantasia* this model divides into nine centers. In "To Have Done with Judgment," Deleuze points out Lawrence's model of the body is a "body without organs":

> an affective, intensive, anarchist body that consists solely of a set of poles, zones, thresholds, and gradients. It is traversed by a powerful, nonorganic vitality. Lawrence paints the picture of such a body, with the sun and the moon as its poles, with its planes, its sections and its plexuses.
>
> (1997: 131)

The Lawrentian conception of the unconscious has no split between body and mind, or body and soul, nor are the different zones hierarchical. Flows of energies stem from the same source and acquire specificity and function in the process of development. The unconscious is thus conceived as a vitalist, creative principle, but not in a universal or general sense: "life is a general force, whereas the unconscious is essentially single and unique in each individual" (Lawrence 2004: 38).

Lawrence insists "the unconscious is never an abstraction, *never to be abstracted*" (2004: 38). Abstraction, idealism and automatism are the greatest dangers threatening modern man and society. Thus, Lawrence's psychology entails a diagnosis and remedy for the discontents of his culture. Due to excessive emphasis on mind, a false hierarchy has been established, disturbing the equilibrium between upper and lower body as well as in society, between men and women, adults and children. The upper consciousness has gotten the upper hand, resulting in perversion, idealism, and static arrest of the creative flux. In the *Unconscious* and *Phoenix* essays, Lawrence proposes rather drastic measures to restore the balance regarding the education of children (based on Rousseauian and Spartan principles) and the relation between the sexes. The importance of sexuality, or true union, lies in its capacity to renew the blood (a recurrent term for the unconscious or the lower consciousness is "blood-consciousness") and to revitalize the subjects.[11] At the same time, since man and woman naturally belong to different spheres, it is equally important to withdraw from union and regain strength in singular, independent existence. For this Lawrence coins the term "singleness."

One of the most striking features of Lawrence's writings on the unconscious is his lack of precision in terms like "conscious," "consciousness," "unconscious," "blood consciousness" or "lower consciousness."[12] Lawrence, who had little or no first-hand knowledge of psychoanalysis, was motivated by a jealous attraction to Freud's conceptual language.[13]

> Lawrence's sensitivity to Freud was in the first place a sensitivity to Freud's language, particularly as it, in Lawrence's view, constituted an unacceptably rigid model of the psyche. It is largely the fixed term, the dominant discourse, that Lawrence finds unacceptable.
>
> (Becket 1997: 47)

It is precisely the fluidity and subtle variety within Lawrence's language that makes him so useful for Deleuze and Guattari. Lawrence does not describe or theorize an unconscious, he lays it out, patiently tracking its details and movements and continually refining his diagnostics in novels, essays, and letters.[14] Lawrence sees the unconscious in physical terms as a current of energy, hence words like stream, flow, flux, vibration and poles, polar attraction and dynamic tension. This view of the unconscious or consciousness as a flow is a typically modernist trope that extends to a writing technique.[15] Lawrence tries to render the pure energy and movement of consciousness in a fluid language of streams or strings of metaphors, symbols and similes, oddly disturbing traditional oppositions and mixing different traditions (oriental and occult symbolism, and modern terminology of electricity, e.g. the symbol of the dynamo, wireless communication like the Marconi message or the telephone). The result is the Lawrentian symbol, which Deleuze studies in Lawrence's *Apocalypse* and "To Have Done with Judgment":

> This is what Lawrence calls a symbol: an intensive compound that vibrates and expands, that has no meaning, but makes us whirl about until we harness the maximum of possible forces in every direction, each of which receives a new meaning by entering in relation with the other.[16]
>
> (Deleuze 1997: 134)

In tune with the sexual revolution, Lawrence's work knew a revival in the late 1960s and 1970s, resulting in new French translations of the critical work.[17] Deleuze and Guattari relish catchy phrases from *Eros et les chiens* like "dirty little secret" (Deleuze and Guattari 1982 [1977]: 49), "sex in the head," "our democratic, industrial order of things whose style is my-dear-little-lamb-I-want-to-see-mommy" (Deleuze and Guattari 1982 [1977]: 177) to state modern sexual hypocrisy. Before quoting Lawrence extensively, they ventriloquize his protest, almost in free direct speech, reactivating Lawrence's passionate critique in glimpses of it rather than summary or analysis.

> D. H. Lawrence—who does not struggle against Freud in the name of the rights of an Ideal, but who speaks by virtue of the flows of sexuality and the intensities of the unconscious, and who is incensed and bewildered by what Freud is doing when he closets sexuality in the oedipal nursery—has a foreboding of this operation of displacement and protests with all his might: no, Oedipus is not a state of desire and the drives, it is an idea, nothing but an idea that repression inspires in us concerning desire, not even a compromise but an idea in the service of repression, its propaganda, or propagation.
>
> (Deleuze and Guattari 1982 [1977]: 115)

In a lengthy quotation from *Psychoanalysis of the Unconscious*, the notion of the incest motive (the initial target of Lawrence's attack) is juxtaposed to "the active unconscious [which] sparkles, vibrates, travels" (Lawrence cited in Deleuze and Guattari 1982 [1977]: 115). Deleuze and Guattari cleverly pick up on Lawrence's statement that analysis should be impersonal. For Lawrence the notion of "personal" seems synonymous with egoism and individualism, as opposed to singleness, which is a positive quality not of the ego but of the lower consciousness. Deleuze and Guattari slightly displace the term "impersonal" to "inhuman" (a term used by Lawrence in his essays on Melville), bringing it closer to their own notion of the machinic production of the unconscious, as antidote to capitalism, fascism, and to oedipal psychology.[18]

In their proposal for a positive schizo-analysis at the end of *Anti-Oedipus*, Deleuze and Guattari cleverly turn to Lawrence's minor essay "We Need One Another" to supplement the *unconscious* essays (Bryden 2000: 110–11). As the title suggests, Lawrence advocates relationships and sexuality (in a very broad sense) as antidote to detrimental individualism in contemporary society. He shows himself at his most liberated and open-minded when discussing relations between men and women.[19] Men and women must be disconnected from their stereotypical role in society. Both are described as soft vibrations or streams that must flow together in the course of a lifetime.

> Woman is like an idol, like a marionette, always forced to play one role or another: sweetheart, mistress, wife, mother. If only we could break up this fixity, and realize the unseizable quality of real woman: that woman is a flow, a river of life, quite different from a man's river of life: and that each river must flow in its own way, though without breaking its bounds: and that the relation of man to woman is the flowing of two rivers side by side, sometimes even mingling, then separating again, and travelling on. The relationship is a life-long change and a life-long travelling. And that is sex.
>
> (Lawrence 1964: 194)

The emphasis in the isotopy of the flow has subtly shifted from the current working through friction and opposite poles, to a more tranquil flowing and occasional intermingling of rivers. This entails a more fluid notion of identity, in terms of intensities (flow, soft vibration, etc.) and change rather than fixed essences. Deleuze and Guattari repeatedly praise this model of sexuality and the unconscious and translate it in terms of partial flows and circuits, e.g. the sex flow, the excremental flow, the chastity flow, the male and female flow, that are not found as such in the essay (Deleuze and Guattari 1982 [1977]: 351, 362, 366). (Thus Lawrence's essay is seamlessly integrated within the positive model for schizoanalysis by Deleuze and Guattari as fluxes of molecular elements.)

Throughout *Anti-Oedipus*, Deleuze and Guattari consider Lawrence an innovative thinker, critic of the Oedipus complex, and "a fellow traveller" (Becket 1997: 64, 67). Still, the straightforward conclusion that Deleuze and Guattari borrowed some of their main ideas from his work, turning Lawrence's imprecise, wild metaphors into motifs or even concepts, must be qualified. While Lawrence's use of language and imagery may be idiosyncratic, it is also in tune with modernist vogues that lasted well into the 1960s and 1970s. This obviously makes it hard to positively identify its traces. In "Nietzsche and Saint John, Lawrence and John of Patmos," Deleuze's sensitivity to the complexity of Lawrence's use of language and his theory of symbols as dynamic and living elements is most apparent. And yet, in his detailed readings of Lawrence, Deleuze is never really faithful, as Mary Bryden demonstrates. He selects and appropriates elements that can be used. Words are shifted and displaced in order to foreground certain notions, while other more embarrassing elements (e.g. the misogynistic attacks on modern women or the isotopy of race and soil) are either softened or completely left out. If Deleuze and Guattari are critical of Lawrence, their criticism is not aimed at the eccentricities in Lawrence's thought, but concerns the literary work. Lawrence and other Anglo-American authors manage to liberate the flux of the unconscious and allow the energy to traverse the body without organs. They nonetheless fail because they somehow prematurely end the process by trying to name or fix a final destiny.[20] Every deterritorialization also involves "an anthropomorphic or phallic representation" (Deleuze and Guattari 1982 [1977]: 315) or reterritorialization. In Lawrence's case, such closure would be the perfect marriage in the early novels, the utopia of the primitive in later novels (Australia, Mexico, Etruscan civilization). Such naming or halting of movement could be seen as a synthesis, turning the movement into a dialectic, leading towards an ideal goal.

The superiority of Lawrence's *Studies of Classic American Literature*

Towards the end of the 1970s, Deleuze and Guattari's interest shifts from Lawrence's critique of psychoanalysis to the literary criticism, poetry and the later novels (especially *Aaron's Rod*).[21] Already in *Anti-Oedipus*, Deleuze and Guattari declare their partiality to Anglo-American literature and its tendency for leaving, shattering boundaries, deterritorialization. In *A Thousand Plateaus* and especially in the *Dialogue* with Claire Parnet on the superiority of American literature, the *Studies of Classic American Literature* are prominently present.[22] Indeed, key notions from Deleuze and Guattari's aesthetics—the opposition between French idealism and Anglo-American empiricism, the line of flight and becoming, and the artist as athlete—are remarkably congruent with Lawrence's essays. In the *Dialogues*, moreover, it is striking how Deleuze selects, displaces and elaborates ideas and conceptions from the *Studies* that resurface in the aesthetics outlined in *What is Philosophy?*

> The French novel is profoundly pessimistic and idealistic, "critical of life rather than creative of life." It stuffs its characters down the hole and bounces them off the wall. It can only conceive of organized voyages, and of salvation only through art, a still Catholic salvation, in other words, a salvation through eternity. It spends its time plotting points instead of drawing lines, active lines of flights or of positive deterritorialization. The Anglo-American novel is totally different. "To get away. To get away, out! ... To cross a horizon ... " From Hardy to Lawrence, from Melville to Miller, the same cry rings out: Go across, get out, break through, make a beeline, don't get stuck on a point.
>
> (Deleuze and Guattari 2004 [1988]: 207)

The imperatives with which the statement ends are a dramatization and radicalization of the phrase from Lawrence's essay on Melville, from which all transcendent applications from the original are carefully left out.[23]

In the introduction to the *Studies*, Lawrence starts from a juxtaposition between nineteenth-century American (and Russian) literature as genuinely extreme and new, as opposed to pseudo-revolutionary, contemporary (modernist) European literature: "The European moderns [i.e. the Italian futurist Marinetti,

Joyce and Proust] are all *trying* to be extreme. The great Americans I mention just were it" (2003: 11–12). Lawrence relates the extremity of American literature to what he calls the "spirit of place", a kind of polarity or "IT" (2003: 17–18). This "IT" is a revolutionary quality of the American land, the land of freedom that gave the Founding Fathers and the great American novelists the courage to explore and break with the old laws of Europe. Deleuze displaces the "spirit" of American literature to philosophical empiricism, incarnated in the English language (Deleuze and Parnet 2003: 40–4). American literature and empirical philosophy share a kind of concreteness. If Lawrence wrote the novel of Spinozism (Deleuze and Guattari 1996: 67), then empiricism is "like the English novel": concrete, *in medias res* (Deleuze and Parnet 2003: 40).

In *Dialogues II* with Claire Parnet, Deleuze limits the scope of Lawrence's opposition of American nineteenth-century literature versus European modernism to American versus French literature, which is obsessed with the "dirty little secret." Picking up Lawrence's minor comment on Proust in "Pornography and Obscenity," Deleuze uses this catch-phrase as a starting point for everything wrong with French literature: neurosis, narcissism, intellectualism, petty critical overinterpretation, nationalism, and finally, the overemphasis of the signifier in structuralism, which all adds up to an arrest of the flux, of creativity in one fixed meaning (Deleuze and Parnet 2003: 35–7).[24] Opposed to the "dirty little secret" is the "line of flight," a highly polysemous term. As Lawrence also points out in the *Studies*, the motif of the flight (as opposed to the voyage) can be understood in a double sense: a movement of running away—from home, from origin, without a fixed end goal in sight—but also of taking off from the ground towards the unknown, the sky, the inhuman. Second, the line of flight is a mathematical term related to perspective in painting. The illusion of endlessness and depth created by virtual (imaginary) but present centrifugal lines in a painting is contrasted with French pointillism, a myopic gazing at details (dirty little secrets). Third, both in *Dialogues* and in *A Thousand Plateaus*, deterritorialization implies movement and speed.

> Cross the wall, the Chinese perhaps, but at what price? At the price of a *becoming-animal*, a *becoming-flower or rock*, and beyond that a strange *becoming-imperceptible*, a *becoming-hard now one with loving*. It is a question of speed, even if the movement is in its place.
>
> (Deleuze and Guattari 2004 [1988]: 207)

The movement of the line of flight is not directed towards a goal. It is a vibration as well as an oscillating movement, a rotation. Rather than ending, the line of flight becomes something else while remaining in the same place. Finally, in the *Dialogues*, Deleuze relates the line of flight to writing. A writer does not arrive; he disappears as a subject in a process of becoming someone or something else while remaining essentially himself.

The notion of becoming could be read as a translation of the Lawrentian concerns with singleness and transformation, summed up in Lawrence's beloved pictorial motif of the phoenix. In his examples, Deleuze often relates Lawrence and becoming: becoming-woman, becoming-eskimo, becoming-animal (in the tortoise or porcupine poems)[25] or becoming-sea, like Melville in *Moby Dick*. In *Studies of Classic American Literature*, the motifs of "the line of flight" and "becoming" are very present in Lawrence's readings of Melville (of *Typee* and *Oomoo*, and of *Moby Dick*).

> Never man instinctly hated human life, our human life, as we have it, more than Melville did. And never was a man so passionately filled with the sense of vastness and mystery of life which is non-human. He was mad to look over our horizons. Anywhere out of *our* world. To get away. To get out, out! To get away out of our life. To cross the horizon into another life. No matter what life, as long as it is another life.
>
> (Lawrence 2003: 124)

Melville attains the non-human in his descriptions of the sea and of the sea-creature Moby Dick: "He isn't quite a land-animal. There is something slithery about him. Something always half-seas-over. In his life they said he was mad—or crazy. He was neither mad nor crazy. But he was over the border. He was half a water-animal" (Lawrence 2003: 122). At the same time Melville fails miserably, because he somehow denies his "underconscious" drawing him to the inhuman, the savage, the primitive: "He even pined for Home and Mother, the two things he had run from as fast as ships would carry him."[26] The two essays on Melville are remarkable because of the lucidity and complexity of Lawrence's response to Melville: utmost admiration coupled with radical rejection of abstraction, idealism, moralism, and mysticism. Moreover, sharp sensitivity to Melville's language and symbolism goes hand in hand with a strong subjective presence that is never biographical or personal.

In all Lawrence's readings, the truth of American literature is located in the artist and the failure in the man as moral being, all the while recognizing that the two cannot be disconnected. The artists almost succeed insofar as they fail as men, because failure prevents the truth of art from becoming abstract or ideal.

> Art-speech is the only truth. An artist is usually a damned liar, but his art, if it be art, will tell you the truth of his day. And that is all that matters. Away with eternal truth. Truth lives from day to day, and the marvellous Plato of yesterday is chiefly bosh today. The old American artists were hopeless liars. But they were artists, in spite of themselves.
>
> (Lawrence 2003: 14)

Deleuze and Guattari's earlier critique of the failure of Anglo-American writers, because they somehow always reterritorialize their flight, belatedly echoes Lawrence's diagnosis of the successful failures of the Americans. In *A Thousand Plateaus*, *Dialogues*, and *What is Philosophy?* the criticism has made way for a positive appreciation of these failures, expressed in the artist as athlete.

It may be that the writer has delicate health, a weak constitution. He is nonetheless the opposite of the neurotic: a sort of great Alive [the French expression *grand Vivant* contains a pun on *bon vivant*, someone who enjoys the good life and perhaps on *le grand mal*, a form of epilepsy—A. M.] (in the manner of Spinoza, Nietzsche or Lawrence) in so far as he is only too weak for the life which runs in him or for the affects which pass in him.

(Deleuze and Parnet 2003: 37)

In *What is Philosophy?* Lawrence is described as "a seer or becomer," whose description of the death of the porcupine is too terrible to bear (Deleuze and Guattari 1996: 171). The becoming of the artist is a direct contact with an excess of experience. This kind of truth entails its own destruction, for becoming entails an obliteration of the subject of the lived experience in an expression from a virtual position. The artist captures life in a monument because he has seen too much life, more than he can bear.

Through having reached the percept as "the sacred source," through having seen Life in the living or the Living in the lived, the novelist or painter returns breathless and with bloodshot eyes. They are athletes ... "an affective Athleticism," an athleticism of becoming that reveals only forces that are not its own—"plastic spectre." In this respect artists are like philosophers. What little health they possess is often too fragile, not because of their illnesses or neuroses but because they have seen something in life that is too much for anyone, too much for themselves, and that has put on them the quiet mark of death.

(Deleuze and Guattari 1996: 172)

In this sense, the artist is an *Übermensch* capable of bearing the unbearable, even at the cost of his own destruction, in both life and work. Art is no longer the expression of a subject, "sensory becoming is otherness caught in the moment of expression" (Deleuze and Guattari 1996: 177). This conception reformulates and raises the stakes of Lawrence's notion of art-speech and truth: rather than a strict separation of art and life, art continually vibrates, overflows with an excess of life that it can barely contain.

Chaos, cosmos, and philosophy

What is Philosophy? is a systematic attempt to distinguish three domains of thinking: philosophy, art, and science. What they share is their struggle with chaos. Order is created by laying out specific planes onto the chaos, by mapping and thus converting wild chaos into territory. However, the three disciplines differ fundamentally in their way of mapping, the kind of planes they lay out. Thus, different forms of thought are created from chaos, the raw material of thinking, by different types of agents. In the book, Deleuze and Guattari unpack the three-fold distinction in a series of characterizations of the three domains.

Although philosophy is not tangible, it is—like the prephilosophical plane of chaos—always of this world. Ideas are never transcendent. Hence, philosophy unfolds on a plane of immanence populated by concepts. Concepts are abstract mental compounds that are nonetheless material; they possess substance. They are infinite, yet they have a history and are directed towards becoming. They have to be continually recreated in thought in order to remain alive. Dynamic and ever-changing, concepts are compounds, mapped out through composites and zones of indeterminacy, and they produce infinite variations of chaos. The agents operating on this plane are conceptual personae, figures or subjects of enunciation who put forth preconcepts that become concepts in a process of institutionaliza-tion, canonization and pedagogy.[27] Science constitutes a plane of reference, where chaos is tamed by relating infinite matter to a finite number of variables, i.e. functions and prospects. Functions and prospects (the specific creations of logics) are coordinates and references related to matter, creating variables that can be classified and allow us to make predictions. In true science, however, functions and prospects are always also placed in a global cosmology, the infinite field of chaos, which is its precondition. The agent of science is the partial observer, who critically observes the reality of which he is a part.

Art, finally, lays out a plane of composition onto the material (language, sound, stone, canvas, etc.). It creates percepts, affects and blocs of sensations. These are the concrete but impersonal results of perceptions, feelings, and sen-sations materialized in the work of art, where they are preserved independent from artist, character or public.[28] Sensations or perceptions must link to aes-thetic figures. The varieties of art are unique, singular results of the activity of composition in relation to concrete matter. The artwork is a monument, not because it commemorates, but because it embodies affects and precepts that are past as well as eternally immanent and that can activate or resuscitate in the future. To put it differently, in the finite form of the artwork, the infinite is perpetually incarnate, active or productive. The percepts and affects, radically distinct from perceptions or affectations of a subject, exceed the material limits of the artistic creation and resonate with the infinite chaos from which it arises.

Chaos is the surface onto which zones and landmarks are created, paths are traced, force fields are activated through the attraction and repulsion of its poles, resulting in dynamism, flows, and life. The revolutionary quality of truly "creative" thinking, whether in philosophy, science or art, lies in this dynamic mapping and hardwiring of the planes laid out onto the chaos (territorialization), in such a way that they do not cover up but instead continually open up the chaos (deterritorialization). By confronting us with chaos, by taking up the challenge posed by chaos, the three domains distinguish themselves from their true "enemy," threatening them both from without and from within: *doxa*, i.e., the fallacious beliefs by which we ignore or repress the inherent chaos of existence to gain a false sense of security and certainty.

> It is as if the *struggle against chaos* does not take place without an affinity with the enemy, because another struggle develops and takes on more importance—

the struggle *against opinion*, which claims to protect us against chaos itself. In a violently poetic text, Lawrence describes what produces poetry: people are constantly putting up an umbrella that shelters them and on the underside of which they draw a firmament and write their conventions and opinions. But poets, artists, make a slit in the umbrella, they tear open the firmament itself, to let in a bit of free and windy chaos and to frame in a sudden light a vision that appears through the rent ... Then come a crowd of imitators who repair the umbrella with something vaguely resembling the vision and the crowd of commentators who patch over the rent with opinions: communication. Other artists are always needed to make other slits, to carry out necessary and perhaps ever-greater destructions, thereby restoring to their predecessors the incommunicable novelty that we could no longer see. This is to say that artists struggle less against chaos (that, in a certain manner, all their wishes struggle forth) than against the "clichés" of opinion.

(Deleuze and Guattari 1996: 204)

Deleuze and Guattari refer here to "Chaos in Poetry," originally the preface to Harry Crosby's *Chariot of the Sun*, published separately in 1929. In the text, Lawrence characterizes poetry's new vision within the known, not in transcendent or sublime terms but in terms of chaos forever surging in the world. This state is unbearable to man. Indeed, "Man must wrap himself in a vision, make a house of apparent form and stability, fixity" (Lawrence 1964: 255). This stable house— a recurrent metaphor in *What is Philosophy?*—is presented as an umbrella, protective but also taking away the vital light of the sun. The poet's task, "enemy of convention," is to make slits in the umbrella, opening a vision of the sun and letting in draughts of chaos. The history of poetry and art, unfortunately, is such that each of these original visions is doomed to become a new umbrella.

Chaos is all shut out. The umbrella got so big, the patches and plaster are so tight and hard, it can be slit no more. If it were slit, the rent would no more be a vision, it would only be an outrage. We should dab it over at once, to match the rest. So the umbrella is absolute. And so the yearning for chaos becomes a nostalgia. And this will go on till some terrific wind blows the umbrella to ribbons, and much of mankind to oblivion.

(Lawrence 1964: 257)

For Lawrence, as for Deleuze and Guattari, the poet is both a seer and a symptom. Poets "show the desire for chaos, and the fear for chaos. The desire for chaos is the breath of their poetry. The fear of chaos is in their parade of forms and techniques" (Lawrence 1964: 257). In Lawrence's analysis of *Chariot of the Sun*, the breath of poetry is also failure: "Failure is part of the living chaos. And the groping reveals the act of attention, which suddenly passes into pure expression" (Lawrence 1964: 261). Here, we encounter the concepts crucial to Deleuze and Guattari's poetics in a preconceptual or, as Lawrence puts it, a naive form.

The essential quality of poetry is that it makes a new effort of attention and "discovers" a new world within the known world. Man and the animals, the flowers, all live within a strange world of ever surging chaos. The chaos we have got used to we call a cosmos. The unspeakable inner chaos of which we are composed we call consciousness, and mind, and even civilizations.

(Lawrence 1964: 255)

The artist as failure transforms into the artist as athlete; the act of attention that passes into pure expression becomes "sensory becoming is otherness caught in the moment of expression" (Deleuze and Guattari 1996: 177); the notions of chaos, cosmos, and consciousness appear as versions of Deleuze's philosophy of immanence and an "image of thinking" (Dosse 2007: 157–8).

The circle of life

Like Deleuze and Guattari, Lawrence returned to the same images, metaphors and symbols in his work, displacing and elaborating them, thus constructing the tissue of his thought, his "metaphysic." The phrase "to rip the veil of the old vision across and walk through the rent," also in the preface to *Fantasia of the Unconscious*, indicates which Lawrence is most dear to Deleuze and Guattari: the visionary, the metaphysic, "the thinker as poet" as Fiona Becket calls him. Both consider art and philosophy as two equal, distinct yet closely related ways of thinking: immanent, dynamic, conflictual and not afraid to face chaos against the false comfort of opinions in bad philosophy and bad art.

Deleuze and Guattari conclude *What is Philosophy?* by pointing out three types of interference of the different planes "that join up in the brain," in other words, three zones where philosophical, scientific, and artistic thinking meet (Deleuze and Guattari 1996: 216). First, there are extrinsic interferences when one discipline looks at another from its own plane, e.g. when philosophy tries to make a concept of a sensation, or when art creates sensations of concepts or functions. Here, there is no real contact, since the different planes are maintained and do not mix. Second, intrinsic interferences occur when elements or agents slip from one plane onto another (e.g. concepts and conceptual personae sliding from the plane of immanence onto the plane of composition). The third, most complex kind of interference has to do with the reference of each kind of thinking to their negative or to their "No." This is ultimately the point where they join in chaos, not in a dialectical sense, but as a constant centrifugal reference.

Philosophy needs a nonphilosophy that comprehends it; it needs a nonphilosophical comprehension just as art needs nonart and science needs nonscience. They do not need the No as beginning, or as the end in which they would be called upon to disappear by being realized, but at every moment of their becoming or their development.

(Deleuze and Guattari 1996: 218)

The relation of forms of knowledge to their negative is for Deleuze and Guattari the most enigmatic type of interference between the three planes. They speak in almost religious terms of "submersion," from which a "people to come" is extracted or summoned forth by art, philosophy, and science. Thus, the notions of concept, function and affect acquire a depth, or a front and a backside—in other words, an existence. While they have their own form and identity on the front side, their back always remains out of sight, in the shadow. This undifferentiated shadow or chaos pushes forth the recognizable shapes of concept, function and affect—like pseudopodia—but it remains their common denominator.

> It is here that concepts, sensations and functions become indecidable, at the same time as philosophy, art, and science become indiscernible, as if they shared the same shadow that extends itself across their different nature and constantly accompanies them.
>
> (Deleuze and Guattari 1996: 218)

Throughout the last chapter, the isotopy of the brain as material object is mixed with a mock-religious or cosmological isotopy of birth and rebirth that is perhaps more comical-occult animation than religious creation.

The dynamics of art, philosophy, and science is the point where thinking comes to life, becomes active in renewal and growth. This is where thinking becomes exciting even if always partly in the shadow. The movement is tilting or flipping rather than sliding. Thoughts arise and disappear, on the verge or brink of thinking, and always already beyond reach. Deleuze and Guattari are, like Lawrence, interested in the point where thinking is captured but not or barely contained by expression. The opening to a cosmos or chaos perpetually exceeds knowledge, it is a constant process of transformation. And yet, neither Lawrence nor Deleuze and Guattari conceive this point as purely mystical or spiritual. It is material, palpable, chaotic, and frictional.

The flow of partial, molecular thought elements can be intuited as an intensity or vibration, or magnified and observed as a symptom on the micro-level of a text or work. The dynamic juxtaposition and repetition of words (colors or sounds) into a texture is present in the experience of actively encountering the point where texts release ideas. This in turn infects and affects the medium, producing vibrations inside the thinking brain, transforming them into something else. From this perspective, whether a philosophical work is interesting, good or successful is no longer a question of form or content, of failure or success, but of vitality, of "a Life." Perhaps then, it is the way Lawrence's oeuvre moves and vibrates through repetitions, contradictions and shifts, revealing how ideas continually exceed language, that is the main, most difficult to pinpoint, motif in Deleuze and Guattari's attraction to Lawrence.

Notes

1 *Deleuze et les écrivains* has a full index of references to Lawrence (Gelas and Micolet 2007: 568), but the relationship is not examined in depth.

2 Deleuze may have been introduced to Lawrence through his wife Fanny's translation of Lawrence's *Apocalypse* essay. Dosse reports Lawrence's *Eros et les chiens* (he mistakenly cites *Les Chiens d'Eros*) and Joyce's *Ulysses* were on Guattari's desk when he died unexpectedly in 1992 (Dosse 2007: 585).

3 Notable exceptions are Mary Bryden's insightful reading of Deleuze's preface to *Apocalypse*, "Nietzsche and Saint-Paul, Lawrence and John of Patmos." See also Gelas and Micolet 2007: 8, 259–65, 340–1. Within Lawrence studies the relation between the two is equally underexamined. Fiona Becket pays attention to the influence of Lawrence's unconscious essays on *Anti-Oedipus*. Beatrice Monaco's Deleuzian reading of *Women in Love* offers very few new insights.

4 This essay focuses mainly on the work written by Deleuze and Guattari, among which I also count *What is Philosophy?* Dosse attributes this work to Deleuze on his own (Dosse 2007: 27).

5 Deleuze and Guattari most frequently refer to *Eros et les chiens*, from 1969. The volume contains a selection from *Phoenix I* and *II*. Among the most frequently quoted essays are "We Need One Another" and "Pornography and Obscenity," from which they borrow notions like the "sex flow" and the "dirty little secret" (see Lawrence 1964: 176–7, 184, 191–4).

6 Key questions in both essays are the ethical-political notions of judgment, power, and singularity or "singleness" versus collectivity. (See Mary Bryden and Michèle Clément in Gelas and Micolet 2007: 259–65.)

7 This is Becket's focus in *D. H. Lawrence: The Thinker as Poet* (Becket 1997). Kinkead-Weekes (1997–8) argues Lawrence's philosophy was extracted from his literary work, rather than the other way around.

8 See Michael Bell (1992: 10–11).

9 On the notion of "speaking *with*, seeing *with*" and sympathy, see *Dialogues* (Deleuze and Parnet 2003: 39).

10 Lawrence is mentioned more than seventeen times (in *A Thousand Plateaus*, there are only six mentions). In footnotes, they refer to *Aaron's Rod*, *Fantasia of the Unconscious* and the later essays, most notably "Art and Morality" and "We Need One Another." The text alludes to "Pornography and Obscenity" and to *Studies in Classic American Literature*. All references are to translations.

11 Armstrong considers this intertwining of sexual emancipation with social reform and spiritual renewal as a typical modernist feature (Armstrong 2004: 72–3).

12 *Studies in American Literature* uses the term "underconscious." In *Women in Love*, there are states like "semi-consciousness."

13 Lawrence's knowledge of Freud was mediated through his wife Frieda and friends like Edith and David Eder, Barbara Low and the dissident Jungian analyst Trigant Burrow. See also the *Preface to the Cambridge edition* (Lawrence 2004).

14 Jean-Jacques Lecercle demonstrates the abundant use of adjectives in Lawrence's novels makes a true writing of the affect in Lyotard's sense, but the argument also holds for Deleuze and Guattari's conception of the affect, which Lecercle is obviously familiar with (Lecercle 2001: 184–5).

15 Borrowed from electricity, it is a typical modernist image, deepened by ancient connotations arising from Greek thought in the wake of Nietzsche, Heidegger, and Bergson. William James' notion of the "stream of consciousness" links a psychological model to one of the most characteristic modernist literary devices (Armstrong 2004: 95–9). Although Lawrence was not directly influenced by Heidegger, Heidegger's philosophy inspires some of the best readings of Lawrence by Becket and Bell.

16 Deleuze extensively comments on the Lawrentian symbol in *Apocalypse* (1997: 48).

17 The second volume, *Fantasia of the Unconscious*, was translated very early into French by Charles Mauron, *Fantaisie de l'inconscient* (Paris: Stock, 1932). In 1969 *Eros et les chiens* appeared with Bourgeois.

18 See the long reference to Lawrence in the positive outline for schizo-analysis, where Deleuze and Guattari offer a Nietzschean reading:

> As Lawrence said, analysis does not have anything to do with the anything that resembles a concept or a person, "the so-called human relations are not involved." Analysis should deal solely (except in its negative task) with the machinic arrangements grasped in the context of their molecular dispersal.
> (Deleuze and Guattari 1982 [1977]: 323)

The linking of the impersonal and the machinic is not incongruent with Lawrence's ambiguous relation with modern society and technology.

19 The traditional dualism of the female–male divide in Lawrence's earlier works and his denouncing of overly independent castrating modern women who should be subordinated by strong phallic men got Lawrence into well-know trouble with feminism in the 1960s, in spite of his pleas for sexual liberation, championed by people like Anaïs Nin and Henry Miller (whose influence on the popularity of Lawrence and particularly of *Aaron's Rod* in France cannot be overestimated). Deleuze underscores this phallic tendency but shows that things are more complex: "Lawrence and Miller are considered to be great sexists: writing, however, drew them into an irresistible woman-becoming" (Deleuze and Parnet 2003: 32).

20 "Strange Anglo-American literature: from Thomas Hardy, from D. H. Lawrence to Malcolm Lowry, from Henry Miller to Allen Ginsberg and Jack Kerouac, men who know how to leave, to scramble the codes, to cause flows to circulate, to traverse the desert of the body without organs. They overcome a limit, they shatter a wall, the capitalist barrier. And of course they fail to complete the process, they never cease failing to do so. The neurotic impasse again closes—the daddy-mommy of oedipalization, America, the return to the native land—or else the perversion of exotic territorialities, then drugs, alcohol—or worse still, the old fascist dream" (Deleuze and Guattari 1982 [1977]: 132–3).

21 Deleuze and Guattari make few references to Lawrence's novels, except the "leadership novels" from the 1920s–1930s, such as *Aaron's Rod* or *The Man who Died*. Deleuze obviously knows the literary work well, yet he never mentions the most famous or critically acclaimed novels.

22 See also Tibaud Trochu in Gelas and Micolet (2007: 341).

23 "To get away. To get out, out! To get away out of our life. To cross the horizon into another life" (Lawrence 2003: 124).

24 "You may read all the novels of Marcel Proust, with everything there in detail. Yet you will not kill the dirty little secret. You will perhaps only make it more cunning" (Lawrence 1964: 184). Lawrence describes "the dirty little secret" as a vicious "narcissus-masturbation circle" that stops the natural sex flow and turns it into "sex in the head." Deleuze and Guattari relish this phrase and associate it with the family theater of Oedipus (e.g. Deleuze and Guattari 1982 [1977]: 49; Deleuze and Guattari 2004 [1988]: 218, 227) and neurosis.

25 Lawrence's poetry is repeatedly cited as a prime example of the becoming. See Deleuze and Parnet 2003: 33, 36–8, 40; Deleuze and Guattari 2004 [1988]: 269, 597; Deleuze and Guattari 1996: 169, 171, 173.

26 This passage is extensively quoted in Deleuze and Guattari 2004 [1988]: 209 and in Deleuze and Parnet 2003: 27–8.

27 Conceptual personae are thus the voices used in philosophy, somewhat comparable to narrators in literature. Examples are Socrates in the work of Plato or Zarathustra in Nietzsche.

28 This impersonal quality is present in the three domains of philosophy, science, and art, but perhaps most problematic for the domain of art, for which it is still hard to let go of the personified author, despite Barthes and Foucault. For Deleuze and Guattari, the activity of thinking is in all three cases executed by the "thought" rather than by persons or people.

Bibliography

Armstrong, T. (2004) *Modernism: A Cultural History*, Cambridge: Polity.

Becket, F. (1997) *D. H. Lawrence: The Thinker as Poet*, London: Macmillan.

—— (1997–8) "Being There: Nostalgia and the Masculine Maternal in D. H. Lawrence," *The D. H. Lawrence Review* 27: 255–68.

Bell, M. (1992) *D. H. Lawrence: Language and Being*, Cambridge: Cambridge University Press.

Brewster, S. (1997–8) "Jumping Continents: Abjection, *Kangaroo* and the Celtic Uncanny," *The D. H. Lawrence Review* 27: 217–32.

Bryden, M. (2000) "Nietzsche's Arrow: Deleuze on D. H. Lawrence's *Apocalypse*," in M. Bryden (ed.) *Deleuze and Religion*, London: Routledge, 101–15.

Buchanan, I. (2000) *Deleuzism: A Metacommentary*, Edinburgh: Edinburgh University Press.

Deleuze, G. (1997) *Essays Critical and Clinical*, trans. D. W. Smith and M. A. Greco, Minneapolis: Minnesota University Press.

Deleuze, G. and Guattari, F. (1982 [1977]) *Anti-Oedipus: Capitalism and Schizophrenia*, trans. R. Hurley, M. Seem, and H. R. Lane, Minneapolis: Minnesota University Press.

—— (2004 [1988]) *A Thousand Plateaus: Capitalism and Schizophrenia*, trans. B. Massumi, London: Continuum.

—— (1996) *What is Philosophy?* trans. G. Burchell and H. Tomlinson, London: Verso.

Deleuze G. and Parnet, C. (2003) *Dialogues*, second edn, trans. J. Tomlinson, B. Habberiam, and E. Albert. New York: Columbia University Press.

Dosse, F. (2007) *Gilles Deleuze Félix Guattari: biographie croisée*, Paris: La Découverte.

Gelas, B. and Micolet, H. (2007) *Deleuze et les écrivains: Littérature et philosophie*, Nantes: Editions Cécile Defaut.

Kinkead-Weekes, M. (1997–8) "The Genesis of Lawrence's Psychology Books: An Overview," *The D. H. Lawrence Review* 27: 153–70.

Lawrence, D. H. (1932) *Fantaisie de l'inconscient*, trans. C. Mauron. Paris: Stock.

—— (1961 [1936]) *Phoenix I. The Posthumous Papers of D. H. Lawrence*, ed. E. D. McDonald, London: Heinemann.

—— (1964) *Phoenix I. The Phoenix Edition of D. H. Lawrence*, London: Heinemann.

—— (1969) *Eros et les chiens*, trans. T. Lauriol, Paris: Bourgeois.

—— (2003) *Studies in Classic American Literature*, ed. E. Greenspan, L. Vasey, and J. Worthern, Cambridge Edition of the Letters and Works of D. H. Lawrence, Cambridge: Cambridge University Press.

—— (2004) *Psychoanalysis and the Unconscious and Fantasia of the Unconscious*, ed. B. Steele, Cambridge Edition of the Letters and Works of D. H. Lawrence, Cambridge: Cambridge University Press.

Lecercle, J.-J. (2001) "La Phrase de Lawrence," in G. Katz-Roy (ed.) *Lectures d'une ouvrage: Women in Love*, Paris: Editions du Temps.

—— (2002) *Deleuze and Language*, Basingstoke: Palgrave.

Monaco, B. (2001) "*Women in Love* and Deleuze: New Insights," *Q/W/E/R/T/Y: Arts, littératures et civilations du monde anglophone* 11: 29–37.

Turner, J. (1997–8) "David Eder: Between Freud and Jung," *The D. H. Lawrence Review* 27: 289–309.

Williams, L. R. (1997–8) "'We've been forgetting that we're flesh and blood, Mother': Glad Ghosts and Uncanny Bodies," *The D. H. Lawrence Review* 27: 233–53.

Deleuze and his sources

Response to Anneleen Masschelein

Ian Buchanan

> When we think in abstractions there is a danger that we may neglect the relations of words to unconscious thing-presentations, and it must be confessed that the expression and content of our philosophising then begins to acquire an unwelcome resemblance to the mode of operation of schizophrenics.
>
> (Freud 1991 [1915]: 210)

> The world is the set of symptoms whose illness merges with man.
>
> (Deleuze 1997 [1993]: 3)

Anneleen Masschelein puzzles very fruitfully over the nature of the relation between Deleuze and D. H. Lawrence. As she points out, Deleuze is simultaneously a close, careful, and knowledgeable reader of Lawrence, as well as a highly selective, subtly distorting, and even negligent reader of Lawrence. He not only ignores the great novels, he also ignores Lawrence's 'misogynistic attacks on modern women' and his 'peculiar ideas on the education of children' (Masschelein). He favours instead the critical and psychological works such as *Psychoanalysis and the Unconscious*, *Fantasia of the Unconscious*, and the essays in the posthumous collection *Phoenix*. He makes occasional mention of minor novels like *Aaron's Rod* and novellas such as *The Plumed Serpent*, but as Masschelein rightly observes these references are always of ambiguous intent and purpose. Deleuze simply extracts resonant catch-phrases, slogans, and tag-lines like 'dirty little secret' from Lawrence, rather than fully formed ideas. Masschelein's critique of Deleuze's treatment of Lawrence directs us to a question well beyond this specific case: that of his relation to his sources in general, be they literary, historical, philosophical or scientific. This issue extends to all of Deleuze's (and Guattari's) concepts.

I will take as my test case a concept which Masschelein describes as one of the most notorious, namely the body without organs (BwO) which appears to have been inspired by literature (Artaud), philosophy (Spinoza), and science (Weismann). The BwO will, via a circuitous route through Artaud and Lewis Carroll, take us to Lawrence and Freud. Here I will state baldly what I think Masschelein suspects, that Lawrence provides Deleuze with a suitably anti-psychoanalytic rhetoric with which to disguise or at least estrange a profound engagement with Freud himself. Deleuze's project has always been to lead psychoanalysis to autocritique and thereby re-engineer it from the inside (Deleuze and Guattari 2004: 90, 128). Lawrence is essential to this project, which in Jameson's terms is fundamentally modernist, because like the many great modernist artists Deleuze is inspired by, he conceives of a mental life that is richer and stranger than Freud's ultimately normative conception. Deleuze explicitly links Lawrence and Artaud in the title of his essay on Lawrence, 'To Have Done with Judgement', which borrows from Artaud. He also attributes to Lawrence an explicit role in making the BwO visible to us. 'Lawrence paints the picture of such a body, with the sun and the moon as its poles, with its sections, and its plexuses' (Deleuze 1997: 131).[1] Lawrence's characters also seemed to Deleuze to give life to the concept. 'Lawrence ceaselessly describes bodies that are organically defective or unattractive – like the fat retired toreador or the skinny, oily Mexican general – but that are nonetheless traversed by this intense vitality that defies organs and undoes their organisation' (Deleuze 1997: 131). But as evocative as these observations are, it is not immediately clear how they clarify the BwO in an analytic rather than descriptive sense. For this reason I want to foreground the problematic relation between Deleuze and his sources that Masschelein so usefully draws our attention to.

While it might seem that we should simply return to the original sources and read Artaud or Lawrence for ourselves, we are effectively barred from doing so by Deleuze and Guattari's theorization of how philosophy works, as laid out in their final collaborative work, *What is Philosophy?* Their central implication is that ideas, concepts, and models drawn from other sources do not retain their original meaning once they are incorporated into another thinker's work. Of course we can and should read Artaud and Lawrence for ourselves, but we can't then treat their work as though it supplies a missing referent for Deleuze and Guattari's work. This is made explicit in their discussion of the plane of immanence, which is effectively a 'sense-regime': it is the 'atmosphere' or 'environment', unique to each philosopher, in which a concept is able to function. Philosophers can co-exist on the same plane and therefore share concepts, but great philosophers – and is not Deleuze a great philosopher? – are defined by the originality of the planes of immanence they institute. The problem becomes more acute when we move outside of philosophy. Art doesn't create a plane of immanence, it creates a plane of composition; science doesn't create a plane of immanence either, it creates a plane of reference; thus any 'concepts' philosophy takes from these non-philosophical sources undergo a radical transformation when they are brought into their new environment.[2] If we cannot read Artaud or Lawrence as a referent, then how can we read them? My answer, drawn directly from Deleuze, is that we should read Deleuze's sources as he does: clinically. That is, we should read them as symptomatologists, specifically of mental illnesses. The BwO is a symptom, that is its first and proper meaning, and this fact must guide us in our analyses of its subsequent permutations in Deleuze and Guattari's work.

It is no coincidence that the BwO, which Deleuze first used in *The Logic of Sense* (1969), is one of the concepts which drew Guattari to Deleuze.[3] He evidently saw something crucial to the understanding of schizophrenic experience in the concept of the BwO that had been overlooked in both clinical and critical discourse. In their subsequent collaborative work, one senses that Guattari brought his clinical experience to bear to confirm Deleuze's original critical insight.[4] Two observations can substantiate this intuition: first, although the concept becomes more complicated in Deleuze and Guattari's collaborative work, its meaning doesn't change; second, in his 1975 entry on 'Schizophrenia' for the *Encyclopaedia Universalis* Deleuze treats the concept in a clinical fashion – that is to say, clinical more in Guattari's therapeutic sense of the term than his own hermeneutic or literary sense. In their different ways, both pieces conform to the more general idea of the clinical Deleuze elaborated in his earlier work on Masoch, which proposed to bring the medical and the literary together in order to form a 'new relationship of mutual learning' (Deleuze 1989: 14). Read together, then, these two pieces make it clear that the BwO should be understood as a condition, something affecting the psychical apparatus rather than a constitutive feature of it. The fact that no psychical apparatus is considered free of its affects shouldn't deter us from seeing the secondary nature of it. Indeed, if we do not take note of this we cannot grasp what is perhaps its most important trait, namely its uncanny ability to rise up and fall back on the operations of the unconscious, or what Deleuze and Guattari refer to as desiring-production, and make it seem that *it* is the true source of its productivity.

Remarkably, the BwO's debut in *The Logic of Sense* is basically unmarked, appearing first in a mere parenthesis. In fact, at this point, it doesn't even amount to a genuine concept; it is more the description of a symptom or condition. Although it will in due course become a fully fledged concept, it is important to keep sight of its pre-philosophical origins.[5] My implication is that Deleuze doesn't take the BwO from Artaud as a ready-made concept – it only becomes so in his own work. Therefore, one cannot use Artaud as a reference point if by that one means his work functions as its signified. The BwO crops up, as it were, in the midst of a comparative discussion of Carroll and Artaud. Deleuze's question is this: is the nonsense of the one the same as the other? Are Carroll's made-up words the same as Artaud's breath-words (*mots-souffle*) and howl-words (*mots-cris*)? Deleuze thinks not. 'A little girl may sing "*Pimpanicaille*"; an artist may write "frumious"; and a schizophrenic may utter "perspendicace". But we have no reason to believe that the problem is the same in all these cases and the results roughly analogous' (Deleuze 1990: 83). The works of these three subjects are not organized in the same way: their sense-regime is different in each case. Artaud's attempt at translating Carroll's 'Jabberwocky' is an indicative case in point. At first, Deleuze says, we have the impression that Artaud's translation conforms with the rules of translation espoused and adhered to by Carroll's other French translators.

> But beginning with the last word of the second line, from the third line onward, a sliding is produced, and even a creative, central collapse, causing us to be in another world and in an entirely different language. With horror, we recognise it easily: it is the language of schizophrenia.
>
> (Deleuze 1990: 83–4)

Carroll's is a language of the surface, whereas Artaud's is a language of depth.

As Deleuze says in a short piece on Carroll: 'It is not that surface has less nonsense than does depth. But it is not the same nonsense' (Deleuze 1997: 22). Surface is what protects non-schizophrenics from depth, which as Deleuze puts it 'is known to any schizophrenic, who lives it as well in his or her own manner' (Deleuze 1990: 86). Depth is the opposite of surface. But it is not something lurking below the surface in the way the unconscious is sometimes depicted as operating beneath the conscious; it is rather its end. Depth is our model and image of death, Deleuze and Guattari argue. 'As the authors of horror stories have understood so well, it is not death that serves as the model for catatonia, it is catatonic schizophrenia that gives its model to death' (Deleuze and Guattari 2004: 363). But it is not just a matter of horror stories and fearful images that we can consign to the dustbin of the imaginary. These images only affect us because they recollect a common occurrence in the unconscious of the experience of death: 'death is what is felt in every feeling, *what never ceases and never finishes happening in every becoming* – in the becoming-another-sex, the becoming-god, the becoming-a-race, etc., forming zones of intensity on the body without organs' (Deleuze and Guattari 2004: 363). Becoming is Deleuze and Guattari's term for the disorienting experience of delirium, which is the experience of the real *for itself*, the feeling for which no words are finally adequate. The Wolf-Man *feels* he is becoming a wolf, although he knows he isn't. Delirium isn't a loss of reality, as it is sometimes described in psychoanalysis, but an excess of reality. 'The real is not impossible; on the contrary, within the real everything is possible, everything becomes possible' (Deleuze and Guattari 2004: 29). Delirium is reality experienced in its full 'intensity'. The Deleuzian concept of 'intensity' is derived from 'intension' rather than 'intense', implying that delirium is a power of selection for which there are no corresponding properties that could explain it (the feeling of being a wolf with no fangs and no fur).

This is why the BwO (i.e. the schizophrenic state) is likened by Deleuze and Guattari to an egg – just as nothing about an egg suggests either where it came from or what it will become, so the schizophrenic is gripped by an inexorable feeling of inner-change for which there is neither an obvious point of origin nor clear sense of destination.[6] More exactly, this feeling can only be sensed and not put into words, and this is something we have all experienced, the vertiginous power of thought itself (Deleuze 1994: 140–2). Here we see why Jameson should want to describe Deleuze as a modernist, for it is precisely in this realm of that which can only be sensed that modernism finds inspiration for its concept of the new. The lesson learned by all the avatars of modernism is that the radically new can only stem from that which is by definition ineffable. Returning to the discussion at hand we can say that man is rooted in the depth of thought. It is, however, a depth that cannot co-exist in the same place as surface: depth is what one falls into when the surface comes undone. When this happens, the frontier between propositions and things vanishes and the body loses its protective shell, becoming a kind of sieve.

The consequence of this is that the entire body is no longer anything but depth – it carries along and snaps up everything into this gaping depth which represents a fundamental involution. Everything is body and corporeal.

(Deleuze 1990: 87)

The effects of this rupture are abrupt, brutal, and terrifying. The first casualty is meaning, or what Deleuze defines more pragmatically as 'the power to draw together or to express an incorporeal effect distinct from the actions and passions of the body, and an ideational event distinct from its present realisation' (Deleuze 1990: 87). Loss of meaning, as it is described here, should not be confused with a neurotic inability to decide the meaning of things. It is more devastating than the situation of meaning-loss Lacan describes in his account of schizophrenia, which Jameson expertly summarizes as the inability to connect signifiers resulting in the breakdown of the signifying chain and the reduction of meaning to a 'rubble of distinct and unrelated signifiers' (Jameson 1991: 26). It is more devastating because the result of schizophrenic meaning-loss is not so much the loss of connection between signifiers, but the loss of the protective ability to stop connections from forming; moreover, the result of schizophrenic meaning-loss is anything but the inert state of a pile of rubble. When words lose their meaning they crumble into their phonetic elements and it is as though a protective sheath has been stripped away to reveal a cluster of highly mobile and aggressive-acting razor blades.

The moment that the maternal language is stripped of its sense, its *phonetic elements* become singularly wounding. The word no longer expresses an attribute of the state of affairs; its fragments merge with unbearable sonorous qualities, invade the body where they form a mixture and a new state of affairs, as if they themselves were a noisy, poisonous food and canned excrement.

(Deleuze 1990: 88)

Under this pressure, the schizophrenic body is unable to hold together – it becomes a sieve through which the unbearable particles of words and sounds flow unimpeded; it fragments into parts which then form new relations with the invading particles, giving rise to all kinds of monstrosities; it disintegrates, the bonds between particles turn inwards and relations of attraction give way to relations of repulsion.[7]

The schizophrenic responds to this threat not by trying to recover the meaning of things and somehow restore them, but by trying to destroy the words themselves. This is the function of breath-words and howl-words – they transform, or better transmute and transvalue (in Nietzsche's sense), the literal, syllabic and phonetic values of words into tonic values. 'To these values a glorious body corresponds, being a new dimension of the schizophrenic body, an organism without parts which operates entirely by insufflation, respiration, evaporation, and fluid transmission (the superior body or body without organs of Antonin

Artaud)' (Deleuze 1990: 88). The schizophrenic thus has two bodies: one that is porous, friable, and scattered, and another that is smooth, steely, and bonded; the one a body in a state of collapse, the other a body in a state of suspended animation. *Both bodies are a product of schizophrenia* – the one an impassioned suffering body, the other a body curled up in a defensive posture, with its mouth, ears, eyes, nose, and anus shut tight, trying to cure itself, or at least defend itself against the onslaught of the word-particles. Deleuze finds a fascinating variation of this felt urgency in the work of Louis Wolfson, an American schizophrenic who wrote in French out of a pathological horror of the mother tongue.[8]

> His procedure is as follows: given a word from the maternal language, he looks for a foreign word with a similar meaning that has common sounds or phonemes (preferably in French, German, Russian, or Hebrew, the four principal languages studied by the author).
>
> (Deleuze 1997: 7–8)

Wolfson guards himself against words by performing an endless labour of transformation on them. He is unable to ignore what he doesn't want to hear. Words are so many nails and screws that bite into his flesh, clawing away at him until he finds the means of transmuting them into something else, a flow of breath-sounds. When that fails, he retreats to his BwO by jacking into his homemade prototype of the Walkman (he claims to have invented) fabricated from a stethoscope plugged into a portable tape deck (Deleuze 1997: 13).

The schizophrenic has two bodies: one is composed of organ-machines and the other is organless, neither of which refers to either the actual body or an image of the actual body (Deleuze and Guattari 2004: 9). As the example given above readily attests, the schizophrenic is torn between the need to construct elaborate procedures to deal practically with the ceaseless torments of reality and the almost irrepressible desire to shut the world out altogether. Either the mother tongue must be converted as rapidly as possible into another language or else it must be drowned out. The schizophrenic oscillates between the discomposed or machinic body, which is plugged into machines, traversed by machines and has for all intents and purposes become a machine itself, and the stoppered-up organless body Deleuze likens to an egg. Bruno Bettelheim's case study of little Joey is exemplary in this respect. He has eating machines, defecating machines, sleeping machines, all of which require power to work properly. So before being able to eat, shit or sleep, Joey must ensure all the circuits of his machines are intact and live.

> Essentially, the schizophrenic is a functional machine making use of left-over elements that no longer function in any context, and that will enter into relation with each other *precisely by having no relation* – as if the concrete distinction, the disparity of the different parts became a reason in itself to group them together and put them to work, according to what chemists call a non-localisable relation.
>
> (Deleuze 2006: 18)

But when these machines break down, or their demands become unbearable, Joey falls into a catatonic state. The frontispiece to *Anti-Oedipus*, Richard Lindner's *Boy with Machine*, provides a pictorial representation of this dual state of being: the boy in question is at once a bloated, organless body lost in its own reality and an organ-machinic body hooked up to an infernal machine which he seems somehow to be powering (Deleuze and Guattari 2004: 8, 51, 392). The organless body is a stationary motor giving life and power to its opposite number and at the same time resisting and repelling the little organ-machines which swarm across its surface.

> If we think of the organless body as a solid egg, it follows that, *beneath* the organisation that it will assume, that will develop, the egg does not present itself as an undifferentiated milieu: it is traversed by axes and gradients, by poles and potentials, by thresholds and zones destined later to produce one or another organic part.
>
> (Deleuze 2006: 21)

Ansell-Pearson insists that the image of the egg is adapted from neo-Darwinist August Weismann's theory of 'germinal life', but in *The Logic of Sense*, at least, no such scientific connection exists (Ansell-Pearson 1999: 4–5). In fact, Humpty-Dumpty is given as the source of the egg-image for the gloriously smooth body. What other reason, Deleuze asks, did Artaud have for confronting this text (Deleuze 1990: 92)? The point to bear in mind here is that the BwO is only one aspect of the schizophrenic body and it doesn't act alone. As Deleuze's discussion of Artaud makes clear, for every Humpty-Dumpty there is an Alice, for every Alice a Humpty-Dumpty: body-sieve and glorious body (Deleuze 1990: 92). Clinically speaking, the two bodies antagonize one another.

> Every coupling of machines, every production of a machine, every sound of a machine running, becomes unbearable to the body without organs. Beneath its organs it senses there are larvae and loathsome worms, and a God at work messing it all up or strangling it by organising it.
>
> (Deleuze and Guattari 2004: 9)

What the BwO objects to is the attempt to organize it made by the organ-machines. The constant pressure of having to translate English words into French or German, together with the pain of failure, compels the student of languages to stopper his ears and retreat to a zone where no such words can reach him. Little Joey, too, succumbs to a catatonic exhaustion brought on by the relentless need to control his environment. As Deleuze and Guattari argue throughout their work, the BwO is often a product of therapy – the psychoanalysts' inability to hear what they are told (not Daddy, a wolf!) and the psychiatrists' fetish for physical therapy send the schizophrenic into a black hole from which there is no return. Artaud's description of a body that has renounced all its organs so as to have done with God's judgement should be seen in precisely this light: it describes the exhausted, dispirited, hopeless state of the schizophrenic who has opted for silence and stillness rather than put up with any further incursions. Now we come to what is one of the most surprising connections to a prior source in Deleuze's work:

> In order to resist organ-machines, the body without organs presents its smooth, slippery, opaque, taut surface as a barrier. In order to resist linked, connected, and interrupted flows, it sets up a counterflow of amorphous, undifferentiated fluid. In order to resist using words composed of articulated phonetic units, it utters only gasps and cries that are sheer unarticulated blocks of sound. We are of the opinion that what is ordinarily referred to as a 'primary repression' means precisely that: it is not a 'counter-cathexis', but rather this *repulsion* of desiring-machines by the body without organs.
>
> (Deleuze and Guattari 2004: 10)

The relationship between organ-machines and the organless body finally takes on an analytic character once cast in its proper light as a rewriting of Freud. I'm mindful of the fact that this is a heretical claim, so I will briefly try to justify it. In Freud's system the ego is the site and the agency of repression – what we see in the quotation above is the BwO inserted in the same functional place as the ego would normally reside. Deleuze and Guattari preserve the structure of the unconscious as Freud conceives it and supplement it with a few conceptual inventions of their own, the BwO being one such invention. The BwO becomes apparent in what Freud described as occasions of ego-loss, this being his sense of what happens in the extremes of schizophrenic delirium. It is in this sense a symptom of schizophrenia, but not a product of schizophrenia – the BwO is what stands beneath the ego, the thin line separating the ego from the id, which Freud says is permeable but more or less distinct. The BwO is what remains, then, after the ego has disintegrated, but it is no mere ruin: in fact, it continues to defend the possibility of an ego by holding back the id and maintaining a place where the ego might come into being. By the same token, in the ego's absence it is also able to take its place and serve as the subject's organizing centre. When I quoted Deleuze saying that Lawrence painted a picture in words of a BwO, it should now be understood that what Lawrence gave us is not the concept of the BwO but one of its productions. His fantasias of the unconscious are precisely examples of the world seen through the lens of the BwO rather than the ego.

Notes

1 Deleuze refers here to *Fantasia of the Unconscious*.
2 See Deleuze and Guattari (1994: 40–1).
3 See Guattari's comments in the interview published in Deleuze (1995: 15).
4 This is confirmed by Guattari's recently published notes.
5 'Pre-philosophical' is Deleuze a Guattari's term in *What is Philosophy?* for ideas they take from art and literature.

6 Kafka's short story 'Mr Blumenfeld' is the perfect example of this: the balls come from nowhere and for no reason. For a discussion of this story see Buchanan 2006: 77–8.
7 'Body-sieve, fragmented body, and dissociated body – these are the three primary dimensions of the schizophrenic body' (Deleuze 1990: 8). These are the three ways in which the body of the schizophrenic suffers or endures its passion.
8 Deleuze provided a preface to Wolfson's book *Le Schizo et les langues* which he later revised an incorporated into *Essays Critical and Clinical*.

Bibliography

Ansell-Pearson, K. (1999) *Germinal Life: The Difference and Repetition of Deleuze*, London: Routledge.
Buchanan, I. (2006) 'Žižek and Deleuze', in G. Boucher, J. Glynos, and M. Sharpe (eds) *Traversing the Fantasy: Critical Responses to Slavoj Žižek*, London: Ashgate, 69–85.
Deleuze, G. (1989) *Masochism: Coldness and Cruelty*, trans. J. McNeil, New York: Zone Books.
—— (1990) *The Logic of Sense*, trans. M. Lester and C. Stivale, London: Athlone.
—— (1994) *Difference and Repetition*, trans. P. Patton, London: Athlone.
—— (1995) *Negotiations*, trans. M. Joughin, New York: Columbia University Press.
—— (1997 [1993]) *Essays Critical and Clinical*, trans. D. W. Smith and M. A. Greco, Minneapolis: Minnesota University Press.
—— (2006) *Two Regimes of Madness: Texts and Interviews 1975–1995*, ed. D. Lapoujade, New York: Semiotext(e).
Deleuze, G. and Guattari, F. (1994) *What is Philosophy?* trans. Hugh Tomlinson, New York: Columbia University Press.
—— (2004) *Anti-Oedipus*, trans. R. Hurley, M. Seem, and H. R. Lane, London and New York: Continuum.
Freud, S. (1991 [1915]) 'The Unconscious', in *On Metapsychology*, Penguin Freud Library Vol. 11 (Harmondsworth: Penguin), 159–222.
Guattari, F. (2006) *The Anti-Oedipus Papers*, ed. S. Nadaud, trans. K. Gotman, New York: Semiotext(e).
Jameson, F. (1991) *Postmodernism, or, the Cultural Logic of Late Capitalism*, Durham, NC: Duke University Press.
—— (2002) *A Singular Modernity: Essay on the Ontology of the Present*, London: Verso.
Marx, K. (1975) 'A Contribution to the Critique of Hegel's Philosophy of Right', trans. R. Livingstone and G. Benton, London: Penguin, 243–57.
Žižek, S. (2006) 'Concesso Non Dato', in G. Boucher, J. Glynos, and M. Sharpe (eds) *Traversing the Fantasy: Critical Responses to Slavoj Žižek*, London: Ashgate, 219–55.

2 Modernism, postmodernism, and the two sublimes of surrealism

Roger Rothman

1

Over the last three decades, no two figures have influenced the intellectual landscape of contemporary theoretical discourse as widely and deeply as have Gilles Deleuze and Jacques Derrida. What makes this dual influence all the more remarkable is that, as Slavoj Žižek has remarked, "Derrida and Deleuze speak different, totally incompatible, languages, with no shared ground between them" (Žižek 2004: 47). Yet he insists their differences are today more salient:

> While Derrida proceeds in the mode of critical deconstruction, of under-mining the interpreted text or author, Deleuze, in his buggery, imputes to the interpreted philosopher his own inner-most position and endeavors to extract it from him. So, while Derrida engages in a "hermeneutics of suspi-cion," Deleuze practices an excessive benevolence toward the interpreted philosopher. At the immediate material level, Derrida has to resort to quo-tation marks all the time, signaling that the employed concept is not really his, whereas Deleuze endorses everything, directly speaking through the interpreted author in an indirect free speech *without* quotation marks. And, of course, it is easy to demonstrate that Deleuze's "benevolence" is much more violent and subversive than the Derridean reading: his buggery pro-duces true monsters.[1]
>
> (Žižek 2004: 47)

Žižek's distinction between Derrida's hermeneutics of suspicion and Deleuze's buggery questions the development of these two trajectories and of Poststructuralism generally. The answer is multidimensional, but the profound, but sometimes indirect, influence of the generation of thinkers which preceded Derrida and Deleuze—the Surrealists—deserves closer attention.

Deleuze, who died in 1995, was born in 1925; Derrida, who died in 2004, was born in 1930. A book on French thought around the time of their births—a book on Antonin Artaud, Michel Leiris, Roger Caillois, or Jean Paulhan—would likely frame the discussion around the two figures who most significantly shaped the discourse of the period: André Breton and Georges Bataille. Like Deleuze and Derrida, Breton and Bataille were united by a few key similarities—above all the importance of reconciling Hegel and Freud. And like Deleuze and Derrida, Breton and Bataille were distinguished by how they set about this reconciliation. I show this is more than mere coincidence; it signifies a deeper alignment of theoretical practices.

With the recent passing of Deleuze and Derrida, and attention shift toward Žižek and Alan Badiou, this moment is particularly suitable to reconsider Poststructuralism.[2] This paper attends to this moment by engaging in a genealogical investigation of the principal divide in the generation preceding the theorists of the 1970s and 1980s—the divide internal to Surrealism. André Breton was born in 1896 and Georges Bataille was born in 1897, making them a generation older than Deleuze and Derrida. In 1925, the year of Deleuze's birth, Breton launched *La Révolution surréaliste*, and in 1929, the year before Derrida's birth, Bataille founded *Documents*, a journal to counter Breton's. One year later, Breton published the "Second Manifesto of Surrealism," in which he explicitly and aggressively attacked Bataille's ideas. That manifesto (and the fact Breton emphatically renamed the journal *Le Surréalisme au service de la révolution*) was in large measure a response to the threat posed by *Documents*.

In the thirty to forty years separating these Surrealist texts from the rise of poststructuralist theory, Breton's and Bataille's influence upon the French intellectual landscape was considerable, and its force is felt in both Deleuze's and Derrida's writings. As Margaret Cohen argued, although Bretonian Surrealism "is certainly a conspicuous absence in [Deleuze and Guattari's 1972] *Anti-Oedipus*," the text nevertheless "proposes a strolling schizophrenic reminiscent of Breton's mad *flâneuse*, Nadja" (Cohen 1993: 112–13). On the other hand, Derrida's debt to the Surrealists is explicit and unequivocal. Under Jean Hyppolite's direction at the École Normale Supérieure in the 1950s, Derrida first read Hegel, Husserl, and Heidegger; he also began reading Bataille under Hyppolite.[3] This early influence manifested most fully in Derrida's 1967 essay in *L'Arc*: "De l'économie restreinte à l'économie générale: un hégélianisme sans réserves."[4] In other words, despite the generational gap separating Surrealists from Poststructuralists, evidence suggests the latter owe the former a considerable and complex debt.

2

Today the Surrealist movement of the 1920s and 1930s is largely perceived as cleaved in two: Breton's "orthodox" members and Bataille's "dissidents" (Foster 1993; Hollier 1990, 1992; Krauss 1985, 1993, 1994). What makes this perception of a bifurcated Surrealism especially important is that it sheds light not only on what Surrealism was in the 1920s and 1930s, but how it was redeployed by the subsequent generation of postwar French theorists. Different aspects of this split are evident not only in Derrida and Deleuze, but also Michel Foucault and Jean-François Lyotard.[5] This is not to say all postwar reflections on Breton and Bataille articulated the divided legacy of Surrealism in the same manner.

Nonetheless, one thing remains constant in all the above: the rarely declared but always palpable sense that one is compelled to align (openly or covertly) with either Breton's *amour fou* or Bataille's *informe*. In fact, it would seem, given their reception, one simply could not have both at the same time.

The sense of having to choose—that is, that the two are fundamentally incompatible—is most clear in the work of Roland Barthes. Indeed, his work above all took on the divided legacy of Breton and Bataille, with Bataille as the more significant of the two. By the end of his career, his dismissal of Breton stood as a principal motif, so much so that apparent similarities between his own writings and those of Breton took on an importance they would not ordinarily have had. In a late interview, Barthes found himself confronted with this very issue. "You write in *The Pleasure of Text*," remarked Daniel Oster,

> "The text has a human form, which is a figure, an anagram of the body"; and further on: "The pleasure of the text is that moment when my body starts following its own ideas." Couldn't we compare this representation of the body with automatic writing? And aren't you proposing a kind of automatic writing?

Barthes's reply was swift and unequivocal: "I don't like the notion of automatic writing at all ... The idea of automatic writing implies an idealist view of man divided into a speaking subject and a profound inner subject." For Barthes, Breton's purported idealism prevents one from registering the full materiality of the body. Simply put, in Barthes's mind, "the Surrealists *missed* the body" (Barthes 1985: 243–5).

Bataille echoes in Barthes's choice of words. It is unmistakable in his rejection of Breton as an "idealist" and his preference for the opacity of the body, for the thickness of pure matter. Bataille first stamped Breton with the "idealist" epithet, and referred to Breton's idealism as "servile" (Bataille 1985: 41).[6] Given that Bataille was still bristling at having been "kissed off" by Breton in the pages of *La Révolution surréaliste*—the frontispiece featured a panoply of red lip-prints on stark white paper—Barthes ought to have taken his words with at least a few grains of salt (Breton 1972a). "All of existence," wrote Bataille, "conceived as purely literary by M. Breton, diverts him from the shabby, sinister, or inspired events occurring all around him, from what constitutes the real decomposition of an immense world" (Bataille 1985: 41). For Barthes, the decomposition invoked by Bataille would refer most pressingly to the human body, that mass of flesh destined for death and decay.

Barthes' debt to Bataille (unmentioned in the interview) is explicit in his "autobiography," *Roland Barthes by Roland Barthes*. In the final chapter, he includes a biographical outline that reads as if Bataillean matter-in-decay were the preferred model of literary self-presentation. In place of the usual resumé-like entries, Barthes provides a laconic history of the author's declining health: "May 10, 1934: Hemophtisis. Lesion in the left lung"; "July 1943: Relapse in the right lung"; "1943–45: Second stay in the Sanatorium de Étudiants" (Barthes 1977a: 183–4).

Elsewhere Barthes refers to Bataille's dystopian discourse of "heterology" and wonders how he, Barthes, can endorse such a program and still maintain "a critique of violence" (Barthes 1977a: 100). In yet another entry entitled "Bataille, la peur," he writes:

> Bataille, after all, affects me little enough: what have I to do with laughter, devotion, poetry, violence? What have I to say about "the sacred," about "the impossible"? Yet no sooner do I make this (alien) language coincide with that disturbance in myself which I call *fear* than Bataille conquers me all over again: then everything he *inscribes describes* me: it sticks.
>
> (Barthes 1977a: 144)

By contrast, Barthes had little interest in Breton. In fact, Barthes entitled an earlier section "Le fantasme, pas le rêve," thereby implicitly distancing himself from the dream-fascination of Breton.[7]

Beneath Barthes' reception of Surrealism—or its reception in general—lies a larger issue, which goes beyond preference for Breton or Bataille. The reemergence of the sublime is at stake, a concept that at least since the publication of Lyotard's *The Postmodern Condition* has become a hallmark of postwar French theory and a leitmotif of postmodernism. This entails reexamining the philosophical distinction between the sublime and the beautiful. In pursuing this distinction, one falls back far beyond the early part of this century to the work of Kant.

The recent reemergence of this issue bears witness to a reversal of the previous prioritization of the beautiful. Whereas for Kant the sublime was "a mere appendage to the aesthetic estimate of the finality of the nature" (1952: 93), of far less philosophical significance than beauty, for recent theory the sublime has taken center-stage. It functions not only to overturn the beautiful in general, but the most beautiful, the most self-contained, all-embracing organic beauty of all modernity—Hegel's dialectic of reason. Undoing Hegel went hand in hand with the return to the sublime. Both gurgle beneath Barthes's famous declaration of the eclipse of the "work" and the rise of the "text." Whereas the "work" is self-contained, internally coherent, "organic," the "text" is unbounded, "dispersed," anti-organic (Barthes 1977b: 157, 161). In other words—although Barthes is not so explicit—the "work" is both beautiful and sublated, whereas the "text" is sublime and unsublateable. Thus it is no coincidence that *both* Breton and Bataille—arguably the first "textualists"—felt compelled to take on Hegel and reformulate Kant.

3

For Breton and Bataille, the crux of the problem with Hegel's "dialectic of reason" was the relative status of the words *dialectic* and *reason*. Hegel was of use only if one of the two terms took precedence. But they disagreed on which term to privilege. Breton rejected Bataille's privileging of reason at the expense of the dialectic: "M. Bataille's misfortune is to reason: admittedly, he reasons like someone who 'has a fly on his nose,' which allies him more closely with the dead than with the living, but he does reason" (Breton 1972a: 184). Conversely, Bataille saw it as Breton's "misfortune" that he had privileged the dialectic: "Since Surrealism is immediately distinguishable by the addition of low values (the unconscious, sexuality, filthy language, etc.), it invests these values with an elevated character by associating them with the most immaterial values" (Bataille 1985: 39). Breton's solution was to push the dialectic until it undoes reason itself; Bataille's was to push reason beyond the dialectic by refusing to shy away from even the most profane and repellent realities.

Such repellent realities are the *excess* that the dialectic cannot manage. The profane, the abject, the material, belong to that class of objects that cannot be sublated: as Bataille writes, "In the [Hegelian] 'system' poetry, laughter, ecstasy are nothing. Hegel hastily gets rid of them: he knows no other aim than knowledge. To my eyes, his immense fatigue is linked to his horror of the blind spot" (Bataille 1988: 111). The blind spot overlooked by a timid reason that knows only lofty knowledge is the opaque scar left by a dead (and now decaying) God, a transcendent blot that resists all intelligibility:

> There is in nature and there subsists in man a movement which always exceeds the bound, that can never be anything but partially reduced to order. We are generally unable to grasp it. *Indeed it is by definition that which can never be grasped*, but we are conscious of being in its power: the universe that bears us along answers no purpose that reason defines, and if we try to make it answer to God, all we are doing is associating irrationally the infinite excess in the presence of which our reason exists with our reason itself. But through the excess in him, that God whom we should like to shape into an intelligible concept never ceases, exceeding this concept, to exceed the limits of reason.
>
> (Bataille 1986a: 40–1; italics mine)

Here, Bataille's anti-positivism confronts negative theology. As Derrida points out, Bataille's theology offers no existent being, no "superessentiality," no "supreme being," no "indestructible meaning" (Derrida 1978: 263). This is why he referred to his theological discourse as an "atheology" and planned to include *Inner Experience*, *Guilty*, and *On Nietzsche* in a larger volume provisionally titled *Summa Atheologica*. In a world in which God is dead, the plane of transcendence remains, but it remains empty, leaving behind only a formless blot or "void" (Bataille 1988: 122). More than anything else, this aspect of Bataille's thought drew Derrida's attention. As Derrida put it:

> [The Bataillean] signifier "matter," ... [is] problematical only at the moments when its reinscription cannot avoid making of it a new fundamental principle which, by means of a theoretical regression, would be reconstituted into a "transcendental signified." It is not only idealism in the narrow sense that falls back upon the transcendental signified. It can always come to reassure a metaphysical materialism ... This is why I will not say

that the concept of matter is in and of itself either metaphysical or non-metaphysical ... The concept of matter must be marked twice: in the deconstructed field—this is the phase of overturning—and in the deconstructing text, outside the oppositions in which it has been caught (matter/spirit, matter/ideality, matter/form, etc.).

(Derrida 1981: 64)

As Derrida notes apropos of his own project:

If I have not very often used the word "matter," it is not ... because of some idealist or spiritualist kind of reservation. It is that in the logic of the phase of overturning this concept has been too often reinvested with "logocentric" values, values associated with those of thing, reality, presence in general, sensible presence.

(Derrida 1981: 64)

Nothing could be farther from Breton's conception. Breton was most frustrated by the chronic misperception of Surrealism as some sort of mystical speculation. In Brussels in 1934, at a public meeting organized by the Belgian Surrealists, he presented a corrective:

A certain ambiguity in the word *Surrealism* is capable, in fact, of leading one to suppose that it designates I know not what transcendental attitude, when on the contrary it expresses—and always has expressed for us—a desire to deepen the foundations of the real; to bring about an ever clearer and at the same time ever more passionate consciousness of the world perceived by the senses. The whole evolution of Surrealism, from its origins to the present day ... shows that our unceasing wish, growing more and more urgent from day to day, has been at all costs to avoid considering a system of thought as a refuge; to pursue our investigations with eyes wide open to the external consequences; and to assure ourselves that the results of these investigations would be capable of facing the *breath of the street*. At the limits, for many years past—or, more exactly, since the conclusion of what one may term the purely *intuitive* epoch of Surrealism (1919–25)—at the limits, I say, we have attempted to present interior reality and exterior reality as two elements in process of unification, of finally becoming *one*.

(Breton 1978: 115–16)

This last sentence resembles a rehearsal of Hegel's final moment of sublation, and it has often been misinterpreted as such. But the invocation of "becoming one" cannot be removed from the matrix of Breton's discourse. One is thus confronted with a curious composite of "the one" and "the many"' subsisting together in a space of non-oppositional contradiction. Breton's *one-and-many* is neither the idealist monism of Hegel nor the dualist materialism of Bataille, but rather like the paradoxical formulation of Deleuze and Guattari: "Arrive at the magic formula we all seek—PLURALISM = MONISM—via all the dualisms that are the enemy, an entirely necessary enemy, the furniture we are forever rearranging" (Deleuze and Guattari 1987: 20).

Thus, Breton confronts the limitations of positivism without recourse to an unsublateable, transcendent Beyond. Instead, he transforms it from the inside, from the position accepted by Hegel—immanence.[8]

> Everything I love, everything I think and feel, predisposes me towards a particular philosophy of immanence according to which Surreality would be embodied in reality itself and would be neither superior nor exterior to it. And reciprocally, too, because the container would also be the contents. Which means, of course, that I reject categorically all initiatives in the field of painting, as in that of literature, that would inevitably lead to the narrow isolation of thought from life, or alternatively the strict domination of life by thought … One rupture, duly recorded and suffered, one single rupture testifies simultaneously to our beginning and our end.
>
> (Breton 1972b: 46)

Within a field of immanence-without-transcendence one cannot embrace a discourse of excess, for there is nothing to exceed. There is simply no beyond—not that there is some "nothing" beyond, some void or blot on the other side of existence, but rather that everything that is, is here: "We wish, we shall have the beyond here and now" (quoted in Balakian 1971: 240). But how does one overturn the dialectic of reason without exceeding it? How, that is, without recourse to something like the transcendence of Bataillean laughter?

The answer, claims Breton, is not to go beyond the dialectic but to bury oneself ever deeper into the thick of it—stretch it to the point of bursting. When one looks closely at reason, picking from it all the minute particulars, it is not reasonable at all. It is "wrinkled like the bud of a poppy" (Breton 1987: 35). In these wrinkles Breton furrows—not beyond the dialectic, but between it. By grasping it "from the inside" (Breton 1978: 139), by caressing it, fondling it gently, the infinitesimal wrinkles peel back to reveal their irrationality—their immanent irrationality "searching in the folds of material, in knots of wood, in the cracks of old walls, for outlines which are not there but which can readily be imagined" (Breton 1960: 121). In a "land without exit," a "medal with no reverse" (Breton 1994: 137), the dialectic of un-reason reveals a single plane of multiplicity with no voids, no cracks, utterly smooth. Breton referred to this ultimate condition as akin to "Words without wrinkles" ("*Les mots sans rides*") (Breton 1988: 284).

Years later Deleuze and Guattari formulated a similar discourse of immanence and made it a central component of their thinking:

> Perhaps there are two planes, or two ways of conceptualizing the plane. The plane can be a hidden principle, which makes visible what is seen and audible what is heard, etc., which at every instant causes the given to be

given, in this or that state, at this or that moment. But the plane itself is not given. It is by nature hidden. It can only be inferred, induced, concluded from that to which it gives rise ... It is a plan(e) of transcendence ...

Then there is an altogether different plane, or an altogether different conception of the plane. Here, there are no longer any forms or developments of forms; nor are there subjects or the formation of subjects ... There are only relations of movement and rest, speed and slowness between unformed elements, or at least between elements that are relatively unformed, molecules and particles of all kinds ... It is necessarily a plane of immanence and univocality ... However many dimensions it may have, it never has a supplementary dimension to that which transpires upon it.

(Deleuze and Guattari 1987: 265–7)

Deleuze and Guattari's collaborative project, in which individual selves become a multiplicity, owes more to Breton, for Breton first proposed—with Paul Eluard and Philippe Soupault—to transform the plane of immanence into a field of multiple subjectivities through the Surrealist collaboration in which "poetry is made by all, not by one" (Breton and Eluard 1990; Breton and Soupault 1985).[9]

4

By way of conclusion, in both cases—Breton/Deleuze and Bataille/Derrida—at the center lies an inescapable paradox. In the case of Breton/Deleuze, the paradox is that the finitude of immanence stands at odds with an endless multiplicity. In the case of Bataille/Derrida, the excess of transcendence stands at odds with a persistent dualism. That each of these logical systems should result in a paradox suggests each is, in its own way, "an outrage on the imagination"— which, for Kant, was the principal criterion of the sublime (Kant 1952: 91). In order to understand the peculiarities of these two distinct paradoxes, it is useful to consider Kant's distinction between the two types of sublime—the *mathematical* and *dynamical* sublime.

The mathematical sublime erupts, claims Kant, when reason demands more than the immediate senses can provide. In the case of contemplating the immensity of the universe, for example, reason posits a totality (the universe must be complete), whereas our senses provide only a fragment of that totality. This coexistence yields the mathematical sublime through the apprehension of an impossible magnitude. The mathematical sublime erupts when the immanent field of experience is expanded beyond its limits in the attempt to make it accord with reason.[10]

The dynamical sublime, however, arises from a different realm of experience. It does not involve the confrontation between sense and reason but rather the confrontation between an observing subject and observed object. The dynamical sublime arises when the excluded subject—that which by its nature must lie beyond the field of objects—is introduced into the realm of objects. When, for example, one looks from a cliff upon a ship dashed against the rocks by an enormous storm, one feels both the destructiveness of the observed event and the safety afforded by the observation. The impossible attempt to reconcile subject (in safety) and object (in danger) into a coherent totality provokes the feeling of the dynamical sublime. In other words, the dynamical sublime erupts as the result of an irreconcilable dualism—which, as Derrida insisted, "must be marked twice: in the deconstructed field—this is the phase of overturning—and in the deconstructing text, outside the oppositions in which it has been caught" (Derrida 1981: 64).

In sum, I argue Breton's *amour fou* and Bataille's *informe* stand opposed not as the beautiful against the sublime (unity against dissimilation) but as two species of the sublime, as two distinct types of dissimilation. That this distinction has remained obscured indicates the polemics that have befallen the reception of Surrealism since Bataille's reappraisal over thirty years ago. It is as if Breton had been, to the subsequent generation, a burden too heavy to bear. He had to be simplified, misread, and made to fit an analysis that would fashion him as the most obvious counter to Bataille. When Barthes, for instance, found the body lacking in Breton, he found nothing more than his own misreading. Indeed, there are too many bodies in Breton, and if Barthes did not see them, it was because he preferred to take Bataille at his word. But to allow either one to speak for the other—to accept Bataille's diagnosis of Breton as having a "pathology of castration reflexes," motivated by "servile idealism," and "Icarian naiveté" (Bataille 1985: 39, 41, 42); to accept Breton's diagnosis of Bataille as an "obsessive" with a pathological "phobia of 'the idea'" (Breton 1972a: 184)—would be to let their polemics determine our retrospective account. It would amount to a superficial dismissal of one for an equally superficial endorsement of the other. It would amount to reducing our own historical reflection to partisan canon-making. But most of all, it would amount to obscuring a history that continues to shape current thought almost as much as it did in the 1930s. If, as Vincent Descombes suggests, one can "trace the passage from the generation known after 1945 as that of the 'three H's' [Hegel, Husserl and Heidegger] to the generation known since 1960 as the three 'masters of suspicion' ... Marx, Nietzsche and Freud" (Descombes 1980: 3), then to this passage one would have to add, tugging at the margins, the two sublimes of Surrealism.

Notes

1 Žižek invokes Deleuzian "buggery" and its production of "monsters" referring to Deleuze's notorious comment that he sees his practice as a philosopher

> as a sort of buggery or (it comes to the same thing) immaculate conception. I saw myself as taking an author from behind and giving him a child that would be his own offspring, yet monstrous. It was really important for it to be his own child, because the author had to actually say all I had him saying. But the child was bound to be monstrous too, because it resulted from all sorts of shifting, slipping, dislocations, and hidden emissions that I really enjoyed.
>
> (Deleuze 1995: 6; cited in Žižek 2004: 46)

2 In his recent study of Alain Badiou, Peter Hallward claims that Badiou is "perhaps the only serious rival of Deleuze and Derrida for that meaningless but unavoidable title of 'most important contemporary French philosopher'" (Hallward 2003: xxii). Hallward is correct: the title itself is trivial. On the other hand, it points to something of considerable significance.

3 For a sketch of Derrida's intellectual formation, see Norris 1987: 239–45.

4 Jacques Derrida, "De l'économie restreinte à l'économie générale: un hégélianisme sans réserves," *L'Arc* 32 (1967) 24–5. This essay was published in English a decade later as "From Restricted to General Economy: A Hegelianism without Reserve" (Derrida 1978).

5 For Foucault's reception of Bataille, see "Preface to Transgression," in *Language, Counter-Memory, Practice* (Foucault 1977: 29–52). Lyotard's endorsement of Breton appears in "The Dream-Work Does Not Think" (Lyotard 1989: 19–55). Lyotard reflects on his early dismissal of Bataille in *The Inhuman: Reflections on Time* (Lyotard 1991: 55).

6 Although penned a short time after Breton's public denunciation, this essay did not appear in print until 1968, when it was published in *Tel Quel*.

7 When Barthes published *Camera Lucida* a few years later, he captioned his photographs in the same eccentric manner in which Breton captioned his photos in *Nadja*. Perhaps Barthes was more influenced by the Magus of Surrealism than he cared to admit.

8 For a genealogy of immanence in modern secular thought, see Yovel 1989.

9 The status of immanence within Deleuze's thought extends beyond his collaboration with Guattari. "The heart of Deleuze's philosophical motivation," notes Todd May, is "the resistance to transcendence" ("Badiou and Deleuze on the One and the Many" in Hallward 2004: 73).

10 For more detailed accounts of Kant's distinction between the mathematical and the dynamical see: Copjec 1994; Lyotard 1994; Žižek 1993.

Bibliography

Balakian, A. (1971) *André Breton: Magus of Surrealism*, New York: Oxford University Press.

Barthes, R. (1977a) *Roland Barthes by Roland Barthes*, trans. R. Howard, New York: Farrar, Straus, and Giroux.

—— (1977b) *Image, Music, Text*, trans. S. Heath, New York: Farrar, Straus, and Giroux.

—— (1985) "The Surrealists Overlooked the Body," *The Grain of the Voice: Interviews, 1962–1980*, trans. L. Coverdale, New York: Farrar, Straus, and Giroux.

Bataille, G. (1985) *Visions of Excess: Selected Writings, 1927–1939*, trans. A. Stoekl, Minneapolis: University of Minnesota Press.

—— (1986a) *Erotism*, trans. M. Dalwood, San Francisco: City Lights Books.

—— (1986b) *The Blue of Noon*, trans. H. Mathews, London: Marion Boyars.

—— (1988) *Inner Experience*, trans. L. A. Boldt, Albany: State University of New York Press.

Breton, A. (1960) *Nadja*, trans. R. Howard, New York: Grove Weidenfeld.

—— (1972a) *Manifestoes of Surrealism*, trans. R. Seaver and H. R. Lane, Ann Arbor: University of Michigan Press.

—— (1972b) *Surrealism and Painting*, trans. S. W. Taylor, New York: Harper and Row.

—— (1978) *What is Surrealism? Selected Writings*, trans. F. Rosemont, New York: Pathfinder.

—— (1987) *Mad Love*, trans. M. A. Caws, Lincoln: University of Nebraska Press.

—— (1988) *Oeuvres complètes*, Vol. 1. Paris: Gallimard.

—— (1994) "Introduction to the Discourse on the Paucity of Reality," trans. R. Sieburth and J. Gordon, *October* 69: 132–44.

Breton, A. and Eluard, P. (1990) *The Immaculate Conception*, trans. J. Graham, London: Atlas Press.

Breton, A. and Soupault, P. (1985) *The Magnetic Fields*, trans. D. Gascoyne, London: Atlas Press.

Cohen, M. (1993) *Profane Illumination: Walter Benjamin and the Paris of Surrealist Revolution*, Berkeley: University of California Press.

Copjec, J. (1994) *Read My Desire: Lacan against the Historicists*, Cambridge: MIT Press.

Deleuze, G. (1995) *Negotiations*, New York: Columbia University Press.

Deleuze, G. and Guattari, F. (1987) *A Thousand Plateaus: Capitalism and Schizophrenia*, trans. Brian Massumi, Minneapolis: University of Minnesota Press.

Derrida, J. (1978) "From Restricted to General Economy: A Hegelianism without Reserve," *Writing and Difference*, trans. A. Bass, Chicago: University of Chicago Press.

—— (1981) *Positions*, trans. A. Bass, Chicago: University of Chicago Press.

Descombes, V. (1980) *Modern French Philosophy*, trans. L. Scott-Fox and J. M. Harding, Cambridge: Cambridge University Press.

Foster, H. (1993) *Compulsive Beauty*, Cambridge: MIT Press.

Foucault, M. (1977) "A Preface to Transgression," *Language, Counter-Memory, Practice: Selected Essays and Interviews*, trans. D. F. Bouchard and S. Simon, Ithaca: Cornell University Press.

Hallward, P. (2003) *Badiou: A Subject to Truth*, Minneapolis: University of Minnesota Press.

—— (2004) "Introduction: 'Consequences of Abstraction'," in P. Hallward (ed.) *Think Again: Alain Badiou and the Future of Philosophy*, London: Continuum.

Hegel, G. W. F. (1977) *Hegel: Texts and Commentary*, trans. W. Kaufmann, Indiana: University of Notre Dame Press.

Hollier, D. (1990) "The Dualist Materialism of Georges Bataille," *Yale French Studies* 78: 124–39.

—— (1992) "The Use Value of the Impossible," *October* 60: 3–24.

Kant, I. (1952) *The Critique of Judgment*, trans. J. C. Meredith, Oxford: Clarendon Press.

Krauss, R. (1985) *The Originality of the Avant-Garde and Other Modernist Myths*, Cambridge, MA: MIT Press.

—— (1993) *The Optical Unconscious*, Cambridge, MA: MIT Press.

—— (1994) "Michel, Bataille et moi," *October* 68: 3–20.

Lyotard, J.-F. (1984) *The Postmodern Condition*, trans. G. Bennington and B. Massumi, Minneapolis: University of Minnesota Press.

—— (1989) *The Lyotard Reader*, ed. A. Benjamin, Oxford: Basil Blackwell.

—— (1991) *The Inhuman: Reflections on Time*, trans. G. Bennington and R. Bowlby, Cambridge: Polity Press.

—— (1994) *Lessons on the Analytic of the Sublime*, trans. E. Rottenberg, Stanford: Stanford University Press.

Norris, C. (1987) *Derrida*, Cambridge, Harvard University Press.

Yovel, Y. (1989) *Spinoza and Other Heretics: The Adventures of Immanence*, Princeton: Princeton University Press.

Žižek, S. (1993) *Tarrying with the Negative*, Durham, NC: Duke University Press.

—— (2002) *Welcome to the Desert of the Real!* London and New York: Verso.

—— (2004) *Organs Without Bodies*, New York and London: Routledge.

The two sublimes, fourth time around

Response to Roger Rothman

Allan Stoekl

Roger Rothman's essay on the "Two Sublimes of Surrealism" is less about surrealism *per se* than it is about the perennial recurrence of the problem of the sublime, in particular, the two sublimes analyzed by Kant in the *Critique of Judgment*: the mathematical and the dynamical. The larger conclusion one can draw from Rothman's essay is that the modern critical tradition in France is condemned—or privileged?—to repeat the Kantian distinction. This repetition goes beyond the apparent dissimilarities between the older "surrealist" approach and the newer "post-structuralist" one. Deleuze and Derrida do not supplant Breton and Bataille but repeat them in a different register. Perhaps we, too, are fated to repeat the dynamical/mathematical opposition; what will be new is not the general structure of the opposition, but the set of concerns with which that opposition is inflected. As Derrida might remind us, we do not simply escape the opposition, but repeat it, parody it, simulate it with a difference. But which difference?

In the many approaches inspired by Kant's analysis of the sublime, it has been insufficiently recognized that Kant was writing primarily about rationality and the power of the human mind, rather than the sublime *per se*. If anything *was* sublime, "absolutely large," it was not nature and the human imagination overwhelmed by it, but the power of human reason to comprehend and go beyond nature's scale. Concerning the mathematical and dynamical sublimes, Kant writes:

> [In the mathematical sublime] we … found, in our power of reason, a different and nonsensible standard that has this infinity [of "the magnitude of nature's *domain*"] itself under it as a unit; and since in contrast to this standard everything in nature is small, we found in our mind a superiority over nature itself in its immensity. In the same way, though the irresistibility of nature's might makes us, considered as natural beings, recognize our physical impotence [the dynamical sublime], it reveals in us at the same time an ability to judge ourselves independent of nature, and reveals in us a superiority over nature that is the basis of a self preservation quite different in kind from the one that can be assailed and endangered by nature outside us.

> (Kant 1987: 120–1)

Kant concludes with this unequivocal statement:

> Hence sublimity is contained not in any thing of nature, but only in our
> mind, insofar as we can become conscious of our superiority to nature
> within us, and thereby also to nature outside us (as far as it influences us).
>
> (Kant 1987: 123)

In the mathematical sublime, we are superior in that we can grasp totality
through the power of reason; in the dynamical, we grasp our mind's freedom
from the overwhelming power and destructive force of nature (Shaw 2006: 82).
What is ultimately sublime, then, is our own reason and judgment: they promise
an escape from the sense of the sublime registered by an imagination that
undergoes "submission, prostration, and a feeling of utter impotence" (Kant
1987: 123) before an overwhelming nature (waterfalls, the stormy sea, etc.).

To go from Kant's sublime to that of Breton and Bataille, a reversal must be
recognized in which nature is valued in its sublimity, in relation to us. This is a
standard Romantic move, dating back to Schelling; we resituate the sublime in
nature, while attuning our mind to that natural sublimity, or attuning nature's
sublimity to our own, in both cases via art (rather than elevating the mind over
it, rendering it supremely powerful but also divorced from nature).

Breton and Bataille approach a very different nature from that celebrated by
Wordsworth or Lamartine. Their primary stress is not the Pascalian infinity (of
great or small) that initially threatened Kant's imagination, or the awe-inspiring
nature of mountain peaks or breathtaking lakes, now positively coded, that carried over from Kant's dynamical sublime to the Romantics. If Breton's and
Bataille's nature is associated with materialism, it is necessarily also a different
matter from that celebrated by contemporaneous Marxists. The sublimity of matter
in Breton is inseparable from the found object: the three-dimensional graph
discovered by Breton in the Paris flea market, in *Nadja*, is incomprehensible in
and of itself—but it is powerful in its opacity (Breton 1960: 52, 54). Moreover,
its phallic shape is simultaneously threatening and liberating, obsessive and
amorous. It both attracts interpretation and repels it; in this way it is sublime,
infinitely remote, defying and seducing the concept. In Bataille's case there is
also a materialism which he calls "virulent"; nature is now sublime in its very
obscenity. In "The Deviations of Nature" (Bataille 1985: 53), nature is that of
freaks, of disturbing prodigies that put the very concept of the well-ordered and
rational—Kantian—human in question.

In both cases this nature is social. Kant's sublime (the false sublime of the
imagination interacting with nature) was an individual event, the effect of nature
on a single consciousness, producing feelings of disproportion or fear. Kant's
theory was mainly a refutation of the sublime in that reason either escaped from
or mastered the sublime.

For Breton and Bataille, on the other hand, there is no easy escape from
nature, which, at the same time, takes a different form: our imagination and
reason, *together*, respond to a sublime materiality—what remains of nature—

socially. The found object challenges our conventions of propriety and rationality; the hideous formlessness of the freak, in Bataille, challenges the ordered world of reason. The event of the material returns not to the imagination but to the "experience" of the individual in a social bond. Sublime materiality *is* the social; *amour fou* in Breton, the sacred in Bataille.

So nature returns, as matter, and, as Rothman argues, Breton affirms the mathematical sublime, Bataille the dynamical. Breton's materiality is that of an infinite web of signification: the drift of signs in society always open to another analysis. Nature is a web of illegible (or constantly re-read) signs; we move from one to another, like Nadja in Paris, always adding one more interpretation, one more vision to coexist with those that have gone before. As in automatic writing, this infinite suggestibility is the freedom of the material body passing through sounds, objects, and urban space. In Bataille, by contrast, materiality is one of a monstrous dualism: through transgression, the sacrificial victim passes from life to death. The sacred object is matter expended, charged with ritual energy because it exceeds the status of stable, useable object. It is dual in its ritual charge. This is the sublime as death-drive.

A similar displacement of the sublime, with an attendant repetition of its mathematical and dynamical aspects, appears in Deleuze and Derrida. Though this is a vast question, we can nevertheless affirm that the *material* in Breton and Bataille shifts into the *textual* in Deleuze and Derrida. The latter are not so concerned with the sublime in society as they are with seeing its operation through an "infrastructure" that is not the locus of sense, but the very material of reading. The textual is now so vast that the social is subsumed by it, just as reason was devoured by the material in Breton and Bataille. I won't belabor the point—Rothman points out that the Deleuzian operation of philosophy is one of "buggery," the production of "monstrous offspring." True, Deleuze writes that "There are only relations of movement and rest, speed and slowness between unformed elements, or at least between elements that are relatively unformed, molecules and particles of all kinds" (cited in Rothman n.d.: 14)—but are these "molecules" phenomenally real or are they effects of interpretation? Can Deleuze analyze these "molecules" apart from reading them, in a text? From the buggery of a text? Can Deleuze write of the play of signs, for example, apart from their interplay in, say, Proust?

The same applies to Derrida; there is no Derridean "philosophy," there are only readings, "by" Derrida, of texts. There is certainly no rationality that reclaims the sublime from its scary material inscription. The text, to put it crudely, "is" the sublime, and, as Derrida famously put it, "there is no 'hors-texte':" nothing can play outside the text's unmasterable movement. In this respect, Derrida, like Deleuze, and like Breton and Bataille before them, breaks with Kant: there is no reassuring space of the human that serves as a respite from the relentless movement of the sublime.

Derrida doubles Bataille in what Bataille called the movement of "non-sense": the affirmation of the dualities inherent in a text or a system, mimed by another position, that is both excluded from the system, and yet necessary to its operations.

In Bataille this was the movement of the Hegelian dialectic, doubled by an "absolute knowledge" that simultaneously completes the movement of knowledge and loses it in a "night" resistant to all meaning. Similarly, for Derrida, the *pharmakon* is written as a supplement both necessary to, and escaping the dualities of, the Platonic system.

Importantly, however, the two sublimes by this point are not easily opposable; they may even contain or imply each other. Just as metonymy cannot be conceived in isolation from metaphor, the mathematical and dynamical sublimes are mutually dependent. Breton's *amour fou* finds plenty of examples in Bataille, and the Bataillean model of sacrifice is not foreign to Breton (Nadja's madness both follows and transgresses the line of social space). The metonymic field proposed by Deleuze is, after all, dependent on "difference and repetition"—movements native to Derrida's orientation, and *"différance"* always already implies "dissemination."

Of most interest here is how the opposition (which is not simply a difference) is to be repeated. If we are condemned only to repeat it—not to generate new structures—we must ask *how* the varieties of the sublime are to be reenacted. I argue that what has been lost in the Deleuze/Derrida repetition is Breton *and* Bataille's stress on the sublime as a catalyst for social analysis and even revolution. The Bretonian surrealist revolution, Bataille's base materialism and accompanying economic analysis, both privilege the utopian model of a radical change in the world we live (and die) in, starting on a very personal level (of dreams, desire, disgust). In Deleuze and Derrida, by contrast, all change and revolt is be put in quotation marks: Deleuze engages in a "philosophical buggery" that possesses texts "from behind"; Derrida repeats texts with the disruption of the deconstructive *différance*. This is likely the inevitable consequence of a transition from the material in society to the textual in repetition (or dissemination). Perhaps the next version (parody? cloning?) of the two varieties of the sublime will take into account Deleuze and Derrida's textual strategies, while attempting to reaffirm the utopian movements of desire and excessive expenditure enacted in different ways by Breton and Bataille.

These projects have not yet been written. But one can foresee new strategies. In the dynamical sublime (Bataille/Derrida), that would mean versions of monstrous nature not only socially but textually inscribed. Bataille already laid the groundwork for this when he proposed a model of energy in society where, in a sense, expenditure and depletion are inseparable. Nature "is" expenditure, but a vast overflow of a resource (such as solar energy) is always doubled by a corresponding radical finitude. Expenditure in a human population—sacrifice—is tied to population or wealth that is surplus precisely because of the environment or economy's limited ability to absorb it. A similar expenditure is legible in a closed intellectual field—say, a philosophy—which is limited by its constitution as a coherent, i.e., finite, truth. There will in this case "be" more truth than can be absorbed in the system—a sacrificial truth will be exuded: a truth that in relation to the system can only be read as noxious defiance or non-sense. This double movement of energetic excess—legible only in the context of radical depletion—and truth both necessary to, and incompatible with, a larger textual and social system may well characterize more than one "approach" in the coming years. How, in other words, does one read excess and scarcity within a system of energy production and consumption? How is it that production/consumption/depletion are legible within the production and depletion of intellectual, political, and social systems? In an era of seemingly endless energy crises and the decline of globalism, these questions will be paramount.

The other sublime—the mathematical—already imbricated, in the dynamical, will have another type of avatar. Breton and Deleuze may well be rewritten in a vast social, ecological and textual analysis of systems of expenditure and entropy. The natural here is inseparable from the social. Oil stocks are "natural" in that they were formed over millions of years by geological forces. The awe-inspiring vastness of this process is certainly sublime, if that word still has any meaning. But sublime is also the "human," social nature of oil resources: refined, stockpiled, traded, shipped, fought over, the sublime is now lodged in a human rationality gone wild. It faces, in one direction, "peak oil" and the revelation of the imminent finitude of resources, and in the other, global warming and the terrifying unthinkability of the future. We see this sublime when we gaze not at a mountain peak but at a six-lane freeway filled with frozen traffic.

This endlessness is not "mastered" by reason—quite the opposite. The mathematical sublime will be rewritten, and lived, as a vast interrelation of systems: of resource consumption, even on the smallest scale, in war, ecstasy, and survival. Intensities will be matched by shortages, which will then generate new intensities. Consumer societies where endless quantities of energy are pumped and dumped may be followed by societies (and ecologies) in which the detritus from earlier days is recycled as the potlatch tokens of new desires and obsessions. Yet at the heart of this vast lateral spread remains the element we saw in the dynamical sublime: expenditure, the movement from sense to non-sense, from isolation to continuity, from hoard to dissemination. This is a model of sustainability, of recycling, in which what is expended always returns in sublime blowback.

The "figure" who embraces this movement will likely reenact both sublimes, since they are inseparable, along with the figures of both preceding eras—the crisis years of the 1930s and 1940s (Breton/Bataille) and the crisis years of the 1960s and 1970s (Deleuze/Derrida). But the future crisis will be on a completely different scale, and its legibility will be contested far beyond the limits of French literary and philosophical discourse.

Bibliography

Bataille, G. (1985) "Deviations of Nature," in A. Stoekl (ed.) *Visions of Excess: Selected Writings, 1927–39*, Minneapolis: University of Minnesota Press.
—— (1988) *The Accursed Share*, trans. R. Hurley, New York: Zone.
Breton, A. (1960) *Nadja*, trans. R. Howard, New York: Grove.
Derrida, J. (1981) "Plato's Pharmacy," *Dissemination*, trans. B. Johnson, Chicago: University of Chicago Press.
Kant, I. (1987) *Critique of Judgment*, trans. and intr. W. S. Pluhar, Indianapolis and London: Hackett.
Shaw, P. (2006) *The Sublime*, London and New York: Routledge.

3 "What true project has been lost?"

Modern art and Henri Lefebvre's *Critique of Everyday Life*[1]

Thomas S. Davis

> The limits of this concept—daily life—are, moreover, those of every concept: none vouchsafes for mastery of what it grasps ... Sometimes a particular concept (for example, art) is born with the end of its referent.
>
> (Lefebvre 2005: 16–17)

1

Like others loosely collected under the banner "everyday life studies," Henri Lefebvre's extensive work on the everyday offers us little by way of strict definitions or clear concepts; rather, it demonstrates the severe demands the everyday places on conceptualization. Maurice Blanchot understood this more than most, and it is the focal point of his 1962 review of Lefebvre's work. The version of everyday life Blanchot deduces from Lefebvre is a provocation riddled with ambiguity: it is "what we are first of all and most often," but also "what is most difficult to discover" (Blanchot 1992: 238). It is a composite of the concrete and abstract, the immediate and the highly mediated, both generative and corrosive for critical thought.[2] How then, should a critical theory of everyday life proceed? Should it amass "histories from below," archiving voices and experiences that have yet to participate in the writing of history? What about a sociological study that would calculate the everyday through facts, statistics, and so forth? Can philosophy be of any use? For Lefebvre, the everyday is enigmatic; it cannot be understood solely through rigorous application of these forms of knowledge. For an alternative whose restlessness exempts it from the disciplinary restrictions of history, sociology, or philosophy, Lefebvre turns to art: "The functions of the critique of everyday life can be determined by reference to an art which immerses itself in everyday life" (Lefebvre 1992: 25).[3] Indeed, a brief inventory of these "references" is telling: the first volume of *The Critique of Everyday Life* opens with a sketch of literary history charting the life of the everyday in Baudelaire, Flaubert, Rimbaud, and French Surrealism and later adds references to Chaplin, Brecht, and Woolf in the reissue; *Introduction to Modernity* engages with Baudelaire and includes a much expanded version of Lefebvre's aesthetico-political essay "Vers un romantisme révolutionnaire"; *Everyday Life in the Modern World* begins with an analysis of Joyce's *Ulysses*; finally, the late works on the everyday—*Critique of Everyday Life Volume III* and *Rhythmanalysis: Space, Time, and Everyday Life*—contain more negotiations with modern(ist) artworks that bear more than a family resemblance to Adorno's writings on art and music.[4] Yet, how do we evaluate this conjuncture of art and critique in Lefebvre's project? I suggest that we think of modern art as a condition of possibility for Lefebvre's critique of everyday life, for situating and framing the everyday as something to be observed, thought, and analyzed critically. In Lefebvre's critique, modern artworks are not obscure objects in need of explanation; they are explanations; they constitute multiple responses to the conditions of everyday life under capitalism.

References to modern art in Lefebvre's critique have not gone unnoticed and they often determine how his critical project is received. Claire Colebrook, Rita Felski, Michael Gardiner, and Ben Highmore have insightfully read Lefebvre's work with an eye towards the importance of art and aesthetics.[5] According to Colebrook and Felski, Lefebvre pursues a transcendence of everyday life and values the quotidian only insofar as it can be radically transformed.[6] Defamiliarizing the entrenched avant-gardism in Lefebvre's work, Felski writes "the conviction that the everyday can be redeemed only by its aesthetic transfiguration will become the leitmotif of a French intellectual and political tradition most prominently represented by Henri Lefebvre and by the Situationists" (Felski 2002: 609).[7] Moreover, this form of aesthetic ideology is particularly modernist: "Those qualities most valued in modernist aesthetics—innovation, formal disruption, self-reflexivity—are transferred without further ado to the domain of everyday life and hailed as the key to its revolutionary transformation" (Felski 2002: 611). These are, of course, serious charges, but, as Highmore and Gardiner show, they are not irrefutable; Highmore rehabilitates aesthetics as a fundamental mode of sociological investigation for Lefebvre. For Gardiner, the very notion that "daily life must be 'liberated' through a transformative praxis that ushers in some sort of idealist utopia, is ... a distorting caricature" (Gardiner 2004: 239).[8] Both rejoinders demonstrate the productivity of reading Lefebvre more closely and, at times, against the grain. Still, Felski's critique remains provocative because it poses two questions: can a critical project that draws from art avoid aestheticizing the everyday? Is Lefebvre touting yet another aesthetic ideology, repeating Schiller's notion that political transformation can only come through the aesthetic?

I think we can answer these questions without either diminishing the importance of art or suspending the political. Modern art has nothing if not a profoundly political function in Lefebvre's critique. For Lefebvre, modern art mediates the antagonisms of daily life and he is interested in the various modes this mediation might take. Thus, it is not my concern to revalorize art for its own sake. Even less do I propose to defend all of Lefebvre's aesthetic judgments; some are short-sighted (Rimbaud and Surrealism) and others motivated by personal conflicts (Breton and Debord). I am more interested in questions that disappear if we accept Felski and Colebrook's arguments. For one, if Lefebvre is not redeploying a general avant-gardiste technique of defamiliarization, how do we characterize the use of modern art for his project? Does modern art's exclusion from both the practices of everyday life and its increasing rationalization lend it a particular way of questioning the everyday? Finally, what is to be learned from modern art's failure to end art's separation from everyday life? These questions allow us to discern more carefully the relation between modern art and critique, and, moreover, the political dimension Lefebvre's project acquires through that relation.

In an oft-cited (and misread) passage from the first volume of the critique, Lefebvre identifies the everyday as a residue, as what is left when all "distinct, superior, specialized, structured activities have been singled out by analysis" (Lefebvre, 1992: 97). Despite what John Frow (2002) rushes to tell us, Lefebvre never intended to detach everyday life from other systems; rather, he understands the everyday as relational—to art, economic formations, the state, historical cir-cumstances—and that relation can be broadly characterized as one of uneven development.[9] He recognizes modern art, which he dates from Baudelaire forward, as an invaluable register of the changing realities of daily life under capitalism. For Lefebvre, the growing disproportions between the technological and eco-nomic development of the modern world and the material conditions of daily life are sedimented into the form and content of modern artworks. In *Everyday Life in the Modern World* he tells us, "the momentous eruption of everyday life into lit-erature should not be overlooked. It might, however, be more exact to say that readers were suddenly made aware of everyday life through the medium of lit-erature or the written word" (Lefebvre 1984: 2). Sorting through the rubble of this "momentous eruption," Lefebvre retrieves a few things: first, he recovers several dialectical models of everyday life as they emerge and expire at different moments of literary history; second, he reads the relation of those dialectics to utopic longings or their absence; finally, he reads art politically, focusing on how it imagines life within and, perhaps, without power. Lefebvre indexes at least three ways art addresses the quotidian, and we can sketch them as the sympto-matic (Baudelaire), the transcendent (Surrealism), and the tactical (Brecht, Constant Nieuwenhuys, and the Situationist International).

2

As his biographers have told us, art and everyday life are bound from the beginning for Lefebvre. Rémi Hess explains how everyday life became a critical category as early as the 1920s through the "confrontation between the Surrealists and the young philosophers [Lefebvre, Georges Politzer, Pierre Morhange, Paul Nizan, Norbert Guterman] animating the journal *Philosophies*" (Hess 1988: 52). Both groups agreed on the importance of daily life but parted ways on how one would mobilize it. Lefebvre remained suspicious of the Surrealist appropriation of the quotidian, but the Surrealists themselves were part of a longer trajectory of French literary and art history. In many ways this explains why the first volume of the *Critique of Everyday Life* opens with a sketch of French literary history from nineteenth-century decadence to twentieth-century modernism.[10] Despite their clamorous proclamations of the new, Lefebvre sees the modernists bewitched by the same spell of the marvelous, or the extra-ordinary, under which "nineteenth-century literature mounted a sustained attack on everyday life" (Lefebvre 1992: 105). This attack begins with France's poet of modern life, Charles Baudelaire. At first blush, Lefebvre's judgment of Baudelaire appears as vicious as Baudelaire's poetics: he "eulogize[s] mental illness" (Lefebvre 1992: 107) and concerns himself only with "pleasure, the organized confusion of the mind which words can so delightfully supply" (Lefebvre 1992: 108); he acutely perceives the duality of modern life, but only to intensify "its painful tensions" (Lefebvre 1992:107), to "leave the mind in ruins" (Lefebvre 1992: 107). Binary oppositions animate all of Baudelaire's poetics, but his "dialectic of opposites ... always ends abortively" (Lefebvre 1992:108). As Georges Poulet (1984) notes, Baudelaire not only fails to resolve or connect these extremities, he makes such an operation impossible. Finally, Lefebvre levies his last charge against Baudelaire for the literary and aesthetic tradition he inaugurates: Rimbaud, Valèry, Mallarmé, Lautréamont, and the French Surrealists all inherit an everyday divested of value; it exists only to be pillaged for shocking manifestations of the extraordinary. Yet, Baudelaire commands Lefebvre's attention for two important reasons: he severs art from the transcendent and relocates it onto the terrain of everyday life; second, as a remarkable physiognomist of social types, his work embodies an aesthetic exigency to look at the everyday.

Fifteen years later, relaxing his combative posture, Lefebvre revisits the *poète maudit* in his *Introduction to Modernity*. He reads Baudelaire's censorious poetics and criticism symptomatically: "It says something other than what it appears to say, something much more extreme" (Lefebvre 1995: 174). Like Walter Benjamin before him, he places Baudelaire within a larger historical scene. In Lefebvre's account, the failure of the 1848 revolution figures most prominently:

> Scarred by the Revolution and its failure, full of loathing for the bourgeoisie and scorn for the bourgeois world, he registered and ratified the failure of revolutionary praxis. He appropriated duality and division. He came to terms with them. He refused to accept them as such ... Like one possessed, he exacerbated them, delving deep within them to unearth the seeds of an idealized transformation which would substitute for the real transformation which had failed to come to pass.
>
> (Lefebvre 1995: 173)

Baudelaire's aesthetics of decline encrypt the agonies of history and the defeat of a world before it came to pass. This results in a double movement. First, he accepts the post-revolutionary bourgeois world "as a 'world'" (Lefebvre 1995: 174); there is no desire for another world in his poetics, no longing for political transformation.[11] Second, Baudelaire submits this world with all of its unresolved contradictions to a radical aesthetic transformation: "There is a demented hope which is disalienating in terms of the everyday life they [Baudelaire and those that come after him] reject ... but alienating and alienated in all other respects" (Lefebvre 1995: 175). This poetic transfiguration elevates literary language to the level of the absolute and, for Lefebvre, Baudelaire opens a space of aesthetic retreat where language itself becomes fetishized, alienated, and guarded from the vicissitudes of history. In short, Baudelaire's aestheticization of everyday life trades one form of alienation for another.

But again, Lefebvre's concern is not to admonish Baudelaire. Uncovering the faint scars of 1848, Lefebvre discerns a key problem in treating the everyday as one side of this or that duality of modern life. He states it baldly in the third volume of the critique, but the same sentiment pulses early on: "Daily life is not some *binary* opposition to the non-quotidian: the philosophical, the supernatural, the sacred, the artistic. A binary schema of that sort forgets a (the) third term—that is to say power, government, the state-political" (Lefebvre 2006: 4). The forgetting of the political in Baudelaire does not denote its absence; rather, Lefebvre suggests a kind of anamnesis to restore the force of the failed revolts of 1848 in Baudelaire's work. The disappointment after 1848 leads to the loss of utopia, of another horizon of possibilities. For Lefebvre, Baudelaire's Satanism, his incessant terrorizing of everyday life, is an act of mourning, the acceptance of a world no longer capable of real transformation.

In the same essay, Lefebvre directs our attention to another figure marked by 1848, Karl Marx. Marx and Baudelaire present two responses to an "identical situation" (Lefebvre 1995:172), and Lefebvre treats those responses dialectically. In contrast to Baudelaire's Satanism, Marx seeks some possibility of redemption:

> The relative failure of 1848 had made him see the limitations of philosophy, including the philosophy of praxis, which was an attempt to supersede philosophy and to realize it practically by emphasizing the unlimited negative and constructive forces of the working class. Without abandoning his programme, but adopting a more "positive" stance than twenty years previously. Marx began to work on economic and historical materials: these would be his basis for formulating what was possible and what would be impossible.
> (Lefebvre 1995: 173).

Marx's disenchantment with philosophy parallels Baudelaire's with politics. Yet Marx never loses sight of the possible. He targets the economic and political formations that produce those painful dualities at the heart of Baudelaire's poetics. The dialectic here suggests the critical tools we might garner from Baudelaire—displacement of transcendence, the pairing of the ordinary and the extraordinary, and a socio-aesthetic way of looking at everyday life—cannot be rallied toward any critical end without the utopic. Yet, for Baudelaire, "history, stimulated by utopianism, killed utopia off" (Lefebvre 1995: 79). With Lefebvre, critique is bound with utopia, which he defines modestly as when "we wish for something different" (Lefebvre 1984: 75).

The logic of Lefebvre's dialectic implies Baudelaire supplements Marx. Lefebvre treats this dialectical movement only briefly and with less precision. Working in the realms of philosophy and then economics, Marx lacks the proximity to the everyday that Baudelaire achieves poetically, even if Lefebvre disapproves of the quotidian's fate in Baudelaire. As Stuart Elden correctly notes, "The 'everyday' as such may not have appeared in Marx, but his work offers us potential for analysis" (Elden 2004: 110) and Baudelaire exhibits a sensitivity to the everyday, an eye for making it appear. The dialectical encounter Lefebvre's essay stages, however, must wait for the Surrealists in the 1920s before it materializes in any tangible literary historical form.

3

Like their predecessors, the Surrealists operate close to the objects and locations of everyday life, "but only to *discredit* it, under the pretext of giving it a new resonance" (Lefebvre 1992: 131). They are "the absurd paroxysm and the end of the methodological disparagement of real life and the stubborn attack on it which had been initiated by nineteenth-century literature" (Lefebvre 1992: 113). Lefebvre reduces Surrealism to a symptom, but not in the same way as Baudelaire. Given the numerous histories of Surrealism, Lefebvre's icy appraisal in 1947 seems hardly sufficient. Lefebvre's comments are part of the generally lukewarm reception Breton received upon his return to Paris from exile in New York after the Second World War. His former colleagues who stayed behind had little interest in reviving Surrealism. René Char refused Breton's invitation to partake in a new Surrealist group; Tristan Tzara unapologetically exclaimed "history has passed Surrealism by" (cited in Lewis 1988: 164) and Eluard characterized Breton as "petrified in a historic pose" (cited in Polizzotti 1995: 573).[12] The Surrealists' volatile relationship with the French Communist Party (PCF) had long ended, and the missing talents of Dalí, Aragon, or Eluard severely weakened Surrealism's chance to recapture its status before the war.[13] Thus, we should keep at bay the personal invectives against Breton in Lefebvre's 1947 text. A more productive point of entry is an important endnote for the "Foreword to the Second Edition" of *The Critique of Everyday Life* issued ten years after its initial publication. Lefebvre redresses his views on Surrealism, but he does not revoke his most poignant critiques:

> In the text below, published in 1947, the reader will find a partially unjust assessment of Surrealism. The author was carried away by his polemic, and consequently his point of view was one-sided. The errors of Surrealism as a doctrine (pseudo-philosophical, with a pseudo-dialectic of the real and the dream, the physical and the image, the everyday and the marvellous) notwith-standing, it did express some of the aspirations of its time … its scorn for the prosaic bourgeois world, its radical rebellion did mean something. And the hypothesis that only the *excessive* image can come to grips with the profundity of the real world—a hypothesis which one can identify just as much with Picasso, Eluard and Tzara as with André Breton—needs to be taken seriously.
> (Lefebvre 1992: 261, n. 49)

Lefebvre's genuine quarrel with Surrealism is over its amateur Hegelian dialectics and "doctrines," which include its transcendence of everyday life, but also Breton's idealism, his emphasis on the revolution of the mind and the sovereign individual. The old problems with Baudelaire—dialectics of everyday life, aestheticization, utopia, the political—resurface, but they are inflected differently, and these nuances require closer inspection.

Lefebvre's rapprochement with the Surrealists bears great import for his critical project in two respects: Surrealism longs for another world beyond the humdrum of daily life and, at least initially, it contests art's separation from the everyday. The Surrealists pressed for a Hegelian synthesis of dream and reality, the quotidian and the marvelous, the individual and the social, but, in Lefebvre's judgment, they moved too hastily from the quotidian. Mary Ann Caws writes Breton's beliefs "are firmly rooted in the future and in the space that imagination creates beyond the borders of everyday life ... Surrealism is a hand pointing away from all that we already know" (Caws 1996: 21). Yet, as Lefebvre reminds us, everyday life is not what we already know and its borders are not self-evident. The Surrealists defamiliarized the everyday "without producing any real enigmas or problems" (Lefebvre 1992: 119). As Rob Shields puts it, "unlike Lefebvre, the Surrealists sought to transcend rather than banish alienation" (Shields 1999: 55).

For all of Surrealism's "research," Lefebvre never viewed their work as critical of everyday life, but as so many games for acceding into *surréalité*.[14] The potential of the "excessive image" (Lefebvre 1992: 261, n. 49), of an aesthetic negativity capable of grasping the contradictions of the everyday without abandoning it, ultimately misfired. Animated by the search for the marvelous, Surrealism's dialectics of everyday life turned away from the quotidian, ending embarrassingly in the occultism of the post World War II years. For Lefebvre, the everyday in Surrealism becomes little more than the staging ground for the marvelous, and this was their fatal flaw. It is no accident that Lefebvre names Tzara for the critical use of the excessive image. In a memoir of Breton and the Surrealists, Lefebvre recalls his admiration for Tzara, and remains as enraptured in 1967 as he did in the early 1920s: "His presence equally calls into question the surreal as well as everyday life ... Thereafter, I could only see in Breton and Eluard (leaving aside Aragon) weakened versions of Tzara ... They attenuated Tzara's poetic radicalism" (Lefebvre 1967: 713).[15] The Pope of Surrealism and his avant-garde faithful not only mishandled the radical energies of Tzara and Dada, but their figuration of utopia as the marvelous smuggled transcendence back into modern art's relation to everyday life. Even Lefebvre's romantic Marxism could not accept this aesthetic transcendence of everyday life.

4

So far, Lefebvre's dialectics of literary history move as follows: Baudelaire initiates a proximity to the everyday, but his poetics are bereft of any utopic longing. The Surrealists generate several means for defamiliarizing the everyday, but the pursuit of the marvelous degrades the quotidian and binds utopia to the transcendence of daily life. Lefebvre's measured objections to Baudelaire and Surrealism open a third way: a tactical aesthetics, or an art that transfers its quotidian "research" into life practices. This third aesthetic modality encompasses Baudelaire's proximity, a less psychoanalytic and surreal defamiliarization, and a concrete utopia. These critical disclosures occur for Lefebvre in the work of Bertolt Brecht, Constant Nieuwenhuys, and the Situationist International. Much of this, however, is already figured in the films of Charlie Chaplin, whom Lefebvre endorses. Chaplin functions as a reverse-image, "an image of everyday reality, taken in its totality or as a fragment, reflecting that reality in all its depth *through* people, ideas and things which are apparently quite different from everyday experience" (Lefebvre 1992: 12). This reverse-image critiques everyday life in "the form of a living, dialectical pair: on the one hand, "modern times" (with everything they entail: bourgeoisie, capitalism, techniques and technicity, etc.), and on the other, the Tramp" (Lefebvre 1992: 13). This discordance elicits a comic effect without condemning or transcending the everyday. Chaplin's comedy, then, is defamiliarizing, distancing us from what might otherwise seem natural, or at least normal, reactions to the situations and contexts of Chaplin's mishaps.

As rich as Chaplin's reverse-image might be, it begins and ends in the cinema and the viewers can only ever be viewers; at the end of the day, Chaplin is still entertainment. By contrast, in Brecht's epic theater, audience participation is the ultimate objective. The events on stage should compel the viewer to form judgments, and, ideally, the theatrical event opens a new critical consciousness among the spectators. Whether or not Brecht's theater ever achieved this is a different matter altogether. What is indispensable is that the "epic" in Brecht's theater is not heroic or mythical, but, like Joyce, the everyday is epic:

> Brecht's epic theatre immerses itself in everyday life, at the level of everyday life, in other words at the level of the masses (not simply the masses of individuals, but the masses of instants and moments, of events and actions) ... It does not purify the everyday; and yet it clarifies its contradictions.
>
> (Lefebvre 1992: 23)

Lefebvre recalls Brecht's well-known analogy between epic theater and an incident on a street corner. A witness to a car accident explains the incident to others by acting the part of the driver, victim, or both.

> The bystanders may not have observed what happened, or they may simply not agree with him, may "see things a different way"; the point is that the demonstrator acts the behavior ... in such a way that the bystanders are able to form an opinion about the accident.
>
> (Brecht 1964: 121)

All depends on a presentation of the facts, not the quality of the performance: "He must not 'cast a spell' over anyone. He should not transport people from normality to 'higher realms'" (Brecht 1964: 122). The narration of the event by one witness, the recollections and conflicting judgments of others, determine how the accident is narrated, who will be deemed at fault, and other consequences; the event depends in part upon their judgment. The spectators are not passive recipients. Ambiguity and difference are essential and Lefebvre credits Brecht for demonstrating "ambiguity is a category of everyday life" (Lefebvre 1992: 19). Brecht attempts to transport this street scene into the theater: "Without being aware of it, and although everything is clearly happening in full view, the spectator becomes the living consciousness of the contradictions of the real" (Lefebvre 1992: 21). In principle, Brecht's theater showcases the contradictions of everyday life, urging its audience to adopt the critical disposition necessary for transferring the critical force of Brecht's art into life beyond the stage.

If Simon Sadler is right to view the Situationist International (SI) "as the ultimate development of twentieth-century experimental theater" (Sadler 1999: 105), it is precisely because the SI imagined new ways of living and new spaces for living as inseparable. The question of space is what sparked Lefebvre's first contact with Debord and the SI. In a letter dated January 3, 1960, Lefebvre acknowledges his great interest in *Internationale Situationniste*. In particular, he was interested in their writings on urban planning, functionalism, and radical critique, topics that would occupy him for the rest of his life. For Lefebvre, the SI exhibited two things that set them apart from their avant-garde predecessors: they believed one could instantiate utopic desires in a very concrete way through urban planning (at least in its first phase 1957–62) and, as a corollary, they sought more than most to supersede the artwork. Life itself should be the work of art.

We are often told Lefebvre exerted a powerful influence over the SI and was the source of their most fundamental and provocative ideas.[16] With the recent publication of Debord's correspondence, we can safely say the SI received much less from Lefebvre's thought than he often claimed. If anything, Lefebvre drew more from the SI than previously thought. The first point of contention is around the idea of the situation.

The situation supplants the artwork for Debord, and it was supposed to safeguard the SI from the pitfalls of the historical avant-garde: "Dadaism sought to abolish art without realizing it and Surrealism sought to realize art without abolishing it" (Debord 1978: 136). The construction of situations, not artworks, was the only possible way to release the creative and critical forces of the avant-garde into everyday life. In this sense, the situation hastened the end of art negatively, as its death or terminus, and positively, as art's goal to merge with everyday life. Michel Trebitsch, Rémi Hess, and others claim Lefebvre's theory of moments as the inspiration for the SI's situation. It is more correct to say the theory of situations cuts its edges against the theory of moments. Debord rightly understood the difference between the two as primarily structural: Lefebvre's moment is "natural," a flash of intense feeling, and it was above all a temporal concept. The situation is, on the other hand, constructed and "completely spatio-temporal" (Debord 1978: 318). The task, as Debord formulates it in his letters to André Frankin, was to find the possible "mix" or "interactions" between the two; that is to say, how might constructed situations give rise to moments that cut through the grey fabric of everyday life, that realize desires or spark unknown or prohibited ones?

   The city was the primary field of application for these constructed situations and, to that end, the SI evolved a number of concepts and practices to construct new settings for lives beyond the society of the spectacle. In his inaugural address to the SI congress in Italy in 1957, Debord explained their activity as such: "We must build new settings that will be both the product and the instrument of new behaviors. To do this, at the outset, requires that we empirically use everyday approaches and cultural forms that presently exist, while questioning their value" (Debord 1978: 42). Among other things, these presently existing forms were urban spaces, primarily the sectors of European cities not entirely organized around the flow of capital. Certain quarters of Paris (Les Halles), Amsterdam, and Venice were exemplary, and the Situationists conducted *dérives*, or drifts, through these cities to connect various areas according to their ambiance rather than geographical proximity. They drew maps charting these vectors of feeling, sketching what they called the psychogeographical relief of the city; in psycho-geography, the sensible experience of the city trumped its rational planning and, moreover, pointed to a city organized around human interests, not financial ones. In "Theory of the Dérive" Debord likens psychogeographical techniques to others from the history of cartography: "With the aid of old maps, aerial pho-tographs, and experimental *dérives*, one can draw up hitherto lacking maps of influences, maps whose inevitable imprecision at this early stage is no worse than that of the first navigational charts" (Debord 1978: 53). There is more than a fortuitous connection between these "maps of influence" and "the first naviga-tional charts," or portolan maps. Cartography historian Tony Campbell notes that the portolan charts vary widely in measurement, scale, perspective, and orientation; however, these navigational charts produce dependable pictures of the Mediterranean coastline. The portolan "preserved the Mediterranean sai-lors' firsthand experience of their own sea, as well as their expanding knowledge of the Atlantic Ocean" (Campbell 1987: 372); these maps could also be followed by others with some success. Where experience and affect fall out of the picture in the functional urbanism the SI criticized, sense orientation and rational knowledge collaborate in these early mapping practices. This lost equilibrium appears again in *Internationale Situationniste* #3 where Mademoiselle de Scudéry's *La Carte de Tendre*, a fanciful map from her seventeenth-century romance novel *Clélie*, sits adjacent to an aerial photograph of Amsterdam. *La Carte de Tendre* attributes emotional or virtuous names to towns, cities, and bodies of water. Following a trajectory similar to a *dérive*, the river, *Inclination Fleuve*, ambles across the landscape, cutting through a series of cities named for one feeling, or "unity of ambiance" in Situationist parlance. The *Inclination Fleuve* forms an arrow ter-minating at *La Mer Dangereuse*, but pointing to *Terres Inconnus* on the other side of the sea. The map suggests the drifter should traverse *La Mer Dangereuse* to sustain the "feeling" of exploration, continuing into the unknown.

   On the opposite page the aerial photograph of Amsterdam offers unhindered visibility. Yet it bears a striking resemblance to its imaginative counterpart; like the *Inclination Fleuve*, the canals point to an unmarked *terre inconnu* untouched by the canals and lost to the photograph. This juxtaposition aligns a geography of affect with a highly technological, objective geography. Following these two geographies, the situationist city would be planned both affectively and objectively. "Unitary urbanism," their program for urban life, collapsed divisions between private and public, work and leisure, and individual and collective life. Theirs was a city for *homo ludens* "who has finally seized the baton from *homo faber*" (Heynen 1996: 28). However, such a city can only follow a refiguration of the material conditions of existence, something Lefebvre believed the Surrealists never quite understood. Constant's New Babylon attempted to realize this project for over a decade. His utopic city requires far more attention than I am able to give here, but his efforts to build it and Lefebvre's admiration are notable.[17] The maps, blueprints, models, and essays concerning New Babylon show it to be a mobile and suspended city, built to accommodate its inhabitants' desires. Moreover, human labor is abolished and automated machines perform all necessary work. The city is fully given over to play and community, with private space reserved primarily for the ill. Needless to say, the city was never constructed. New Babylon resides on the far side of utopia, somewhere art and situations were not able to take us either before or after the SI's denouement in May 1968.

Lefebvre's interest in unitary urbanism, Constant's New Babylon, and the emphasis on life as art cuts across his work long after his friendship with the SI ended in 1962. But Lefebvre's abiding interest in urbanism and an affective, non-rational relation to the city occurs alongside his rethinking of power in the 1970s and 1980s. By the time he completed his final works on the everyday, he had produced a four-volume study on the state and rethought the machinations of political power. Neither the liberal capitalist state nor the socialist state offered a means for addressing the very real problems of daily life; both were technocratic mechanisms bent on managing populations and increasing their shares of global power and the world market. In 1981, Lefebvre concludes "the left critique of the state is closely akin to the critique of everyday life" (Lefebvre 2006: 52). The state for Lefebvre was a complex sequence of administrative (not ideological) apparatuses that could integrate and defang any revolutionary movement. He termed this process recuperation: "an idea or project regarded as irredeemably revolutionary or subversive … is normalized, reintegrated into the existing order, and even revives it. Shaken for a brief moment, the social relations of production and reproduction—that is to say, domination—are reinforced" (Lefebvre 2006: 105). State power's elasticity redefines what forms resistance might take and, in the era of global capital, they would not be based on a model of mass revolt. His final and posthumously published work on rhythmanalysis can be read as a meditation on the dynamics of power and life in late capitalism.

Lefebvre's "science of rhythms" echoes Situationist ideas of an affective relation to the city. He studies the links between the rhythms of life and spatial organization, but also how the linear time of technological production stitches itself onto the cyclical time of biological life: "Rhythm appears as regulated time, governed by rational laws, but in contact with what is least rational in human beings: the lived, the carnal, the body" (Lefebvre 2004: 9). This defamiliarization uses the body "as a metronome" (Lefebvre 2004: 19) to capture its inaudible rhythms, moving deeper into the murmurs and static of everyday life. Thus, the rhythmanalyst "garbs himself in the tissue of the lived, of the everyday" (Lefebvre 2004: 21). Lefebvre is after the same thing he pursued with artworks: a dialectic of everyday life that investigates it on its own level, hoping to change it for the better. Rhythmanalysis continues this, pursuing a traditional project of philosophical aesthetics that considers the SI's urbanism: an exploration of the sensible as a form of cognition. Rhythmanalysis relies on sense experience, or *aisthesis*, as an alternate means of comprehending the spatial and temporal experience of daily life. "The sensible, this scandal of philosophers from Plato to Hegel, (re)takes primacy, transformed without magic (without metaphysics) ... Knowledge of the lived would modify, metamorphose, the lived without knowing it" (Lefebvre 2004: 18). Recovering a sensible orientation to the everyday world appears to be a minor form of contestation to the rational administration of life. "Without claiming to *change life*, but by fully reinstating the sensible in consciousness and in *thought*, he would accomplish a tiny part of the *revolutionary* transformation of this world and this society in decline. Without any declared political position" (Lefebvre 2004: 26). Embodied experience acts as both a register of late capitalism's claims on the biological and as a site of potentiality, as a way of defamiliarizing those forms of power grafted onto the most intimate areas of daily and biological life.

5

I close with an interview Lefebvre gave not long before his death. Discussing the turbulent 1960s, he marks out his principal differences with the avant-gardes of the day and, in particular, Herbert Marcuse, who adopted some of their ideas: "I disagreed with him on the fact that one could change society through the aesthetic. In fact, it was already an idea underwriting the Surrealists when they wanted to make the aesthetic practical" (Latour and Combes 1991: 70).[18] Of course, these comments come late in his life after witnessing the false starts and painful dissolutions of the last century's most storied avant-gardes—Dada, Surrealism, COBRA, Situationist International. As we see in the posthumously published *Rhythmanalysis*, Lefebvre hardly loses his "revolutionary romanticism"; as Blanchot writes, "having entered a romantic, Lefebvre exits a romantic" (Blanchot 1997: 84). What Lefebvre sees, what he always saw, was the danger of relying on art and aesthetics alone for social transformation. However, art and aesthetics function as vital references for construing the multiple ways power penetrates the extremities of everyday life. As Lefebvre and many Marxist aestheticians saw it, the exclusion of modern art from both the practices of everyday life and its rationalization lend it a peculiar capacity for calling the everyday into question, for making claims about how life is lived. Lefebvre takes these claims seriously, even if he judges them at times to be failures or horribly misguided. Modern art constitutes a unique and legitimate way to understand everyday life as it is, on its own level, and what it might mean to live otherwise.

Contrary to his detractors, Lefebvre's references to art cannot be explained away as yet another aesthetic ideology. I ask why their dismissal of the aesthetic is often accompanied by a dismissal of critique. In lieu of critique, we are asked to "make peace with the ordinariness of daily life" (Felski 2000: 95), but what does such pacification entail? Are we left with any way to account for the social, economic, and political forces that enable certain forms of life and prohibit others? Do we have any way of recording this "ordinariness", much less evaluating what it means to live an ordinary or deviant life? We may wonder what critical project for everyday life exists without some relation to the aesthetic and, moreover, why liberal quietism seems such an appealing alternative. We may indeed wonder what project has been lost.

Notes

1 The title line is from Guy Debord's 1961 film *Critique of Separation*. See his *Oeuvres cinématographiques completes: 1952–1978* (Debord 1978).
2 Blanchot's review initially appeared in the June 1962 issue of *La Nouvelle Revue française* 10 (112): 1070–81. A revised version entitled "Le Parole quotidien" was collected in *L'Entretien infini* (Paris: Gallimard, 1969) and translated as "Everyday Speech" in *The Infinite Conversation* (1992).
3 Lefebvre lacerates a number of others whom I do not have space to treat: Beckett, Ionesco, Robbe-Grillet and the *nouveau roman*, and others.
4 "Vers un romantisme révolutionnaire" appeared first in *La Nouvelle Revue française* (in 1957) and was republished as the final chapter in *Introduction to Modernity* four years later.
5 See Felski (2000: 77–98) and (2002: 607–22), Highmore (2002), Langbauer (1999), and Sherringham (2006). It is interesting that Felski's "The Invention of Everyday Life" reads Lefebvre both generously and critically. Her later essay leaves little place for critique as such, opting instead for a model influenced by phenomenological description and American pragmatism. Highmore pursues a similar question to mine but his is directed towards establishing an avant-garde sociological tradition for thinking the everyday and continuing it: "How do different forms of representation produce different versions of the everyday? In what way are certain aesthetic practices seen to produce a specific version of everyday life and how do these thinkers marshal them?" (Highmore 2002: 21). See also Highmore (2004).
6 See also, from the special issue Felski edited, Claire Colebrook's "The Politics and Potential of Everyday Life." Colebrook makes a sweeping generalization in an endnote that links Lefebvre, Agnes Heller, and Maurice Blanchot to a "tradition" of thinking the everyday as inauthentic that stems from Heidegger. While both Lefebvre and Blanchot have their own complicated relations to Heidegger, the everyday is never inauthentic in Lefebvre's work; it is always relational. Moreover, Lefebvre's open refutations of Heidegger's *Alltäglichkeit* make such a genealogy impossible.
7 See John Frow (2002). If Felski reads this form of redemption as aesthetic, Frow's highly selective reading notes a standard theological narrative of redemption. The best response is Michael Gardiner, "Everyday Utopianism: Lefebvre and His Critics" (Gardiner 2004).
8 There are other problems with Felski's intellectual biography of Lefebvre and the Situationist International as well. For one, Dada and Surrealism present two very different approaches to everyday life and Lefebvre and the Situationist International had their own misgivings about the political efficacy of the historical avant-garde.
9 *The Critique of Everyday Life Volume II* elaborates the everyday as a mediating level. See also his summary of the first volume in the "Introduction" to *The Critique of Everyday Life Volume III*, especially pages 10–16. This element is missing from John Frow's "'Never Draw to an Inside Straight': On Everyday Knowledge."

10 I refer to the 1947 text and not the lengthy foreword that precedes it in the later editions.
11 Of course, Walter Benjamin takes another line altogether on Baudelaire. See the two versions of his "Paris, Capital of the Nineteenth Century" and "Convolut J: Baudelaire" in *The Arcades Project* (1999: 3–26; 228–387), and *Charles Baudelaire: A Lyric Poet in the Era of High Capitalism* (1973).
12 See Polizzotti (1995), particularly pages 535–64 on Breton in the years immediately following the liberation. For a review of Surrealism, its postwar politics and postwar legacy, see Lewis (1988: 164–75).
13 After the round of excommunications in 1929, the Surrealists could number new talents such as Salvador Dali, René Char, and Georges Hugnet among their ranks. Yves Tanguy and Man Ray were also more active.
14 This is highly debatable. Ben Highmore (2002: 45–59) mounts a compelling argument for rethinking Surrealism as a kind of social research into daily life. In addition, Michael Sherringham's recent *Everyday Life: Theories and Practices from Surrealism to the Present* (2006) lends a great importance to Surrealism. Walter Benjamin's 1929 essay "Surrealism: The Last Snapshot of the European Intelligentsia" offers another counterpoint to Lefebvre (Benjamin 1999b: 207–21). Also, see the group of essays in Lacosse and Spiteri's *Surrealism, Politics, and Culture* (1991).
15 These are my translations from Lefebvre (1967).
16 See Trebitsch's "Preface: The Moment of Radical Critique" in Lefebvre (2002), Hess (1988: 215–28), and Latour and Combes (1991: 67–72).
17 See Chapter 3 in Sadler (1999), Heynen (1996), and Kofman and Lebas (2000).
18 My translation.

Bibliography

Benjamin, W. (1973) *Charles Baudelaire: A Lyric Poet in the Era of High Capitalism*, trans. H. Zohn, London: NLB.
—— (1999a) *The Arcades Project*, trans. H. Eiland and K. McLaughlin, Cambridge, MA: Harvard University Press.
—— (1999b) *Benjamin: Selected Writings Volume II, 1927–1934*, ed. M. Bullock and M. W. Jennings (eds), Cambridge, MA: Belknap Press.
Blanchot, M. (1992) *The Infinite Conversation*, Minneapolis: University of Minnesota Press.
—— (1997) *Friendship*, trans. E. Rottenberg, Stanford, CA: Stanford University Press.
Brecht, B. (1964) *Brecht on Theatre: The Development of an Aesthetic*, ed. and trans. J. Willett. New York: Hill and Wang.
Campbell, T. (1987) "Portolan Charts from the Late Thirteenth Century to 1500," in J. B. Harley and D. Woodward (eds) *The History of Cartography*, Chicago: University of Chicago Press.
Caws, M.A. (1996) *André Breton*, New York: Twayne Publishers.
Elden, S. (2004) *Understanding Henri Lefebvre*, New York: Continuum.
Felski, R. (2000) *Doing Time: Feminist Theory and Postmodern Culture*, New York: New York University Press.
—— (2002) "Introduction," *New Literary History* 33: 607–22.
Frow, J. (2002) "'Never Draw to an Inside Straight': On Everyday Knowledge," *New Literary History* 33: 623–37.
Gardiner, M. (2004) "Everyday Utopianism: Lefebvre and His Critics," *Cultural Studies* 18 (2/3): 228–54.
Hess, R. (1988) *Henri Lefebvre et l'aventure du siècle*, Paris: Métallié.
Heynen, H. (1996) "New Babylon: The Antinomies of Utopia," *Assemblage* 29: 24–39.

Highmore, B. (2002) *Everyday Life and Cultural Theory: An Introduction*, New York: Routledge.
—— (2004) "Homework: Routine, Social Aesthetics, and the Ambiguity of Everyday Life," *Cultural Studies* 18(2/3): 306–27.
Kofman, E. and Lebas, E. (2000) "Recovery and Reappropriation in Lefebvre and Constant," in J. Hughes and S. Sadler (eds) *Non-Plan: Essays on Freedom Participation and Change in Modern Architecture and Urbanism*, Oxford: Architectural Press, 80–90.
Lacosse, D. and Spiteri, R. (2003) *Surrealism, Politics, and Culture*, London: Ashgate.
Langbauer, L. (1999) *Novels of Everyday Life: The Series in English Fiction, 1850-1930*, Ithaca, NY: Cornell University Press.
Latour, P. and Combes, F. (1991) *Conversation avec Henri Lefebvre*, Paris: Messidor.
Lefebvre, H. (1967) "1925," *La Nouvelle Revue française* 172: 707–19.
—— (1984) *Everyday Life in the Modern World*, trans. S. Rabinovitch, New York: Transaction Publishers.
—— (1992 [1947]) *Critique of Everyday Life Volume I: An Introduction*, trans. J. Moore, New York: Verso Press.
—— (1995) *Introduction to Modernity: Twelve Preludes September 1959–May 1961*, trans. J. Moore, New York: Verso Press.
—— (2002) *The Critique of Everyday Life, Volume II: Foundations for a Sociology of the Everyday*, trans. J. Moore, New York: Verso Press.
—— (2004) *Rhythmanalysis: Space, Time and Everyday Life*, trans. S. Elden and G. Moore, New York: Continuum.
—— (2005 [1981]) *The Critique of Everyday Life, Volume III: From Modernity to Modernism (Towards a Metaphilosophy of Daily Life)*, trans. G. Elliott, with a preface by Michael Trebitsch, New York: Verso Press.
Lewis, H. (1988) *The Politics of Surrealism*, New York: Paragon House Publishers.
Polizzotti, M. (1995) *Revolution of the Mind: The Life of André Breton*, New York: Farrar, Straus, and Giroux.
Poulet, G. (1984) *Exploding Poetry: Baudelaire/Rimbaud*, trans. F. Meltzer, Chicago: University of Chicago Press.
Sadler, S. (1999) *The Situationist City*, Cambridge: MIT Press.
Sherringham, M. (2006) *Everyday Life: Theories and Practices*, Oxford: Oxford University Press.
Shields, R. (1999) *Lefebvre, Love, and Struggle: Spatial Dialectics*, New York: Routledge.

Disdained everyday fields

Response to Thomas S. Davis

Ben Highmore

If a family resemblance exists across works of visual and literary modernism, across some forms of vernacular culture and modern theory (including various forms of philosophy, anthropology, psychoanalysis, and so on), then what propensities would we need to stress, what personality traits would we have to emphasize, to make this resemblance evident? Focusing on political positions, social themes, and cultural values, will take us reeling back into the unmanageable world of ceaseless heterogeneity. More productively, a case could be made for a shared set of technical and procedural resources; *devices* for attending to the modern world.

I suggest that modern theory shares with modernist literature and art a set of procedures or proclivities that could be roughly described under three overlapping headings. First, the modernist (historian, artist, philosopher, etc.) has to find a field and form of attention, an orientation towards the world often aimed at what has hitherto been deemed unworthy of serious attention. Chance encounters, daily life, routines, lowly environments, commercial entertainments, mistakes, and so on, while not constituting new ingredients for works either of theory or of fiction, take on an intensified status for many modernists. This might include what Siegfried Giedion, the historian of modern architecture and technological forms, described as 'disdained everyday fields' (Giedion 1995: 85). Giedion was attentive to 'grey buildings', to 'humble things, things not usually granted earnest consideration' (Giedion 1995: 85) for his accounts of technological and aesthetic modernism. This included sheds and factories, domestic appliances and ordinary technologies (such as plumbing), items that would pepper the paintings of people like Francis Picabia, the sculptures and prints of Eduardo Paolozzi, and the photographic archives produced by Hilla and Bernd Becher. Similarly, when T. J. Clark suggests that modern art is often marked by 'a taste for the margins and vestiges of social life; a wish to celebrate the 'insignificant' or disreputable in modernity' (Clark 1985: 55), he might just as well have been talking about Walter Benjamin as about Charles Baudelaire, or about Georges Bataille as much as Eduard Manet.[1]

'Disdained everyday fields', then, can be seen as the operational field of a host of artistic and theoretical adventures that emerge in the late nineteenth and early twentieth century. While phenomenology, existentialism, psychoanalysis, impressionism, feminism, cultural anthropology, and so on, have not been even in their attention to the socially marginal, they all attend to what has been deemed 'things not usually granted earnest consideration'. For Freud (for instance), it was the day-to-day, night-to-night world of routine occurrences that offered the best examples of the very ordinariness and obstinacy of the unconscious. Persuading the world of the importance of psychoanalysis meant stressing the terrain of the banal: the unexceptional world of lost keys, forgotten names, seemingly random dreams, and misremembered places.

Second, the modernist is engaged in a search for an adequate way of rendering these often maligned objects of attention; or in a more qualified sense, the modernist is engaged in a search for ways of rendering that are less inadequate to the world being scrutinized. The links between art and literature (where formal considerations are immediately more evident) and the production of theory become clearer when we recall that a sociologist like Georg Simmel was described as a sociological impressionist, or when we take seriously Benjamin's demand for a historical methodology that would utilize a montage aesthetic. Montage allows fragments and fractures to connect without having to supply a narrative of causality; it allows micro-descriptions to sit suggestively and awkwardly on a stage of an ill-disciplined totality.

Perhaps the form of rendering most central to the modernist enterprise is the activity of 'making strange'. If it is a 'disdained everyday field' being rendered, the first thing necessary to bring it into clearer focus is to lose this sense of 'disdain': to take it out of the world of the 'already known', to allow it to rise above a horizon of social invisibility. There is nothing essentially modern about the activity of estrangement. As Carlo Ginzburg has shown, estrangement as a poetic device stretches from Marcus Aurelius to Tolstoy. His example of Aurelius's description of heterosexual intercourse as the 'attrition of an entrail and a convulsive expulsion of mere mucus' (Marcus Aurelius cited in Ginzburg 1996: 11), produces something of the same effects and affects as Freud's description of kissing:

> Moreover, the kiss ... between the mucous membrane of the lips of the two people concerned, is held in high sexual esteem among many nations (including the most highly civilized ones), in spite of the fact that the parts of the body involved do not form part of the sexual apparatus but constitute the entrance to the digestive tract.
>
> (Freud 1983: 150)

Freud's rendering of kissing in terms of digestive tracts and mucous membranes brings as many sexual conventions as possible into the realm of perversion to reveal perversion in all its ordinariness as the basis for mature sexuality. This is, of course, the other side of the technique – to bring the seemingly extraordinary or highly valued into the realm of the ordinary.

What makes estrangement central for characterizing artistic and theoretical modernism is not its novelty, but its ubiquity. The Russian formalist critic Victor

Shklovsky might find estrangement (*ostraneniye*) in specific works (Tolstoy's novels or Sterne's *Tristram Shandy*), yet he theorizes estrangement as a central device of literature in general, a cornerstone of his critical architecture. He does this at the same time as a host of Soviet photographers and artists are about to become singularly interested in the practice of estrangement (Watney 1982: 154–76). In modernism, estrangement is the constant (unfinished) work that preoccupies cultural producers. This is to suggest that the problem with modernity is not the constant emergence of new social forms (since this is in itself a form of estrangement), but rather that such changes become part of the taken-for-granted world so quickly. While the device of estrangement is sustainable, specific mobilizations of estrangement have shorter life-spans: the readymade, for instance, has to be constantly remade to provide a defamiliarizing jolt. Yet if the device of defamiliarization is seen as the motor of modernism, it is not just for its ability to render vivid that which is in danger of slipping into invisibility, it is because it is able to alter the value of an object and a form of evaluation. Freud's kiss is just one example of estrangement's use in the modernist enterprise of the transvaluation of value.

But 'ways of rendering' aren't just about figural devices; they are also about the vehicles of communication themselves, in all their practical, social forms. In the arts, the impact of technologies is particularly vivid: cinema and photography, in particular, had a decisive role. Yet, for the critics and theorists, the more important media were radio, newspapers, and magazines. These media provided their own vernacular rhythms that the modernist adopted and adapted. Thus, a writer like Siegfried Kracauer displayed his incendiary little dialectic snapshots in the *Frankfurter Zeitung*. As one of the editors of the newspaper, Kracauer regularly wrote about modern life and the new forms of culture, with a critical lightness and invention that owes as much to the newspaper form as it does to the tradition of critical thinking that Kracauer is engaging.

Third (and most tentatively), the project of the modernist seems ineluctably marked by doubt and the concomitant need for self-reflection. One way of characterizing this aspect of modernism is to suggest that modernist work nearly always includes a meta-literary or meta-disciplinary ingredient. Modernist literature, like modernist psychology, or modernist anthropology, is insistently a commentary on the state of the discipline, of the field of research. This sense of doubt is not often marked by self-doubt, but a doubt aimed at an underlying foundation for thought and belief. If the modernist pulled the rug from under traditional values, this wasn't immediately to be replaced by a new carpet of belief, a new dogma of certainty. More important was the constant self-searching disciplinary uncertainty that accompanied modern thought.

Thomas S. Davis's essay on Henri Lefebvre provides a detailed and lively topography of the part that forms of modernist art played in Lefebvre's thought. He argues that Lefebvre's critique of everyday life emerges in the work of modernist writers and artists. Offering an analysis of Lefebvre that stretches across his voluminous writing, Davis perceives a tripartite schema that divides modernist attention to the everyday into the symptomatic (Baudelaire), the transcendent

(Surrealism), and the tactical (Brecht, Constant and the Situationists): all of which are necessary for the critique of everyday life. Yet, it is the tactical that allows modernism to move from symptom to diagnoses, and Brecht primarily offers Lefebvre a practice that can be inhabited by critical thinking in its attention towards the 'disdained field of the everyday'.

In his 1958 'Foreword' to the second edition of *Critique of Everyday Life: Volume One*, Lefebvre reframes his initial critique by attending to changes in society that have occurred since the first edition in 1947. In the 'Foreword' it is Brecht who allows Lefebvre to see the critical potential of Charlie Chaplin's film, that, in turn, provides him with the mechanism for suggesting the possibility of 'reverse-images' for reflection on the everyday. This offered a way of setting alienation against alienation in a form of negative dialectics. In his 1962 book *Introduction to Modernity*, the references to Brecht are implicit, but are evident in the variety of forms of Lefebvre's writing (the letter, the dialogue, the dreamlike description, the exposition, etc.), using popular forms and humour alongside didactic writing.

If Brecht vividly demonstrates the productivity of the project of modernism, it is partly because the devices he provides are exportable into areas that aren't purely literary or artistic. Brecht, I would argue, isn't simply an influential play-wright, poet or theorist of drama. His work provides a condensed exemplification of what it means to bring together 'disdained everyday fields', a concern with ways of rendering this field, with a concentrated reflection on this process. Brecht is a champion of popular forms of culture and mass-media, a writer of and for the socially marginal and perhaps the pre-eminent theorist of defami-liarization. His critical doubt fashions a form of didacticism that doesn't try to rhetorically persuade or recruit, but to enable the audience to take the role of critical thinkers. But as we have briefly seen, none of this is specific to Brecht alone. In this way, Brecht isn't a progenitor but a contained nucleus of moder-nist energies. Brecht is shorthand for this project of modernism, a synecdoche for a more diverse and dispersed set of approaches.

In 1954 and 1955 Brecht took the recently formed Berliner Ensemble to Paris, on the first visit to perform *Mutter Courage* and on the second *Der kaukasische Kreidekreis*. In 1956, the year of Brecht's death, the Ensemble visited London to perform *Leben des Galilei*. The tours were a sensation and generated intense cri-tical discussion in newspapers and among the theatrical communities. In London, for instance, the visits coincided with the first publication of *Encore* magazine, the magazine that would become the main forum for the New Wave of British theatre. Brecht's energy is felt in Joan Littlewood's work and in her formation of the Theatre Workshop. But the echo of Brecht can be felt in more dispersed ways. First, the beginnings of what became known as Cultural Studies emerged at this time, in consort with a sense of Brechtian energy. In the work of Raymond Williams, but also in the work of the artists, historians, and critics who met in London's ICA in the 1950s (the Independent Group), we find a history for the emergence of Cultural Studies, infused with Brecht's sense of popular engagement, critical openness, and inventive poetics (Massey 1995).

In France, Lefebvre's friend and neighbour Roland Barthes was fascinated by the Berliner Ensemble and wrote enthusiastically of their work. This is another emergence of a putative Cultural Studies. Nowhere is the Brechtianism of Barthes more seriously felt than in his essays in *Mythologies*. Here, Barthes' micro studies of 'disdained everyday fields' (plastic, wrestling, etc.) or of 'things not usually granted earnest consideration' (cars, toys, etc.) turn on the figure of estrangement. Degraded materials like plastic are given god-like properties. It is worth recalling that Barthes' writing first appeared in newspapers and magazines, before being collected together as a volume of mini-essays framed by intense self-reflexivity.

Brecht didn't cause the emergence of Cultural Studies, didn't refashion Lefebvre into a different kind of theorist and didn't form the Barthes of *Mythologies*. But I suggest the Brecht-affect was such that any number of people with a range of different (but often aligned) political positions could recognize Brecht as an important family member. At the beginning of this piece, I said that a family resemblance wouldn't be found by looking at political positions or social values. But perhaps this could be framed in a dialectical reversal: is there something about the formal proclivities that I've sketched, which belong to modernism, which would act as a safeguard to forms of fascist thinking or to the untrammelled seductions of the commodity form? It is exceptionally foolhardy to give cultural forms the job of inoculating us against vicious and invidious politics, but it may recognize the nebula of 'the political' to see its aesthetics and counter-aesthetics in operation. The practices mentioned here (Lefebvre's, Brecht's, Barthes', the Independent Group's) still offer a form of attention that is energized, critical, and capable of an amazing array of forms. This is not to mark out a canon of named writers; more quietly, it is to suggest that 'disdained everyday fields' are still worth tending.

Note

1 These pairings are, of course, hardly incidental: Benjamin wrote extensively on Baudelaire, Bataille on Manet.

Bibliography

Barthes, R. (1973) *Mythologies*, trans. A. Lavers, London: Granada.
Clark, T. J. (1985) 'Clement Greenberg's Theory of Art,' in F. Frascina (ed.) *Pollock and After: The Critical Debate*, London: Harper Row.
Freud, S. (1983) 'Three Essays on Sexuality', in *On Sexuality Volume 7: Pelican Freud Library*, Harmondsworth: Penguin.
Giedion, S. (1995) *Building in France, Building in Iron, Building in Ferro-concrete*, trans. J. D. Berry, Santa Monica: The Getty Centre for the History of Art and the Humanities.
Ginzburg, G. (1996) 'Making Things Strange: The Prehistory of a Literary Device', *Representations* 56: 8–28.
Lefebvre, H. (1995) *Introduction to Modernity*, trans. J. Moore, London: Verso.
Kracauer, S. (1995) *The Mass Ornament: Weimar Essays*, trans. T. Y. Levin, Cambridge, MA: Harvard University Press.

Massey, A. (1995) *The Independent Group: Modernism and Mass Culture in Britain 1945–59*, Manchester: Manchester University Press.

Shklovsky, V. (1965 [1917]) 'Art as Technique', in L. T. Lemon and M. J. Reis (trans.) *Russian Formalist Criticism: Four Essays*, Lincoln and London: University of Nebraska Press.

—— (1965 [1921]) 'Sterne's *Tristram Shandy*: Stylistic Commentary', in L. T. Lemon and M. J. Reis (trans.) *Russian Formalist Criticism: Four Essays*, Lincoln and London: University of Nebraska Press.

Watney, S. (1982) 'Making Strange: The Shattered Mirror', in V. Burgin (ed.) *Thinking Photography*, London: Macmillan.

4 Time and its countermeasures

Modern messianisms in Woolf, Benjamin, and Agamben

Hilary Thompson

Ends

Virginia Woolf didn't always want the party to end, but she had no illusions that the people there didn't often want to die or kill each other. The climactic party of *Mrs Dalloway*, concluding the novel without fully concluding itself, goes further, deviating from what Stella McNichol calls Woolf's "normal writing habits" (Woolf 1973: 10) by reappearing in stories composed later, thus pursuing an afterlife. Woolf's party novel is never alone: it grows from preceding stories and carries on in later ones, forever textually surrounding itself. Why does the party state carry a peculiar charge that exceeds even Woolf's notorious need for closure on projects? We can think of the party as both a predestined culminating point and a protracted end state, and we can look to Woolf's handling of it, despite the deviance from normal habit, as a model for her conception of end time, an occasion to meditate on ends' ethics, and a rendezvous for modernism and theory.

Exploring Woolf's conception of ends can bring our own ethics of reading sharply into view, since readings of Woolf, especially her most canonical works, are among the most overdetermined. In pedagogically hasty moments, we quote her out of context to tell us when a new era began, what the new aesthetic was to be, what women writers really need, what language they speak—and usually in ways made to fit our prior commitments. Frequently, readings of her are set up specifically to tell us something about modernism, modernity, psychology, or femininity, which is to say, Woolf's sense of teleology is rarely alone. We are often aware of its having company, and too often the companions exert an influence more sovereign and restricting than sociable and reciprocal. Our tendency to come to Woolf's work over-prepared might explain why Woolf is one of modernism's most famous yet frequently rediscovered, even rehabilitated, writers, a case of our continually striving to refind what was already there. Our different phases of "Woolf recovery" even index the progress of new waves of modernist study. But to see modernism and critical theory each as party to the other's inquiries presents an opportunity to reconsider what meaning we find and how our means change when we entertain applying a writer's own conception of ends. Placed in the company of two crucial theorists of ends and end time, her contemporary Walter Benjamin and his latter-day advocate Giorgio Agamben, Woolf shows herself uniquely foresightful: where they see a history in which messianism strikes or stalls exceptionally, she projects a peopled dimension opened up by our extreme visions' interceptions.

Volatile states

The imagined guests of the stories collected in *Mrs Dalloway's Party* (1944), whether feeling like terrorized birds (Woolf 1944: 70), fantasizing massacring and decapitating interlocutors (Woolf 1944: 33), or actually tearing the wings off flies as they chat (Woolf 1944: 42), all attest to a party behavior pattern of threat, defense, assault, and recoil. In an oft-quoted diary entry, Woolf describes the condition she explores as one

> where people secrete an envelope which connects them & protects them from others, like myself, who am outside the envelope, foreign bodies. These states are very difficult (obviously I grope for words) but I'm always coming back to it. The party consciousness ... You must not break it. It is something real. You must keep it up; conspire together. Still I cannot get at what I mean.
>
> (1944: 12–13)

Woolf is not satisfied with her description but clearly sees this state in organic, psychic, and political terms. It involves secretion of a shell, a drive towards self-cohesion, and a defense from "foreign bodies." Perhaps the term Woolf lacks is *extimacy*, a paradoxical play of inner and outer, in this case, the process by which one's "envelope" is constructed out of one's innermost secret treasure, which then, having been externalized as one marshals the prized resources that ought to give the self coherence, is betrayed and degraded, taking its guardian self down with it. Woolf certainly knows her "party consciousness" is a state of defense in which inner and outer are confused and in which selves contravene their normal rules of engagement in their very attempt to restore normalcy and balance. Woolf examines within the realms of the psyche and social world what Benjamin and Agamben analyze politically as the state of emergency or exception. Small wonder her investigation was without end.

The eighth thesis

The essential text for recent discussions of the state of exception is Benjamin's eighth thesis in "On the Concept of History":

> The tradition of the oppressed teaches us that the "state of emergency" in which we live is not the exception but the rule. We must attain to a conception of history that accords with this insight. Then we will clearly see that it is our task to bring about a real state of emergency, and this will improve

our position in the struggle against fascism. One reason fascism has a chance is that, in the name of progress, its opponents treat it as a historical norm.— The current amazement that the things we are experiencing are "still" possible in the twentieth century is *not* philosophical. This amazement is not the beginning of knowledge—unless it is the knowledge that the view of history which gives rise to it is untenable.

(Benjamin 2003a: 392)

Benjamin writes in 1940, and as Agamben points out, in 1933 Hitler had come to power and suspended crucial articles of the Weimar constitution, "so that from a juridical point of view the whole Nazi regime can be considered a state of emergency that lasted for twelve years" (Agamben 2005a). We can see Benjamin's concept of the exception as the rule in concrete terms, but we need to go further to grasp the concept of history he advocates. Agamben claims that modern totalitarian governments work by creating states of emergency that enable "physical elimination not only of political adversaries but also of whole categories of citizens who for some reason cannot be integrated into the political system." But even further, he adds "the willing creation of states of emergency seems to have become one of the essential tasks of contemporary states, including so-called democratic ones" (Agamben 2005a: 285). We cannot look at extreme measures and exceptional states with mere shock and outrage that this can happen "here" and "now." Benjamin and Agamben enjoin us to see what these states lay bare.

Traditional theories of the state of exception, Agamben maintains, entail inextricable paradoxes. Benjamin's philosophical opponent, Carl Schmitt (whose *Political Theology* appears in 1922, when Woolf is working on the Dalloway stories and novel), writes of the sovereign as "he who decides on the state of exception" and is "*at the same time* outside and inside the juridical order" (cited in "Messiah"; Agamben 2005a: 161, emphasis Agamben's). Not only is the state of exception a legal way states can operate beyond their usual legal constraints, but the sovereign, as the figure endowed with the power to declare this state, becomes the figure who is outside the law and who *is* the law. The loophole possibility of the state of exception speaks, for Agamben, about what has always been true of sovereign states and is fundamental to the structure of the law. Thus he makes pointed use of Schmitt's statement that "The exception is more interesting than the regular case. The latter proves nothing; the exception proves everything. The exception does not only confirm the rule; the rule lives off the exception alone" (cited in Agamben 1999: 162). Benjamin's eighth thesis, Agamben proposes, is a "conscious alteration" of Schmitt: rather than the rule living off the exception, we are living in a state of exception that has really always been the rule.

The paralyzed messiah

Benjamin calls on us to see the law's functioning throughout history for what it is and to "bring about a real state of emergency." Agamben believes, remarkably, that the state of exception has become ever more expansive, encompassing "the entire planet" and "every part of our culture, from politics to philosophy and from ecology to literature" (Agamben 1999: 170). As it has gobbled up all zones, this state has ceased being "the hidden foundation of the system" and now "has fully come to light" (Agamben 1999: 170). And yet this illumination has not created the "real state of emergency" Benjamin called for, his advent of the messianic or the "blast" that was to "open the continuum of history" (Benjamin 2003a: 396). Instead, for Agamben, "We can compare the situation of our time to that of a petrified or paralyzed messianism" (Agamben 1999: 171). For Benjamin, the revolutionary "on the locomotive of world history" was trying to "activate the emergency brake" (Benjamin 2003b: 402), and the heroic historical materialist was to have seen the present, not as part of a story of progress, but as an instant "in which time takes a stand [*einsteht*] and has come to a standstill" (Benjamin 2003a: 396). But for Agamben our arrested state is where the truth becomes ever more obvious and ever less transformative: a stalemate. We reach an impasse where Benjamin and Agamben give counter-descriptions of the standstill. Woolf, too, envisions a moment of arrest where messianic potential and paralysis clash, but she gives a more precise profile of the petrified emissary.

When *Mrs Dalloway*'s two major characters first converge, the scene also contains all the major figures and concepts that obsess Benjamin from the 1920s up until his last writing in 1940. As Mrs. Dalloway shops for party flowers, a pistol-shot sound fires in the street, and then, as the sovereign, perhaps the Queen, the Prince, the Prime Minister, passes by in a car, we meet the returned, shell-shocked soldier Septimus Warren Smith, who is "unable to pass," for whom "Everything had come to a standstill" (Woolf 1925: 15). Everyone, including Mrs Dalloway, stares, looks to spot the sovereign in the suddenly stopped traffic, but Septimus thinks, "It is I who am blocking the way" and considers whether he is "not weighted there, rooted to the pavement, for a purpose?" (Woolf 1925: 16). But to discern for what purpose he must wait. A sky-writing airplane races above, and just as we must wait for "antiquaries sifting the ruins of time" for the moment when "The face in the motor car will then be known" (Woolf 1925: 17–18), so the plane seems "destined to cross from West to East on a mission of the greatest importance which would never be revealed" (Woolf 1925: 23). For Lucrezia Warren Smith, merely getting her rattled husband to cross the street is a mission. And onlooker Mr Bentley sees both the plane and the cross in St Paul's Cathedral as symbols of "man's soul," the drive to "get outside his body" or to soar and become "all spirit" (Woolf 1925: 30–1). While others hear the airplane, Septimus responds to "the voice which now communicated with him who was the greatest of mankind, Septimus, lately taken from life to death, the Lord who had come to renew society" (Woolf 1925: 27). We begin with a blast (in fact, a car backfiring), in the wake of the shock, the sovereign appears and everyone's movements are arrested, Septimus confuses himself with the sovereign and the standstill with his own presence, the atmosphere is charged with the sense of a mission, and the air echoes with the ringing of an unknown message. Emergency, sovereignty, theology, and teleology are present here, and we can even read Woolf's scene as a staging of the seeming impasse between Benjamin and Agamben: if Septimus embodies and carries a message, it is messianic paralysis itself. But if Septimus is a harbinger of arrested messianism, what will be revealed when his fate runs its course? What will our final judgment be on the standstill and his stand?

Divine justice?

Septimus is the bearer of several seemingly contradictory truths: that "there is no crime" (Woolf 1925: 108), that he has been given a death sentence for a crime, that "there is no death," that there is universal love, that "there is a God," that there is an all-embracing tree, that "Men must not cut down trees," that "No one kills from hatred" (Woolf 1925: 26), that "it might be possible that the world itself is without meaning" (Woolf 1925: 97), and, most painfully, that his task is to hold back the coming of Evans, his spectrally returning fallen comrade. One way of understanding these countering truths is to say that Septimus is ensnared in the terms of mythic justice but is forever seeking a realm of divine justice.

In his "Critique of Violence" Benjamin explores the question of what constitutes violence, or force, and, taking up the customary legal concepts of justice, ends, and means, argues that "violence can first be sought only in the realm of means, not in the realm of ends," a proposition that is, he adds, more far-reaching than we would guess (Benjamin 1996: 236). In the last stages of his essay, he considers violent "outbursts" that are not tied to "a preconceived end" and claims prime examples may be found in myth (1996: 248). When the gods unleash violence, it is not to punish the transgression of a known law, nor is it to make their will known, but rather it is simply to make their presence known and to draw a line between us and them. Thus their violence is a "manifestation" not a "means," and it enacts a law rather than upholds one (Benjamin 1996: 248).

Both Lucrezia and Septimus see themselves as victims of a fate that operates without justification. Lucrezia asks herself why she must suffer, repeats to herself that she has "done nothing wrong" (Woolf 1925: 71), protests to the esteemed doctor Sir William Bradshaw that Septimus "has done nothing wrong whatever" (Woolf 1925: 105), and considers that her "lot" is to "be rocked by this malignant torturer" (Woolf 1925: 72). When the backfire blasts and the traffic halts, Septimus believes that the "world has raised its whip" and he helplessly wonders, "where will it descend?" (Woolf 1925: 15). Septimus sees himself as "the scapegoat, the eternal sufferer" (Woolf 1925: 27) at one moment and at another imagines that a "divinely merciful" heaven has "spared him, pardoned his weakness" (Woolf 1925: 74). This ever-present tension might explain why Septimus must utter and write down "truths": because he sees fate exacting retribution from him for a transgression that is without specific origin, he understands that he exists at the point where law enacts itself, and thus, like the ancient Greeks in Benjamin's account (and it is tellingly in Greek that Septimus hears birds speak to him), he must seek to evade the snares of unwritten law by struggling to write law. He is hounded by a mythic verdict, a death sentence that, because it issues from "human nature" for a crime against this nature, seems to define, delimit, and thus arise from outside humanity, an exceptional verdict by all means. To escape this mythic judgment, Septimus must appeal to a higher authority by seeking divine justice.

But the term Benjamin opposes to mythic lawmaking violence (and ultimately Benjamin sees all enacting and making of law as mythic violence at its root) is not so much divine justice as divine violence. In keeping with his unsettling figures of shocks and blasts, Benjamin often envisions a divinity whose force is destructive:

> Far from inaugurating a purer sphere, the mythic manifestation of immediate violence shows itself fundamentally identical with all legal violence, and turns suspicion concerning the latter into certainty of the perniciousness of its historical function, the destruction of which becomes obligatory. This very task of destruction poses again, ultimately, the question of a pure immediate violence that might be able to call a halt to mythic violence. Just as in all spheres God opposes myth, mythic violence is confronted by the divine. And the latter constitutes its antithesis in all respects. If mythic violence is lawmaking, divine violence is law-destroying; if the former sets boundaries, the latter boundlessly destroys them; if mythic violence brings at once guilt and retribution, divine power only expiates; if the former threatens, the latter strikes; if the former is bloody, the latter is lethal without spilling blood.
>
> (Benjamin 1996: 249–50)

In divine violence, according to Benjamin, lies revolutionary potential, space for true human political action because divine violence acts without preconceived ends but, unlike mythic violence, does not end up instating ends in the form of law, thus becoming identical with lawmaking and the "assumption of power." Rather, divine violence calls a halt to these ends, so that, "Justice is the principle of all divine endmaking, power the principle of all mythic lawmaking" (Benjamin 1996: 248). Benjamin's divine violence becomes one mode of the messianic for Agamben, who speaks of it as violence that as "pure means" dissolves the "relation of violence and law" or the exceptionality that the rule lives off of. By deactivating law, divine violence brings it to "messianic fulfillment" (Agamben 2005b: 63).

Septimus has known mythic violence at its sharpest, and its power is both exacerbated and dislocated in him. Isn't he, like Benjamin, reaching for a force, pure and immediate, that would clear out, deactivate the rule of falsely justifying ends? This would be one meaning for his principle that "there is no crime" and one explanation for his need to communicate his truths to the sovereign who decides on and presides over states of exception. Septimus sees himself as taking on the burden of civilized history's supreme secret truth, "the meaning, which now at last, after all the toils of civilization—Greeks, Romans, Shakespeare, Darwin, and now himself—was to be given whole to ... ' To whom?' he asked aloud, 'To the Prime Minister,' the voices which rustled above his head replied" (Woolf 1925: 74). It is as though he believes he can lift his death sentence, indeed lift society's death sentence, the cycle of transgressions it is doomed to be juridically, violently enmeshed in, if he articulates the right expiating universal truth, the maxim that will embody the God's eye point of view.

In Benjamin's vision, though, divine violence is potentially lethal, and Septimus dangerously identifies himself not only with messianism but with sovereignty and exceptionality. He sees himself as designated to receive the law because he feels he is outside the law and, he fears, illegally so, a marked man. Thus he decides it is he who is blocking the way. To have lived through law at its furthest extreme—that is, war, licensed killing—and to see this extreme as revelatory, the truth behind civilization, and to no longer even register shock, is to have arrived at the knowledge that the view of history that would have given rise to shock has become untenable. But to lay bare exceptionality is to risk making life unbearable. Septimus becomes the emissary of a message he can't carry. In one of his last visions, Septimus transposes divinity onto Lucrezia, seeing her as "a flowering tree" through whose branches he can see "the face of a lawgiver" (Woolf 1925: 162). But this glimpse of God's gaze doesn't remove the "verdicts" of the "judges," the doctors who "saw nothing clear, yet ruled, yet inflicted" (Woolf 1925: 162). Sir William Bradshaw, whom Clarissa later describes as the man having to "decide questions of appalling difficulty" (Woolf 1925: 200) has become (as Agamben will later argue of doctors in our time) another figure for the sovereign, and he has ruled to restrict Septimus's mobility, to detain him in a state of rest. In Bradshaw's view, "It was a question of law" (Woolf 1925: 106). Because Septimus has threatened suicide, given clear signs of violent internal turmoil, his usual caregivers, Lucrezia and their general physician Holmes, can be dismissed, relieved of authority in this time of extraordinary measures. Threatened with being dragged out of his heightened state of constant exception and back into the banal emergency, Septimus chooses to enact a real emergency. Much as he doesn't want to "spoil" the bread-knife and resents "the tiresome, the troublesome, and rather melodramatic business of throwing himself out," he gives in to the window knowing that it "was their idea of tragedy, not his" (Woolf 1925: 163). This submission to "their" terms becomes not only lethal but blood spilling, as his leap from the window becomes a fall onto the rails. It as though he is never allowed to attain the realm of pure means, the truly divine endmaking he seeks. While Benjamin's messianism in the form of divine violence can describe the terms of Septimus's struggle, it can't account for the totality of his sacrifice. In his last leap, Septimus no longer simply embodies an impasse between messianism and paralysis; now he traces an arc that gestures towards a realm of the divine even as it lets itself fall into myth. This arc introduces the element of time.

The rest of time

Just as the emissary airplane of *Mrs Dalloway* crosses over St Paul's Cathedral, in *The Time that Remains*, Agamben crosses Benjamin's concept of messianic time with the Pauline epistles. Distinguishing "the time of the end" from "the end of time," messianism from eschatology, Agamben suggests that messianic time is not only the time left to us, but that (drawing from linguist Gustave Guilluame) it can also be seen in the lag-time leftover produced by the noncoincidence of our representations of time and the time it takes us to make them. Instead of a tacked-on supplement, this end time becomes "a time within time—not ulterior but interior" and its messianic fulfillment would be our grasping the fact of this non-coincidence as it exerts its pressure from within time (Agamben 2005c: 67–68).

Agamben's disentangling of messianism from eschatology also allows him to challenge one definition of modernity: that messianism is eschatological and that modernity is the epoch antithetical to such culminations, the time when we cannot believe in ultimate salvation (Agamben 2005c: 63). In differentiating messianism from eschatology, Agamben tries to retrieve it for modernity. Nonetheless, to fully "achieve" or apprehend temporally our representing of time would seem to radically rework time as we know it. Indeed, a concept of unworking is crucial to Agamben's vision of both messianism and modernity. Retracing the path of the apostle Paul's concept of *katargesis* or deactivation through Luther to Hegel and on to Benjamin, Agamben argues that this term Paul uses repeatedly to describe the impact of the messianic on the law is a Greek word whose perhaps most striking prior use was in "the form *argeo* in the Septuagint, a translation of the Hebrew word that signifies rest on Saturday" (Agamben 2005c: 96). In effect, Paul claims the messianic puts earthly law on a "sabbatical suspension" (Agamben 2005c: 96). And here, moving neatly from Septuagint to Septimus, we recall that Woolf's bearer of the truth of the law is also named as the seventh and ordered into the indefinite sabbatical of the rest cure. Tracking *katargesis* in the German tradition, Agamben reveals that Paul's word for unworking, abolishing yet conserving, becomes the German dialectical *Aufhebung*, and this "genealogy" means

> not only is Hegelian thought involved in a tightly knit hermeneutic struggle with the messianic—in the sense that all of its determining concepts are more or less conscious interpretations and secularizations of messianic themes—but this also holds for modernity, by which I intend the epoch that is situated under the sign of the dialectical *Aufhebung*.
>
> (Agamben 2005c: 100)

We could extend Agamben's terms to call modernity the epoch of undone time we may still grasp. If the state of exception as the limit-point of the law, its potential laying bare or implicit undoing, can be the harbinger of the messianic, messianism would be an apprehending of the very terms of modernity. Or, extending this model, we might say modernism would become a feature of the epoch of messianism, rather than either its aegis or its antithesis. For Agamben, then, Benjamin, with his historically urgent analysis of the state of exception, calls for the halting of ends, and political use of the theological, becomes the constellating text required for Paul's work to come to "full legibility" (Agamben 2005c: 145).

To attend to such a culmination, thousands of years in the making, is not to be ahistorical; it is to be messianically historical: that is, to be attuned to the critical "now-time" of each text's truth brought to light by their intertwining. Again, extending Agamben's terms, we might say messianic reading becomes the most modern form of historical reading.

Saving time

Yet the airplane over St Paul's progresses in a counter-Hegelian direction (West to East), and its mission of greatest importance, far from becoming illuminated, is destined never to be revealed. Nor is conversion the epiphany for Clarissa that it is for Paul. Is it that we want to insist on historical specificity rather than a trans-temporal macro-narrative, even one of ingenious asynchronies, as we read the novel? And yet *Mrs Dalloway* also insists on spawning times out of times. Its historical moment, the Great War's immediate aftermath with all the standing down from emergency this period ought to entail, is crucial without having to be sovereign. Likewise, although Big Ben resounds throughout the narrative, punctuating key episodes, it is not the commanding monolith one might assume. Time has been slackened, stretched out, reconfigured and saved (that is, both abolished and conserved), but at the expense of carrying over some of what ought to have ended. Freedom goes hand in hand with subtle continuing violence. In public life, for example, battle rhetoric persists and pervades. As the time to arrive at the Dalloways' draws near, Peter Walsh, fresh from the East and guest by last-minute invitation, has a telling reverie:

> I resign, the evening seemed to say, as it paled and faded above the battlements and prominences, moulded, pointed, of hotel, flat, and block of shops, I fade, she was beginning, I disappear, but London would have none of it, and rushed her bayonets into the sky, pinioned her, constrained her to partnership in her revelry.
>   For the great revolution of Mr Willett's summer time had taken place since Peter's last visit to England. The prolonged evening was new to him.
>
> (Woolf 1925: 177)

Held over after the war, this seasonal one-hour advance of the clocks saves more daylight time for entertainment, more sunny liberty from work hours, but the revolution is not emancipating for evening itself, who favors early retiring yet is forced into compulsory sociality as if pressed into service. And daylight saving time is not traditional time's only "revolution."

When Clarissa fixates on her daughter's tutor, the dreaded, zealous Miss Kilman and the cruelty of religious conversion, she sees through the window the "old lady" who lives opposite, and then she thinks of love. At this moment Big Ben is countered:

> Love—but here the other clock, the clock which always struck two minutes after Big Ben, came shuffling in with its lap full of odds and ends, which it

dumped down as if Big Ben were all very well with his majesty laying down the law, so solemn, so just, but she must remember all sorts of little things besides.

(Woolf 1925: 140)

What better instance of a time beside time? The other clock doesn't complete the hour, sounding time when Big Ben does. It instates and reveals an asynchrony rather than confirms a sovereignty, and Big Ben's upstaged majesty is equally necessary for the apprehension of this asynchrony. Further, the lagging clock tells of another teleology, since it is not the clock of ends so much as "odds and ends" or remnants, the tasks that are left. Little things and oddments are freed from law and majestic final strokes. What has happened in the narrative to loosen time?

The force that would have held several times in a seeming unity is Conversion (the demon that drives Miss Kilman, and also Sir William Bradshaw), but Conversion acting covertly as Proportion. When Bradshaw's goddess of Proportion—good health, restrained habits—is revealed to have a sister who is not as pleasant and who controls him "under some plausible disguise" (Woolf 1925: 110), we meet the goddess Conversion in all her mythic fury. Conversion loves human blood, devours human will, and admires "her own features stamped on the face of the populace" (Woolf 1925: 109). Once Conversion is no longer concealed by Proportion and the Warren Smiths leave Bradshaw, time audibly splinters:

> Shredding and slicing, dividing and subdividing, the clocks of Harley Street nibbled at the June day, counseled submission, upheld authority, and pointed out in chorus the supreme advantages of a sense of proportion, until the mound of time was so far diminished that a commercial clock, suspended above a shop in Oxford Street, announced, genially and fraternally, as if it were a pleasure to Messrs Rigby and Lowndes to give the information gratis, that it was half-past one.
>
> (Woolf 1925: 112)

Oneness, be it monochrony or a power's monopoly, is halved and almost past. The motley chorus signals Proportion's loss of majesty, the fall of Conversion's figurehead and puppet, and this fall allows even the forces of commerce an opportunity to give the Warren Smiths time free. As with Benjamin's concrete experience of a constant state of emergency, there are ways to see specific historical references in these examples. Alex Zwerdling would remind us of the moribund Conservative governments in 1923 and of the disintegrating empire. And Vincent Sherry argues that Woolf's outrageous portrayal of Bradshaw and his law of Proportion makes a mockery of British Liberalism's wartime rhetoric of rationalism and ratio, a rhetoric the Great War laid bare (Sherry 2003: 289–90). But whatever references to party politics we see in Woolf's pillorying of proportion, we miss part of the point if we overlook the accompanying ethical quarrel with conversion. For Clarissa, the subordination of others to one's own ends is the callous conversion exemplified by the idea rather than person of Miss Kilman. But the very militancy of her own party as counter-campaign undermines both Clarissa's claim that party-giving is an end in itself and her attempt to use it as pure, immediate force, divine endmaking separate from others' terms. Small wonder the end of another, Septimus, told through the brute barking of Lady Bradshaw, will appear at the "middle" of the party, the center where death and ends were to be held at bay.

The window

If Woolf's characters entertain but don't attain divine violence, how else might she foresee the messianic entering? Woolf doesn't give us Benjamin's famous "small gateway," the potential opening for the messiah in every moment, but she returns repeatedly to the window, and someone always appears there. Clarissa often watches for the old lady opposite, and paradoxically, this woman becomes emblematic of the soul's privacy, its right not to be converted, made emblem; the paradox's resolution is that while Clarissa converts the woman into her own meaning, she maintains a privacy, since the woman need never know. Clarissa will return to the window when the party winds down and she has been struck by the story of Septimus, as though she must look for something in the same space he has thrown himself out of. And just before he hurls himself, Septimus has a vision analogous to Clarissa's: "Coming down the staircase opposite an old man stopped and stared at him" (Woolf 1925: 164). But Septimus's vision stops there. Clarissa picks up the vision imaginatively and follows the pattern of Woolf's short story characters, contemplating her life's prized moments as a defense. But at the point she spies the lady opposite seeming to stare "straight at her" (Woolf 1925: 203), her response shifts. After watching her and feeling seen by the woman (and Clarissa never knows whether the woman in the dark has actually seen her at the moment their lines of vision meet), Clarissa decides she feels "somehow very like him—the young man who had killed himself." Not only that, but she feels "glad that he had done it; thrown it away while they went on living" (Woolf 1925: 204).

What about the window enables these strange connections, and why does the window scene culminate and draw out the party section? It is because in the window you see someone "opposite" seeing you, and these opposite figures, whether they put out the light or witness your fall, conjure up the other side of life for you, so that it sees you. We have the sight of something held within a frame yet impinging from another side; it remains other but affords us a vision of ourselves beheld from beyond. We have the messianic not simply as time but as sight, human sight.

The ends meet?

What does such a convergence suggest about the grounds on which epochs and movements might meet? In "On the Concept of History" Benjamin claims that a moment of "causal significance" becomes "historical posthumously" through even "events that may be separated from it by thousands of years." He advocates that we stop viewing history as a "sequence of events like the beads on a rosary" (Benjamin 2003a: 397). If we take this caution seriously, we must ask ourselves what priority we should give to chronology in our modes of historical reading. Benjamin calls on the historian to grasp "the constellation into which his own era has entered, along with a very specific earlier one. Thus, he establishes a conception of the present as now-time shot through with splinters of messianic time" (Benjamin 2003a: 397). This is to say, a messianically attentive historian may at times jump beads, and this is also why Agamben finds, through Benjamin, that Paul's letters are utterly timely. Do we feel Paul had to wait for Benjamin or, borrowing a metaphor from Woolf, Big Ben had to wait for tellingly asynchronous little Agamben? What is revealing about Woolf's climactic window scene is that Clarissa doesn't need the old woman to have seen her; they are not waiting for each other. Clarissa may see in the old woman a projected image, a possible future self, she may even feel acknowledged by this presence, but she doesn't need the acknowledgement actualized concretely; it doesn't need to happen in real time. This is the model of the best messianic reading. If modernism and theory are to meet on even ground, we cannot simply reclaim theory for modernism on the basis of temporal priority or we risk falling into a triumphal procession of victors bearing spoils. Nor can we allot ourselves the position of privileged avatar apprehending fully the sight of another. Rather, Woolf's interceptional time suggests that we must catch the transformations produced by sight lines that come into collision without outright collusion.

The envisioning of the state of exception is an extraordinary case in point. Woolf writes her Dalloway texts in the time of the Great War. Benjamin lays the foundations of his theory of time in the same period, but crystallizes his conceptions while the Nazis are in power. Agamben writes now in the midst of our "war on terror." Each of these states provides the writing's concrete circumstances. But if we take each state singly as the writing's sovereign reference point, we make them all isolated, exceptional cases and miss the binding rule to which they might want to alert us. If we take seriously the possibility that Woolf, Benjamin, and Agamben have intersected, theorized a similar time and condition, we can't look to each one's history for a sense of peculiar shock or singular recognition. At the same time, we may have qualms about all too easily aligning them. We may be wary of Agamben's belief in the globalization of petrified messianism and, at times, in a seeming monism of exceptionality. We might wince at some of Benjamin's invocations of destruction, of blasting. We might feel uncomfortable simply equating Woolf's social world with a state of emergency. Nevertheless, in the midst of times of extreme measures, all three have entertained ethics of pure force and pure means. And so they all can speak to us as cautions on the risks of reading reductively for end-driven meanings even when these take the form of privileging immediate historical context. Perhaps it is in eruptions of the extreme that we most need to attack ends, our sense of being strung along as history's mere beads. In such moments, we often imagine the opening up of another time, and, as Woolf shows, here we are bound to encounter the vision of others looking in our direction. They are not singling us out. They need for a moment to try to see themselves at the place where we might meet them. Writings of the exception and Woolf's unfolding of interceptional time are pointed reminders that in the midst of historicizing, from time to time, we must interhistoricize.

Bibliography

Agamben, G. (1999) "The Messiah and the Sovereign: The Problem of Law in Walter Benjamin," in *Potentialities: Collected Essays in Philosophy*, trans. D. Heller-Roaze, Stanford: Stanford University Press, 160–74.

——— (2005a) "The State of Exception," trans. G. Agamben and K. Attell, in A. Norris (ed.) *Politics, Metaphysics, and Death: Essays on Giorgio Agamben's* Homo Sacer, Durham, NC: Duke University Press, 284–97.

——— (2005b) *State of Exception*. trans. K. Attell, Chicago: Chicago University Press.

——— (2005c) *The Time that Remains: A Commentary on the Letter to the Romans*, trans. P. Dailey, Stanford: Stanford University Press.

Benjamin, W. (1996) "Critique of Violence," trans. E. Jephcott, in M. Bullock and M. W. Jennings (eds) *Walter Benjamin, Selected Writings, Vol. 1, 1913–26*, Cambridge, MA: Belknap Press, 236–52.

——— (2002) "Theological-Political Fragment," trans. E. Jephcott, in H. Eiland and M. W. Jennings (eds) *Walter Benjamin, Selected Writings, Vol. 3, 1935–38*, Cambridge, MA: Belknap Press, 305–6.

——— (2003a) "On the Concept of History," trans. H. Zohn, in H. Eiland and M. W. Jennings (eds) *Walter Benjamin, Selected Writings, Vol. 4, 1938–40*, Cambridge, MA: Belknap Press, 389–400.

——— (2003b) "Paralipomena to 'On the Concept of History'," trans. E. Jephcott and H. Eiland, in H. Eiland and M. W. Jennings (eds.) *Walter Benjamin, Selected Writings, Vol. 4, 1938–40*, Cambridge, MA: Belknap Press, 401–11.

Sherry, V. (2003) *The Great War and the Language of Modernism*, Oxford: Oxford University Press.

Woolf, V. (1992 [1925]) *Mrs Dalloway*, ed. S. McNichol, intr. E. Showalter, New York: Penguin.

——— (1973 [1944]) *Mrs. Dalloway's Party*, ed. and intr. S. McNichol, Orlando: Harcourt.

Zwerdling, A. (1986) *Virginia Woolf and the Real World*, Berkeley: University of California Press.

Time's exception

Response to Hilary Thompson

Pamela Caughie

> Every image of the past that is not recognized by the present as one of its own concerns threatens to disappear irretrievably.
>
> (Benjamin 1968: 255)

"We hear these days that the 'moment of theory' is over," writes Stephen Ross in his prospectus for this collection. We have been hearing this claim for some time now. "The day of high theory is passing," the *Chronicle of Higher Education* proclaimed in October 1993. Thirteen years later, at the time of this writing, Toril Moi opens her essay on the state of feminist criticism today (2006) by declaring that "the poststructuralist paradigm is now exhausted" (Moi 2006: 1735). Perhaps we have been beating a dead horse for two decades, but Stephen Ross provides an alternative perspective, one worked through in these essays, when he questions this commonplace, arguing that the statement reflects "a change in how theory is studied" rather than its demise as a practice. "Scholars are now beginning to regard theory as something that has a history," he writes.

The "historical turn" in recent academic scholarship, following in the wake of the "linguistic turn," is often understood as an alternative practice that returns to materialist analysis after decades of textual play, returns to the referent said to be banished by poststructuralism. What this (re)turn to history indicates, however, is less a departure from the days of high theory than, in Jane Elliott's words, "the temporalization of knowledge" (Elliot 2006: 1699). In that same *PMLA* issue cited above, Elliott—writing specifically on feminist theory, though her insights pertain to theory more generally—notes that "as the repeated declarations of feminism's death in the mainstream media and the academy make clear," especially insofar as academic feminism has been tied to poststructuralist theory, "the production of the new [is] a signal intellectual value" (Elliott 2006: 1700), a point that echoes one of the preeminent poststructuralist theorists, Roland Barthes.[1] Such a value requires closer attention, she says, to the complex relations among "the new, the politically useful, and the intellectually compelling" (Elliott 2006: 1697). The question then becomes not "Is theory over?" but "What does it mean to proclaim the passing of theory?"

I want to stay with Elliott's essay another moment because her focus on feminism will return later in this essay. Because feminism wants to change the world,

Elliott continues, "feminist theory has a profound investment in timeliness" (2006: 1700): "For feminist theory, the timely and the important are even more deeply implicated than they are in modernity at large, and thus we tend to assume that theory that is no longer novel is no longer useful" (Elliott 2006: 1701). Thus, Elliott asks what it might mean "to produce feminist theory outside its 'appropriate' moment, to risk the genuinely untimely" (2006: 1701). This risk is one assumed by Hilary Thompson in her essay in this volume, and a risk I will run in turn in my response. We have "to interrupt the contemporary moment," writes Elliott, and "such interruptions need not appear historically new," she says, citing as an example the many recent returns to Walter Benjamin's "Theses on the Philosophy of History" (Elliott 2006: 1701), to which we can now add Thompson's essay. When we assume familiar approaches no longer serve "to dislodge the present," we show how much we are implicated in "the modern logic" that equates the new with the politically effective (Elliott 2006: 1701). "In so doing, we sidestep the difficult realization that while intellectual work should be exciting, political work may be dull, that things may stay true longer than they stay interesting" (Elliott 2006: 1701).

Staying within "the modern logic," I have argued elsewhere, has prevented critics from grasping the implications of contemporary theory for reading modernist literature. The "temporalization of knowledge" requires not just the study of theory as "having a history," as the essays in this collection do so well, but also the adoption of a different set of assumptions about history and narrative than those that have informed much modernist criticism. One way of effecting such a shift in attitude is to risk the untimely, to write outside the "appropriate" moment by embracing Thompson's challenge to "interhistoricize" (p. 98). In addition to the interhistoricizing Thompson and I both engage in by reading the modernist writer with the contemporary theorist, I want to interhistoricize Thompson's and my readings as well, brushing them against the grain of history.[2]

By "Time's Exception," I mean to suggest that time should—and in a sense, does—make a difference between Thompson's reading of Virginia Woolf in "Time and Its Countermeasures" and my reading in *Virginia Woolf and Postmodernism* nearly two decades ago, but not the difference we may expect. This difference manifests itself in the texts we cite, the language we use, and the passages we select as significant in Woolf's writing. Thompson cites Benjamin and Agamben, I cite Barthes and Derrida; she discusses temporality, I discuss textuality; she emphasizes passages in *Mrs Dalloway* where time is suspended, I emphasize passages where language is strained. To adopt Ross's division of modernist scholars, we might say that Thompson belongs to the first group that "follows the fortunes of modernism into the realm defined by the Frankfurt School," while I fall into the second, those Ross calls the "instrumentalists," who use theory as a tool for revealing how theoretical modernism really was, how much like the contemporary theory that we now see as *of* its moment rather than as its heir.

Yet our differences strike me as more generational than theoretical or methodological, generated by the moment in which each of us writes rather than by the theorists on whom we draw. I wrote *Virginia Woolf and Postmodernism* (1991) in the shadow of the "linguistic turn," the time of the "ascendancy of the signifier," as Marianne DeKoven characterizes that moment (2006: 1692); Thompson writes in the time of our turn to history. Still, Thompson's and my readings both work against efforts to read chronologically, for "temporal priority" (see Thompson, p. 97), thereby, and paradoxically, undermining the difference time makes, and the assumption that time marks the difference in our work. Time's exception, a case to which the rule may not apply. To better understand this difference that is at once genuine and merely nominal or symbolic, I will begin by returning to a prior moment in Woolf criticism when poststructuralist theory enters the scene, keeping in mind that that prior moment is posited and constructed retroactively, not something "there" to be retrieved.[3]

"In or about December 1985 Virginia Woolf criticism changed." So begins *Virginia Woolf and Postmodernism* (Caughie 1991), which demonstrates how post-modernist and poststructuralist theories can change, and have changed, the way we read Woolf—that is, the kinds of questions that motivate our readings, the objectives that guide our analyses, and the contexts in which we place her works. In 1985, Toril Moi published *Sexual/Textual Politics* and first articulated "feminist postmodernism" as a new methodology that disrupted the cultural consensus among feminist critics of the 1970s. In her introduction, "Who's Afraid of Virginia Woolf?", Moi interrogates the theoretical assumptions about the rela-tionship between aesthetics and politics that made so many American feminist critics resistant to Woolf's modernist style. In contrast, Moi locates Woolf's poli-tics *"precisely in her textual practice"* (1985: 16), focusing on the *politics of language* rather than on the politics *expressed* by Woolf's language. Moi was the first to articulate the difference poststructuralist theory makes for feminist literary criticism. What this change in thinking means for reading Woolf is the subject of my book.[4]

Yet the change in Woolf criticism signified by the date 1985 was neither sudden nor decisive. To conceive that change as a shift from misguided modernist readings to enlightened postmodernist ones, or from limiting (liberal) feminist readings to liberating (poststructuralist) ones is to remain in "the modern logic." It is precisely this kind of story, I argue—a narrative of progressive enlight-enment or a narrative of a radical break—that postmodern theory forsakes. In seeking to change the way we approach Woolf's writings in the wake of post-modernism, and not to argue that Woolf was a postmodernist *avant la lettre*, *Virginia Woolf and Postmodernism* does not attempt to narrate a continuous history, explaining how Woolf's writing comes to resemble a postmodern aesthetic or postmodern theory of the subject. Rather, through a series of related explorations, it deliberately disrupts the chronological treatment of Woolf's novels in many critical studies and instead organizes chapters around the problems in Woolf criticism that postmodernist theories can help us to unravel. In that book, I argue that Woolf felt the strains in a changing literary as well as social and political climate, and that in working through some of the tensions in the novel form itself, she experimented with some of the same structures and concerns that have come to characterize postmodern fiction and poststructuralist theory (Caughie 1991: 20).

In this sense, that 1991 book adopts an approach similar to the one Thompson takes here. What makes Woolf "postmodern," then, is not her position in history, as a transitional figure between the modern and the postmodern, but the way she makes us read, and specifically, as Beth Carole Rosenberg says, "makes us read history as a series of unrelated moments, moments whose unity comes through a narrative that tells us more about its own construction than it does about the past" (2000: 1128). The assumption that the text and its historical moment exist prior to and apart from our reading of them; that all texts grouped under the same rubric (e.g. modernism, postmodernism, or feminism) share certain common features; that these features are properties of the texts themselves rather than effects created by the method of reading; and that the text bears a reflective relation to its historical moment—that is, the assumptions informing much of the 1980s criticism I was reading against—these assumptions belong to a modern paradigm that my reading of Woolf in terms of theory had tried to dislodge.

For example, the fragmentation of Woolf's last novel, with its numerous interruptions and abrupt breaks, has often been read as an expression of Woolf's loss of faith in the efficacy of art or as reflecting the social disruptions brought about by the advent of war. But if we read for the theoretical, critical, and aesthetic implications of the novel's structural principles, the "orts, scraps, and fragments" of *Between the Acts* can be read as the logical consequence of a narrative in which the concepts of history as progress, narrative as continuous, and culture as homogeneous are no longer credible. *Between the Acts* confronts the tension between the historical need to recognize diversity in the polity that was increasingly thrust upon modernist writers in the interwar period, and the equally compelling psychological need to seek identity in the collectivity. In confronting the possibility that outsiders may not come to share a social vision, Woolf was compelled to face what postmodernist theorists identify as the crisis of the collectivity. Such a crisis need not produce despair but rather can serve to create a willingness to tolerate the incompatibilities and discontinuities that any collective concept engenders. Fragmentation and discontinuity, suspended moments and odd juxtapositions, can be understood as elements of, not obstacles to, the reading of literature and history that do not, to draw on Benjamin's understanding of language and history, point beyond themselves. To stage an engagement between modernism and theory, then, to read Woolf's fictional texts the same way we read theoretical texts rather than taking theory as offering explanatory paradigms for the fiction, is to change our *ways of reading*, not just our readings of Woolf. It is, to return to Thompson's essay, to stage an interruption in the historical progression.

Similarly, Thompson writes:

> If modernism and theory are to meet on even ground, we cannot simply reclaim theory for modernism on the basis of temporal priority or we risk

falling into a triumphal procession of victors bearing plundered spoils. Nor can we allot ourselves the position of privileged avatar apprehending fully the sight of another. Rather, Woolf's interceptional time suggests that we must catch the transformations produced by sight lines that come into collision without outright collusion.

(p. 97)

What it means to read from this interceptional time, a time that interrupts the progressive narrative of history, putting time beside itself, is the subject of Thompson's essay. This kind of reading is not just evident in the writings of Woolf, Benjamin, and Agamben, it is also enacted in Thompson's own reading, making her essay what I would call a performative, as opposed to a discursive, reading.[5] Or, to use Thompson's words, a reading that enacts rather than upholds a way of proceeding (p. 90). To read modernism and theory together, "each as party to the other's inquiries," Thompson says, requires that we reconsider how our readings change when we apply a writer's "own conception of ends" (p. 86).[6]

Thompson begins by reading *Mrs Dalloway* through the "major figures and concepts" of Benjamin (p. 89). Like Benjamin, as well as Agamben, Woolf provides a scene of time suspended, "a moment of arrest" charged with messianic potential (p. 89). But rather than using Benjamin's concepts to interpret Woolf's narrative, Thompson reads Woolf's narrative as staging the "impasse" between Benjamin's and Agamben's notions of messianic time:

> While Benjamin's messianism in the form of divine violence can describe the terms of Septimus's struggle, it can't account for the totality of his sacrifice. In his last leap, Septimus no longer simply embodies an impasse between messianism [Benjamin] and paralysis [Agamben]; now he traces an arc that gestures towards a realm of the divine even as it lets itself fall into myth.
>
> (p. 92)

It is here that time's exception comes into play.

What time are we in when we represent time? That time, the time of writing, is a time beside time, as Thompson puts it. The historical materialist, writes Benjamin, "cannot do without the notion of a present which is not a transition, but in which time stands still and has come to a stop," and this is the time of his writing of history ("Theses" 16). This time, the time of our representation of time, is, says Agamben, "the time *that* we ourselves are, is the only real time, the only time we have" (Agamben 2005c: 68).[7] To grasp this time is to undo time as we currently understand it, the kind of thing modernist texts such as Woolf's do. Indeed, Thompson's image for this time is the second clock in *Mrs Dalloway*, "the clock which always struck two minutes after Big Ben" (Woolf 140; cited p. 94), one that "instates and reveals an asynchrony rather than confirms a sovereignty" (p. 95). This is what we might call unofficial time rather than chronological time, providing a different conception of ends. As Thompson puts it so well: "the lagging clock tells of another teleology, since it is not the clock of ends so much as 'odds and ends' or remnants, the tasks that are left" (p. 95). What Thompson refers to as "the most modern form of historical reading" is where the "truth" (or we might say the "subtext," using Jameson's terminology) of different texts, and times, is "brought to light by their intertwining" (p. 94). "What better instance of a time beside time," Thompson writes, than that "other clock" (p. 95). Thompson and I, in our different ways, put texts beside each other to show how texts situated in different times may be responding to similar conflicts and concerns and thus read together not anachronistically or ahistorically but interceptionally. Thompson calls this time beside time in Woolf's novel "interceptional" time, a time figured in the window through which Clarissa sees the old woman across the way, "a vision of ourselves beheld from beyond" (p. 96).

If we are to follow Benjamin and Woolf and stop seeing time chronologically, stop seeing history as "a sequence of events like the beads on a rosary" ("Theses" 18, quoted (p. 97), then, Thompson asks, "what priority [should we] give to chronology in our modes of historical reading" (p. 97)? Thompson's own reading encourages us to "jump beads" by reading texts of different times as intersecting, "theoriz[ing] a similar time and condition" (p. 97) but not coming together in a shared view or in "real" time (p. 97). It is a reading Thompson has learned as much from Woolf as from Benjamin, Jameson, and Agamben—that is, as much from modernism as from theory. All of these writers caution us, says Thompson, on "the risks of reading reductively for end-driven meanings" (p. 97).

Even though I begin from a very different place—the poststructuralism of Barthes and Derrida rather than the historical materialism of Benjamin, Jameson, and Agamben—my reading of Woolf raises Thompson's question about what role chronology plays or should play in our histories of modernism and theory. Historicism, the target of Benjamin's "Theses," returns to the origin as if to something that once was, a "real" to be recuperated by the writing of history; in contrast, Benjamin emphasizes taking "the past from its context, destroying it, in order to return it, transfigured, to its origin" (Agamben 1999: 152). So what happens when we "interhistoricize" and read, in this case, my reading of Woolf with Thompson's? That is, what do we risk in being untimely?

One way to interhistoricize would be to read my work as enacting an "arrested moment" insofar as it interrogates a state of Woolf criticism I date from 1985. The year 1985 for me, like 1910 for Woolf, is not a telos, a goal or an end point toward which Woolf criticism or literature has been progressing; rather, such dates signify a turning point, or, in the terms of Thompson's essay, an arrested moment in which we can grasp the time of our representation of Woolf's time and her writing. Criticism in this moment attends to its own narrative of Woolf's writing.

Another way of thinking about arrested moments and the time of the representation of time is through Jacques Derrida rather than Giorgio Agamben. Derrida's concept of iterability presented in "Signature, Event, Context" ("SEC") similarly disrupts conventional notions of time and ends. "For my written communication to retain its function as writing, i.e., its readability," Derrida writes, "my communication must be repeatable—iterable—in the absolute absence of the receiver or any empirically determined collectivity of receivers. Such iterability ... structures the mark of writing itself" (Derrida 1982: 7). Although Derrida notes that *iter* comes from the Sanskrit term for *other*, and thus "ties repetition to alterity," the term also has its roots in narrative theory's concept of the "iterative," as articulated in Gérard Gennette's *Narrative Discourse*, a term which refers to a repeated event that is narrated only once. The effect generated by the iterative tense is precisely what Derrida elaborates in "SEC": for an event to have significance, it must invoke a prior occasion. There is no "first time." But what is prior is never simply there but is produced in language. This is not to say that language gives us a "fiction" of a prior event, but that the fictional or narrative process itself structures the prior event as an historical past.

Or take, as another example, Barthes's *The Pleasure of the Text*, a work that has taught me much about textuality and desire, but that also has much to say about history. Writing on the difference between pleasure and bliss, Barthes says that how we will write "the history of our modernity" depends on the way we see their relation:

> For if I say that between pleasure and bliss there is only a difference of degree, I am also saying that the history is a pacified one: the text of bliss is merely the logical, organic, historical development of the text of pleasure; the avant-garde is never anything but the progressive, emancipated form of past culture: today emerges from yesterday, Robbe-Grillet is already in Flaubert, Sollers in Rabelais [Agamben or Barthes in Woolf] ... But if I believe on the contrary that pleasure and bliss are parallel forces, that they cannot meet, and that between them there is more than a struggle: an *incommunication*, then I must certainly believe that history, our history, is not peaceable and perhaps not even intelligent, that the text of bliss always rises out of it like a scandal (an irregularity), that it is always the trace of a cut ... and that the subject of history ... is never anything but a "living contradiction": a split subject, who simultaneously enjoys, through the text, the consistency of his selfhood and its collapse, its fall.
>
> (Barthes 1975: 20–1)

This "incommunication" would be a time outside of time, the time of our representation of time, the time, in Thompson's words, "the noncoincidence of our representations of time and the time it takes us to make them" (p. 93). Time not as telos or terminous but as a cut, scandal, irregularity, or blast.

That is to say, the linguistic turn may have been a (re)turn to history all along, that Thompson's focus on temporality and mine on textuality may be different ways of effecting the same end, so to speak, however resistant we are to ends. My reading of *Mrs Dalloway*, for example, also looks at "exceptions," not the state of exception that Thompson explores but the exceptions to the repeated claims that critics make about Woolf's novel. Many critics take Woolf at her word, accepting what she says about the novel (e.g. it is an expression of her unifying vision of life, a luminous halo of consciousness that transcends individual minds), therefore taking her writing for granted, mistaking Woolf's claims for results. Such readings, I argue, "do not account for the 'exceptions' that make up a significant portion of the novel and that undermine its seamless quality" (Caughie 1991: 73–4). The narrative draws attention to "the mediation of scenes and thoughts," blurring distinctions between characters and between characters and narrator, making the source of a thought doubtful, and undermining our tendency to attribute a character's or narrator's insights to the author. Clarissa's intimacy-yet-detachment, her participation in scenes she also stands apart from, observing—such as the window scene that in Thompson's essay represents interceptional time—parallels the narrative strategy with all those forced transitions that function to emphasize "the art by which these scenes are created" (Caughie 1991: 75). Critics who value unity decry these "contrived" transitions as intrusive, disruptive (Caughie 1991: 75). Yet in these "arty" transitions, the *process* of creating unity or effecting an end is brought to the fore. "We are aware at once of some kind of narrative unity and of the process of constructing such unity … We are aware of things existing side by side and of the associations that can link them" (Caughie 1991: 75). Putting things side by side rather than linking them in a narrative is what Thompson calls Woolf's interceptional time.

The arrested moment, whether in Woolf's novel (1924) or Woolf criticism (1985), is the time of the writing, a moment suspended, transfigured, and given back to us as an origin. For Woolf, as for the theorists with whom Thompson and I read her, "there is no end goal toward which we are progressing, no common ground on which we can rest, no plot that liberates us or reveals hidden truths" (Caughie 1991: xiii). What we find in Woolf's writing is not "there", prior to our readings, but "posited by and constructed in the very course of our readings" (Caughie 1991: xiii). It is in this sense that the arrested moment is the time of our writing, the time of our *own* representation of time (p. 89). Thus we must pay as much attention to our own motives, strategies, and contexts as to Woolf's (Caughie 1991: xiii). Or rather, we must understand our context, what we think lies outside us in the historical moment of our writing, as reconstructed by our writing, in Jameson's words, its ideological subtext.

This time, the arrested moment, happens in language; it is a writing *effect*. It is Proust's intermittence. In "The Image of Proust," Benjamin describes this moment:

> We know that in his work Proust did not describe a life as it actually was, but a life as it was remembered by the one who had lived it … The important thing for the remembering author is not what he experienced, but the weaving of his memory, the Penelope work of recollection. Or should one call it, rather, a Penelope work of forgetting? Is not the involuntary recollection, Proust's *mémoire involontaire*, much closer to forgetting than what is usually called memory? And is not this work of spontaneous recollection, in which remembrance is the woof and forgetting the warf, a counterpart to Penelope's work rather than its likeness? … Only the *actus purus* of recollection itself, not the author or the plot, constitutes the unity of

the text. One may even say that the intermittence of author and plot is only the reverse of the continuum of memory, the pattern on the back side of the tapestry.

(Benjamin 1968: 202–3)

This time is not only not objective, not "real time" or the historicist's time. This time, the arrested moment, is also not genderless. It is figured here as a woman weaving, but elsewhere Benjamin describes this other time as a man in a whore house:

> The historical materialist cannot do without the notion of a present which is not a transition, but in which time stands still and has come to a stop. For this notion defines the present in which he himself is writing history … The historical materialist leaves it to others to be drained by the whore called "Once upon a time" in historicism's bordello. He remains in control of his powers, man enough to blast open the continuum of history.
>
> (Benjamin 1968: 262)

The gendered language brings up other issues to consider, and returns us to the discussion of feminist theory with which I began. Modernity is not only "the epoch of undone time we may still grasp," as Thompson so nicely puts it (p. 93): it is also, we might quip, the epoch of undone women.

So much of modern literature is represented through feminized figures— Flaubert's maid, Baudelaire's prostitute, Balzac's castrato, Proust's Françoise, modernism's "New Woman." It is hard to believe that feminism, which emerged as a concept in English c. 1913, was ever *not* a part of modernism as it was represented by contemporary critics, that women could have been written out of that history. A return to feminism as an origin of modernism, the kind of work that characterizes the "new modernist studies," however, need not entail the historicist's "Once upon a time," where the past is redeemed, "restore[d] to its true dignity" (Agamben 1999: 153), as a whore might be redeemed by faith or charity. It need not simply require recovering forgotten texts or reading retroactively to show how modernist women writers anticipated what will be termed a poststructuralist critique. It can mean instead interhistoricizing, as Thompson shows us, reading feminism and modernism together, "each as party to the other's inquiries" (p. 86). In terms of my reading of Woolf, it means understanding feminism not as content or even form, but as function or strategy. As Griselda Pollock puts it:

> An art work is not feminist because it registers the ideas, politics or obsessions of its feminist maker. It has a political effect as a feminist intervention according to the way the work acts upon, makes demands of, and produces positions for its viewers [or readers]. It is feminist when it subverts the normal ways in which we view art and are usually seduced into a complicity with the means of the dominant and oppressive culture.
>
> (Pollock 1987: 363)

Pollock's "seduced" recalls Benjamin's bordello of historicism, where the historian is seduced by a concept of time as continuous and history as progress, and her "complicity" recalls my critique of feminist critics of Woolf whose readings, I argue, are complicit with the assumptions about language, narrative, and history informing writings by the very masculinist modernists whom they criticize. Here, though, it is not a man who "blast[s] open the continuum of history" but a feminist who makes, we might say, an untimely appearance and intervenes to change the way history acts upon, or seduces, us. If feminism subverts the "normal ways" of the "dominant and oppressive culture," as Pollock says, that function can be read through Thompson's "deviance from normal habit" (p. 86), that is, as subverting the desire or need for closure.

It may seem untimely, if not unseemly, to claim today to be a postmodern feminist. If I continue to ride that dead horse, it is because I believe that "things may stay true longer than they stay interesting." There remains the need for a feminist intervention informed by the insights of poststructuralist theory that would have us question notions of collective identity or action, end-oriented narratives, or the past as redeemable. Where a notion of progress returns in our history of theory is not in the notion of ends, as if there is a goal to be realized, but in the realization that feminism is what cannot pass, or become passé. I am not simply arguing that the work of postmodern feminism is not yet done (though I believe that); I am arguing that we have never been postmodern—though, to echo Bruno LaTour, we think that we were in claiming to have moved beyond postmodernism.[8] As Wendy Brown says of critical theory in general, I would say of postmodern theory in particular: we need it "to keep the times from closing in on us," to reclaim the present from "the conservative hold on it that is borne by the charge of untimeliness" (Brown 2005: 4). In the weeks following September 11, 2001, many commentators and columnists read in the attacks on the World Trade Center in New York City and on the Pentagon in Washington DC the demise of postmodernism. In articles such as "Attacks on U.S. Challenge Postmodern True Believers" (*New York Times*, 22 September, 2001) and "After the Attack, Postmodernism Loses its Glib Grip" (*Chicago Tribune*, 27 September, 2001), writers proclaimed postmodernism the latest victim of the horror of the terrorist attacks. But as Thompson points out at the end of her article, "it is in the eruptions of the extreme that we most need to attack ends, our sense of being strung along as history's mere beads" (p. 97).[9] The very fact that these claims could be made shows how little we have learned from postmodernism, and from history.

Since endings are so difficult, it might be appropriate to end with a statement about modernism and politics from the time of the arrested moment in *Mrs Dalloway*, the year 1924. In her essay on Gertrude Stein (1924), Mina Loy writes:

> The pragmatic value of modernism lies in its tremendous recognition of the compensation due to the spirit of democracy. Modernism is a prophet crying in the wilderness of stabilized culture that humanity is wasting its aesthetic time. For there is a considerable extension of time between the visits to the

picture gallery, the museum, the library. It asks "what is happening to your aesthetic consciousness during the long intervals?"

The flux of life is pouring its aesthetic aspect into your eyes, your ears— and you ignore it because you are looking for your canons of beauty in some sort of frame or glass case to tradition. Modernism says: Why not each one of us, scholar or bricklayer, pleasurably realize all that is impressing itself upon our subconscious, the thousand odds and ends which make up your sensory every day life?

(Loy 1990: 244)

Woolf's suspended moments in *Between the Acts* make us self-conscious about "what is happening to [our] aesthetic consciousness during the long intervals," about the aesthetics of everyday life. This is that other teleology, not of ends but of the "odds and ends," "the tasks that are left" (p. 95). The point of efforts to dislodge the "modern logic," the point of interhistoricizing, is not to get it right and thus end, but rather to learn how to go on.[10]

Acknowledgements

I am indebted to Steven Venturino for a discussion of Agamben, Benjamin, and Jameson which stimulated many of the ideas in this essay.

Notes

1 "The New is not a fashion, it is a value, the basis of all criticism" (Barthes 1975: 40). Elliott might have noted that not long after feminism entered the English language, it was declared dead. In 1913, feminism was so new it wasn't in the dictionaries yet (in fact, it was not in the *OED* until 1933), yet in 1914 Beatrice Hale published *What Women Want: An Interpretation of the Feminist Movement*. See Nancy Cott, *The Grounding of Modern Feminism* (New Haven: Yale University Press, 1989).

2 In his seventh thesis Walter Benjamin writes that the historical materialist "regards it as his task to brush history against the grain" (1968: 257). Here, it seems, I am trying to pass as the historical materialist rather than the poststructuralist feminist.

3 Kenneth Burke emphasizes a symbolic act as at once genuine, capable of producing real change, even if only symbolic, and "merely" symbolic, leaving the real untouched (Jameson 1981: 80).

4 Some of the material in this essay is drawn from my chapter on postmodernist and poststructuralist approaches to Woolf in *Palgrave Advances in Woolf Studies*, edited by Anna Snaith (2007).

5 *Discursive* is one of those ambiguous words that poststructuralists love, meaning both a rational analysis that moves coherently from topic to topic and an explanation that rambles. Although I mean it here in the first sense, a poststructuralist would remain sensitive to the implications of the alternate meaning, which cannot simply be set aside but which marks the difference within this concept. Thus, the distinction I am drawing here between the discursive and the performative is useful, not ontological. A performative approach is not an alternative to the discursive but rather one that brings out the double meaning of that concept.

6 In "Postmodernism, or the Cultural Logic of Late Capitalism," Fredric Jameson argues that the "last few years have been marked by an inverted millenarianism, in

which premonitions of the future, catastrophic or redemptive, have been replaced by senses of the end of this or that" (Jameson 1991: 1).

7 This notion of "real time" recalls Jameson's discussion of reality in *The Political Unconscious*:

> The literary or aesthetic act therefore always entertains some active relationship with the Real; yet in order to do so, it cannot simply allow "reality" to persevere inertly in its own being, outside the text and at distance. It must rather draw the Real into its own texture, and the ultimate paradoxes and false problems of linguistics, and most notably of semantics, are to be traced back to this process whereby language manages to carry the Real within itself as its own intrinsic or immanent subtext ... That history—Althusser's "absent cause," Lacan's "Real"—is *not* a text, for it is fundamentally non-narrative and nonrepresentational; what can be added, however, is the proviso that history is inaccessible to us except in textual form, or in other words that it can be approached only by way of prior (re)textualisation.
>
> (Jameson 1981: 80–1)

8 In *We Have Never Been Modern*, Bruno LaTour argues that modernity is defined by dichotomous thinking, especially the absolute distinction between the human and the nonhuman, society and nature, but that that is not the way the world is, only how it has been represented to be. Thus, we have never been modern in the sense that nature and society have always been interdependent and co-produced.

9 "The current amazement that the things we are experiencing are 'still' possible in the twentieth century," Benjamin writes, "is not the beginning of knowledge—unless it is the knowledge that the view of history which gives rise to it is untenable ("Theses" VIII).

10 In my conclusion to *Virginia Woolf and Postmodernism*, which I entitle "Issuing" to emphasize process over ends, I quote Wittgenstein on this point. For Wittgenstein's philosophical attitude is not "I have gotten it right" but "Now I know how to go on!" (*Philosophical Investigations* #154).

Bibliography

Agamben, G. (1999) *Potentialities: Collected Essays in Philosophy*, ed. and trans. D. Heller-Roazen, Stanford, CA: Stanford University Press.

Austin, J. L. (1975 [1962]) *How To Do Things with Words*, ed. J. O. Urmson and M. Sbisà, Cambridge, MA: Harvard University Press.

Barthes, R. (1975) *The Pleasure of the Text*, trans. R. Miller, New York: Hill and Wang.

Benjamin, W. (1968) "Theses on the Philosophy of History," in *Illuminations: Essays and Reflections*, ed. H. Arendt, trans. H. Zohn, New York: Schocken Books, 253–64.

Brown, W. (2005) "Untimeliness and Punctuality: Critical Theory in Dark Times," in *Edgework: Critical Essays on Knowledge and Politics*, Princeton, NJ: Princeton University Press, 1–16.

Caughie, P. L. (1991) *Virginia Woolf and Postmodernism: Literature in Quest and Question of Itself*, Urbana and Chicago: University of Illinois Press.

—— (1999) *Passing and Pedagogy: The Dynamics of Responsibility*, Urbana and Chicago: University of Illinois Press.

—— (2007) "Postmodernist and Poststructuralist Approaches," in A. Snaith (ed.) *Palgrave Advances in Virginia Woolf Studies*, London: Palgrave/Macmillan, 143–68.

DeKoven, M. (2006) "*Jouissance*, Cyborgs, and Companion Species: Feminist Experiment," *PMLA* 121(5): 1690–6.

Derrida, J. (1982) "Différance," in *Margins of Philosophy*, trans. A. Bass, Chicago: University of Chicago Press, 1–27.

—— (1988) *Limited Inc.*, ed. G. Graff, trans. S. Weber, Evanston, IL: Northwestern University Press.

Elliott, J. (2006) "The Currency of Feminist Theory," *PMLA* 121(5): 1697–1703.

Gennette, G. (1980 [1970]) *Narrative Discourse: An Essay in Method*, trans. J. E. Lewin, Ithaca, NY: Cornell University Press.

Jameson, F. (1981) *The Political Unconscious: Narrative as a Socially Symbolic Act*, Ithaca, NY: Cornell University Press.

—— (1991) *Postmodernism*, Durham, NC: Duke University Press.

LaTour, B. (1993) *We Have Never Been Modern*, trans. C. Porter. Cambridge, MA: Harvard University Press.

Loy, M. (1990) "Gertrude Stein," in B. K. Scott (ed.) *The Gender of Modernism*, Bloomington: Indiana University Press, 238–45.

Moi, T. (1985) *Sexual/Textual Politics: Feminist Literary Theory*, London: Methuen.

—— (2006) "'I Am Not a Feminist, But … ': How Feminism Became the F-Word," *PMLA* 121(5): 1735–41.

Pollock, G. (1987) "Feminism and Modernism," in R. Parker and G. Pollock (eds) *Framing Feminism: Art and the Women's Movement 1970–1985*, London and New York: Pandora, 79–122.

Rosenberg, B. C. (2000) "Virginia Woolf's Postmodern Literary History," *MLN* 115(5): 1112–30.

Snaith, A. (ed.) (2007) *Palgrave Advances in Virginia Woolf Studies*, London: Palgrave/Macmillan.

Steiner, G. (1967) *Language and Silence*, New York: Athenaeum.

Part II

Modernism's theory

Abstract affiliations

Introduction

Continuing in the direction indicated by Part I, especially Thompson's and Caughie's cogitations about "interceptional time" and the need to "inter-historicize" modernism and theory, the papers in Part II ask about the more abstract relationship obtaining between modernism and theory. They do so in part through key theorists of modernism and modernity—Fredric Jameson, Theodor Adorno, Jean-François Lyotard, Louis Althusser, and Paul de Man—exploring how modernism and theory have been constructed and how those constructions have influenced common critical understandings of them. Concerns with timeliness, periodization, and the event; nominalism and the new; and theory versus philosophy pervade the papers in this section.

Of the several interlacing sets of terms and concepts in this section, timeliness is the most central. Behind the notion of timeliness as it is used here by Neil Levi, Glenn Willmott, and C. D. Blanton is the Marxist notion that cultural production expresses its historical moment's dominant relations of production. It never does this completely, just as its historical moment is never fully homogenous. Rather, the remains of previous modes of production continue to influence the present, just as possible future modes of production begin to be felt. Both mix with the dominant configuration to shape its characteristic cultural production. As such, every cultural product contains residues of past modes of production (and the social and class formations that went with them) along with inklings of future modes and their attendant formations. Timeliness becomes relevant whenever we try to read texts from an earlier moment as relevant to a later moment (or vice versa), as Thompson and Caughie showed with regard to Woolf, Benjamin, Agamben, and feminism in Part I. Questions of anachronism crop up almost immediately, as do issues of how it can be possible for a text from an earlier mode of production to speak productively to subjects inhabiting a later one. Levi and Willmott take this up in relation to Fredric Jameson's apparently paradoxical affinity for particular modernist texts as relevant to our postmodern moment, and Blanton speculates that the characteristic feature of modernism is its consciousness of its own untimeliness, what he calls its "non-contemporaneity of the contemporaneous" (p. 149).

Tied to the issue of timeliness is the question of periodization: the process by which we allocate historical parameters to cultural phenomena like modernism. Though Jameson may well be right when he contends that "we cannot not periodize" (2002: 29), we must nonetheless acknowledge that periods are narrative categories: they allow us to break up the flow of history into manageable segments. Even if the impulse to narrate (and by implication to periodize) is fundamentally human (Jameson 1981: 13), a series of tricky questions about periodization still emerges: how do we characterize a given period? What licenses us to choose start and end dates for a period? What kinds of events constitute the beginning and ending of a period? Can legal, political, chronological, or military events usefully punctuate artistic, philosophical, or cultural periods? Or, if periods emerge gradually, when can we say we have a new period, rather than a subsidiary element of the previous period? What's at stake in setting the temporal limits of a period? And what do we do with the vastly more complex issues that arise when we expand our vision to include other locales that seem to be on different timelines? This last question in particular has come to the fore of modernist studies lately: scholars no longer ask only when modernism begins and ends, but where it begins when and when it begins where. The answers have problematized periodization, as critics assert multiple modernities and multiple modernisms that resist assimilation to a singular modernism. As a consequence, critics are testing out new approaches to timeliness and periodization. These approaches seek to account for the anomalous existence of texts bearing all the characteristics of periods other than their own (e.g. *Tristram Shandy*'s [1759–69] infamous postmodernism), and to account for claims that texts remain relevant decades— even centuries—after publication.

One such approach, taken here by Levi, relies upon Alain Badiou's notion of the event: a singular happening that ruptures the given order and necessitates a new way of being. Like the state of exception, messianic time, divine violence, and the sublime, the event is punctual and singular. It does not belong to the order of history that can be divided and debated under the rubrics of timeliness and periodization. Rather, it steps outside of those rubrics, resisting and troubling their compartmentalizing logics. As such, it provides a way to think particular moments as resonating truly beyond their contexts. In essence, the event lets us eschew the logic of periodization in favour of punctual happenings to which we can remain faithful even when their contexts recede. Such fidelity to the event, insistently seeing the world from the new perspective it opens up, is the essence of ethics for Badiou. For Levi, it provides a means of resolving the paradox he detects in Jameson's work, and of asserting the relevance of modernism beyond its historical and geographical limits. If certain events of modernism thus articulate Utopian energies that have not been realized, as Jameson contends, we need not abandon them, but can remain faithful to them. In this sense, we might even say that the fundamental thesis of *Modernism and Theory* is that theory remains true to the event of modernism by preserving and advancing its critique of modernity.

Relevant in this context is the modernist fascination with the new, and specifically Adorno's notion of nominalism (which Jameson has called an event in its own right [*Late Marxism*; Jameson 2007: 157]). First, the new. Pound's famous call to modern artists to "make it new" stands in this regard as a call for an event, for a radical break with the past and the establishment of new possibilities. As Gelikman shows, for Adorno this translates into rejecting universals in favour of the social nature of art: nominalism. Nominalism holds that instead of expressing eternal truths, art embodies social realities that are particular to when and where it is produced. Art's very form, Adorno contends, encodes real social contradictions that must be read in their particularity and not as universals. For example, the broken-backed form of Joseph Conrad's *Lord Jim* articulates not a universal claim about the conflict between man and nature, but the real contradictions arising from imperialist ideology, the transition from the age of sail to the age of steam, and the rise of global capitalism. The uneasy fusion of modernist psychologism with adventure romance marks these tensions formally, without necessarily taking them up as features of the novel's content. Such a nominalist reading thus insists on specifics rather than universals, embedding the works' very form in its immediate context. The attention it brings to specifics, and to the signs of the new encoded in them, aligns nominalism with the new, and both with the notion of the event, challenging existing epistemological, ontological, and political models, and making imaginable wholly new possibilities.

The tension between existing systems and ruptural interventions approached in various ways by notions of timeliness, periodization, the event, the new, and nominalism helps characterize another set of terms: theory and philosophy. The distinction can be difficult to maintain (Shiach suggests that it may be ideological rather than historical), especially because so many theorists have philosophical training, and refer to philosophy in their work. It is complicated further by the intuitive association of modernism with philosophy and postmodernism with theory. Nevertheless, there is a pertinent distinction between them, and good reason for aligning modernism with theory: as Jameson puts it, philosophy

> is always haunted by the dream of some foolproof self-sufficient system, a set of interlocking concepts which are their own cause ... Theory, on the other hand, has no vested interests inasmuch as it never lays claim to an absolute system, a non-ideological formulation of itself and its "truths"; indeed, always itself complicit in the being of current language, it has only the vocation and never-finished task of undermining philosophy as such, by unravelling affirmative statements and propositions of all kinds.
>
> (Jameson 2006)

Not just distinct, then, theory and philosophy are opposed to one another, with theory articulating intellectual events that disrupt philosophy's cozy dream of Truth. This quest to precipitate events, to "make it new," and to break with existing paradigms in favour of hitherto unimaginable possibilities aligns theory with modernism. For Blanton, modernism is inherently theoretical in its *eidaesthetic*[1] dimension: its capacity both to think its own conditions of possibility and to break with existing epistemological or ontological systems through its formal innovations.

The common concerns of the essays in this section—timeliness, periodization, and the event; nominalism and the new; and theory versus philosophy—expand the scope of our consideration of modernism and theory, challenge the very terms of this collection, and lay the groundwork for Part III's forum.

Note

1 From the Greek *eidos* for idea and *aesthetic* for things perceptible by the senses.

Bibliography

Badiou, A. (2005 [1988]) *Being and Event*, New York: Continuum.
Jameson, F. (1981) *The Political Unconscious: Narrative as a Socially Symbolic Act*, Ithaca, NY: Cornell University Press.
—— (2002) *A Singular Modernity: Essay on the Ontology of the Present*, New York: Verso.
—— (2006) "First Impressions," *London Review of Books*, 7 September; online at www.lrb.co.uk/v28/n17/jame02_.html (accessed 23 January 2008).
—— (2007) *Late Marxism: Adorno: Or, The Persistence of the Dialectic*, New York: Verso.

5   The persistence of the old regime

Late modernist form in the postmodern period

Neil Levi

Throughout his extraordinary oeuvre, but perhaps most clearly in *A Singular Modernity*, Fredric Jameson's views on artistic and particularly literary modernism display profound ambivalence. Put simply, the *idea* of modernism usually arouses Jameson's antipathy, yet his work is rife with appeals to and defenses of the legacies of individual modernists. This ambivalence points to a larger tension. On the one hand, Jameson has a strong and well-known commitment to *timeliness* or even *temporal propriety*; without it he could not begin *A Singular Modernity*, with his denunciatory chapter on the "Regressions of the Current Age."[1] On the other hand, he wants to find a past that can, in Walter Benjamin's phrase, "blast open the continuum of history" (Benjamin 2003: 396).

This persistent tension in Jameson's thought produces in his arguments a strange, oscillating movement that lacks the cohesive force of the dialectic. The opening lines of *A Singular Modernity* evoke all that a postmodern consensus denounces in modernism: asceticism, minimalism, authoritarianism, aesthetic teleology, the cult of the genius, and a lack of concern for pleasure. Jameson endorses this denunciation as a "healthy movements of disgust and revulsion" for an unusable past; these healthy movements Jameson contrasts with the apparently unhealthy resurgence of such traditional fields of inquiry as aesthetics, ethics, and theology. Such rhetoric already gives an indication of the extent to which Jameson's own thinking reveals a kind of modernist, but perhaps more precisely avant-gardist tendency: the rhetoric of health, disgust, and purging echoing, no doubt self-consciously, the manifestoes of the Futurists and Vorticists. Yet, Jameson is more historically responsible than Marinetti and Lewis, and points out that the postmodern denunciation misses its target. He argues that what postmodernism perceives as the undesirable features of modernism are actually the features of the *ideology* of modernism, where ideology is understood both pejoratively, as "false consciousness," and descriptively, as the theory of the practice (Jameson 2002: 197). The ideology of modernism appears in the theories of Clement Greenberg and the literary practice of such late modernists as Nabokov and Beckett. Postmodernism imagines itself to break with high modernism, but it is actually, according to Jameson, breaking with late modernism (Jameson 2002: 210).

Jameson does not, however, rescue "classical modernism" from postmodernist incomprehension; classical modernism too has its distinctive features, and they too have become obsolete and must be disavowed. Jameson's *magnum opus*, *Postmodernism*, already teaches that many of the characteristics of the postmodern emerge when modernism becomes impossible: we get them when we can no longer share, for example, the Futurists' excitement about the machine, or when psychic and linguistic fragmentation make Expressionist anxiety and alienation "no longer appropriate in the age of the postmodern" (Jameson 1991: 14). In other words, with a period break comes a normative decision about what does and does not belong in the realm of art and culture.

A Singular Modernity continues Jameson's insistence upon definitive and normative breaks between the modern and the postmodern. Whatever problems he acknowledges about periodization itself, they are not obstacles to his assertion of "at least one clear dividing line between the modern and the postmodern, namely, the refusal of concepts of self-consciousness, reflexivity, irony or self-reference in the postmodern aesthetic and also in postmodern values and in philosophy as such" (Jameson 2002: 92–3). The rejection of what he also calls "that now ancient category of self-consciousness" is of a piece with his denunciation of the category of the subject as the unrepresentable locus for contemporary narratives of modernity (Jameson 2002: 55).

Yet while classical or high modernism may be inappropriate to the postmodern experience, the same cannot be said for the works of high modernists. *A Singular Modernity* concludes with a call for a "Poundian mission to identify Utopian tendencies with a Benjaminian geography of their sources and a gauging of their pressure at what are now multiple sea levels. Ontologies of the present," continues Jameson, "demand archaeologies of the future, not forecasts of the past" (Jameson 2002: 215). We need only turn to Jameson's 1998 *Brecht and Method* to show how Brecht's legacy, the very "idea of Brecht," remains *useful* for the present. At the start of that book, the theorist who instructs us to always historicize acknowledges, somewhat sheepishly, the anachronism in claiming the modernist Brecht is relevant to postmodern times, a problem he does his best to resolve dialectically. Accompanying these strenuous dialectical maneuvers are repeated efforts to show the singularity (one could hardly say individuality) of Brechtian modernism: "the only legitimate form … of modernist innovation as such" (Jameson 2000: 127). Thus, where other modernists cultivated a personal, expressive *style*, Brecht produced an antisubjective *rhetoric*. Even as Brecht's innovations are celebrated, the modernist canon is delegitimized (with the exceptions of Benjamin and Adorno, Pound and Joyce and who knows who else; but this is precisely my point).

How can modernists be relevant to the present when modernism in general is not? Certainly the generalizations of period concepts are never adequate to any particular instance, but, as Maxim One of *A Singular Modernity* declares, "We cannot not periodize," which means that one cannot *not* see modernists as modernists, even if one (if one is Jameson) would prefer to call them Utopians. How to negotiate between Jameson's normative ideas about periodization and modernism, and his pleas for a certain classical modernist pantheon bearing potential for social change? How, in short, to distinguish the unhealthy movement backwards that Jameson calls regression from the healthy movement backwards that is a way forwards, an archaeology of the future?

It is difficult to read Jameson on modernism and postmodernism without wondering whether and how modernism might persist in the postmodern period. Can one even call literature produced in the 1980s "modernist," or is that already to fail to periodize? Can we identify distinctively modernist features in contemporary literature without accusing such works of being "regressive"? Could we not, inspired by Alain Badiou, see them as exhibiting a fidelity to the event of modernism?

In *Ethics*, Badiou denounces the contemporary "ethical turn" in favor of an "ethics of truths" that emerges in relation to specific realms and, more precisely, as a result of encounters with particular events:

> [i]f there is no ethics "in general," that is because there is no abstract Subject, who would adopt it as his shield. There is only a particular kind of animal, convoked by certain circumstances to *become* a subject—or rather, to enter into the composing of a subject.
>
> (Badiou 2001: 40)

The circumstances in which something might happen to transform the human animal into a subject emerge in four principal domains: science, art, love, and politics. In these domains an "event" can take place, "something that cannot be reduced to its ordinary inscription in 'what there is.'" By "what there is" Badiou means the ordinary order of things, that is, of opinion and knowledge. The event ruptures this order of things and "compels" those who recognize it as the manifestation of a truth to "decide a *new* way of being" (Badiou 2001: 41). The event places a demand upon one that by remaining faithful to the truth of that event one becomes a subject. Badiou's examples include the French revolution, the meeting of Heloise and Abelard, Galileo's creation of physics, Haydn's invention of classical style, as well as the Chinese cultural revolution, Schoenberg's invention of twelve tone, and the mathematical inventions of Cantor. Badiou's list is, however, not universally binding—a point to which I shall return. Badiou himself raises the question of fidelity to modernism in particular:

> Berg and Webern, faithful to the musical event known by the name of "Schoenberg," cannot continue with fin-de-siècle neo-Romanticism as if nothing had happened ... An eventual fidelity is a real break (both thought and practised) in the specific order within which the event took place.
>
> (Badiou 2001: 42)

By treating artistic events—Schoenberg's invention of serialism, Brecht's epic theater, Joyce or Woolf's exploration of the languages shaping consciousness, or Picasso's dismantling of Western perspectivism—as events after which one cannot continue as if nothing has happened, one might display fidelity to the events of modernism. On Badiou's account, one need not be faithful to the whole realm of modernism but can treat distinct events, can recognize the singularity of modernist events, can follow Brecht but not Joyce, Schoenberg but not Stravinsky, and so on. Yet, each of these events displays the logic of modernism as a radical break with the modes of representation that preceded it.

If we follow Badiou, to remain faithful to a modernist event is not anachronistically to imitate modernist models but to see modernist works as events whose implications demand continued investigation. Nothing in Badiou's conception of fidelity requires us to ignore the conditions that lead Jameson to call the specific modes and themes of modernist representation "no longer appropriate" (Jameson 1991: 14). Fidelity to modernism does not mean pretending still to be excited about machines when they have become omnipresent but, rather, working out what modernism means after the machine has lost its hold on the imagination while the event of the Futurist Manifestoes (or *Ulysses*, or *Mrs Dalloway*, or ...) has not. Badiou claims "[t]o be faithful to an event is to move within the situation that this event has supplemented, by *thinking* (although all thought is a practice, a putting to the test) the situation 'according to' the event" (Badiou 2001: 41–2). A change in political, economic, and technological conditions does not mean that art can no longer be modernist. It means it must be modernist differently. Artistic periodization need not be reducible to the stages of capitalist development; modernism need not become postmodernism when modernity becomes postmodernity.

What fidelity to modernism requires is, therefore, a more dialectical understanding of the temporal situation of works of art and literature produced in fidelity to modernism. The paradox such works try to solve is of the continuity of the break: "An evental fidelity is a real break ... in the specific order within which the event took place" (Badiou 2001: 42). What comes before a break is, after all, not always destroyed: one could ignore or simply not be taken by Schoenberg, and continue with neo-Romanticism; one could remain unmoved by Joyce or Stein and persist with the classical *Bildungsroman*. The break is a break only for those who continue to recognize and treat it as such.

Sensitivity to the continuity of the break means that Badiou's conception of fidelity to the event is refreshingly free of the quasi-existentialist anxiety about authenticity that dogs Jameson. Badiou would not accept Jameson's distinction between modernism and late modernism as pure event and corrupt ideological institutionalization. Institutionalization is, for Badiou, unavoidable, even desirable, if the event is to remain consequential, is to persist. Just as Pauline Christianity is not, for Badiou, a perversion of the purity of Christ's teachings but one mode of perpetuating and stabilizing them, so too the late modernism that Jameson denounces as the transformation of modernism into aesthetic ideology could be a serious attempt to "keep going" with modernism in the aftermath of its founding events.

Put simply, I suggest that where Jameson's fetishization of the narrative break and the "no longer possible" leaves him without a vocabulary to conceptualize a modernist-inspired "archaeology of the future," Badiou usefully articulates the value of relationship and continuity with modernist works. Badiou gives us a way to take seriously the idea of a contemporary perpetuation of artistic modernism in the age Jameson insists can only be postmodern. Furthermore, in explaining the role of the event in subject formation, Badiou offers an account of the decision for rupture or continuity: that is, an account of precisely that abyssal decision that is central to Jameson's own theory but that remains, in his work, simultaneously arbitrary and perpetually biased toward narrative break.

This decision is not, in Badiou, a subjective universal. Whereas Jameson repeatedly invokes what "we" can and cannot believe about the condition of contemporary culture and, particularly, the transition from modernism to post-modernism as if each were the only apt response to its historical conjuncture, Badiou's events do not demand consent from everyone. Whatever one might say about the authoritarianism of Badiou's political views, his account of fidelity to the event allows one to see, for example, Schoenberg as a wrong turn in the history of music. In other words, those events to which one might best display a kind of aesthetic fidelity are precisely those to which fidelity is not a given, for which recognition cannot be taken for granted. Despite the abstractness of Badiou's model, there is an acknowledged specificity and contingency: the event is an event for a particular subject—is, indeed, only an event insofar as it pro-duces a subject who will recognize it as such. Thus Badiou might briefly be aligned with a thinker such as Ernst Bloch, whose theory of nonsynchronism begins from the premise that "we do not all live in the same now" (Bloch 1977: 22–38). If, as Jameson says, we cannot not periodize, one might still ask the fundamental question: for whom are those periodizations meaningful or even binding?

Ironically, then, the notion of fidelity to modernist events solves the problem I identify in Jameson's writings—the tension between his commitment to concep-tions of periodization, progress, and historical obsolescence, and his loyalty to Adorno and Benjamin, Brecht and Pound. Jameson proclaims and disavows that loyalty in the same breath: disavows it because of the problem of periodization, and proclaims it because these works are the objects of his affective investment and his methods are shaped by them, from his approach to the historico-political significance of form to his preoccupation with identifying the new. Yet, Jameson leaves himself no language with which to account for that fidelity.

What I see as Jameson's dilemma is not least the product of his refusal to accommodate the subject in his account of modernism and periodization. Although the two would have agreed on precious little else, the liberal pragmatist Richard Rorty's criticism of Jameson resonates strikingly with the one I extract from the militant Leninist Badiou. *In Achieving Our Country*, Rorty writes against Jameson:

> You cannot … find inspirational value in a text at the same time that you are viewing it as the product of a mechanism of cultural production … If it is to have inspirational value, a work must be allowed to recontextualize much of what you previously thought you knew; it cannot, at least at first, be recontextualized by what you already believe.
>
> (Rorty 1998: 133–4)

Inspirational value functions for the self in Rorty much as the event functions for the subject in Badiou: as the encounter with something that transforms, and by transforming creates, the subject. Tellingly, Rorty and Badiou, for all their differences, both expose the gap in Jameson's work by his unequivocal refusal to consider the effect of the work of art upon the subject. In the story we might generate from Badiou's conception of fidelity to the event of modernism, there would be no such prohibition. While Badiou's history of modernism might not be written as a history of the individual subject, it would include events that constituted particular kinds of subjects. The subjectivities in question would not be the inaugural, unrepresentable word in such a history, but the necessary supplements to the events that constituted them in the first place: be they austere, market-shy late modernists committed to investigating the consequences of the discoveries of Stein, Joyce, or Kafka (e.g. Samuel Beckett and Paul Celan), or cunning followers of Adorno, Brecht, and Benjamin, devoted to investigating montage, estrangement, and history in the rapidly changing contexts of postwar writing and cinema (e.g. Jean-Luc Godard, Alexander Kluge, and Chris Marker).

To consider what fidelity to the event of modernism might look like in practice, we need only ask how we might think about some English writers as contemporary, or, if you like, postmodern, modernists. Even in Jamesonian terms, England is perhaps not too implausible a site for something like a postwar modernism. Given time, one might speculate on the peculiar historical conditions that created space for postwar English modernism. One might emphasize how the use of models drawn from continental European modernism should be understood as disrupting a national cultural identity predicated on self-differentiation from Western Europe. Furthermore, the relative weakness of an indigenous English modernism allows the radical potential of actual modernist works to persist in England long after the ideology of modernism has made the repetition and imitation of modernist models appear a reactionary or even academic gesture to more jaded eyes in more initially receptive nations.

It would also be important to bear in mind the experience of shock and transition in England's loss of Empire and, with it, the status of global power. If, as Jameson, Perry Anderson, and many others have claimed, modernism is what you get when modernization is incomplete and postmodernism is what you get when it is complete, what do you get when, perhaps through a kind of trick of international perspective, you feel that your own modernization has started to slow, even head backwards, and come undone? Is this not, in reverse, the period of incomplete modernization that is the precondition for modernism? At the same time, as Jed Esty reminds us in *A Shrinking Island*, postwar England also conceived of itself as "the country where industrial, imperial capitalism hit first and hit hardest [and] … also the country first out the other side [of …] the very paradigm of demodernization" (Esty 2004: 21). Note the double temporality at work: to demodernize is to go backwards, but to be first out the other side of modernity is to remain in some sense, if not the most modern, still the most advanced. English conditions might be peculiarly ripe to experience going backwards as a form of going forwards.

Postwar English modernism then: between the middlebrow late modernism of Anthony Burgess, the experimental postmodernisms of B. S. Johnson, Ann Quin, and Angela Carter, and the more commercial postmodernisms of Amis, Ishiguro, and Self, lie the works of a dramatist such as Howard Barker, with his "Theatre of Catastrophe," and a novelist such as Nicholas Mosley, with his five-novel sequence *Catastrophe Practice*. Figures such as Barker and Mosley lack the attributes that Jameson has taught us to think of as postmodernist, and manifest many of the attributes that he says are distinctively modernist: an individual, idiosyncratic *style*, a preoccupation with epistemology rather than ontology, depth rather than surface, consciousness and self-consciousness rather than, say, fragmentation or cognitive mapping. Like Jameson's late modernist icons Beckett and Nabokov, Barker and Mosley follow the models of the classical modernists, but unlike Beckett and Nabokov, they are less interested in what Jameson calls the modest aesthetic autonomies of the late modern than in the Absolutes of the modernists (Jameson 2002: 200): in revealing truth, and in fostering the formation of new human beings and new human communities, in examining and creating the conditions for social change. Indeed, Mosley appears to treat the classical modernist heritage, in particular that left by Brecht, as a resource with which to overcome late modernist aesthetic and ideological taboos, such as those against meaning and hope, which he identifies as Beckett's legacy.

Contemporary modernists return to the resources of classical modernism to undo the disabling taboos imposed by late modernism. Mosley's *Catastrophe Practice* quintet reworks this distinctively modernist strategy in a manner that nevertheless transcends the individualism and subject-centered thinking for which Jameson critiques it. Mosley shares with Jameson's hero Brecht a deep interest in art as pedagogy, in scientific ideas, and in the elaboration of modes of acting that would both reveal and undo the ways in which we are all actors in everyday life. As the concept of "catastrophe practice" implies, however, Mosley departs from the idea that after World War II received forms of self-understanding disclosed their capacity to annihilate life on this planet. In response to both the fact of catastrophe, and what he sees as the probability of its repetition, Mosley continues the modernist project of searching for new forms of literary representation appropriate to contemporary life and renews the avant-garde call for "a new human type" capable of surviving, or even circumventing, the worst forms of catastrophe.[2] The political stakes of Mosley's work appear in the fact that the characters of the *Catastrophe Practice* series converge for the first time at an anti-nuclear demonstration outside an American airbase. As the hope implicit in such resistance might suggest, Mosley also means to refer to catastrophe in the evolutionary sense, in which punctual radical change bears both the promise of and the demand for radical transformation.

The last novel published in the *Catastrophe Practice* series is *Hopeful Monsters* (1990), which offers a prehistory of the novels published before it. Mosley summarizes *Hopeful Monsters* as telling the stories of Max and Eleanor,

> students growing up in the 1920s in Cambridge and Berlin. They have to
> come to terms with the rise of Communism and Naziism [sic], the crack up

of old ways of thinking in science and philosophy, the self-destructiveness of
the Spanish Civil War, the making of the Bomb. What they learn can be
passed on, eventually, to the protagonists of the books that follow.

(Mosley 1990: postscript, unnumbered)

The subsequent books mentioned here are *Imago Bird, Serpent, Judith*, and *Catastrophe
Practice*, the main protagonists of which are mentored by Max and Eleanor. Max
and Eleanor's lessons are learned, in short, during the historical period that Eric
Hobsbawm has taught us to think of as "the Age of Catastrophe."[3] At the same
time, the story told by the *Catastrophe Practice* sequence cannot be parsed as
simply a twentieth-century *Bildungsroman*. It is, rather, the story of how what Max
and Eleanor have learned can be transmitted to later generations.

What Max and Eleanor transmit is not some particular content so much as a
style of thought, a highly self-conscious attitude towards experience that is manifest most conspicuously in the ornate mode in which they communicate their
thoughts to each other, and in such *leitmotifs* as that drawn from an image used
to explain the theory of relativity: Mosley's characters repeatedly suggest that
people's efforts to break out of the bonds of their own vision as leading views of
the backs of their own heads. There is some optimism in this thought: "I suppose
it might be by seeing that they can't get out of their own vision, that people
might get out" (*Hopeful Monsters*; Mosley 1990: 13, 27). Both the distinctive, cerebral, questioning tone of the narrators and the stakes of *Hopeful Monsters'* version
of self-consciousness are on display as Eleanor writes to Max of her time as an
anthropologist in West Africa:

> We have not asked—What are we doing here recording and classifying the
> customs of a society? Might we not simply be exercising the customs of our
> minds? To ask this would be to step back from the protective mechanisms of
> our own tribe: it would be to risk, perhaps, stability of mind.
>   But as we—you and I—have said before, might there not be an anthro-
> pology in which the observer is seen as part of what he observes: in which
> his observing is taken into account as affecting what he observes? If it is by
> not asking such questions that stability is maintained, then by asking them
> might there not be some anthropology to do with change? If we stand back
> from the part of ourselves that is part of what we see—between these two
> parts of ourselves might there not be freedom for change?
>
> (Mosley 1990: 293–4)

Such meditations show that in *Hopeful Monsters*, self-consciousness is not predicated
on the representability of the subject that Jameson rejects but on recognition of
its divisions and gaps. It appears not in the stereotypically modernist guise of an
unaddressed, individual solitary stream of consciousness, but as an inter-
subjective, dialogic reflection on processes of cognition and feeling: "as we—you
and I—have said before." Mosleyan self-consciousness is less about the construction of an autonomous self than it is about making strange and decathecting

certain representations in order to bring about change, a project explicitly conceived in fidelity to the event of Brecht's theatrical innovations.

With this version of self-consciousness, Mosley contends one can go forward, have a future, practice for and even survive catastrophe, through a kind of going back and undoing of the learned, conventional responses of the past. The historical narrative of *Hopeful Monsters* and, by extension, the *Catastrophe Practice* series might therefore offer just what Jameson calls for, an archaeology of the future, by means of precisely what he rejects: the typically modernist and therefore supposedly obsolete technique of self-consciousness. For it is just this new understanding of self-consciousness that promises a new, potentially redemptive relationship to historical time and something like a utopian social organization.

Maxim Number One of *A Singular Modernity*, if not of Jameson's entire *oeuvre*, is that one cannot not periodize. Maybe so. But there is an enormous leap from the recognition that to write history is to tell a story of breaks and continuities, to the insistence that artistic practices and forms can be socially and politically meaningful only in a particular period, and that those with a healthy historical consciousness will be able to read the use-by dates of works and styles, and know when to throw them, proudly disgusted, onto the dustbin of history. Mosley's project indicates that the formal properties Jameson sees as distinctively and exclusively modernist can work in ways strikingly at odds with his attempt to fix them firmly within a particular historical period. While there is undoubtedly a place for ideas of timeliness and untimeless and for such concepts as "period style," Jameson's ideas about these matters are ultimately too rigidly bound to a normative, linear framework to be either intellectually convincing or politically useful. Indeed, Jameson himself is arguably at his most interesting when his passionate literary and philosophical attachments come into conflict with his historico-ideological commitments, as when he makes the case for Brecht as a figure who speaks to the present, or even Pound as a model Utopian. These ideas come not because of but *despite* the demand for periodization that is Jameson's most well-known thesis.

Given his strategic appeal at the end of *A Singular Modernity* to a Benjaminian geography of the sources of utopianism, we should remember that Jameson's inability to see continuity as radical is distinctly at odds with an important strand in Benjamin's own thought.[4] Certainly Benjamin encourages us to blast open the continuum of history and instructs that "[a]rticulating the past historically ... means appropriating a memory as it flashes up in a moment of danger" (Benjamin 2003: 391). But these flashes and explosion should not distract us from the fact that Benjamin's "On the Concept of History" is fundamentally a meditation on the importance to revolutionary thought of a sense of continuity with the past suffering of the oppressed. Recall the famous interpretation of Klee's *Angelus Novus*:

> Where a chain of events appears before *us*, *he* sees one single catastrophe, which keeps piling wreckage upon wreckage and hurls it at his feet ... The angel would like to stay, awaken the dead, and make whole what has been

smashed. But a storm is blowing from Paradise and has got caught in his wings; it is so strong that the angel can no longer close them. This storm drives him irresistibly into the future, to which his back is turned, while the pile of debris before him grows toward the sky. What we call progress is *this* storm.

(Benjamin 2003: 392)

Redemption, for Benjamin as for Mosley, requires learning to see what is behind one's back: what we think we are beyond, what we can no longer see properly, what is outside our line of sight. My argument has been that this task is antithetical to that of periodization and vitiates all declarations of modernism's obsolescence.

Notes

1 "Preface" to *A Singular Modernity* (Jameson 2002).
2 Mosley suggests human survival lies in, among other things, transforming one's attitude to apparent evil, even to acts of aggression (see *Serpent* [1981] in particular), in part by dismantling traditional modes of communal sense-making such as tragic conflict and the logic of sacrifice.
3 See Part One of Hobsbawm (1994).
4 Jameson's recent recourse to Benjamin reveals the contradictions of his thought. In 1999 he suggested the contemporary obsession with Benjamin might be symptomatic of an "anti-theoretical time, which is to say an anti-intellectual time" (Jameson 1999: 267).

Bibliography

Badiou, A. (2001) *Ethics: An Essay on the Understanding of Evil*, trans. P. Hallward, London/ New York: Verso.

Benjamin, W. (2003) "On the Concept of History," *Selected Writings: Volume 4 1938–1940*, ed. H. Eiland and M. W. Jennings, trans. E. Jephcott *et al.*, Cambridge, MA: Belknap Press.

Bloch, E. (1977) "Nonsynchronism and the Obligation to Its Dialectics," trans. Mark Ritter, *New German Critique* 11 (Spring): 22–38.

Esty, J. (2004) *A Shrinking Island*, Princeton, NJ: Princeton University Press.

Hobsbawm, E. (1994) *The Age of Extremes: A History of the World, 1914–1991*, New York: Vintage.

Jameson, F. (1991) *Postmodernism, or, The Cultural Logic of Late Capitalism*, Durham, NC: Duke University Press.

—— (1999) "The Theoretical Hesitation: Benjamin's Sociological Predecessor," *Critical Inquiry* 25 (Winter): 267–88.

—— (2000) *Brecht and Method*, New York: Verso.

—— (2002) *A Singular Modernity: Essay on the Ontology of the Present*, New York: Verso.

Mosley, N. (1990) *Hopeful Monsters*, Elmwood Park, IL: Dalkey Archive Press.

Rorty, R. (1998) *Achieving Our Country*, Cambridge, MA: Harvard University Press.

In the time of theory, the timeliness of modernism

Response to Neil Levi

Glenn Willmott

Is Modernism timely now? Does periodization, which assigns to all the modernisms of the early twentieth century their entrances and exits on the stage of literary history, and leaves them, in a later act, merely to putter in the background—there to serve, like Prufrock's "attendant lord," to "swell a progress, start a scene or two, / Advise the prince; no doubt, an easy tool" in the hands of some post-modern Hamlet—undercut their timeliness? Neil Levi argues that Fredric Jameson's periodization of Modernism (that is, of its own, ironic periodization of itself, as an age committed to subjectivity, irony, and style, from the perspective of a late modernism) leads to just this disenchanting possibility for Modernist scholars.[1] And perhaps Jameson would wryly affirm our resulting boredom as a symptom of the deflation of Modernist escapism, of our desire to "make it new" in a specialist idiolect. Yet to muddy the issue, there is Levi's further suggestion that Jameson, notwithstanding, actually cherishes varieties of modernism; that he regularly draws upon modernist names and texts in the articulation of his uto-pian project. Levi reads this inconsistency as a symptom of the periodization dilemma that Jameson himself strikingly identifies in his historicist approach to Modernism, and whose contradictions Jameson allows necessarily to persist in his own work.

I will not here follow the path opened up for Levi by this dilemma, which is an invitation to supplement Modernist periodization with notions of a persis-tence and authenticity of modernist "events" beyond period breaks. It may be worth noting Jameson's own answer to the dilemma in his first major study of Modernism, posed in the fiery language of Wyndham Lewis: canonical moder-nists are but paper radicals, puppets of a capitalist empire they cannot escape except in sublime or tortured extrusions of new forms of personal language and style, new expressive figures that become the ascetic, verbally imprisoned, yet consubstantial phantoms of a liberal culture only too easily tethered to the jus-tification of violence and oppression; and yet, to the extent modernists know this, and can like Lewis boundlessly (dialectically) self-satirize, they may teach us a still timely truth—if an ugly one, yet unresolved—of our own intellectual and artistic institutions in the world at large.[2] This dialectical truth, and the ambivalent politics of its expression and reception—one utopian wingtip lifted to the beyond, the other pinioned in the mire—also reflects a more enduring pattern.

Jameson treats all texts before, during, and after Modernism as dialectical structures in which utopian and repressive forces inhere. One might productively wonder why modernisms attract his faintest enthusiasm, and so make a rhetorical rather than logical question of their utopian timeliness as opposed to regressive lure.

I would like to focus on something rather different from the politics of the "subjective" in which this dilemma of timeliness and modernism is enmeshed, and turn the problem around to another of its sides: narrative. Throughout Jameson's work, which has charted the "political unconscious" of literary history from the age of chivalric romances (and earlier, if we count his sketches of archaic oral literature) to a postmodern present, past writers are folded into a grand narrative, a self-conscious, Marxian romance of market growth, state transformation, geopolitics, and class struggle. Narrative has always been Jameson's key formal concept for the mediation of past writing and the situations of the present-day Left. History as structural narrative, not local content, allows us to grasp the timeliness of symbolic acts. If this narrative is characterized by periods and period breaks, as Jameson says it must be, then the consequence for timeliness is that past writers are timely insofar as they illuminate, not first and foremost their own colorful episode, but as necessary joints and segments, the total story relevant to us today. We have heard something like this before:

> The historical sense involves a perception, not only of the pastness of the past, but of its presence; the historical sense compels a man to write not merely with his own generation in his bones, but with a feeling that the whole of the literature of Europe from Homer and within it the whole of the literature of his own country has a simultaneous existence and composes a simultaneous order ... No poet, no artist of any art, has his complete meaning alone ... You must set him, for contrast and comparison, among the dead.
>
> (Eliot 1976: 49)

For Eliot, writing these words in 1920, this simultaneous order was "timeless" and metaphysical; one found one's complete meaning in the phantom identity of a textual men's club. For Jameson, it is narrative and material. Dead labors and struggles still live in our bones, feeding the life of writing.

I propose this comparison, distasteful in most respects, because I believe it is symptomatic of their otherwise diverse commitments to the modern that both Eliot and Jameson seek to place the timely writer in a relation to a past tradition that is not evidently given, and struggle to understand the estranging pastness or presentness of this past. Both, in so doing, have found themselves waging war on the inward turn of the modern writer (or scholar) and insisted on the ineluctable burden of (either pre-modernist or modernist) inheritance, as well as on an unattractive labor of impersonality or depersonalization required for its recognition.[3] Yet if we draw back from Eliot's own platitudes about inheritance itself (as if it meant little more than a borrower's card to a Borgesian library of the universal human imagination), we may consider the economic legacy of inheritance and its cognate, heritage, for all its curious relation to the very narrative of capitalist modernity here at issue. Inheritances are largely controlled by modern private property law, but the exchanges thus regulated are not commodity transactions but gift transactions, and *inheritance* remains one of the most durable vestiges of kinship-based pre-capitalist societies—emanating from a shrunken domestic sphere—in modern times. Cultural *heritage* similarly refers to intellectual property—of imaginative, ethical, and/or informational kind—as well as that material property in which it is mnemonically embedded (whether Tsimshian ceremonial poles, Irish Ascendancy big houses, European patriarchal surnames, or books), that are passed inter-generationally within social groups via transactions of stories, manners, cherished objects, and other social objects that constitute collective identities and ethical horizons for those indebted to their givers. While it is of course possible to speak alternatively of a commodified heritage, the latter can only refer to a secondary or parasitic appendix to a non-market process of interpellative gifting, since such a "heritage," without prior imaginary identification as such, and fueled only by alienated purchasing mechanisms, would always feel fundamentally elective, that is alienable, rather than necessary or obligatory. This is an important distinction, since one of the most daring and unsettling projects undertaken by modernists was the claim of a heritage or heritages in conflict with that of liberal imperialism—heritages not their own, but discovered especially in the new portraits of tribal life (ancient and contemporary) of a new anthropology and classicism. Yeats' free appropriations from Celtic, East Indian, and other lore, like Joyce's unexpected forging of a conscience for his "race" from a cosmopolitan, but just as insistently Dublinian, plethora of myths and histories, or H. D.'s syncretic and dialectical vision of American Christian and pagan religions, all act on Pound's forthright assertion in Canto 81: "What thou lov'st well is thy true heritage." What distinguishes such projects from a surrounding, cruder array of cultural appropriations and primitivisms is a modernist understanding that such love is not merely elective or affective, but embedded in a long, violent multicultural history from which the writer cannot detach him or herself, and which he or she typically expresses as a euphoric, spiritual, tragic, or absurd fate.

It is in this context that Levi's passing observation, that in its progressivism, its commitment to "make it new," Jameson's "own thinking reveals a kind of modernist" tendency, may here be revisited. Though rare enough, it is a stunning capacity of Jameson's prose, when speaking of the most uncompromised utopian visions, to drift into a kind of gorgeous, earthly mysticism, to evoke never-before-seen colors, new bodily senses and organs, or undreamt-of types of personhood—not as literal ground-plans for the future, of course, but as metaphorical tokens for us in the present to redeem, if they are to have value, in a progressive *engagement* beyond writing. However metaphorical, it is easy to see that such moments belong to the same futurist cloth in which are denounced, in darker hues, regressions to recognizably past social forms, and past or residual modes of production, as so much errant utopianism. Yet if Jameson seeks to "make it new" as such, I doubt that this allies him with Modernism, which must be understood for its backward turn as much as for its inward turn, as the origin of Pound's rule in a pre-capitalist (nearly two-millennia-old) Chinese washbasin inscription already implies. It would seem more evident that Jameson's progressivist narrative—in which pre-capitalist modes and heritages normally appear as things of the past, and play no vital role in a (however uneven or conflicted) present grasped as an "archeology of the future"—has its genealogy in the longer modernity of Marxism and its Enlightenment heritage, rather than in Modernism itself.

The axiom to be introduced here, then, is that Modernism is not only a period, but also a heritage, one with its own material history and political unconscious. Modernism remains timely, not only because one might be able to trace the persistence of Modern events and crises into the material battlefield, the historicity of the present, but also because its very utopian fabric, for the first time in history, comes into ideological being under the pressure of a narrative totality. It emerges, that is, from the unraveling of an evidently inadequate, yet imaginatively necessary and ruthlessly useful, totalizing humanist narrative supplied by the imperialist realization of capitalist modernity, along with the agonized, innovative remaking of this story when brought into myriad dialectical contact with its repressed antitheses, with the otherness of real and vital, coeval social formations having different modes of production, and of segments within capitalist societies where such modes endure. It is true that such segments may suffer a paralyzing containment, in which social power is flattened into compensatory, aesthetic gesture, but this containment may be permeable, its walls flammable, so that identity-based terrorism or revolution, not always liberal, may erupt. Yeats was right to worry, as he stepped into the fin-de-siècle, whether his neo-Celtic dreams of heroic exchanges, politicized eros, and non-market production (from Aran to Emain Macha) were little more than irrelevant, vague ornaments of a bourgeois outcaste. Yet he was also right to worry, as the century went on, that such dreams might play a part in social history, justifying the human sacrifices, the gifts of life as well as the takings, to which a still blood-ridden Ireland's independence was partly due.[4] Today, human sacrifice, heroic kinship, and non-market labor, mediated by languages of heritage, remain fused in segments and strata across the capitalist world, and it is surely timely to rethink them as modern, as material inheritance rather than mere ideological fantasy, and appropriate them to authentically utopian ends. Better this than dismiss their gregarious nostalgia, or overlook their terrifying violence, which meet capital on its own regressive terms.

In his *Archaeologies of the Future*, Jameson tells us how utopian writing may be usefully rather than mistakenly understood as political, in the interests of a contemporary Left politics. His starting point is the problem of "situatedness"—the terrible limitations, indeed, prejudices and blindnesses—that any utopian text must have, growing as it must out of a particular social formation, geography, and history (Jameson 2005: 170). To historicize the utopian is seemingly to muck it in its pasts and presents, and sever it from the radical leap to a future it insists upon imagining. The *mistaken* way to understand its radical politics is to cobble together the various positive themes and ideas, the bits and pieces of utopian floorplans, from a variety of utopian texts that are thus unfortunately but inevitably "situated" in ideological prejudices and local or historical blindnesses, with the idea that all could sit comfortably together in a kind of disinterested or relativistic unity. He is scathing on the subject of different cultures or social groups in the world "communicating" (Jameson 2005: 221) together in order to produce a utopia he terms *reflexive* (Jameson 2005: 213)—yielding the image of a universal (but not homogeneous) culture always locally negotiating, translating, and adapting itself to the internal differences cast up in symbolic form by, or "thematized" (Jameson 2005: 180) by, a globalized world (Jameson 2005: 215–16). This is mere aesthetic resolution at best, and Disneyfication at worst, of a political reality that remains unresolved and unjust at an economic level. Liberal multiculturalism and pluralism are his explicit targets here, but these have cousins on the Left, and in the latter context infect a utopian literary criticism that is satisfied to excavate and celebrate the distinctly progressive content in art according to broadly Left social values. This kind of utopian reading—a net in which, I suppose, many of us may be caught—implicitly

> presuppose[s] that there is ultimately somewhere a correct view of Utopia which is to be attained by allowing for the author's partiality or even by triangulating a variety of different Utopias in order to determine their common emplacement. But there is no such correct Utopia; and all the familiar ones we have are irredeemably class-based.
>
> (Jameson 2005: 171)

Presumably this is because "correct" Utopia for the Marxian historian will be some kind of laborious product of, rather than fantastic alternative to, such worldly conditions. It is an unfortunate paradox, Jameson concludes, that utopian writers must be committed to the "professional effacement, in advance and by definition, of all these concrete determinants [of race and class, of language and childhood, of gender and situation-specific knowledge] of a properly Utopian ideology," because "it is an effacement which is a repression rather than a working through" (Jameson 2005: 171).

But working through does not have its end point in anything like affirmation of such situated knowledges. Two important propositions, for readers of modernism, are connected with Jameson's portrait of a *mistaken* view of the politics of the utopian text. The first is that a genuine, which is to say a currently progressive, radical politics should understand utopian writing principally for its *negative* representation, for its structure of critique or form, rather than its content. He deploys a Greimasian square to diagram a vanguard political interpretation that would cast a cold eye on the positive utopian content synthesized from different utopian visions (the "complex" solution generated by resolving an ideological quarrel or contrast, utopian this vs utopian that), and would seize instead on the *implied* but unrepresented perspective whereby we might resolve contrasting utopian critiques (the "neutral" solution, resolving an opposition of dystopian anti-this vs. dystopian anti-that) (Jameson 2005: 181). He asks us to imagine a utopian perspective—an imaginary "situation," if you like—from which we could launch, that is ourselves escape, both utopian critiques; and this perspective by definition always remains formal, without symbolization. Hence this first proposition challenges us to reread what is utopian in modernisms, and to be strictly suspicious of all utopian content, rather than to celebrate it at the cost of its always situated and compromised material history, and to pursue instead a chiaroscuro dialectics of negative representation uniquely opened up therein. This is not likely to sit well with those of us who would like to hold onto some of that content, even when situated (though the problem of how to do so without being anachronistic is one forced terribly upon us). Jameson will suggest that only such a "non-communicating" world vision allows the real problem of economic, as opposed to merely cultural, justice to be solved (Jameson 2005: 221).

The second proposition, however, is that the *mistaken*, "complex" ideology, this mistaken or "bad Utopianism, founded on the illusions of representation and of affirmative content" (Jameson 2005: 179), is distinctively Modernist. For it affirms contraries, brackets commitments from perspectives understood relativistically, and hence imposes Modernist "irony" and aesthetic "reflexivity" in order to imagine a cultural solution carefully displacing itself from, even while acknowledging or lamenting, real material conflicts (178–9). Put crudely, Modernism enables the bad, "complex" or syncretic method, and Postmodernism the good, "neutral" or negative method, of understanding utopian ideology and the way forward for the Left today.

A ready response to Jameson's strategic periodization is to propose that while Modernism as a panoply movement may well be strongly characterized by this kind of irony and reflexivity (aesthetic and political), it is no less plausible to show how agonized it is by the "neutral" strategies of double negativity Jameson denies to it. Some canonical works, like *The Waste Land*, are surely as easy, if not easier, to see as structures of multiple negation implying some unresolved perspective (one actually figured there by an utterly chameleonic Tiresias, and in Eliot's further pursuit of a totalizing and totally estranged voice, one that half vanishes into the mystical, transcendental addressee of his later poetry, its other half left to the plodding, inconsistent discourse of a "Christian society" in prose), than as structures of multiple content ironically affirmed. Or, leaving the text in-itself aside, it is just as plausible from a reception-based perspective to see such works as teaching machines for the former political aesthetic as for the latter. The same could be said about novels like *Nostromo* or *Tarr*. Consequently we might well find it defensible to dissolve period distinctions enough to preserve Jameson's larger historico-political theory, in the hypothesis that Modernism *already* mobilizes the whole contradictory and contrary structure of complex/ neutral managing of Utopian expression, and that some writers drift decidedly toward the neutral, while others—ironically, those closest to the Left (for example, I believe, Woolf and Joyce)—lean toward the complex "resolutions" of a political unconscious that Jameson stages rather as respectively Modernist and Postmodernist acts in the drama of modern cultural history.

Such a response would merely open up—indeed, why deny it, would redeem—Modernism for the kind of political criticism and timely *engagement* that Jameson assigns to the properly utopian. But there is another and more (I hope) interestingly dialectical objection to be ushered forward: why not affirm situated utopian content? Must it always be class-based? If not class-based, must such content belong anachronistically to the past? Could the unevenness of uneven development be a motor rather than a drag upon change? No doubt the present world is a different place from the one the modernists inhabited, yet just as surely the continuities between the two are many and foundational for the lived experience of, and the systemic limits that impinge upon, most people today. We need not make such a sociological or historical argument to make the logical one, however: why cannot a post-class-based utopia be imagined from a collage or synthesis of positive utopian content, or more simply, from looking at what is valuable in the present and the past, in the many, different, presents and pasts? Such a utopian synthesis, Jameson warns us, is an untimely, regressive "chimera":

> If true, this principle [the great empiricist maxim, nothing in the mind that was not first in the senses] spells the end, not only of Utopia as a form, but of Science Fiction in general, affirming as it does that even our wildest imaginings are all collages of experience, constructs made up of bits and pieces of the here and now: "When Homer formed the idea of Chimera, he only joined into one animal, parts which belonged to different animals; the head of a lion, the body of a goat, and the tail of a serpent." On the social level, this means that our imaginations are hostages to our own mode of production (and perhaps to whatever remnants of past ones it has preserved). It suggests that at best Utopia can serve the negative purpose of making us more aware of our mental and ideological imprisonment.
>
> (Jameson 2005: xiii)

But this view seems to me somewhat pessimistic, first, about empirical science, which can be considered to produce its new knowledge and new objects or beings, for better or worse, precisely through the incremental combination of existing knowledges (insofar as all new knowledge and experience is created by, or calculated by, inherited and existing bits and pieces physical or mathematical). Science viewed thus, as a creative collage of "bits and pieces of the here and now," is after all clearly realized in the many new gene-spliced creations of today, but significantly, is already foreseen by Wells' vanguard vivisectionist, the modernist Dr Moreau. Second, "on the social level," it is a risky gambit for the purposes of argument to assimilate all social work and generation to a single mode of production. Think of areas of gift or other kinds of exchange, of non-market zones of semi-autonomous activity—as small and trans-local as the nuclear family, or as large and more situated as the social institutions created by contemporary American and Canadian Native peoples that build on a continuous history of non-market modes of production and social life (in Canada, there is an entire Northern province or "territory" with a semi-autonomous

Native government)—that take part in the complicated web of ideologies, non-government organizations and institutions, and ruling bodies that affect how diverse modern people value, think, and act on their wealth and desires, ruthless or utopian. The latter reference to contemporary aboriginal sovereignty politics reminds us, indeed, that Jameson's apparently dismissive assessment of the "remnants" of past social forms effectively excludes such institutions from his critical analysis of "new social movements," and infelicitously echoes a primitivist view of aboriginal people (and by extension, all pre-capitalist heritages) as frozen in a dead past, not forces in the Modern. I do not mean that these aboriginal examples, or any other non-market heritages, are inevitably in harmony with the aims of the Left, or innocent of oppressive social relations, but only that they have demonstrable social power and continuity in modern history, and can offer compelling, actually existing models of a still undecided struggle against capitalism for outsiders to them.

In short, we can certainly look further back, to the situated pasts of various modernities, to find utopian elements drawn from pre- or anti- (e.g. in the case of aboriginal peoples) or non- (e.g. in the case of certain domestic spheres and women's institutions) capitalist heritages, all recombined or newly activated in Modernism. And Jameson's important work on Modernism and Fascism will already have suggested the dialectical care that must be brought to evaluating the mixture of modes of production thus mobilized. Beyond this, it may be in Modernism as such, for reasons I have suggested above, that we may find a vast array of programmatic attempts to leap over or shatter unified images of the present with a motley army of re-animated ruins and specters of pasts and presents lured from the shadows of capitalist production. Chimeras, new beings generated from the intercourse of such beings, within or without the marketplace, may be exactly what we need.[5]

To take the notion of uneven development in its most radical sense is to unfold a latent dimension in Jameson's general observation,

> that it is still difficult to see how future Utopias could ever be imagined in any absolute dissociation from socialism in its larger sense of anti-capitalism; dissociated, that is to say, from the values of social and economic equality and the universal right to food, lodging, medicine, education and work.
>
> (Jameson 2005: 196–7)

Present social groups are still able to recall and to a greater or lesser sense reproduce, from their own heritages (as present pasts), semi-autonomous realms that are immeasurably closer to this definition of "socialism in its larger sense" than is the liberal culture of imperialist heritage in its global villager/policeman guise. The political obstacle to "socialism in its larger sense" is perhaps not one of reflexive triangulation at all—of "communication"—but of semi-autonomous material resources pitted against the forces of imperialist assimilation inevitable to capitalist development. When Jameson sketches his view of a contemporary, utopian "archipelago," he explains with rare optimism that imperialist expansion would no longer be a threat because there is nothing left to conquer (whereas, one might well worry, that even or especially in a system of "non-communicating" societies, there is always an *other* with valuable resources: why not just take them?). Imperialism, as a state form of increasing wealth through aggressive territorial expansion, is intrinsic to market capitalism—but also older than capitalism, from whose pre-history it draws its us–them, human–animal, clean–unclean ideologies of sexual, ethnic, or racial distinction. It is hard to see a materialist utopia working without producing and reproducing an array of "communicative" ideologies that imagine transcending such durable dispositions. In any case, there are surely both capitalist and non-capitalist utopian chimeras, both modern and postmodern. And I have wanted to suggest that it is still worth reading across the modernisms for those utopian laboratories hidden in its cellars and closets, busy giving birth to chimeras in which life under capitalism has been productively mated with (not replaced by) devalued, degraded, and obsolete realizations of other modes of life.

If Jameson is right about Modernism, then I am tempted to see Theory itself in the long shadows cast by its twilight. If Theory is the specialized, scholarly, dialectical push and free-fall into boring, repressed, and otherwise unassimilated historical *givens*, which keep a door open in today's literature classroom, in its very utopian historicity, then as such it may be seen as an inheritor of the Modernist fight for ongoing, mundane epiphanies wrought by heretofore degraded ready-mades, overlooked passions, rejected tastes, and anachronized devotions, an inheritor that will affirm all their relative negations as the formal perspective, the utopian *pour-soi* or reflective subjectivity, of a now unrepresentable but unavoidable planetary totality.

Notes

1 I will use forms of the term "Modernism" to suggest substantive period and disciplinary concepts, and forms of the term "modernism" to suggest the range of possibly incommensurate forms of modern writing of the chronological period whose widest scope would range from 1890 to 1960, and whose canonical range would restrict itself to the decades bracketed by the South African and Second World Wars.

2 See the conclusion to Jameson (1979: 176–7).

3 It is tempting, indeed, to see Jameson's deflating assessment of late and early modernists, the immediately preceding generations for writers of the 1960s, as comparable to Eliot's of his preceding Victorians and Romantics. To either side of these respective generations, the one finds stronger fuel in either an earlier Balzac or contemporary LeGuin, the other in an earlier Dante or contemporary Joyce, to ignite their utopian blasts. One might also historicize the modernist heritage for the 1960s in alternative ways: Joan Didion, a canonical 1960s commentator and Jameson's contemporary, expresses in exemplary fashion the paralyzing ironies Jameson finds in the ideology of late modernism:

> I suppose I am talking about ... the ambiguity of belonging to a generation distrustful of political highs, the historical irrelevancy of growing up convinced that the heart of darkness lay not in some error of social organization but in man's own blood. If man was bound to err, then any social organization was bound to

be in error. It was a premise which still seems to me accurate enough, but one which robbed us early of a certain capacity for surprise.

(Didion 1979: 206)

Compare this with an evocation of modernist heritage of the same period by Susan Stanford Friedman, one decade-generation younger:

"What was modernism" to a graduate student in English and American literature in the heady days of the 1960s? Modernism was rebellion. Modernism was "make it new." Modernism was resistance, rupture. To its progenitors. To its students. Modernism was the antidote to the poison of tradition, obligation

(Stanford Friedman 2001: 493)

4 Like most gift-centered economies, the older worlds celebrated by the Celtic Revival were not egalitarian but hierarchical. They were not, however, exploitative by Marxist definition, so that their utopian expression has to be judged in relation both to capitalist society and to those still thriving inheritances from older modes, such as patriarchy and clan/kin superiority.

5 I insist here on the durability of the marketplace because I take the evils of capitalism to derive from a transcending, reified culture of the market in capitalist imperialism, not from the commodity economy itself which is present in many non-exploitative societies where varieties of gift economy, rather, are reified as a primary order and horizon of values. It is worth noting, too, that the figure of the chimera can be sought in the property objects of such economies, perhaps even more starkly than in subject types. Douglas Mao's study (1998) is an exercise in this kind of historical anthropology, trying to get inside those real and imagined objects produced in, by, or for modernist tastes which harbor shadows and forces resistant to capitalist assimilation.

Bibliography

Didion, J. (1979) *The White Album*, New York: Farrar, Straus, and Giroux.
Eliot, T. S. (1976) *The Sacred Wood: Essays on Poetry and Criticism*, London: Methuen.
Friedman, S. (2001) "Definitional Excursions: The Meanings of Modern/Modernity/ Modernism," *Modernism/Modernity* 8(3): 493–513.
Jameson, F. (1979) *Fables of Aggression: Wyndham Lewis, the Modernist as Fascist*, Berkeley, Los Angeles, London: University of California Press.
—— (2005) *Archeologies of the Future: The Desire Called Utopia and Other Science Fictions*, New York: Verso.
Mao, D. (1998) *Solid Objects: Modernism and the Test of Production*, Princeton: Princeton University Press.

6 Invisible times

Modernism as ruptural unity

C. D. Blanton

As regards art, it is well known that some of its peaks by no means correspond to the general development of society; nor do they therefore to the material substructure, the skeleton as it were of its organisation ... It is even acknowledged that certain branches of art, e.g. the *epos*, can no longer be produced in their epoch-making classic form after artistic production as such has begun; in other words that certain important creations within the compass of art are only possible at an early stage in the development of art. If this is the case with regard to different branches of art within the sphere of art itself, it is not so remarkable that this should also be the case with regard to the entire sphere of art and its relation to the general development of society. The difficulty lies only in the general formulation of these contradictions.

(Marx 1970: 215–16)

Practicing modernism

Struggling in 1939 to distinguish the varieties of cultural production of a "capitalism in decline," Clement Greenberg famously divided the notion of modernism into two agonistically related fields: "One and the same civilization produces simultaneously two such different things as a poem by T. S. Eliot and a Tin Pan Alley song, or a painting by Braque and a *Saturday Evening Post* cover" (Greenberg 1986–93, vol. 1: 6). Originating as the cultural logic of industrialized mass production and urbanization, Greenberg's *Kitsch* is not less valid or even less ambitious than its more experimental other. Indeed, to the degree it maintains illusions of content, literacy, and communication, it is perhaps more so. *Kitsch* merely lacks the capacity to reflect its own enabling conditions. For the *avant-garde*, conversely, such reflections become the very substance of art, a last protest against the mechanical formalism of a "motionless Alexandrianism," launched by a class fraction "unwilling to accept this last phase for our own culture" (Greenberg 1986–93, vol. 1: 6):

A society, as it becomes less and less able, in the course of its development, to justify the inevitability of its particular forms, breaks up the accepted notions upon which artists and writers must depend in large part for communication with their audiences. It becomes difficult to assume anything. All the verities involved by religion, authority, tradition, style, are thrown into question, and the writer or artist is no longer able to estimate the response of his audience to the symbols and references with which he works.

(Greenberg 1986–93, vol. 1: 6)

Deprived of any assurance of common reference, art ultimately forsakes reference altogether, sacrificing communication to the emancipation of technique. For Greenberg, art begins to refract mimesis back upon itself, undertaking the "the imitation of imitating" (Greenberg 1986–93, vol. 1: 9):

> In turning away from subject matter of common experience, the poet or artist turns it in upon the medium of his own craft. The nonrepresentational or "abstract," if it is to have aesthetic validity, cannot be arbitrary and accidental, but must stem from obedience to some worthy constraint or original. This constraint, once the world of common, extraverted experience has been renounced, can only be found in the processes or disciplines by which art and literature have already imitated the former. These themselves become the subject matter of art and literature.
>
> (Greenberg 1986–93, vol. 1: 8–9)

Greenberg's argument is incipiently dialectical, partially registering what Adorno later named "the crisis of semblance," that turn through which modern art entrusts itself to "signs that have forgotten themselves and become absolute" (Adorno 1997: 101, 95). Modernist art, under such an account, undertakes the passage of form into content. But perhaps paradoxically, *Kitsch* does the same, albeit by different and less complicated means, reproducing a sense of form scavenged from "a fully matured cultural tradition, whose discoveries, acquisitions, and perfected self-consciousness kitsch can take advantage of for its own ends" (Greenberg 1986–93, vol. 1: 12). In either case, art proceeds by imitation—the imitation of imitating or the imitation of what has been imitated already—reframing itself invariably as an elaboration of its conditions of production: "If the avant-garde imitates the processes of art, Kitsch, we now see, imitates its effects" (Greenberg 1986–93, vol. 1: 17). What is perhaps most notable in either of Greenberg's formulations is that art imitates, but without imitating anything in particular. No longer defined by reference to an object, both *avant-garde* and *Kitsch* mimic a negation, attempting (in T. J. Clark's paraphrase) "to capture the lack of consistent and repeatable meanings in the culture—to capture the lack and make it over into form" (Clark 1982: 154). For an *avant-garde* compelled by "the necessity of an escape from ideas" that can themselves be reproduced and exchanged, the very ease of imitation requires "a new and greater emphasis on form" (Greenberg 1986–93, vol. 1: 28). The simple question that is never quite answered, of course, is what happens next. For the last stage of the formalist argument is not about art at all, but swerves rather toward the broader field of culture that organizes artistic production. Looking to socialism "*simply* for the preservation of whatever living culture we have right now"

(Greenberg 1986–93, vol. 1: 22), Greenberg abandons all claims for autonomy: "Here," he argues, "as in every other question today, it becomes necessary to quote Marx word for word" (Greenberg 1986–93, vol. 1: 22).

In fact, Greenberg never manages to quote Marx directly. Five years later, however, responding to Eliot's own increasingly austere cultural polemic, he would return to the apparent contradiction between modernist poetry and Tin Pan Alley again, and to the mildly desperate, seemingly dated dream of a future socialism.

> Now, however, that Western industrial capitalism is in the process of establishing a global economy with coordinated methods of production on all continents, the possibility of a global Culture appears. Only socialism can realize such a Culture, and it could do so only by accepting and even encouraging regional variations. Meanwhile our deteriorating Western Culture duplicates—and will do so increasingly—the imperialist and exploitative role of Western capitalism. The colonial Cultures, more of them decrepit in any case, are being done to death by mass-produced, ready-made commodities exported from New York and California. There will soon be little diversity of Culture for Mr Eliot's common religious faith to unify. There will just be greater and lesser degrees of backwardness; and the unifying agents will be movies, comic books, Tin Pan Alley, the Luce publications (with editions in all languages), Coca-Cola, rayon stockings, class interests, and a common boss.
>
> (Greenberg 1986–93, vol. 1: 219–20)

There is much else to linger over in Greenberg's melodramatic plaint: the specter of an emergent global economy predicated on the reorganization of an imperial model under American hegemony; the now predictable conversion of mimesis into mass-production, ready-mades back into commodities, signs in either case of an ongoing cultural degeneration; the reduction of the printed word to a series of trademarked abstractions like *Time*, *Life*, and Coca-Cola. There is the keen critical sympathy that leads Greenberg (quite rightly) to sense "the omnipresence of Marx" even in Eliot's conservatism, counter-intuitively aware (as he would put it in *Art and Culture* some years later) that the poet's account of culture "has the merit of sending us back to Marx and his beginning" (Greenberg 1989: 26). But perhaps most notably, those ideas from which artists once sought to escape have become "unifying agents" instead, evidence of the power of a single idea—Western industrial capitalism, backed by military force and bad taste—that displaces all others. Subordinated to such a structure, diverse elements of culture assume another aspect, each functioning as the particular and partial manifestation of a concept that regulates production in general. Yoked together as discrete components of an emergent system, previously unrelated phases and planes of development are rearticulated as "greater and lesser degrees of backwardness," incremental deviations from an American industrial norm newly codified in the global institutions of the postwar world.

Momentarily at least, Greenberg's language is more Leninist than Marxian. The products of culture—art or *Kitsch* almost indifferently—incorporate the systemic fact of industrial reproduction not by referring to its concept but rather by including it, cumulatively forming a global index of backwardness. Culture itself becomes an abstraction that can only be approximated metonymically, an almost Lukácsian totality that nevertheless informs each of its provisional instantiations. It is here of course that Greenberg's argument notoriously verges into difficulty. If it is *Kitsch* rather than the *avant-garde* that most effectively usurps art's mimetic logic, forcing modernism into a tortuously attenuated "imitation of imitating," then modernist art itself threatens to lapse into a secondary phenomenon: Kitsch once mediated. Modernism's famous isolation of medium, it turns out, conceals not only the materiality of aesthetic form, but also and more decisively encodes the very system of production that it resists. Each artistic medium, on such a premise, specifies not only an artistic practice but also a distinct historical temporality, a coefficient of "backwardness" measurable by its non-correlation to "coordinated methods of production on all continents."

More fully even than autonomy or medium, it is this odd unity of discrepant times that allows the general formulation of modernism as a contradiction. And it is this unity—what I will ultimately follow Louis Althusser to term a "ruptural unity" (Althusser 2005: 99)—that simultaneously marks the site at which critical theory emerges as the dialectical counterpart of any coherent account of modernism more broadly, passing beyond the limit of mere formalism in order to recognize in artistic practice a fundamentally conceptual enterprise. By 1960, Greenberg's own negotiation of that tension would collapse, with the insistence that "Modernism has never meant, and does not mean now, anything like a break with the past" and the announcement of his most portable critical axiom: "Modernist art develops out of the past without gap or break, and wherever it may end up it will never cease being intelligible in terms of the past" (Greenberg 1986–93, vol. 4: 92). But in the exploitation of "the characteristic methods of a discipline to criticize the discipline itself, not in order to subvert it but in order to entrench it more firmly in its area of competence" (Greenberg 1986–93, vol. 4: 85), Greenberg's vision of the critical project of a post-Kantian modernity also sketches the first movement of an immanent theoretical enterprise, a thinking of the aesthetic "from the inside, through the procedures themselves of that which is being criticized" (Greenberg 1986–93, vol. 4: 85). That claim, needless to say, is familiar enough. For Paul de Man, "theory can be said to come into being ... when the object of discussion is no longer the meaning or the value but the modalities of production and of reception of meaning and of value prior to their establishment" (de Man 1986: 7). More recently, Fredric Jameson has argued that "theory begins to supplant philosophy (and other disciplines as well) at the moment it is realized that thought is linguistic or material and that concepts cannot exist independently of their linguistic expression" (Jameson 2004: 403). In that sense, theory too marks a turn into medium, one more domain cast back on its own practices.

But it is that other sense of abstraction—the real abstraction (echoing Marx again) against which a history of backwardness emerges—that I wish to measure here. If modernism initiates the incipiently dialectical movement away from figuration to surface that culminates in the almost unqualified autonomy of the individual work and the several arts—what Jameson has termed the "ideology of modernism" (Jameson 2002: 169)—it also marks the coalescence of an art oriented toward the unified concept of production. At a surreptitious second degree, the liberation of technique proclaims the emergence of art as such, only to requalify that notion of art as the imprint of an idea of production gone universal. Lodged within this double account of abstraction, with its passage from the language of art to that of a distinct materialism, is a movement that usurps even the autonomy of conceptual language, reinscribing philosophy itself as a medium for the metonymic description of a global concept of production in its particular effects.

Practicing theory

I began this essay by quoting Marx word for word, with a famous fragment in which the history of art emerges as the site of a distinct contradiction between the seemingly autonomous developmental rhythm of discrete "branches" of art and the larger social totality of which it forms an uneasy and heteronomous part. Art, Marx suggests, not only resists the notion of progress "understood in the usual abstract form"; it also and more pointedly formulates a contrary insight, foregrounding the *"unequal development of material production and, e.g. that of art"* (Marx 1970: 215). Artistic form's capacity to cut across and complicate developmental narratives, to inhabit multiple and distant historical moments at once, inevitably disrupts and disorders even the most subtle of dialectical models. For Marx, art is the tenacious problem that gives rise to a thought of uneven development. In another sense, however, it is also the mechanism through which a "general formulation of these contradictions" becomes possible. It is precisely *through* art's non-correlation with the normative fact of universal reproduction that uneven development can be measured. The sensuous particularity of art thus marks and maintains a temporal lag that resists the notion of development, even as the gap between the various arts or between society and "the entire sphere of art" assumes the structure of a philosophical concept, rigorously confounding, even systematically negating, the universal with the particular. Modernism's liberation of the particular will in this sense become not only a mode of resistance to imitation but also, and far more importantly, a strategic possibility to be renewed long after its moment has seemingly passed, a theoretical practice that inclines precisely *toward* a certain backwardness constantly in the process of disappearing. Or to say the same thing another way, modernism entails the work of theory.

This is not to argue that the need to grapple with the conceptual fact of modernism imposes some ongoing discursive obligation to theory as a critical code, that we must in some fashionable (or perhaps now unfashionable) way speak theoretically. Nor is it to suggest that the emergence of critical theory as a discursive mode belongs strictly to the strange historical and aesthetic phase that modernism represents, arising in opposition to that traditional theory that Horkheimer described as "stored-up knowledge, put in a form that makes it useful for the closest possible description of facts" (1972: 188) or as the vestige, in Adorno's phrase, of a pallid philosophy that "lives on because the moment to realize it was missed" (1973: 3). Both of these may be quite true, but the invocation of theory in any of these senses implies a particular and limited notion of its work, reinscribing the idea of a belated hermeneutics aspiring in the wake of modernism to the methodological self-sufficiency of a practice. Both presume, in other words, that modernism, once finished, merely bequeaths the conditions of theory and that theory deals retrospectively in questions of meaning. I propose the converse: that modernism also *presupposes* a domain—and more importantly, a practice—of theory, takes theory in fact as its first object of imitation and ultimate negation.

To put it more crudely, the overlapping and occasionally skewed involutions of form that have been patched together for the last century (or more) into a roughly textured historical concept of modernism must be conceived also as an onset of theory. Figures as otherwise diverse as Stanley Cavell and Thierry de Duve have insisted that the very idea of a modernist practice is predicated upon a prior structure of criticism or judgment, upon some need—renewed with every work that would claim to be art at all—to decide exactly what art is (see Cavell 2002: 188–9; de Duve 1996: 3–85). The obvious impossibility of rendering any such judgment definitively, of fixing art to an affirmative concept, only underscores the restless movement by which a sensuous particular strains after the general. So understood, the work of art necessarily exerts a conceptual claim, inevitably partial and perhaps tendentious, even as it casts any self-sufficient concept of art as such into question. More recently, Jacques Rancière has discerned in this necessary self-questioning an emergent "aesthetic regime of the arts," describing the displacement of older platonic or mimetic definitions by a modernity "that strictly identifies art in the singular and frees it from any specific rule, from any hierarchy of the arts, subject matter, genres" (Rancière 2004: 23). Detached from classical canons of representation and shaped by "the concept … of a historically determinate unstable disjunction" (Rancière 2007: 72), such an art remains caught in the gap, bound to the conceptual even as it fails to define its own concept. In effect, it reduces philosophy to its own medium and, in the process, forces its collapse back into an account of the history of production. To speak of aesthetic theory, then, is to note the philosophical work that art fails to do, constituting itself as art by that very failure.

In the shadow of modernism, proclamations of theory's death will thus not be wrong so much as irrelevant: confessions of an inability to account not merely for modernism, but also for art, oblivious to the pressure of the unifying agent that predicates the individual work of art. Noting the critical advent of "new modernisms," attended by the organizing orthodoxies of "modernist studies," I therefore insist that (for all its abundant contradiction and apparent diversity) modernism remains conceptually singular, as resistant to the fraying effects of a fashionable but scholarly positivism as it is to the banality of "study" itself. Modernism cannot in any simple sense be studied as an object or even strictly delimited in time, though it may be practiced and it may be thought. What is at stake, then, is not an end of theory but a beginning, a procedural crossing point at which conventional logical categories of form and content suddenly invert, inverting too the anchorages of aesthetic form. In this sense, an account of modernism undertaken in its historical wake begins from the problem of art as a determinate theoretical activity that calls critical concepts into being. Modernism becomes a stage in the dialectic of theory as such.

Crucial to this understanding is the Althusserian reimagination of the Marxian dialectic as an epistemological break from the spiritual unities of Hegelian historicism, predicated on the fundamental non-correspondence of determinant fields within any given historical conjuncture. Theory in this sense undergoes its own effect of non-correspondence: assuming both a discrete demotic meaning (a "theoretical practice" that "works on a raw material (representations, concepts, facts) which it is given by other practices, whether 'empirical', 'technical', or 'ideological'" [Althusser 2005: 167]) and an ultimate one (as Theory in general, "the materialist dialectic which is none other than dialectical materialism" [Althusser 2005: 168]). Between these spontaneous and scientific senses of theory, however, lies a transformative zone of labor, where knowledges are both broken down and reconstituted, a region of autonomization through which various social domains must, in a sense, find their own historical way. Among what Althusser terms "these risky but existing *avant-garde* domains" (2005: 172) concerned with culture and ideology, domains such as art, "theory" (distinguished by inverted commas) thus delineates something distant from a speculative move into abstraction, instead indicating "a specific practice which acts as its own object and ends in its own *product*: a *knowledge*" (Althusser 2005: 173).

In Althusser's sense, the problem of art is both like and unlike that of other theoretical domains. Almost uniquely, its materials and techniques range broadly across the field of social production in general, without ever becoming merely reducible to that system. Indeed, Althusser seems to maintain the Kantian premise that allowed Greenberg to specify art's modernity when he argues

> the real difference between art and science lies in the *specific form* in which they give us the same object in quite different ways: art in the form of "seeing" and "perceiving" or "feeling," science in the form of *knowledge* (in the strict sense, by concepts).
>
> (Althusser 2001: 153)

The moment art begins to formulate the components of its own production explicitly, however, and take those components or media as its own material, something else transpires: production itself—understood as the totality of theoretical practices—begins to function as a universal, as the very concept or purpose that Kant's account of judgment denies to the aesthetic. Where a Kantian account would continue to locate art's critical power in its innocence of the concept, Althusser suggests a theoretical break, a sudden transposition from the spontaneous language of taste to that of "theory" in another register:

> Like all knowledge, the knowledge of art presupposes a preliminary *rupture* with the language of *ideological spontaneity* and the constitution of a body of scientific concepts to replace it. It is essential to be conscious of the necessity for this rupture with ideology to be able to undertake the constitution of the edifice of a knowledge of art.
>
> (Althusser 2001: 154)

Yet, such a rupture becomes a moment of production itself, reconstellating the work of art as the particular instantiation of a totality nowhere fully available, nowhere representable as such. Such an art forsakes transparency, rejects the ideologically mannered aspiration to simple plausibility, and abandons familiar mimetic forms naturalized by habit. In a movement already visible in Hegel, art is both abstracted and anatomized, set free as an idealist absolute by its engagement with the concept but ushered simultaneously into the domain of determination rather than reflection (Greenberg 1986–93, vol. 1: 106–10).

It is just such a theoretical labor, a systematic reconceptualization of poiesy as a model of production, that Phillipe Lacoue-Labarthe and Jean-Luc Nancy trace as the history of an eidaesthetics: an artistic practice capable of recuperating the idea beyond philosophy, under the broader trope of theory. The reorientation of art as a privileged site of conceptual production, under such an account, "determines the age we live in as the *critical* age *par excellence*" (Lacoue-Labarthe and Nancy 1988: 16), precisely by "charting the space of what we now refer to … as theory" (Lacoue-Labarthe and Nancy 1988: 16). For Lacoue-Labarthe and Nancy, the literary absolute that impels a Kantian modernity from its romantic origin depends not only on its capacity for autocriticism but also on the resulting construction of an art that "produces the truth of production in itself" (Lacoue-Labarthe and Nancy 1988: 12) and accordingly inaugurates the history of modern dialectical thought. In its very claim to a certain autonomy, the literary (and by implication the broader aesthetic sphere of which it constitutes a privileged vanguard) begins to figure a model of production, something like an abstract diagram of social labor in the radically depersonalized form of romantic genius. What Lacoue-Labarthe and Nancy fail to specify in the history of such a dialectic, however, is its properly dialectical moment, that point of transfiguration at which the alignment of poiesy with production opens the possibility of a subsequent break, one that reattaches the work of art and the concept not to the subject but to the object, to the determinate material substrate that labor and production transform. Conceived as a theoretical practice, modernism might well be taken as eidaesthetics under the sign of negation, as the constitution of a knowledge of production that inheres in the work itself.

Construed on the basis of such a knowledge, art remains distant, not so much artificial as impossible or inhuman. More importantly, it silently encodes the universality of a concept of art that it cannot name, initiating a counter-poiesy that Clark describes as "a work of interminable and absolute decomposition" (Clark 1982: 153), nothing more than "the fact of negation" (ibid.: 154). Greenberg understood this gamble, even if he failed to track its full consequence. Insofar as modernist forms specify their own media as zones of technical inquiry and dissolution, they presume the ultimately hypostasized category of Art upon which Greenberg would increasingly insist, even as they generate the concrete mechanisms through which such categories are conceptually decomposed. Modernism becomes the rough name of that dialectical phase in which the Absolute begins to negotiate a new and different relation to the truth of production, no longer mimetic but, as Adorno suggests, monadic: "The relationship of the work and the universal becomes the more profound the less the work copes explicitly with universalities, the more it becomes infatuated with its own detached world, its material, its problems, its consistency, its way of expression" (Adorno 1992: 297). Modernism is simply the art that no longer *represents* production as a universalizing fact but preserves and incorporates it theoretically as ground, the concept that was always already there.

Vanishing medium

Broadly speaking then, modernism initiates a second order or phase in the history of an eidaesthetics, a negation that amounts also to a theory of production. Its relentless specification of medium separates aesthetic practices from one another, breaking art into atomically distinct but parallel crafts—Kandinsky's point, Pound's line, Le Corbusier's plane, Brecht's gesture, Schoenberg's series—even as it detaches art more generally from the duty of representing other conceptual systems. The work of art is set loose, desubordinated from the incursion of alien hierarchies that would correlate it with external procedures and impose the need to depict, even as the philosophical unity of some grander notion of art enfolds upon itself. As Daniel Albright puts it,

> everything changes as soon as the artist or the critic renounces the goal of mimesis. Suddenly the arts fly apart, because there is no common focal point: sculpture recedes into stone, painting into dyestuff, poetry into depictorialized syllables—each regarding the others with suspicion or hostility.
> (Albright 2000: 13)

The diffusion, however, only permits a different and higher order of concentration: a *"testing of the limits of aesthetic construction"* (Albright 2000: 29, italics in original) that initiates a dialectic of consonance and dissonance, pitting "arts that try to retain the propriety, the apartness, of their private media" against those "that try to lose themselves in some pan-aesthetic whole" (Albright 2000: 33). The grinding force of this tension—already visible in Lessing's attempt to distinguish the specific ranges of expression proper to the various arts—shapes a field of jaggedly contradictory and even incommensurable forms.

But as Rancière insists, this aesthetic regime of the arts entails an immediate contradiction. By suspending the law of representation, art "destroys any pragmatic criterion for isolating this singularity," blurring any distinction between "the autonomy of art and the identity of its forms with the forms that life uses to shape itself" (Rancière 2004: 23). The medium to which art turns permits its ultimate devolution into the world it seeks to evade. By refusing to represent the world, art engages it in other ways. In this sense, any claim for autonomy immediately generates a contrary insight, in the dialectical inversion through which Jameson has recently recuperated and qualified the long narrative of aesthetic autonomy. Reconceiving the trope ironically, Jameson proposes a narrative of "autonomization" instead, renaming the longer eidaesthetic history through which an ideologically constructed Absolute also mediates a relation with the messier elements of the real: "if the autonomy of art means some absolute spiritualization or sublimation beyond the figural, it can dialectically equally well be represented in terms of an absolute materiality" (Jameson 2002: 173).

The trope of autonomization thus preserves the imprint of a notion of aesthetic autonomy while also foregrounding the stricter sense of production captured in the medium itself. Individual arts are not so much freed, therefore, as cut loose from a transcendental mooring, left to float to ground and re-encounter the disparate and contradictory social contents and experiences that they wish to renounce. Under Jameson's argument, a second moment of rupture therefore emerges within the field of art, "achieved by a radical dissociation within the aesthetic itself: by the radical disjunction and separation of literature and art from culture" (Jameson 2002: 176). In one sense, that fissure is the reflexive tension Greenberg describes between *Kitsch* and *avant-garde*, renamed as a function of ideology and recast as "a disjunction internal to the very sphere of the cultural itself, internal to the aesthetic in its widest sense" (Jameson 2002: 177). But, as Jameson insists, such a gap symptomatically marks modernism's ending, the signal announcement of a process of canonization and settlement more properly to be identified with the political and economic situation of late modernism.

But this, after all, is exactly the point at which Greenberg left us in 1944, at the boundary between an art that aspires to some different future and a global system of production that forecloses the aspiration in a nightmarish glut of comic books and Coca-Cola. It is certainly no accident that Greenberg's prophecy of a deferred global culture, like the Eliotic provocation to which it responded, emerges as the modernist interval fades. Indeed, Greenberg seems haltingly to register the translation of modernism into late modernism, discerning the disconcerting potential identity of T. S. Eliot and Tin Pan Alley within a system of abstract aesthetic equivalence and exchange. With the collapse of *avant-garde* into *Kitsch* and the rise of a postwar order, that is, the claim for autonomy has already become a narrative of autonomization. The first effect of the revision lies in a recorrelation of aesthetic terms as political ones. *Avant-garde* and *Kitsch* have now become generic markers of an impossible socialism and an inevitable imperialism respectively, each adopting a different relation to those "unifying agents" of a late capital in which all objects, from stockings to class interests, have become imitative fantasies and *objets d'art*. Even if the socialist gesture remains empty, and even if the strain of Greenberg's increasingly tortured position would only mount as the Cold War reinscribed economic dialectic as political antinomy, the argument leaves open a crucial insight. Recalling Jameson's insistence that "aesthetic autonomy did not yet exist in the modernist period, or only as a by-product and an afterthought" (Jameson 2002: 208), it becomes clear that the critical myth of autonomy was never more than the shifting formal affirmation of a determinate negation, attached all but indifferently to modernist art or socialist politics, but rooted in the coordination and reduplication of methods of production. In a moment of global integration, a moment in which the function of the Absolute has been usurped by the economy itself, autonomization emerges as the counter-intuitive sign of a deeper loss of autonomy, of an ever more complete absorption of figuration itself into the commodified signification of a unitary and singular regime of cultural production. The conclusion is both unyielding and impossible to articulate: any ultimate resistance to the normative and unifying forces would require both the displacement of its productive apparatus *and* an abandonment of the premise of art's autonomy. In order to survive, art must embrace the determinate force of some other system no longer (or not yet) in existence.

What Greenberg's prophecy could describe but not name was nothing less than the emergent mode of production of late capital. If the possibility once known as modernism has ceased to offer any meaningful resistance to *Kitsch*, has in fact been reincorporated as the secondary *Kitsch* of late modernism, it is simply because no material possibility on the order of what Greenberg termed socialism has arisen to reconceive production as such, leaving only the triumphant globalism of mass culture that both Jameson and Andreas Huyssen have identified with the postmodern. In retrospect, however, this ironically postmodern Greenberg opens another possibility. For what is perhaps most valuable in the account of autonomization lies in the reclamation of modernist art not as pure form but rather as vestigial deposits held over from a penultimate historical moment. Recast as "greater and lesser degrees of backwardness," variable markers of distance on the unrelenting way to a world of pure *Kitsch*, *avant-garde* works provide evidence out of time, confirming that modernism itself was but a threshold moment. If *avant-garde* and *Kitsch* have been realigned as the terms of an economic history, across the historical threshold of modernism's ending, and are accordingly reconceived in the light of an endlessly mimetic total system, then modernist art, with its relentless specifications of medium and its programmatic negations, becomes vestigial, outmoded to the point of social obsolescence by its theoretical adherence to a question that is no longer a question. But it is just such an art that, by opening a small space of non-correspondence in a global expanse of pure imitation, maintains the thought of unevenness noticed by Marx.

Within a global economy, then, even modernism is eventually rendered archaic and turned against itself. Out of step with their moment, modernist forms begin to remediate a truth of production that is no longer true, embodying in its place a set of increasingly mysterious forgotten technical operations. Such forms are thus defined by their paradoxical attachment to a process of vanishing. No longer determined in idealist fashion by the sensuous presentation of the idea, they testify instead to the field of the invisible, registering the presence of a lost theoretical practice within a purely synchronic present. In a system of such effacements, the merest reminder of such histories constitutes an anachronistic puncture or (in a provocative phrase of Paul Piccone's) an "artificial negativity" (Piccone 1978: 43), a knowledge now available only as theory. Art, therefore, begins to constitute the visible evidence of an invisible historical break, less a gap than a surplus knowledge that holds the place of a still vacant future. But it is just this remembrance of invisible times that constitutes its remaining work, perhaps even its purpose.

Invisible times

To this point, my argument has involved two basic postulates. First, modernism and the art that it propounds, with its abrogation of the referential structure of imitation, are best understood not as sensuous presentations of the idea but as theoretical practices. Second, such a theoretical practice presupposes a functional universal, an operative concept that turns out to be—even in a formalist vocabulary—nothing less than an entire system of production. In essence, this modernism transposes a romantic Absolute into a materialist register, thereby inverting the concept of art and binding it to an invisible social totality. Autonomization, in this sense, is merely a mode of production in its aesthetic aspect, the shape of an art no longer able to figure production as an image, but forced instead to incorporate the idea in some other way, as knowledge. Recalling Nancy's distinction between an art constituted in images and one conceived in terms of the vestige—a sensible impression by which art captures the movement of something larger and imageless—one might even discern a formula for the expression of a new and global sublimity (Nancy 1996: 96–8). But the Absolute that such vestiges mutely acknowledge is a purely economic concept. If the ideology of autonomy is taken to mean anything at all, it must indicate above all else the paradoxical collapse of a range of more classical semiautonomous conceits, those systems of mediation and determination that Greenberg grouped as the "verities of religion, authority, tradition, and style," and the corollary exposure of art to the more diffuse but more encompassing logics of an incipiently globalized system of exchange. Modernism, in this sense, remains little more than the phenomenal marker of a threshold, delineating the interval between a moment at which an economy of planetary scale becomes possible in the abstract and one at which it emerges in the concrete—the lag between possibility and necessity.

Modernism thus retains its historical specificity only as a transitional term, a symptom of "incomplete modernization" in Jameson's phrase, torn between the fully elaborated logic of late capital and the full range of broken social formations cleared in its path. I have argued also that this reformulation of the problem of the aesthetic, as an ideology of autonomy or an aesthetic regime, should effectively invert our sense of the place of theory, divulging how works of art constitute a theoretical practice that refracts the conceptual edifice of production. If so, the task is not to theorize modernism but to discern what modernism has already theorized. I have recalled already Marx's intimation that art's theoretical uniqueness lies in its tendency to reproduce the problem of historical unevenness at an escalating level of generality: within the media of various arts, across the arts generally, and still more abstractly, as a general form of historical contradiction. Each art, in Marx's sense, follows its own twisting and contradictory history, even as the arts in general seem to lag behind, stretch ahead, or flatly contradict any orderly developmental narrative that would correlate dialectically to their correspondent social forms.

Locally of course, this is simply the historical problem of modernism in its most canonical form, of a conjuncture defined by the extreme confrontation of the archaic and the new, and by all the partial accommodations reached as imaginary resolutions along the way. But the notion of a modernism that collects and mixes the contradictions of multiple social orders, each in the process of assimilation to an emergent economic totality defined by the fundamental invisibility of production, should also alter the problem of periodization that underpins any account of modernism. This contradiction within modernism is familiar enough, echoed in Ezra Pound's claim that "we do not all of us inhabit the same time" (Pound 1968: 87) or in Ernst Bloch's declaration that "[n]ot all people exist in the same Now" (Bloch 1977: 22). If the experience of modernity means anything at all, it is certainly in this simultaneous contemporaneity of the non-contemporaneous and non-contemporaneity of the contemporaneous—and in the construction of an organizing system within which such contradictions become possible. But the labor done by art in such a situation lies precisely in the acknowledgment of the rough striations that history would smooth. At stake is not an opposition between the timeless and the timely, Greenberg's famous claim for a modernism without break, but rather what Peter Osborne describes as "a paradoxical temporal doubling inherent in the conceptual structure of the 'modern' that Greenberg's criticism found increasingly hard to negotiate" (Osborne 2000: 93). The growing incommensurability between an *avant-garde* practice that is "radically temporalizing and historicizing" and a more conventional logic of *Kitsch* that insists on "an evacuation of temporality from the object" (Osborne 2000: 92) renders art an all but unique site of mute historical memory, gathering a multitude of concrete temporalizations, each in a state of material non-correspondence with the other. It is not the autonomy of arts, of forms, or of media, that modernism ultimately acknowledges and asserts against pure contemporaneity, but rather the simultaneous autonomy and coalescence of times.

The periodization of modernism, indeed of the entire history of post-Kantian art, thus entails the delineation of that larger uneven history through which individual theoretical practices are progressively subsumed within a singular global temporality and the corollary recognition of the aesthetic itself as the vestigial field of semiautonomous regions of production in the process of disappearance. Modernization marks not the rise of an autonomous aesthetic but the paradoxical eclipse of autonomy, the slow accession of any exteriority to the reproductions of a culture that belatedly imposes the normative conditions of a transcendental aesthetic, of a unitary space and time, as intuitive orders. Theoretically speaking, the thought of aesthetics, the problem of modernism, thus lies in the retrospective task of assembling the arts as posterior evidence of multiple times of production, "a co-presence of heterogeneous temporalities" that Rancière identifies as "the temporality specific to the aesthetic regime of the arts" (Rancière 2004: 26). This insight completes the theoretical inversion promised by Althusser, the final displacement of an art without purpose into a field that conceives its own product as a knowledge. What such an art shows is time, the structure of temporalization that *Kitsch* obscures and commodifies; what it practices is a materialist dialectic already. To speak of medium, to speak of the imitation of imitating, is to use art as Marx used it, as the evidence of general contradiction, and thereby to take the problem of periodization as a symptomatic index of labor and resistance, the formal trace of a history describable in no other way. It is to take art, as Althusser suggested, as the ground of historical method.

> It is not enough, therefore, to say, as modern historians do, that *there are* different periodizations for different times, that each time has its own rhythms, some short, some long; we must also think these differences in rhythm and punctuation in their foundation, in the type of articulation, displacement, and torsion which harmonizes these different times with one another. To go even further, I should say that we cannot restrict ourselves to reflecting the existence of *visible* and measurable times in this way; we must, of absolute necessity, pose the question of the mode of existence of *invisible* times, of the invisible rhythms and punctuations concealed beneath the surface of each visible time.
>
> (Althusser and Balibar 1997: 100–1)

But what of theory now? Having anchored theory in the thought of modernism rather than in a thought about it, and having consigned that same modernist practice to a transitional phase now certainly past, I have seemingly left little space of operation in the present, little still to be done. Conceptualizing modernism as an endstage of unevenness, or even as a more durably subterranean and invisible time in the present, will certainly amount to little at a moment when culture and *Kitsch* have become fully exchangeable. Rather than reclaiming some contemporary relevance for a modernist practice, I have seemingly guaranteed that even the prospect of an aesthetic theory will follow it into obsolescence. In the identification of modernism as a conjuncture on the threshold of a global economy, however, forced into the negation of representation in order to represent an invisible but determinate system of production, lies a transformative element.

Attempting to solve the Marxian problem of unevenness and devise a general formulation of the form of contradiction that it entails, Althusser hit on the notion of a constellation of semi-autonomous contradictions that under the pressure of a particular moment amass in concert: "an accumulation of 'circumstances' and 'currents' so that whatever their origin and sense … they *'fuse'* into a *ruptural unity*" (Althusser 2005: 99, italics in original). For Althusser, this moment is political and revolutionary, the Leninist instant at which the exacerbated contradictions of relations of production become a material force, able to *"reconstitute* and complete their basic animating unity" in a "contradiction inseparable from the total structure of the social body in which it is found" (Althusser 2005: 100–1, italics in original), both determined and determinate. But if this structure of over-determination describes the political moment of modernism, then it also captures its aesthetic break differently: a unity of formal ruptures as much as a rupture of formal unities, each bound to the formal conditions of its own production and making, to its own semiautonomous contradiction.

To the degree that modernism merely names the arts in a state of ruptural unity, it renders unevenness available as a knowledge, even now. The description of this modernism requires not only the reconstruction of its archive, but also the restoration of its predicates, those temporalizations no longer available except as artistic traces. As such, modernism provides the ground for an elaboration of that social totality that absorbed it, even while maintaining the possibility of an artificial negativity that subsists as a record of invisible times still to come. The difference between *Kitsch* and *avant-garde* was never more than the disparity between practices that reproduce the present and practices that imitate a future we have now failed to inhabit but must continue to know.

Bibliography

Adorno, T. (1973) *Negative Dialectics*, trans. E. B. Ashton, New York: Continuum.
—— (1992) *Notes to Literature*, 2 vols, trans. S. Weber Nicholsen, New York: Columbia University Press.
—— (1997) *Aesthetic Theory*, ed. and trans. R. Hullot-Kentor, Minneapolis: University of Minnesota Press.
Albright, D. (2000) *Untwisting the Serpent: Modernism in Music, Literature, and Other Arts*, Chicago: University of Chicago Press.
Althusser, L. (2001) *Lenin and Philosophy and Other Essays*, trans. B. Brewster, New York: Monthly Review Press.
—— (2005) *For Marx*, trans. B. Brewster, London: Verso.
Althusser, L. and Balibar, E. (1997) *Reading Capital*, trans. B. Brewster, London: Verso.
Bloch, E. (1977) "Nonsynchronism and the Obligation to Its Dialectics," trans. M. Ritter, *New German Critique* 11 (Spring): 22–38.
Cavell, S. (2002) *Must We Mean What We Say?* Cambridge: Cambridge University Press.
Clark, T. J. (1982) "Clement Greenberg's Theory of Art," *Critical Inquiry* 9(1) (September): 139–56.
de Duve, T. (1996) *Kant after Duchamp*, Cambridge, MA: MIT Press.
de Man, P. (1986) *The Resistance to Theory*, Minneapolis: University of Minnesota Press.
Greenberg, C. (1989) *Art and Culture: Critical Essays*, Boston: Beacon Press.
—— (1986–93) *The Collected Essays and Criticism*, 4 vols, ed. J. O'Brian, Chicago: University of Chicago Press.
Hegel, G. W. F. (1998) *Aesthetics: Lectures on Fine Art*, 2 vols, trans. T. M. Knox, Oxford: Clarendon Press.
Horkheimer, M. (1972) *Critical Theory: Selected Essays*, trans. M. J. O'Connell, New York: Herder and Herder.
Huyssen, A. (1986) *After the Great Divide: Modernism, Mass Culture, Postmodernism*, Bloomington: Indiana University Press.
Jameson, F. (2002) *A Singular Modernity: Essay on the Ontology of the Present*, London: Verso.

—— (2004) "Symptoms of Theory or Symptoms for Theory?" *Critical Inquiry* 30 (Winter): 403–8.

Lacoue-Labarthe, P. and Nancy, J.-L. (1988) *The Literary Absolute: The Theory of Literature in German Romanticism*, trans. P. Barbard and C. Lester, Albany: State University of New York Press.

Marx, K. (1970) *A Contribution to the Critique of Political Economy*, ed. M. Dobb, trans. S. W. Ryazanskaya, New York: International Publishers.

Nancy, J.-L. (1996) *The Muses*, trans. P. Kamuf, Stanford: Stanford University Press.

Osborne, P. (2000) *Philosophy in Cultural Theory*, London: Routledge.

Piccone, P. (1978) "The Crisis of One-Dimensionality," *Telos* 35 (Spring): 43–54.

Pound, E. (1968) *Literary Essays*, New York: New Directions.

Rancière, J. (2004) *The Politics of Aesthetics: The Distribution of the Sensible*, trans. G. Rockhill, London: Continuum.

—— (2007) *The Future of the Image*, trans. G. Elliot, London: Verso.

More than a hint of desperation – historicizing modernism

Response to C. D. Blanton

Morag Shiach

Dan Blanton stages a fascinating argument about the temporality of modernism that reads modernist cultural practice in and through the dominant paradigms of literary and artistic critical practice in the second half of the twentieth century. He is thus engaging in a double sense with modernism as both a movement and a moment that exists through the particular discursive regimes that attempt to understand and to some extent to master it. One might perhaps wish to signal a certain unease about the geographical confines of this modernism, and its too comfortable placing within a specific and partial tradition. But that would, I think, be to mistake both what is valuable and what is problematic about Blanton's overall argument. He is engaged precisely in a struggle with the tradition that provides his own critical and theoretical categories, and that is what generates much of the force of his argument. But he is also hoping to find within the oppositions, conflicts and resistances of his chosen texts not simply 'the capacity to reflect [their] own enabling conditions' (p. 137) but also a capacity for historical critique.

Blanton's approach is dialectical in the formal sense that it proceeds through setting in play oppositions that generate a third term or concept, which is then seen to be inadequate or incomplete. From the beginning, for example, the analysis of Greenberg's opposition between kitsch and the avant-garde, also described as an opposition between high and mass culture, sets the tone of Blanton's argument. The opposition is not real in the sense that neither term sustains what is asked of it by Greenberg. Rather, the resistance, the theoretical and historical friction, generated by this separation, is what Blanton finds most productive in Greenberg's work. The opposition, its non-sustainability, the resistance it enables or at least articulates, are all aspects of what Blanton values in Greenberg's thinking. Greenberg is simply the first in a line of critics and theorists who fascinate Blanton because they try to articulate a cultural practice that might, in advanced capitalism, preclude unmediated reincorporation under a regime of consumption. Of course, they fail.

Blanton lays out the apparently inflexible trajectory of Greenberg's position, which leads him ultimately to be caught by 'the simple question that is never quite answered … of course, of what happens next' (p. 138). Greenberg is driven into posing what can only ever be an imaginary, or formalist, understanding of the possibilities of critical or historical resistance. It is here, Blanton argues, that 'Greenberg's argument notoriously verges into difficulty' (p. 140): forcing modernism into a tortuously attenuated "imitation of imitation", then modernist art itself threatens to lapse into … a secondary phenomenon' (p. 140), this 'odd unity of discrepant times' (p. 140) allows Blanton to formulate modernism as contradiction, but also generates for Greenberg, and for Blanton, more than a hint of desperation in the continuing attempt to answer 'the simple question that is never quite answered' (p. 138).

Despite this logic of desperation, Blanton endorses much of Greenberg's project, deeming that in spite of himself Greenberg laid out the productive tensions within any materialist account of modernism. Greenberg, Blanton argues, could not solve the complexity of the relationships and practices he identified, and even veered increasingly away from the true logic that underpinned them. But this veering away was the condition of possibility, Blanton argues, for the belatedly modernist enterprise of theory.

'Theory' here becomes the new terrain on which the desire for a productively historical critique is played out. It represents the possibility of an immanent critique within the ideology of modernism. Blanton also, through a particular reading of Jameson, proposes that the defining feature of 'theory' is its disjuncture from philosophy: theory is able to articulate what philosophy has occluded, which is the understanding that thought is material and generated through and in the linguistic medium of its expression.

Blanton is not arguing that theory is simply a tool that will allow us better to capture the unfolding logic of modernist cultural practice. Blanton's claim for and of theory seems to me to be much stronger than this. It is, he argues, rather the case that the emergence of modernism must also be understood as the beginning of 'theory': modernism is thus an inherently theoretical cultural mode. Blanton's own theoretical frame for this argument is familiar, ranging from Paul de Man, Louis Althusser and Immanuel Kant to Philippe Lacoue-Labarthe and Jean-Luc Nancy. The names are shorthand for complex theoretical work, whose significance and relevance to Blanton's overall argument are not in any doubt.

But is it really possible to range these voices so confidently along the front of 'theory', particularly when theory is seen as something so distinct from philosophy? Here, I think, Blanton demonstrates something of his own hint of desperation to articulate a distinct space of sustainable cultural knowledge and critique. How would his argument be different if we were to insist that this tradition he is invoking is in fact one of philosophy? Continental philosophy certainly, but Kant, Althusser, and indeed Marx to whom he also refers frequently and effectively certainly have a claim to be read most coherently as part of a philosophical tradition with a much longer historical trajectory than the one Blanton offers for theory.

'Theory' risks in this analysis becoming an ideological rather than a historical category. Blanton seems to need the rupture between theory and philosophy to underpin the logic of his argument: but is it really either defensible or sustainable? When did we begin to think in terms of 'theory' as a distinct practice? And how did it come to be articulated as something distinct from, and even beyond, philosophical inquiry? The notion of such a definitive rupture certainly appears in a text such as Tel Quel's *Théorie d'ensemble* (1968) and then seems to gather momentum in the diffuse Althusserianism of the 1970s. By the 1980s it had become the space in which a range of fundamental arguments about culture, history, politics, and the academy were played out. 'Theory' in that sense matters, and is certainly worth defending as a form of cultural and critical practice that was capable of disruption as well as insight.

But theory as a mode of inquiry that has left the domain of philosophy and entered into a uniquely productive relationship with modernism seems to me to be a much more problematic category. It is really only in the Anglo-American tradition that we have made this cultural practice so concrete and embedded it in curricula and in texts. Maybe that does not matter for Blanton's argument, as this is the very cultural space he is seeking to understand. But I am still uneasy with the extent to which this rupture is rhetorically invoked, when I am not sure that it can be either theoretically or philosophically maintained.

Across Blanton's chapter a fascinating set of dialectical oppositions are teased out, worked through and then ultimately displaced, leaving a sense of the potential and the frustrations of the 'uneven development' with which his argument began. These oppositions begin with the invocation of moments of rupture, which are the energetic and historical cause of the complex historical unfolding of modernism in Blanton's analysis.

As I have suggested above, the epistemological and historical contours of some of these ruptures need fuller exposition if we are not to find ourselves driven by the desperation that underpins our desire for sustainable critique onto what is in the end just another twist in the tail of the logic of reproduction. But there is also more than one way to read a rupture, which takes me finally to the 'Eliotic provocation' to which Blanton refers so tantalizingly. Invoking Eliot reminds us sharply that rupture can be experienced, or theorized, as loss, rather than as the possibility of knowledge or of a genuinely critical practice as Blanton prefers. When Eliot conjured up the notion of a 'dissociation of sensibility' in his 1921 essay 'The Metaphysical Poets', he was naming a rupture that had produced in his view a kind of cultural and historical slackening. As Eliot put it in this essay, 'a dissociation of sensibility set in from which we have never recovered' (Eliot 1975: 64). If, as Blanton concludes, modernism 'names the arts in a state of ruptural unity' how can we be sure whether this rupture signals the movement of a dialectical logic or the stasis and cultural pessimisms of the Eliotic loss?

Bibliography

Eliot, T. S. (1975) 'The Metaphysical Poets', in *Selected Prose of T. S. Eliot*, ed. F. Kermode, London: Faber and Faber.

7 "This new evolution of art"

Adorno's modernism as a re-orientation of aesthetics

Oleg Gelikman

In contrast to virtually everything said on the subject of modernism, Theodor Adorno maintained that the nineteenth-century equation of the modern with the new had introduced a negative, reductive, contentless term that must not be allowed to dominate the critical discussion of modernism in an unanalyzed form: "The new is a blind spot, as empty as the indexical gesture 'look here'" (Adorno 1997: 20).[1] Making it new, modernism gestures toward the void that propels it. As a privative concept, the new indicates the absence of the old, the familiar and the expected. Because the new must always be determined anew, the content the category received in various modernist reincarnations conceals the stagnation in the overall historical process. This stasis is the dialectical counterpart to the velocity of modernist innovation, and a key to its reinterpretation. The value of Adorno's *Aesthetic Theory* today consists in delivering a comprehensive analysis of modernism guided by the critique of the new as the blind spot in its critical self-understanding.

Despite and, no doubt, by virtue of being unfinished, Adorno's treatise holds considerable promise, not least because its analysis of modernism conducts a meta-critique of traditional aesthetics. I argue that Adorno's conception of modernism as a normative condition of art, his account of the negative dialectic of tradition in modernism, and his materialist theory of the artwork collectively provide a viable alternative to the unhappy choice that the criticism of modernist art makes vis-à-vis its recalcitrant objects: either to apply extrinsic explanatory schemes or to employ the reflexive discourse of the artists as a basis of analysis.

Given Adorno's considerable attachment to the concept of the gesture (and especially an empty one), the depreciation of the new in *Aesthetic Theory* is not to be mistaken for a suppression of this category. The inability of the new to account for the *metaphysical* significance of modernism does not disqualify this concept from a theoretical reconstruction.[2] On the contrary. Pursuing a dialectical strategy, *Aesthetic Theory* grants the new the considerable authority of a failed attempt to master the experience of modernity of art. Adorno appeals to the historical experience of this failure as the source of conceptual material absent in the concept of the modern as the new:

> The experience of the modern says more, even though its concept, however qualitative it may be, labors under its own abstractness. Its concept is

privative; since its origins it is more the negation of what no longer holds than a positive slogan.

(Adorno 1997: 21)

According to Adorno, the experience of the modern, when distilled to its historical essence, consists in the exaggerated wish to banish the past which has become intolerable simply for being the past. Modernism treats the past as an instance of magical guilt adhering to the historical process as such. In Adorno's analysis, the following (rather familiar) paradox confirms modernism's ignorance of its mythical relation to the past: when modernist art tries to exhibit the new aesthetic or metaphysical content promised by its concept, it becomes a collection of experimental techniques unable to last in their newness. These innovations somehow grow even older than the tradition they wish to abolish and thus become disposable. Because the newness secured through purely technical experimentation remains a product of a decision, intentionality attaches itself to the formal techniques and thereby dissipates the objectivity the artwork requires. Plagued by the contradiction between the voluntarist interpretation of the new and the intentionless nature of the artwork (its entelechy), the ideological claim of the modern to the new insures that the new becomes modernism's nemesis:

> By exigency, the new must be something willed; as what is other, however, it could not be what is willed. Velleity binds the new to the ever-same, and this establishes the inner communication of the modern and myth. The new wants non-identity, yet intention reduces it to identity; modern art constantly works at the Munchhausean trick of carrying out the identification of the nonidentical.[3]

(Adorno 1997: 22–3)

Adorno insists that the cult of the new that, on Baudelaire's authority, served to make modernism into a movement has to be taken for a self-defeating proposition first imposed upon early modernism by the forces of historical development, and then erected into a self-evident truth feeding off the semantic tautology of the modern and the new. Provocatively insisting on the regressive function of the new, Adorno laments that its mythic "inevitability usurps the truth. Innumerable artworks suffer from the fact that they lay claim to being a process of self-transformation and development and yet subsist as timeless sequence of what is ever-the-same" (Adorno 1997: 129).[4] Surrealist automatic writing succinctly illustrates Adorno's point. Originally summoned by André Breton and Phillipe Soupault to enable registration of spontaneous psychic processes, the procedure of jotting down anything that comes to mind at the highest possible speed quickly grew predictable and was abandoned. As stylistic examination of automatic writing shows, it is bound by the law of "semantic incompatibilities." This law, rather than incarnating spontaneity, happened to be the first convention that came along during Breton-Soupault 1919 sessions for *Les Champs magnétiques*.[5] Instead of being an instance of liberation, automatic writing dramatically re-asserted the power of convention—a case of the return of the "ever-the-same" in Adorno's terms. One cannot will the new into being, and spontaneity ossifies into an arbitrary rule precisely when pursued for its own sake. Neither a property of the object nor a manifestation of the subject, the new eludes the dialectic of identity altogether. The new is a historical variable and as such it exhausts the metaphysical thinking in the German Idealist cast.

Because the new cannot be an object of the will, Adorno denies that formal innovation is a primary distinguishing feature of modernism. Instead, he treats technical experimentation as a surface phenomenon that, when absolutized, leads to the narrowly subjectivist, voluntarist interpretations of modernism or the formalist histories predicating the autonomy of art on the increasing mastery of its medium.[6] These two seemingly opposed narratives of modernism—modern art as a chapter in the progressive emergence of autonomous subjectivity, or as a struggle for the minimal convention the medium would tolerate—share a fatal flaw of conceding that modernism is reducible to a set of individual aberrations or a temporary condition of art practice. As a result, these narratives of modernism obscure what Adorno posits as the historical essence of their object—the entanglement of modernism with tradition:

> Given that the category of the new was a result of historical process that destroyed a specific tradition and then tradition as such, modern art cannot be an aberration susceptible to correction by returning to foundations that no longer should or do exist.[7]
>
> (Adorno 1997: 23)

Rather than a conquest of the new, Adorno's modernism is a contradictory negotiation between the social, economic, and psychological reality that the industrial age forced onto art and the imperatives of the tradition the artists of the industrial epoch could neither fulfill nor dismiss.

The historical relevance of Adorno's conception of modernism is borne out by the fact that, without being equally committed to formal innovation, the early French modernists—Baudelaire, Flaubert, and Manet—display commitment to tradition as a (potentially) infinite continuum of interrelated artworks that appears exorbitant in comparison with the complacency of their Romantic peers. Arguably, because of this exorbitance they registered the conflict that threatened the practice of art with anachronism, and assumed a genuinely modernist stance vis-à-vis preceding art.

The unraveling of the tradition was an event more uncanny than the heroic narratives of modernism's origin allow. *Pace* Valéry, it is not that someone or something named Baudelaire destroyed the tradition because he was dissatisfied with the possibilities it handed down to him.[8] Has a writer who felt otherwise ever existed? Doesn't the dissatisfaction with those traditional possibilities confirm the vitality of one's faith in the regenerative powers of tradition? As if catching himself in the act of addressing someone who is no longer there, Baudelaire was overcome by a sense that tradition had already left the historical space of art. The images of death and mortification that dominate *Les Fleurs du mal* thus are products of the displacement of the objective situation of poetry into a metaphysical category. Rather than designating an object, Baudelaire's nomination of the new as the telos of *l'art moderne* has its positive content in the implicit assertion that one could no longer expect the tradition to supply constraints or grounds of comparison that will last into the future, or expect that the misunderstandings attendant upon the immediate reception of the artwork will eventually be redressed.

The cult of the new, then, reacts to a realization that the withdrawal of tradition leaves the practice of art defenseless and perishable, and consequently marks the moment when tradition and traditional art diverge. Modernism emerged at the precise historical point when traditional art was no longer viable as a social practice but reference to tradition was still subjectively necessary. According to Adorno, the qualitative difference between modernism and traditional art resides in the fact that modernism does not "negate previous artistic practices, as styles have done through the ages, but rather the tradition itself" (Adorno 1997: 21). What does it mean to "negate the tradition as such"? What difference does the difference between negating a past style within the framework of tradition and negating the tradition as such make for our understanding of modernism? I approach these questions by way of a text distinguished by the intensity of its commitment to the modern as the new—Mallarmé's presentation of Edouard Manet to the British public in 1876.

Mallarmé's swimming lesson: navigating modern painting

Looking back at *Olympia* and *Déjeuner sur l'herbe* after Malraux, Bataille, Aby Warburg, T. J. Clark, Michael Frieds and many others, we have grown accustomed to seeing Manet as the original modernist. But Manet already seemed the revelation of modernism to the speculative eye of his friend Stéphane Mallarmé. On September 30, 1876, the French poet presented his vision in a London art magazine, *Art Monthly Review*, as "The Impressionists and Edouard Manet." The essay develops an argument about the task and history of modern art based on a statement Mallarmé attributed to the painter:

> Each time one begins a picture one plunges headlong into it, and feels like a man who knows that his surest plan to learn to swim safely is, dangerous as it may seem, to throw himself into water. No one should paint a landscape and a figure by the same process, with the same knowledge, or in the same fashion; nor, what is more, even two landscapes or two figures. Each work should be a new creation of the mind. The hand, it is true, will conserve some of its acquired secrets of manipulation, but the eye should forget all else it has seen, and learn anew from the lessons before it. It should abstract itself from memory, seeing only that which it looks upon, and that as for the first time; and the hand should become an impersonal abstraction guided only by the will, oblivious to all previous cunning.[9]

(Mallarmé 1994: 232)

Having expressed appreciation for Baudelaire's art criticism earlier in the essay, here Mallarmé issues a call (via Manet's ambitions) to undo the dark sarcasm of "Le Voyage," the final poem of *Les Fleurs du mal*:

> Nous voulons, tant ce feu nous brûle le cerveau,
> Plonger au fond du gouffre, Enfer ou Ciel, qu'importe?
> Au fond de l'Inconnu pour trouver du *nouveau*!
>
> (Baudelaire 1975: 134)

This exhortation is addressed to Death, the "old captain," thereby confirming the intertwining of the old and the new (or: modernism and sacrifice) as a primary datum of Baudelaire's historical consciousness. Equally disturbing is the fact that, for Baudelaire, historical progression was an agent of debilitation of artistic faculties; earlier in the same poem, he exclaims: "Aux yeux du souvenir que le monde est petit!" Content to deliver the curse of the new, the envoi of Baudelaire's "Le Voyage" delegated to subsequent art the task of breaking the impasse that constituted its climax. The pitch of Mallarmé's language reveals that his painter is possessed by a fever commensurate with the one attacking Baudelaire's crew. Can a different navigation toward the new take place? If, as Mallarmé asserts, modernity renders the traditional foundations of art obsolete, how does Manet offset this loss?

Modernism swims dangerously, choosing to risk going under over forfeiting the claim to complete emancipation from the historical duration that gave rise to it. The peremptory declaration informs the public that now—i.e. as of Manet— the value of art can no longer be apprehended on the basis of genre conventions like those of landscape or the nude. Now art will no longer live through comparison with its past. Now the time of art will be measured by works, not by periods, schools or even artists. Each work separates the artist from all that he has learned and all that he has seen. What he cannot forget, the "acquired secrets of manipulation," must be put in the service of an unmediated view of the virginal experience that lies before him, as yet unknown even to the artist himself. The artist must be a creature of the will before being a sensate body or a member of his guild. To produce art suited for his age, the artist of modern life must become inhuman—"an impersonal abstraction guided only by the will."

This eloquent advocacy of the new, however, engendered in Mallarmé as much anxiety as it was meant to relieve; besides, taking swimming lessons from the poet famous for allegorical treatments of shipwrecks and drownings might not be the safest occupation. In the comment Mallarmé appends to this passage, the poet retreats into traditional piety before the masters of art and delivers the pre-emptive slap on the wrist: "Such a result cannot be attained at once. To reach it the master must pass through many phases ere this isolation can be acquired, and this new evolution of art be learnt" (Mallarmé 1994: 233).

The dramatic finale of Mallarmé's presentation of Manet offers a representative sample of the self-defeating logic evinced by Adorno's dialectical analysis of the equation of the modern with the new. From the standpoint of *Aesthetic Theory*, Mallarmé's statement is valuable not by virtue of documenting the historical fact of Manet's breakthrough to visual experience unmediated by aesthetic construction, but by presenting the ideological conditions through which art remained a meaningful practice at a critical point in the history of modernity. The theses of "The Impressionists and Edouard Manet" articulate a normative *fiction* constitutive of the condition of art known as modernism. In the quotation above, this fiction exists in Mallarmé's predication of the possibility of art on the total effacement of its prior poetics or eradication of the tradition. It subtends his recommendation of the willful forgetting of the lessons of the hand in favor of the apprenticeship to the eye. It underlies his endorsement of "impersonal abstraction" as the real signatory of the hypothetical work of art and his positing the heuristic suspension of the genre conventions as the origin of the new evolution of art. In the guise of evident practical imperatives, these lines are an apology of the pure experience as the surrogate for the tradition in its function of the medium of continuity of art.

Mallarmé posits experience as the new totality capable of making modern art as meaningful a practice as traditional art used to be. The notion of experience, then, would negate the "tradition as such." Though one can neither articulate nor carry such a negation out coherently, the fiction of this benevolent catastrophe demarcates modernism from previous art. But the poet's description of the origin of this new totality remains caught in an unresolved contradiction between radical voluntarism and persistence of the past. He first tries to evade the problem by instituting a division of labor between the hand and the eye, the experiential equivalents of remembrance and will, of the unwanted past and the desired present. But in vain. The contradiction returns in Mallarmé's warnings that even the "*new* evolution of art" must be *learned*, that no matter how much one wishes to consign to oblivion the "acquired secrets of manipulation," experience reveals its regenerative power only to those who took the time to absorb them.

Instead of supplying guidelines to the study of modernism, the riverside scene painted by Mallarmé apropos Manet leaves critical engagement with modernism beset with the following questions: How should one study art driven by the modes of self-awareness as contradictory and self-defeating as these? If the innovation of modernism cannot be discerned on the basis of its overt rhetoric of the new, what are the historical and hermeneutic consequences of this failure? Should one sidestep modernist stress on the obsolescence of tradition and place modernism into a chronological niche on the continuum of period styles that begins in the Renaissance and extends to the present? Or should one continue to be guided by the self-presentation of modernism as a conquest of experience, the "realization of the senses," in Cezanne's well-known phrase, no matter how incoherent such self-presentation may be? If, as Adorno maintains, modernism did not articulate itself coherently because something in modernism remained unfulfilled, how could we gain access to the inner claim that modernism's immediate history only helped to veil?

Adorno's materialist theory of the artwork and modernism

Aesthetic Theory's reliance on the idiom of German Idealism appeared anachronistic, awkward even, already in 1969 when the manuscript was nearing completion. I suggest we do not rush to take this stylistic peculiarity for a sign of a theoretical regression. It has the practical merit of evading the unsatisfactory alternatives between reproducing the theoretical language of artists or relying on extrinsic explanatory schemes with no connection to the historical material at hand. For instance, Adorno's critique of the modernist cult of the new didn't dismiss the category of the new as a mere self-mystification. On the contrary, his analysis discloses the new as a version of the limit that the immanence of the social imposes upon consciousness of subjects: "In the immanence of society, consciousness of its negative essence is blocked, and only abstract negation acts as a substitute for truth" (Adorno 1974: 95). By refusing to fill the category of the new with experiential or conceptual content, Adorno makes intelligible the abstraction inherent in this category and the disruption in the continuity of the social practice of art to which the persistence of this abstractness corresponds. Thus, Adorno's dialectical approach treats modernist art and theory seriously without taking them literally. It is now time to address the second layer of the book's argument, the one charged with converting the historical diagnosis of modernism into a conceptual resource for the re-orientation of aesthetics.

Adorno opens *Aesthetic Theory* by referring to the rift between the modern practice of art and the tradition that preceded it: "It is self-evident that nothing concerning art is self-evident anymore, neither its relation to the whole, nor even its right to exist" (Adorno 1997: 1, trans. modified). Like Bloch or Marcuse, Adorno recognized the full gravity of the fact that in the nineteenth century art lost the capacity to think of itself as timeless (Marcuse 1978; Bloch 1974). Inasmuch as the traditional practice of art made this belief a condition for the production and reception of art, this transformation meant that socio-economic development placed art at odds with the means of its reproduction. The ensuing migration of theory into the artwork signaled the recognition of the fact that the historical context of art practice had begun to erode its ideological infra-structure. The modernist compulsion to construct totalities out of specific artistic techniques finds its historical justification in the vacuum left by the unraveling of the tradition. These developments set the stage for short-circuiting the relationship between aesthetic structure and the concept of art. The pursuit of the immediate identity between individual work and the schema of practice drove modernist works to extreme forms of nominalism. Adorno sketches out the initial stage of this process via Wagner:

> Wagner is the first instance of consistent musical nominalism … I mean by this that his work is the first in which the primacy of the individual work, and, within individual work, that of the concrete, formed shape (*durchgebildeten Gestalt*), is made to prevail against every convention (*gearteten Schema*) of whatever kind, against every externally prescribed pattern (*Form*). He was the first composer to draw the logical conclusion from the contradiction between forms that had been handed down, indeed the traditional formal language of music as such, and the artistic tasks that he concretely faced.
> (Adorno 2003: 119)

The new at stake in modernism has less to do with the use of unusual techniques, elimination of representation or theoretical justifications erected on behalf of the artworks, than with the kind of thing the artwork has been compelled to become. Nominalism represents the qualitative determination of modernism that alters the conditions of critical understanding. As a result, practical criticism receives the lead in the reconstruction of aesthetic theory which modernism requires simply by being what it is.

Modernism and its criticism share the following predicament: how does one define art if art no longer appears to have timeless essence? This question provoked considerable anxiety as early as Flaubert. Adorno set out to devise an analytical strategy to elicit the truth revealed in the fact that art, and even great art, has nonetheless been produced. The truth at stake is both a truth about truth and a truth about art: "Nietzsche's late understanding, developed in opposition to traditional philosophy, that even what has become can be true, is axiomatic for the re-oriented aesthetics" (Adorno 1997: 2).[10] By means of total historicization of its aesthetic structure, the modernist work of art has secured the knowledge that truth is but a determinate configuration of historical becoming.

Adorno's thesis that, in becoming fully historical, modernist art has also revealed the historicity of truth, leaves his aesthetic theory with a twin burden. He must differentiate his account of the artwork from conventional historicism, either in positivist or Marxist veins. Yet he also must reconcile his assertion that the specifically aesthetic in modernism derives from concrete historical material with the abstractness of modernist artwork. What kind of history speaks through the overwrought formal structures of works like those of Flaubert, Kandinsky or Schoenberg?

Adorno's treatment of historicism in *Aesthetic Theory* begins inauspiciously, grudgingly acknowledging its right to exist: "Nevertheless, there is no contesting the cliché cultural history is so fond of, that the development of artistic processes, usually classed under the heading of style, corresponds to social development" (Adorno 1997: 5). While accepting the overall premise of sociological study of art, Adorno targets its practical vehicle—the doctrine of reflection. Presuming that art's primary contribution is to illuminate extrinsic social processes, this doctrine thereby denies that art constitutes a social process in its own right. Objecting to this overeager reduction of art to the medium of reflection, Adorno draws a consequence crucial for criticism—the fact that the proponents of reflection are bound to ignore what amounts to art's primary claim: to be an original form of coherence as expressed in the immanent purposiveness (or entelechy) of the artwork's materials. To bring this point home, Adorno quotes Schoenberg: "one paints a painting, not what it represents" (Adorno 1997: 4). Since, like other commodities, aesthetic artifacts are produced, branded, distributed, sold or destroyed, Adorno admits that aesthetic relations of production contain mimesis of relations of production *tout court*: "The aesthetic force of production is the same as that of productive labor and has the same teleology; and what may be called aesthetic relations of production ... are sedimentations or imprinting of social relations of production" (Adorno 1997: 5). But to produce an aesthetic artifact is not yet to produce a work of art. While artworks are objects of productive process, they acquire the entelechy indispensable to their identity through processes contrary to production. This is why the relationship of the artworks to the social process out of which they emerge cannot be specified by studying the process of production alone.

Having thus undercut the picture of art as a mirror of social development, Adorno does not draw the idealist conclusion that his argument appears to invite, and refuses the view that artworks are autonomous by virtue of possessing a unique principle of constitution. Consequently, he also opposes the notion that the study of aesthetic values and immanent properties of form from the standpoint of aesthetic entelechy can secure an adequate grasp of the character of art. Against the Platonism inherent in traditional aesthetic thinking, he contends that these values and properties themselves maintain their aesthetic efficacy and durability only as "after-images," "sediments" or "traces" of the contradictory social forces at play in the historical development of Western societies. Adorno's critique of determinism in aesthetics culminates in the following view: the identity of the particular work of art can be established neither on a formal nor on a causal basis, but only by analyzing the structure organizing—Adorno's own term is "mediating"—its formal-aesthetic and extrinsic-material elements. Because its normative pressure equally overdetermines the material and formal strata of the artwork, this structure cannot be adequately described as aesthetic. Its essence is metaphysical, and concerns a specific configuration in the ongoing dialectic of totality whose terms are the spirit and the world, the configuration of non-coercion:

> The artwork is related to the world by the principle that contrasts it with the world, and that same principle by which the spirit has organized the world. The synthesis achieved by means of the artwork is not simply forced onto its elements; rather, it recapitulates that in which these elements communicate with one another; thus, the synthesis is itself a product of otherness. Indeed, synthesis has its foundation in the spirit-distant material dimension of works, in that in which synthesis is active. This unites the aesthetic element of form with non-coercion.
>
> (Adorno 1997: 7)

By locating the spiritual substance of the artwork in the non-coercive relationship to the experiential content of the world it opposes, Adorno positions the materialist theory of form (as dialectic of material and construction) at the center of his reconstructive meta-critique of aesthetics. Departing from the idealism that vitiated traditional aesthetics, Adorno denies that works of art are spiritual because they elude determination by the world. They are spiritual because they rebound on the world that masters them so as to organize it in the manner of spirit, i.e. non-coercively and in accordance with the impossible claim of all things to becoming in freedom. Against the protestations of rationality (that are also an inalienable element of its substance), art takes this unrealizable claim of all the existents as its highest practical priority, and thus makes artworks simultaneously more material and more spiritual than anything one may compare them to.

When the traditional work of art claims to organize its material exclusively in terms of aesthetic values, it implicitly asserts the infinite malleability of historical experience. This assertion is a cipher of the project of total domination of nature that Adorno identifies with the modern stage in the natural history of Western reason. By making the metaphysical and the material components of aesthetic structure interdependent ("synthesis has its foundation in the spirit-distant material dimension of works, in that in which synthesis is active"), Adorno's aesthetic theory breaks with its historical antecedents. Against the phantasm of total domination that the idealist aesthetics purvey, Adorno argues that the heterogeneous elements lodged in the material of the work—implicit value judgments, naturalized ideological assumptions, pre-formed aesthetic contents and structures, historically-specific mental schemata misrecognized as nature, etc.—continue to organize the work despite, and alongside, its pretension to total self-organization.[11] *Aesthetic Theory* readily admits that every artwork is incomplete if judged by the standards of aesthetics; but, unlike other appeals to *désoeuvrement*, Adorno's does not suggest that this incompletion can be mastered in the element of form.[12]

Because it does not take the claim of art to complete mastery of experience at face value, the materialist theory of form espouses a view of mimesis different from the traditional one. Adorno argues that the artwork refracts historical contents regardless of whether it contains a representational stratum, i.e. of whether it has an identifiable historical experience as its theme, object or referent. Therefore, the shape of content, not its representational value, becomes the most dynamic element of the modernist work when it reaches for autonomy.

Though all art refracts historical contents, modernist art is distinct by virtue of its determination to confront this dependence on the historicity of its material, sometimes even to abjure this dependence by means of the flight into the pre-spiritualized realms of the esoteric, archaic, exotic, technical, or occult. When the temptation of this flight is averted, the stage is set for the work of art that may become autonomous precisely as a result of making the refractory features of its historical material into functional elements of its law of form. For Adorno, Flaubert's *Madame Bovary* is such a work of art because it derives its aesthetic character from the non-coercive synthesis of the historically-conditioned material and formal construction:

> The fanatic linguistic perfection of *Madame Bovary* is probably the symptom of precisely the contrary element; the unity of both, of reportage and linguistic perfectionism, accounts for the book's unfaded actuality. In artworks, the criterion of success is twofold: whether they succeed in integrating thematic strata and details into the immanent law of form and in this integration at the same time maintain what resists it and the fissures that occur in the process of this integration.
>
> (Adorno 1997: 7)

The success of *Madame Bovary* consists in the fact that, rather than opting for the pseudo-journalistic reportage or esoteric preciosity, the novel recognized in the opposition between the two an antinomy defining the possibility of literature in the commodity age, and mastered this antinomy by means of its aesthetic structure. Flaubert's compulsive reliance on the stylistic device of the *style indirect libre* forces the reader to become conscious of the dependence of authorial irony on the persistence of the heterogeneous linguistic elements it purports to master. Furthermore, by bestowing on the abject tale of adultery out of boredom the dignity of linguistic form that past art reserved for gods and heroes, Flaubert suspended the rule of Aristotelian aesthetics that required serious art to eliminate everything extra-aesthetic from its material, and thereby reasserted the complete control of nature as a goal to which all production should aspire.

Contrary to the canonical reading of Flaubert as an apostle of pure art, Adorno maintains that, to the extent that his formal aestheticism gleefully accepts the abject and the exalted alike, Flaubert's prose initiated an undoing of the complicity of art in the fiction of production as absolute domination. While serving as a highly productive constraint for traditional art, this fiction had also the less salutary effect of severing the traditional aesthetic categories from the historical contents that made them meaningful.

Having located the theoretical significance of Flaubert's anti-generic stance, Adorno argues that the ideal of total integration challenged by *Madame Bovary* had been a fiction that led traditional aesthetics to construct history as the narrative of progressive increase in the mastery of the medium. However, from the perspective of the materialist history of form Adorno espouses in *Aesthetic Theory*,

> Integration as such does not assure quality; in the history of art, integration and quality have often diverged. For no single select category, not even the aesthetically central concept of law of form, names the essence of art and suffices to judge its products. Essential to art are defining characteristics that contradict its fixed art-philosophical concept.
>
> (Adorno 1997: 7)

These refractory "characteristics" are none other than the marks of the immersion of art into extra-aesthetic materials that the fixed, art-historical notion of art as domination ignores. In becoming modernist, art reveals itself as an integrally historical process driven by the same dialectic of spirit and existence as the historical world that it dares to oppose. Thereby modernism, as Adorno understands it, demonstrates that the central problem of aesthetics, the question of aesthetic constitution, will remain unsolvable as long as art is conceived as an essence rather than a temporal relation:

> The definition of art at every point is indicated by what art once was, but it is legitimated only by what art became with regard to what it wants to, and perhaps can, become ... Because art is what it has become, its concept

refers to what it does not contain. The tension between what motivates art and art's past circumscribes the so-called question of aesthetic constitution.

(Adorno 1997: 2)

Adorno attributes the distinctness of art to the temporal nucleus of the art object, i.e. the tension (*Spannung*) the artwork generates between its reference to past art-practice and the metaphysical claim to be a species of praxis asserting a spiritual relationship between the existents. This is a radically historicist position, arguing that one does not experience the work of art without approaching the image of the past the artwork has reflected into itself so as to negate it better. But this historicism is divested of idealism since it does not assume that the past in question can be consulted like a dictionary. This is because the autonomous work of art refers to a historical datum that, though objectively necessary, for reasons social, political or cultural, was not directly embodied. By displacing mimesis from representational stratum into the interstices of construction, modernist artwork projects the image of production its own production denied it. In a stunning recasting of the oldest aesthetic concept, Adorno calls this image "nature that has been repressed and drawn into the dynamic of history. Nature, to whose *imago* art is devoted, does not yet in any way exist; what is true in art is something non-existent" (Adorno 1997: 131). The Romantic conception of nature wanted to approach this liberated mode of practice as if it already existed, as if one could merge into it by regression or abstraction. By imitating a virtuality of the non-existent, the modernist artwork transcends the romantic longing for otherness content to remain a sentiment:

> Artworks would be powerless if they were no more than longing, though there is no valid artwork without longing. That by which they transcend longing, however, is the neediness inscribed in the figure in the historically existing. By retracing this figure, they are not only more than what simply exists but participate in the objective truth to the extent that what is in need summons its fulfillment and change.
>
> (Adorno 1997: 132)

By making the image of practice the object of art, modernism faced up to the guilt accrued by the concept of mimesis whose many guises—the plausible, the probable, *le vraisemblable*—serve as so many veiled endorsements of the already existent. The pathos inherent in modernist formalism demands that, having lost its claim to being worthy of imitation, the world should imitate art:

> The elements of this other [i.e. the image of practice dissenting from actual conditions of production] are present in reality and they require only a minute displacement into a new constellation in order to find their right position. Rather than imitating reality, artworks demonstrate this displacement to reality. Ultimately, the doctrine of imitation should be reversed; in a sublimated sense, reality should imitate the artworks.
>
> (Adorno 1997: 132)

Surveying the history of modernism from the vantage point of the materialist theory of form, one cannot mistake the modernist tendency to eliminate identifiable content for an escape from history or a breakthrough to a spiritual worldview. In hindsight, this negative gesture entrenched the modernist artwork even further in the historical configuration from which it sprang; today, modernist works that hanker after the spiritual appear the most dated and vulnerable to appropriation by New Age *kitsch*. To remedy this, the affirmative element contained in modernist practice must be distinguished from the abstract negation of art or culture that the ideology of modernism contains. Modernist artworks reject extant conditions of art while conjuring a dissenting mode of artistic practice as their realized antithesis. Modernist art delivers this affirmation via the non-coercive synthesis of the thematic and aesthetic elements it derives from its historical world. Therefore, the formal fanaticism of modernism militates against the view that modernism really wanted to create an autonomous aesthetic sphere. Modernist artworks like *Madame Bovary* or *Le Spleen de Paris* can denounce artfulness *and* display the excess of form without self-contradiction because their aesthetic structures harbor the concept of art—the image of production freed from the requirement of domination—that the historical situation of art denied them.

While *Aesthetic Theory* discloses how the phenomenon of modernism transformed the discourse of aesthetics, Adorno's conception of a work's structure as an image of a dissenting art practice furnishes the positive content of the modernist resistance to the status quo. Skeptical of any providential interpretation of history, Baudelaire in "Le *Confiteor* de l'artiste" prophesies that, short of reclaiming social legitimacy, art, finding no other support than the inwardness of the artist, devolves into a self-consuming hysteria:

> Toutefois, ces pensées [i.e. aesthetic reactions to landscape], qu'elles sortent de moi ou s'élancent des choses, deviennent bientôt trop intenses. L'énergie dans la volupté crée un malaise et une souffrance positive. Mes nerfs trop tendus ne donnent plus que des vibrations criardes et douloureuses. Et maintenant la profondeur du ciel me consterne; sa limpidité m'exaspère. L'insensibilité de la mer, l'immuabilité du spectacle, me révoltent ... Ah! faut-il éternellement souffrir, ou fuir éternellement le beau?
>
> (Baudelaire 1975: 278–9)

If Adorno was right to read the "formal fanaticism" of modernist artwork as a *de facto* re-orientation of aesthetics, then the future of modernism concerns not only art but also the theory of art. Once we begin to think modernism as a condition in which the practice of art actively undermines the philosophical foundations of aesthetics, translating this practical critique into theoretical discourse becomes the ongoing task of aesthetic theory.

Notes

1 "Das Neue ist ein blinder Fleck, leer wie das vollkommene Dies da" (Adorno 1972: 38).

2 The claim to the new has a long critical past. In the American context, its meaning became especially contentious with Clement Greenberg's conception of modernism as elimination of conventions dispensable to the medium. See Clark (1982), Fried (1982), and Melville (1998). For a systematic study of Adorno's uses of negativity in aesthetic argument, see Menke (1998) and Bernstein (1991).

3 "Das Neue ist, aus Not, ein Gewolltes, als das Andere aber wäre es das das nicht Gewollte. Velleität kettet es ans Immergleiche; daher die Kommunikation von Moderne und Mythos. Es intendiert Nichtidentität, wird jedoch durch Intention zum Identischen; moderne Kunst übt das Münchhausenkunststück einer Identifikation des Nichtidentischen ein." (Adorno 1972: 40–1)

4 "Seine [i.e. mythical] Unausweichlichkeit usurpiert die Wahrheit. Ungezählte Kunstwerke laborieren daran, daß sie als ein in sich Werdendes, unablässig sich Änderndes, Fortschreitendes sich darstellen und die zeitlose Reihung von Immergleichem bleiben" (Adorno 1972: 19).

5 For the "semantic incompatibility" of automatic writing, see Riffaterre (1979).

6 Recently, both brands of the orthodox narrative of modernism—the voluntarist (H. Read, H. Rosenberg, A. Malraux, H. Friedrich) and the formalist (R. Jakobson, Cl. Greenberg, J. Pauhlan)—have been increasingly subject to critical re-examination. The milestones are: Compagnon (1990), Jameson (2002), and Rancière (2002).

7 "Wie die Kategorie des Neuen aus dem historischen Prozeß resultierte, der die spezifische Tradition zuerst und dann eine jegliche auflöste, so ist Moderne keine Aberration, die sich berichtigen ließe, indem man auf einen Boden zurückkehrt, der nicht mehr existiert und nicht mehr existieren soll" (Adorno 1972: 41).

The conclusion of the sentence is worth citing if only because it brings out in no uncertain terms that, for Adorno, modernism is normatively, rather than causally, dependent on a dialectical relation to tradition: "das ist, paradox, der Grund von Moderne und verleiht ihr normativen Charakter."

8 I refer to Valéry's canonical description of "Baudelaire's problem" in "Situation de Baudelaire":

> Il s'agit de distinquer à tout prix d'un ensemble des grands poètes exceptionnellement réunis par quelque hasard, dans le même époque, tous en pleine vigueur. Le problème de Baudelaire pouvait donc,—devait donc,—se poser ainsi: 'être un grand poète, mais n'être ni Lamartine, ni Hugo, ni Musset.' Je ne dis pas que ce propos fut conscient, mais il était nécessairement en Baudelaire—et même essentiallement Baudelaire. Il était sa raison d'Etat.
>
> (Valéry 1957: 600)

This statement must count as one of the most literal anticipations of Harold Bloom's theory of the anxiety of influence.

9 For the relevant commentary, see Rubin (1994: 127–43); Fried (1996: 205–6); Durand (1998: 19–32). The French original of Mallarmé's essay has not yet been found. Vincent Descombes's incisive treatment of Mallarmé's 1874 article on Manet, "Le Jury de peinture pour 1874 et M. Manet" (Œuvres Complètes 695–700), is found in Descombes (1992: 93–104).

10 "Axiomatisch ist für eine umorientierte Ästhetik die vom späten Nietzsche gegen die traditionelle Philosophie entwickelte Erkenntnis, daß auch das Gewordene wahr sein kann" (Adorno 1972: 12).

11 These two processes—subordination to the exigencies of the material and overcoming of its resistance in the medium of form—condition each other with such intricacy that no aesthetic theory worthy of the name would presume to be able to determine their interrelationship in advance. The relevance of Adorno's thinking about art today derives from its inability to produce the aesthetic theory its title promises, and from the promise of the theoretical articulation of this impossibility that comes in its stead.

12 I refer to the Romantic cult of the fragment revisited by Maurice Blanchot, Jean-Luc Nancy and Lacoue-Labarthe. See Blanchot (1969) and Nancy and Lacoue-Labarthe (1978).

Bibliography

Adorno, T. (1972) *Asthetische Theorie, Gesammelte Schriften* 7, second edn, ed. G. Adorno and R. Tiedemann, Frankfurt am Main: Suhrkamp.

—— (1974) *Minima Moralia*, trans. E. F. N. Jephcott, London: New Left Books.

—— (1997) *Aesthetic Theory*, trans. R. Hullot-Kentor, Minneapolis: University of Minnesota Press.

—— (2003) "Wagner's Relevance Today," in *Can One Live After Auschwitz?* Stanford: Stanford University Press.

Baudelaire, C. (1975) *Œuvres Complètes*, vol. 1, Paris: Gallimard bibliothèque de la pléiade.

Bernstein, J. M. (1991) *The Fate of Art: Aesthetic Alienation from Kant to Derrida and Adorno*, Cambridge: Polity.

Blanchot, M. (1969) *L'Entretien infini*, Paris: Gallimard.

Bloch, E. (1990 [1974]) *Ästhetik des Vor-Scheins*, Hrsg. Gert Ueding, Frankfurt am Maine: Suhrkamp; trans. J. D. Zipes and F. Mechlenburg, *The Utopian Function of Art and Literature*, Cambridge, MA: MIT Press.

Clark, T. J. (1982) "Clement Greenberg's Theory of Art," *Critical Inquiry* 9(1): 139–56.

Compagnon, A. (1990) *Les Cinq Paradoxes de la modernité*, Paris: Seuil.

Descombes, V. (1992) *Proust. The Philosophy of the Novel*, trans. Catherine Macksey Stanford: Stanford University Press.

Durand, P. (1998) *Crises: Mallarmé via Manet de "The Impressionists and Edouard Manet" à "Crise de vers"*, Leuven: Peeters.

Fried, M. (1982) "How Modernism Works: A Response to T. J. Clark," *Critical Inquiry* 9(1): 217–34.

—— (1996) *Manet's Modernism: or, The Face of Painting in the 1860s*, Chicago: University of Chicago Press.

Jameson, F. (2002) *A Singular Modernity*, London: Verso.

Mallarmé, S. (1994 [1876]) "The Impressionists and Edouard Manet," in J. H. Rubin (ed.) *Manet's Silence and the Poetics of Bouquets*, London: Reaktion, 231–42.

Marcuse, H. (1978) *The Aesthetic Dimension: Toward a Critique of Marxist Aesthetics*, trans. H. Marcuse and E. Sherover, Boston: Beacon Press.

Melville, S. (1998) "Kant after Greenberg," *Journal of Aesthetics and Art Criticism* 56(1): 67–74.

Menke, C. (1998) *The Sovereignty of Art: Aesthetic Negativity in Adorno and Derrida*, Cambridge, MA: MIT Press.

Nancy, J.-L. and Lacoue-Labarthe, P. (1978) *L'Absolu littéraire*, Paris: Seuil.

Rancière, J. (2002) "The Aesthetic Revolution and its Outcomes: Employments of Autonomy and Heteronomy," *New Left Review* 14 (March–April): 133–51.

Riffaterre, M. (1979) "Incompatibilités sémantiques dans l'écriture automatique," in *La Production du texte*, Paris: Seuil, 235–50.

Rubin, J. H. (ed.) (1994) *Manet's Silence and the Poetics of Bouquets*, London: Reaktion.

Valéry, P. (1957) *Oeuvres*, vol. 1, Paris: Gallimard.

What's new? On Adorno and the modernist aesthetics of novelty

Response to Oleg Gelikman

Martin Jay

In his trenchant and insightful response to Theodor W. Adorno's *Aesthetic Theory*, Oleg Gelikman highlights the ambivalent role Adorno assigns to novelty in the modernist break with traditional aesthetics. Although he applauds the modernist intent to abandon exhausted models of universalizing aesthetic normativity, Adorno accuses the fetish of newness for its own sake, the need always to innovate and leave behind the past, of complicity with the very forces it tries to negate. First, in its haste to plunge headlong into the future, it mimics the logic of capitalist fashion, where profits follow from planned obsolescence and new commodities demand to be bought by consumers wanting to be "up to date."[1] It has a mimetic relationship to the reproduction of capital through the ceaseless expansion of the market. Second, by becoming an abstract and transcendental invariant, the need for newness loses its connection with genuine historical change, becoming instead paradoxically a mark of repetition. It partakes of a kind of mythical thinking that operates on the ahistorical level of the eternal return. Third, by over-emphasizing the voluntarist and subjectivist role in creating novelty, which suggests total mastery of aesthetic material, it duplicates the technical domination of nature in the dialectic of enlightenment. And finally, by devaluing all that went before, discarding the past as without merit, it severs its ties with the redemptive energies revealed when the past is rubbed against the grain; a past whose residues, as Walter Benjamin knew, can be recombined in new and arresting constellations in the present and future. Seeing itself instead as liberated from the fetters of the past, conceptualizing the future as unconquered territory for appropriation, it rushes headlong into the abyss.

The real historicity of artworks, Adorno claims, lies in the heterogeneous residue of the traditions out of which they emerge and against which they measure themselves, their sedimented materiality, not their claim to total novelty. Although shapable by formal construction in the present, this aesthetic material is irreducible to the dominating innovation of the current creator, who is wrong simply to negate and devalue what went before. The substance of the work is never, however, a timeless essence, hovering above historical change. Nor can the smooth continuity of tradition be repaired once it is ruptured, contrary to revival efforts such as neo-classicism.[2] Genuine art, Adorno insists, is a negative dialectic of tradition and innovation, of historicism and formalism, of a past that is—luckily—not fully overcome and a future that is not yet born.

The one-sided cult of the new in modernism is evident as early as the operas of Richard Wagner, which Adorno calls "the first case of uncompromising musical nominalism" (Adorno 2002: 589),[3] the first time in which generic normativity or even the precedent of historical convention is left behind entirely in favor of new formal innovation: "Art has been caught up in the total process of nominalism's advance ever since the medieval *ordo* was broken up. The universal is no longer granted art through types, and older types are being drawn into the whirlwind" (Adorno 1997: 1999). How can artworks survive the utter destruction of their traditional substance, the sedimented residue of past practice? Gelikman sees Adorno providing an answer by defending a modernism that is rescued from its fetish of absolute newness and its nominalist destruction of essential truth. Instead, he provides a vision of an art that restores a non-dominating balance between past material and present innovation, one which is itself a model for a redeemed society beyond the present "administered world." In the words of *Aesthetic Theory* cited by Gelikman, "ultimately, the doctrine of imitation should be reversed; in a sublimated sense, reality should imitate the artworks."

Gelikman provides us a cogent reading of Adorno's argument about the dangers of the cult of newness in modernism, but doesn't take it far enough in a critical direction. I will suggest several ways in which Adorno's claims can be enhanced through a more complex reading of the varieties of modernism than he posits in the work drawn on by Gelikman. In particular, I want to focus on the issue of nominalism as a source of the cult of novelty, which negates the value of tradition and supports subjective innovation above all else. There were in modernism, I hope to show, other variants of nominalism that led it in a different direction.

Before investigating those alternatives, one point must be made about the modernist attitude towards tradition itself. "Tradition," Adorno urges, "is not to be abstractly negated but criticized without naïveté according to the current situation: Thus the present constitutes the past" (Adorno 1997: 41). Modernism, he charges, fails to acknowledge this necessity; it does not "negate previous artistic practices, as styles have done throughout the ages, but rather tradition itself; to this extent it simply ratifies the bourgeois principle of art" (Adorno 1997: 21). Adorno was not alone in advancing this claim.[4] But the generalization is too sweeping, failing to recognize, for example, the importance of what Stephen Spender called the "revolutionary traditionalists" among the leading English-language modernist poets. Whereas unreflecting traditionalists doggedly upheld past standards that had become hollow or wallowed in nostalgia, poets like T. S. Eliot and Ezra Pound found a new tradition in works like Joyce's *Ulysses*: "The revolutionary traditionalists were eclectic drawing on the whole European Hellenic and biblical culture, and sometimes going still further afield to the art and literature of China and other parts of Asia, to Buddhism as well as Christianity" (Spender 1963: 225). Moreover, as Harold Rosenberg argued in the 1960s, "the famous 'modern break with tradition' has lasted long enough to have produced its own tradition," although "the new cannot become a tradition without giving rise to unique contradictions, myths, absurdities—often creative absurdities" (Rosenberg 1965: 9).

One of those creative absurdities concerns how the nominalist impulse in modernism could work not to obliterate the past and generate a fetish of newness, but to undermine precisely that impulse.[5] Rather than unleashing the sovereign will of the self-assertive, dominating subject by denying the prior existence of rational universals, which is how nominalism has often been understood,[6] it could also lead to the evacuation of the strong creative self, capable of radically negating the past and starting *ex nihilo*. It needs to be remembered that ever since Duns Scotus stressed the *haecceitas* or "thisness" of an object over what Aquinas and the Scholastics had seen as its *quidditas* or generic "thatness," nominalism has meant not only the denial of real universals, but also privileging absolute particularity over typical exemplarity.[7] That is, objects, including aesthetic ones, were not to be understood as organic wholes derived deductively from a series of eternal aesthetic principles. Although Platonic aesthetics attempted to restore such principles during the Renaissance, by and large nominalism won out, with new, unfocused genres like the novel carrying its banner. As Umberto Eco put it,

> all that remains is the intuition of particulars, a knowledge of existent objects whose visible proportions are analyzed empirically ... as for artistic inspiration, this consists in an idea of the individual object which the artist wants to construct, and not of its universal form.
>
> (Eco 1986: 189)

The constructive impulse in nominalism could certainly lead to the modernism that Adorno rightly saw as abstractly negating tradition and elevating the sovereign will of the creator. But it could also be challenged by that valorization of "existent objects" as intuited particulars Eco sees as another part of the nominalist legacy. This counter-current in modernism is most evident in the provocations of a seminal artist Adorno never seriously discusses, Marcel Duchamp, who, in fact, came to call his own work "pictorial nominalism."[8] By this term, Duchamp seems to have meant a number of overlapping things. It indicated a self-conscious repudiation of the belief that works of art expressed the genius, or even the craftsmanlike talent, of the artist. It suggested that works were not metaphors for deeper meanings or new languages that might be direct expressions of spiritual distinction. It referred to the artist's indifference to the intrinsic beauty of the object or lack thereof, as well as the good taste or lack thereof of the beholder. It meant the abandonment of the quest for the masterpiece, the perfect embodiment of the entelechy or essence of a medium.[9]

Perhaps most importantly, it meant the selection of objects from the already existing world, found not made (at least, not by the artists), and designating, judging, *naming* them art objects worthy of display. Duchamp abandoned painting and invented the "readymade" to become, in Thierry de Duve's words, "the nominalist of a past culture" (de Duve 1991: 142). Also named for the first time, in addition to the object as artwork, was the enabling context of the institution of art. Now, *who* had the power to give the name, *who* had the cultural capital to designate and judge, was itself understood to be a function of that institution, whose discrete and contingent existence was itself named by Duchamp's transgressive gesture. The creative will of the artistic genius, his sovereign forming power over the material world, was replaced by a weaker enunciative power granted by the institution, which allowed only choice from an already given menu of possibilities.

For these reasons, de Duve can write of the readymade that "it reinterpreted the past with such a pertinence that it endowed it with a new resonance. From this came the emphasis I put on the link with tradition and on a 'progressive' rehabilitation of that word" (de Duve 1991: 188). Duchamp's resistance to the cult of the new, his disdain for the creative genius and the authentic, original work of art, helped produce the condition that obtains in what is now called postmodernism: denial of the narrative of constant innovation and refusal to grant any one movement the status of a genuine *avant-garde*. Gelikman neglects the distinction between modernism and postmodernism, and finishes his essay by ruminating on "the future of modernism," as if it really has one. Rather, its troubled future was already present in high modernism's bifurcation of the nominalist impulse: one part going toward formalist constructivism, the sovereignty of the artist's self-asserting will, and the abstract negation of tradition; and the other resisting beautiful form, foregrounding the power of the institution, abandoning the fetish of the new, and accepting the recycling of what was already made (and not by the creative genius). We might call one aesthetic nominalism and the other its anti-aesthetic twin. Adorno only helps us so far in realizing these alternatives as latent in nominalism itself, which he identifies too quickly with only the former.

The real task is grappling with the difficulty of representing or evoking the past in contemporary art, now that the abstract modernist fetish of the new has been pretty much laid to rest. Tradition in any conventional sense of smooth continuity was already undermined during the era of Spender's "revolutionary traditionalists." The provocation of the readymade, recycling in citation marks the artifacts of everyday life, is also clearly a spent force. Despite the foolish pronouncements of certain theorists who interpreted victory in the Cold War as "the end of history," we are clearly still struggling to come to terms with both the past as doggedly alive and the present as itself part of history. Artists in the twenty-first century are inventing new ways to address these challenges,[10] but whether they find a way to create works (or post-works) that will justify Adorno's injunction for reality to imitate art remains to be seen.

Notes

1 Adorno's reduction of one to the other earned him Peter Bürger's reproach:

> Adorno pays for his failure to precisely historicize the category of the new. Since he neglects to do so, he must derive it directly from the commodity society. For Adorno, the category of the new in art is a necessary duplication of what dominates the commodity society … But it must be borne in mind that in the commodity society, the category of the new is not a substantive but merely an

apparent one. For far from referring to the nature of the commodities, it is their artificially imposed appearance that is involved here.

(Bürger 1984: 61)

2 See Adorno (1992–3).

3 Gelikman cites this line in a slightly different translation.

4 See, e.g., Renato Poggioli's discussion of the modern artist's "*alienation from tradition*" in Poggioli (1968: 127).

5 As Rosalind E. Krauss (1985) demonstrated, the alleged fetish of novelty and original-ity in modernist art was often belied by a reliance on techniques of reproduction and copying, which are embodied in the ubiquitous figure of the non-narrative grid. The Duchampian readymade, of which more in a moment, was also a mass produced item with no original aura of authenticity.

6 For a trenchant discussion of the links between medieval nominalism and the freeing of the willing, self-asserting subject, see Part II, Chapter 3 of Blumenberg (1983).

7 For a useful account of the impact of nominalism on medieval aesthetics, see Chapter 8 of Eco (1986).

8 The term was used by Duchamp in a 1914 note from *The White Box*, and is developed by Thierry de Duve into a general theory of his work in *Pictorial Nominalism* (1991).

9 For an account of this quest, see Beltung (2001).

10 See, for example, the exhibition catalogue for the show *Ahistoric Occasion: Artists Making History*, curated by Nato Thompson at the MASSMoCa in 2006–7, and especially my introductory essay, "Aesthetic Experience and Historical Experience: A 21st-Century Constellation."

Bibliography

Adorno, T. (1992–3) "On Tradition," *Telos* 94 (Winter): 75–82.

—— (1997) *Aesthetic Theory*, trans. R. Hullot-Kentor, Minneapolis: University of Minnesota Press.

—— (2002) "Wagner's Relevance for Today," in R. Leppert (ed.) *Essays on Music* Richard Leppert, Berkeley: University of Califonia Press.

Beltung, H. (2001) *Invisible Masterpiece*, trans. H. Atkins, Chicago: University of Chicago Press.

Blumenberg, H. (1983) *The Legitimacy of the Modern Age*, trans. R. M. Wallace, Cambridge, MA: MIT Press.

Bürger, P. (1984) *Theory of the Avant-garde*, trans. M. Shaw, Minneapolis: University of Minnesota Press.

de Duve, T. (1991) *Pictorial Nominalism: On Marcel Duchamp's Passage from Painting to the Readymade*, trans. D. Polan and T. de Duve, Minneapolis: University of Minnesota Press.

Eco, U. (1986) *Beauty and Art in the Middle Ages*, trans. H. Bredin, New Haven: Yale University Press.

Krauss, R.E (1985) *The Originality of the Avant-Garde and Other Modernist Myths*, Cambridge, MA: MIT Press.

Poggioli, R. (1968) *The Theory of the Avant-Garde*, trans. G. Fitzgerald, Cambridge, MA: Belknap Press.

Rosenberg, H. (1965) *The Tradition of the New*, New York: McGraw Hill.

Spender, S. (1963) *The Struggle of the Modern*, Berkeley: University of Califonia Press.

Thompson, N. (2006) *Ahistoric Occasion: Artists Making History* (exhibition catalogue), North Adams, MA: MASSMoCa.

8 Fables of progression

Modernism, modernity, narrative

Andrew John Miller

By the time that modernist studies witnessed the emergence of a programmatically historical trend, the movement known as New Historicism had long since expanded beyond its initial beachhead in Renaissance studies and had made significant gains in most other areas of literary scholarship. An indication of the lagging response of modernist studies to the New Historicist insurgency is that, over the course of the 1980s, *Representations*, the journal most closely identified with New Historicism, published only two essays devoted to thoroughly modernist topics.[1] It is therefore not surprising that, in the introduction to the 1989 collection *The New Historicism*—a collection that can be seen to have marked New Historicism's apex as a theoretically self-reflective movement—the editor, H. Aram Veeser, does not so much as allude to modernism. Nor is it surprising that Jane Marcus, the one contributor who engages directly with modernism, is concerned less with the impact of New Historicism on modernist studies than with its impact on feminist studies. At the moment of New Historicism's peak, modernism seemed hopelessly far from the red-hot center of critical inquiry. Yet subsequent developments make it apparent that modernist studies is one of the areas in which New Historicism has had its most enduring impact. This impact, however, has encouraged the rejection not only of the theoretical dimension of New Historicism but also of the very idea of theory as a legitimate basis for literary interpretation.

This reversion to the norms of scholarly conservatism, though widespread throughout literary studies, has had a particularly damaging effect on modernist studies, a field that stands in an unusually intimate relation to the questions associated with critical theory. Even if we limit ourselves to a narrowly conservative view of the history of ideas, we are compelled to include, in the matrix of modernism, the writings of Freud, Weber, Wittgenstein, Husserl, Heidegger, Benjamin, and Mannheim. How could anyone deny the pertinence of theory to a field that is thus implicated in more or less the same network of concerns that can be found in the work of such formidable French theorists as Derrida, Foucault, Lacan, Althusser, and Lyotard? And yet, in the present climate, writings on modernism that accord a prominent place to theory tend to be treated as anachronistic.[2] Exceptions, it is true, are sometimes made for writings in which the theoretical elements are subordinated to a historical framework, and in which there is a self-abnegating reverence for fact. But theory is regularly ignored when most needed: that is, in those cases in which, in the pursuit of an enhanced sense of verisimilitude, there is an uncritical fetishization of factual data and diachronic contiguity. The desire to tell lucid stories with orderly beginnings, middles, and endings has all but supplanted the desire to engage with the uncanniness and uncertainty that arise from sustained theoretical reflection on the hermeneutics of literary interpretation.

Marcus's contribution to Veeser's 1989 collection can be seen to provide an early illustration of the way in which anti-theoretical stances have regularly been justified using the surprising claim that, in abandoning the notion that truth is absolute and essential, we simultaneously abandon all hope of effecting social change. Adopting a stance that reflects the broader backlash against theory that, by the late 1980s, was already gathering momentum, Marcus attacks the New Historicism for being excessively invested in what she terms "the postmodern suspicion of 'truth value'" (Marcus 1989: 133). As vindication for her claims regarding the nihilistic tendencies of "the postmodern intellectual," Marcus points to "the recent revelations about the anti-Semitic and collaborationist essays written by the late Yale critic, Paul de Man, in Belgium during the Second World War" (Marcus 1989: 132). Blurring a variety of conceptual and institutional distinctions, Marcus produces an ideology critique in which Sandra Gilbert—a feminist scholar who is not a New Historicist—is treated as the prime example of how "[f]eminist versions of New Historicism" are tainted by "presentist concerns" (Marcus 1989: 133).

In her focus on the alleged betrayal of historical truth, Marcus directly anticipates how an anti-theoretical set of historical impulses would come to attain hegemonic status within modernist studies. She rejects the interpretive skepticism associated with the theoretical dimension of the New Historicism. Using the specter of de Man to ascribe sinister, reactionary motives to those who indulge in "an insecurity about human agency over language" (Marcus 1989: 132), she complains that "New Historicism plays with history to enhance the text" (Marcus 1989: 133). Yet, citing in a laudatory way "[t]he reprinting of women's novels about World War I," she encourages the material recovery of archival materials that ostensibly enable "historians to answer historicists" (Marcus 1989: 148). Marcus dubiously assumes that the answer to historicist skepticism can be found in a faithful resuscitation of texts and documents whose testimonial authenticity lets us circumvent the constraints of interpretive mediation. In thus envisioning a form of historical reconstruction that would bracket out the epistemological distractions of historicism, she ignores the extent to which, as Hayden White notes elsewhere in Veeser's collection, "there is no such thing as a specifically historical approach to the study of history, but a variety of such approaches" (White 1989: 302). Marcus voices a desire for a way of narrating history that, by abolishing the need to theorize the conditions of historical knowledge, would allow unmediated access to factual historical experience. With the best intentions, she contributes to the intellectually conservative turn toward history and away from theory that, by the early 1990s, set the dominant tone for modernist studies.

In this context, theory comes to be regarded not only as a matter of secondary concern but also as a dangerously destabilizing force that, by questioning the epistemological status of historical "fact," undermines the ontological foundations of scholarly labor. The ensuing valorization of historical immanence can be seen simply to constitute part of the broader rejection of the ostensibly ahistorical tendencies of deconstruction. Though predicated on clichés and misrepresentations, this rejection was inevitable, given the degree to which many American deconstructionists appropriated Derrida's radicalization of Saussurean difference in ways that, though conducive to formal interpretation, often treated political and historical concerns as mere distractions. In the case of modernist studies, however, both the embrace of history and the flight from theory took unusually intense forms. We regularly observe, in the most visible recent work on modernism, a meticulous effort to reconstruct historical context, the assumption being that, because of the exceptional amount of information about the modernist period that is available, we can understand it in a way that is impossible for earlier periods.[3] Modernist studies thus come to rely on fables of progression that reflect a quasi-Hegelian view of the privilege conferred by our historical vantage point. The modernist period is tacitly treated as if it marked the end of literary history and the beginning of an era in which the domain of literary history can no longer be distinguished from the more broadly inclusive domain circumscribed by cultural materialism. Far from eliminating the need for theory in modernism, the issues raised by this shift in disciplinary focus call for intensified exploration of modernism's place in theory. But this is not the current direction of modernist studies, either as institutional construct or discursive formation. Instead, prevailing standards and practices valorize a pragmatic style of interpretation in which theoretical reflection is almost taboo. Whereas a New Historicist such as Stephen Greenblatt remained concerned with the theoretical problems stemming from the degree to which "cultural poetics is conscious of its status as interpretation" (Greenblatt 1980: 5), recent historical scholars of modernism tend to assume that self-conscious reflection on interpretive concerns hampers analysis of the concretely material conditions that gave rise to modernism. Fredric Jameson has articulated a radically different approach to historicist concerns when exploring modernist writers—notably, Joseph Conrad, Wyndham Lewis, and Wallace Stevens—using a sophisticated Marxist methodology. In Jameson's most influential book, *The Political Unconscious* (1981), Althusser's structuralist Marxism provides a revivified view of the relation between broad paradigmatic shifts in the means of production and more local, immanent shifts in the dominant structures of cultural representation. Jameson's engagements, however, range far beyond modernism, and his work had its most significant impact on postmodernism, postcolonialism, and globalization. Retrospectively, though, Jameson laid the groundwork for connecting the highly autonomized and aestheticized work of modernist writers with the contingencies of historical experience. For example, in a 1984 essay in the *New Orleans Review*, Jameson sketches a historicist reading of the work of Wallace Stevens, a figure who, by virtue of his extreme insistence on imaginative autonomy, continues to serve as the most challenging test case for anyone who would seek to undertake historicist readings of modernist work. More recently, in *A Singular Modernity*, Jameson has revisited "modernism" and "modernity," suggesting possibilities for moving beyond the various conceptual blockages that impeded recent discussions of modernism in theory.

Jameson reminds us that "Marxism is ... not a mechanical but a historical materialism; it does not assert the primacy of matter so much as it insists on an ultimate determination by the mode of production" (Jameson 1981: 45). Far from being the manifestation of an embrace of Marxist methodology, the cultural materialist flight from theory assumes that sustained theoretical reflection fosters corrosive self-consciousness without providing an adequate means of distinguishing truth from falsehood. The good critic, it is assumed, shuns what Lawrence Rainey once dismissively termed "rebarbative jargon" (Rainey 1999: 9). For Rainey, good critics of modernism reject the unbearable ugliness of theory and pursue the enlightened elegance of narration. His key claim is that "[s]tories *are* analysis—by other means" (Rainey 1999: 9).

Turning from theory to storytelling, Rainey breaks with the theoretical self-reflexivity that played an important role in New Historicism. Although Greenblatt, for example, typically followed a critical formula in which localized anecdotes served broader thematizations, he always understood the coherence of those anecdotes to be contingent on the hermeneutic assumptions that framed them rather than on anything inherent in the historical record. By contrast, the tendency in historicized studies of modernism has been to treat the historical record as something that, through the sheer weight of its material immanence, possesses an intrinsic authority. In addition to eliding a wide range of significant theoretical questions regarding the epistemological grounds of historical knowledge, this logic ignores the degree to which the archive is unable to convey to us more than a vaguely enunciated intimation of the considerably vaster body of unwritten acts of witness and behavior toward which Foucault gestures when he acknowledges "[t]he archive cannot be described in its totality" (Foucault 1972: 130). As Giorgio Agamben perceptively puts it, "the archive," in Foucault's formulation, "is the unsaid or unsayable inscribed in everything said by virtue of being enunciated" (Agamben 2002: 144). Foucault's profoundly anti-positivistic conception of the archive stands at a vast remove from the pervasive tendency, in recent work on modernism, to treat the archive as if it were a pure and unadulterated fountainhead of "fact" from which we can derive a sense of veridical certainty.[4]

The triumph of a self-proclaimed historicist tendency in modernist studies, in short, almost entirely rejects the theorization that, during the 1980s, played a crucial role in defining the cultural poetics of the New Historicism. In part, this is the result of a practical desire to get down to business by producing historicized readings rather than metadiscursive analyses of how one might best go about producing such readings. But, curiously, this flight from theory reflects a growing awareness of the degree to which the concerns identified with theory, far from being belated byproducts of a burgeoning postmodernism, were in fact intimately bound up with the concerns of key figures associated with modernism. In the controversies surrounding the Nazi affiliations of de Man and Heidegger, it was often assumed that theory cast doubt on the political implications not only of modernism but of the critical theory that prevailed in literary studies. This ignored the extreme degree of contingency that informed the alleged link between the horrors of fascism, and the skeptical view of truth in the work of contemporary theorists and certain high modernists. Yet the case against theory, though almost entirely circumstantial, proved highly persuasive to the numerous literary scholars who, tired of struggling with the intricacies of French and German philosophical vocabularies, were eager to return to more familiar, commonsensical territory.

I

In the widespread retreat from theoretical readings of modernism, there was an intellectual tendency to classify the modernist period via simplistic binarisms that treated modernism as the embodiment of outmoded attitudes that needed to be rejected and surpassed. In attempting to make sense of this tendency, we confront periodization, a problem that draws us into the labyrinthine issues of the genealogical ties that bind diachronically organized periods to modernity itself. As soon as one manages to define one's periodizations in a stable and systematic way, one finds those periodizations challenged as merely reflecting the historical blindnesses of the moment from which they emerged. How modernism has been periodized is a particularly acute illustration of this process. Over the course of the 1980s, for example, there developed a pervasive sense of an insurmountable divide between the tangible, contemporary experience of the postmodern and the irretrievably lost experience of the modern: an experience that was widely seen, in crucial ways, to have become less relevant than the temporally more remote experience of the Renaissance.

Jean E. Howard draws on this assumption when, in 1986, she invokes the transition to the postmodern as an explanation for "the uncanny way in which, at this historical moment, an analysis of Renaissance culture can be made to speak to the concerns of late twentieth-century culture" (Howard 1986: 15). Modernism, by contrast, seemed hopelessly *passé* and was widely regarded as (at best) a target-rich environment for ideology critique. Even the complex theoretical legacy associated with the modernist moment was regularly depicted as irremediably tainted by fascism and racism. The most obvious target was Heidegger, briefly a member of the Nazi party. But there were also concerns about the degree to which, for example, Theodor Adorno, who uncompromisingly opposed fascism, based his critique of jazz on racially based stereotypes. It was not only the theoretical legacy of modernism, both right and left, that was retroactively classified as irredeemably tainted. As most publicly occurred in the case of de Man's wartime journalism, there were claims that poststructuralist and/or postmodern theory possessed a covert genealogy that could be traced to the most dangerously reactionary tendencies of the modernist era. In other words, many of the least desirable aspects of modernism could evidently be discerned in theoretical discourses widely portrayed as breaking with modernism. Far from redeeming the theoretical dimensions of modernism, this charge increased suspicions that modernist texts did not deserve to be interpreted from a theoretically engaged perspective but only to be diagnosed historically. As part of this discursive shift, there developed a view that the common denominator between modernism and theory could best be understood as a shared penchant for obscurity and irresponsibility.

In this anti-theoretical vein Rainey's *Institutions of Modernism* advocates rejecting "rebarbative jargon" and historicist self-consciousness in favor of historical storytelling based on adherence to archivally verifiable facts. This pejorative view of theory grows out of the reaction against deconstruction in the wake of the revelations regarding de Man. The connection is made painfully explicit in the still more emphatic explanation provided in *Ezra Pound and the Monument of Culture*, which epitomizes the empiricist bias of anti-theoretical tendencies in the "new" modernist studies. There Rainey invokes only one theorist in an unequivocally favorable way: Clifford Geertz, for the concept of "thick description," which had been crucial to Greenblatt's New Historicist work on the Renaissance (Rainey 1991: 3). It is glaringly apparent, however, that Rainey conceives of thick description not as a means of carefully sifting through the layers of sedimentation that mediate our access to local knowledge but, rather, as a means of substituting facts for theories. Rainey explains that his approach to fascism will have little use for any of the key terms associated with critical theory: as he derisively puts it, for "Desire, Language, Intertextuality, Representation, Mimetic violence—the bloated abstractions that dominate contemporary literary studies" (Rainey 1991: 3). Although Rainey, in a fashion reminiscent of Pound's Imagist tactics, thereby frames his attack on theory as a broad attack on the hollowness of abstraction, it soon becomes obvious that the de Man affair is what provides him with his sense of urgency and polemical purpose. The underlying implication is that, while Pound's sins against historical accuracy are enormous, it is not Pound but contemporary literary theory, particularly as epitomized by de Man, that constitutes a clear and present danger.

It would be tedious to document all of the cases in which the de Man affair was instrumentalized in this way. In singling out Rainey, I am not suggesting that he is uniquely responsible for the shift in attitudes toward theory. Instead, I illustrate how, in the climate of the de Man affair, it became possible for some of our most erudite scholars of modernism to discuss the relation between modernism and theory in a way that suggested not merely that poststructural and/or postmodernist theorists were wrong but that the practitioners of such theories were engaged in a directly malevolent enterprise. Although most scholars did not adopt such extreme language, there was a widespread acquiescence to the notion that the relation between modernism and theory was irreparably plagued by scandal.

There is, however, no need to frame the intellectual commerce between modernism and theory in condemnatory terms. As Barbara Herrnstein Smith points out in "Pre-Post-Modern Relativism," there is abundant reason to believe many of the allegedly new and menacing aspects of what is often called postmodern theory were already integral to the intellectual milieu in relation to which modernism took shape:

> [F]rom the end of the nineteenth century and increasingly to the eve of the
> Second World War, a notable feature of theory in virtually every field of
> study was a more or less radical questioning of traditional objectivist, absolutist
> and universalist concepts and a related effort to develop viable alternative—
> non-objectivist, non-absolutist, non-universalist—models and accounts.
>
> (Smith 2005: 19)

In other words, as Smith observes, throughout "the era we call 'Modernist,'"
there was significant space devoted to the same "sort of radical questioning and
related theoretical production" that, under the rubric of postmodernism, has
recently come to be stigmatized as entailing nothing less than a self-destructive
refusal to believe in reality. The crucial element in Smith's argument is her refusal
to accept that there is something sacrosanct about such periodizing divisions as
those that fence off modernity from postmodernity, and modernists from post-
modernists. Unhesitatingly rejecting the narrowly diachronic notions of intellectual
period and milieu that, in recent years, have stultified modernist studies, Smith
rightly observes that the currently accepted temporal boundaries prove pre-
cariously difficult to maintain or justify, when one seriously traces the genealogy
of those views labeled postmodern. Noting that "the periods of the emergence and
prevalence of such views remain open questions for intellectual history," Smith proposes "that any presumed or asserted historical specificity is suspect" (Smith
2005: 18–19). In these richly succinct remarks, Smith touches on a barrier to
revivifying the theoretical dimension that informs modernism: namely, the extent
to which modernist studies adopted a diachronically restrictive model of its
legitimate area of inquiry. The paradox is that, in order to restructure the field
in a way that would permit us to foreground theoretical questions in any thor-
oughgoing fashion, we would have to abandon entirely the binary opposition
between modernism and postmodernism that has come to define the field's
relation to the construction of knowledge. It would not be enough simply to
collapse this binarism, since, as we have seen, in attempting to treat postmodernist thought as simply a variation on modernist thought, critics often end
up retaining a reductivist view of modernism that is itself a byproduct of the
construction of postmodernity as a category of periodization directly opposed to
modernity. Instead, following Smith's lead, we must question all of our current
assumptions about how modernism should (or should not) be periodized.

In other words, to address meaningfully the place of theory in modernism, we
must entertain the possibility that "modernism" has outlived its usefulness—
particularly to the degree that it has come to represent, in quasi-Aristotelian
fashion, a period whose tragic trajectory can be narrated in relation to a relatively clear process of development in which there is a discernible progression
from beginning to middle to end. We would also need to rethink "modernity,"
which has become so capacious as to have lost virtually any sense of specificity.
Jameson's recent critique of the postcolonial interest in defining alternative
modernities is pertinent here. By redescribing modernity as another word for
capitalism, it limits the incantatory power associated with "modernity": "for

Marx modernity is simply capitalism itself" (Jameson 2002: 80). Although such a definition has serious limitations, it has the advantage of compelling us to avoid the pitfalls of pluralistic models of modernity that rob the term of analytic power. Also pertinent is Jameson's maxim that "[w]e cannot not periodize," a maxim that, as Jameson observes, "while acknowledging the objections to periodization as a philosophical act, nonetheless finds itself brought up short against its inevitability" (Jameson 2002: 29). This maxim compels us to think seriously about the evasiveness of how, under the rubric of "new modernisms," we have been encouraged to tell factually detailed stories about localized manifestations of modernism, and to disregard the pressing need to explore the epistemological basis for those stories.

What is it, after all, that authorizes us to tell stories based on the ostensibly stable and homogeneous status of modernism and modernity as periodizing categories? If we choose to tell stories about aspects of something that we choose to call modernism, and if we choose to treat these stories as a subset of something that we choose to call modernity, what periodizing assumptions are we tacitly making about the temporal and historical status of modernism and modernity? Where (if anywhere) should we draw the boundaries of modernist studies as a genre of academic discourse? Given the degree to which our prevailing concepts of literary tradition were produced during what we now retroactively describe as the modernist period, and given the degree to which our prevailing concepts of literary theory are anticipated in the philosophical discourse of what we now retroactively describe as the modernist period, is it not perfectly reasonable to argue that all existing genres of literary study should be regarded as, in effect, subgenres of modernist studies? In raising these questions, I do not mean to suggest that modernist scholars should attempt to colonize the entire discipline of literary studies. Instead, I wish simply to point out that, in forsaking the risks of theoretical confrontation for the quiet pleasures of the archive, modernist scholars deny themselves the opportunity to ask questions that are likely to transform literary studies in unpredictable ways, and that, by interrogating the basis for disciplinary constructions, would possibly shatter the seemingly self-evident assumption that modernist studies necessarily deserves to be described as modernist studies.

II

Given the fecundity of Jameson's observations regarding the contingencies of periodization, it helps to consider the degree to which Jameson's version of historicism is profoundly distinct from the New Historicism and the less theoretically grounded forms of cultural materialism proliferating in modernist studies. As Carolyn Porter observes with reference to *The Political Unconscious*, it is amply apparent that "any serious attempt to historicize literary studies cannot ignore the issues raised by his discussion" (Porter 1988: 750). But although Jameson's famous injunction—"Always historicize!"—formed part of the same intellectual climate that had nurtured the New Historicism, the New Historicist project was dominated by an anti-Marxist ethos that left little place for the synthesizing, structural analogies that characterize Jameson's use of the concept of totality.

Bluntly recognizing this distinction, Joel Fineman praises the New Historicists for their effort to break out of "the encyclopedically enclosed circle of Hegelian historical self-reflection," and proposes that "the New Historicism amounts to a gesture which is the very opposite of Fredric Jameson's essentially ahistorical injunction in *The Political Unconscious* to 'always historicize'" (Fineman 1989: 60). In accusing Jameson of being ahistorical, Fineman tacitly builds on the assumption that, in any effort to frame the play of historical contingency by means of theoretical constructs, we can discern the importation of criteria that are trans-cendental rather than historical. Jameson touches on the same issues in the course of his analysis of the New Historicism, albeit from a perspective that, in a symmetrically antithetical fashion, calls into question the historical credentials of the New Historicists. Analyzing the work of Walter Benn Michaels, he suggests the New Historicism embodies a style of interpretive practice in which theory, having been rejected for relying on an apodeictic vision of critical self-consciousness, is replaced by a nominalistic pursuit of the immanence of cultural forms of sig-nification. As Jameson observes, this rejection of "interpretive distance" (Jameson 1991: 188) exhibits a kinship with Lévi-Strauss's anthropological exegeses in which, by means of "the method of the homology," connections are drawn between "various local and concrete 'texts'" (Jameson 1991: 187).

A related perspective on New Historicist methodology is advanced by Alan Liu, who, alluding to the influence of Lévi-Strauss, suggests, from the vantage point of 1989, that New Historicist "models compose a *bricolage* substituting for what was once the more methodical *narratio* or presentation of facts in history of ideas: the recording of such master paradigms, for example, as the Chain of Being, the Mirror, and the Lamp" (Liu 1989: 721–2). Jameson evokes this shift from the rule of metaphor via the category of the homology. In the New Historicist rejection of all totalizing paradigms, Jameson discerns a radically nominalistic fusion of homological method with the neo-pragmatist logic influentially propounded by Walter Benn Michaels and Stephen Knapp in their polemical essay "Against Theory." Jameson suggests that, in some of its applications within the New Historicism, this logic has been understood simply "as a call to return to a pre-theoretical procedure" (Jameson 1991: 188). But Jameson also notes that the broader trajectory of New Historicism demonstrates just how readily this logic is able "to open up a whole post-theoretical set of operations that retain the discursive conquests of a range of heterogeneous materials while quietly abandoning the theoretical component that once justified their enlargement" (Jameson 1991: 188).

As a result of his decision to base his discussion of New Historicism primarily on Michaels's example, Jameson elides the degree to which, in the writings of such earlier figures as Stephen Greenblatt, there was a persistent attempt to resist the fall into pure immanence by means of a redemptive focus on Foucauldian theorizations regarding the circulation of social energy. However, by the early 1990s, when the influence of the New Historicism at last came to be felt in a decisive way, the New Historicist interest in theories (and histories) of the subject had evaporated. Instead, emphasis was placed on pragmatic forms of cultural materialism in which, as in the work of Michaels, there was "something like a ban or taboo on theoretical discussion and on the taking of interpretive distance from the material" (Jameson 1991: 188). In a manner well beyond Michaels's post-theoretical nominalism the modernist acolytes of historical criticism tended to fetishize factual information and treat theory as a potentially unhealthy diversion into enfeebling skepticism and relativism. This discursive shift recognized the limits of what, in a pragmatist critique of New Historicism, Howard Horwitz identifies as a "model of self-reflection ... adopted specifically from European leftist social science (the Frankfurt school and critical theory)" (Horwitz 1988: 799). Once the practice of historically based forms of Geertzian "thick description" became professional routine, there no longer appeared to be any pressing need to reflect, in a theoretically comprehensive way, on methodology.

In making these observations, I do not pretend that the field of modernist studies is now dominated by practitioners who completely reject the legitimacy of theoretically based criticism. If pressed, even the most fastidious believer in the supremacy of historical context will acknowledge the legitimacy of reading modernist texts in ways that foreground theoretical questions and do not rely on a restrictively periodizing framework. Yet the hegemonic dominance of diachronically strict notions of historical periodization has created a climate in which the future of modernist studies is widely imagined as entailing a continued emphasis on the historical specificity of materially grounded processes of cultural production, and, in a directly related way, on the narrativization of factual detail. One need not revive the old quarrel between New Critics and traditional historical scholars to recognize that the result is descriptive—almost stenographic— literary criticism that aims to tell coherent stories based on clear, linear notions of causality. In a manner regularly invoked in the controversy surrounding de Man's wartime journalism, the active assertion of theoretical sovereignty became widely regarded as irresponsible, undemocratic elitism. In a curious reversal of Sidney's *Defence of Poesy*, we are asked to reject the inventive, sovereign powers of the poet in favor of the sober, secretarial virtues of the historian, who is "loaden with old mouse-eaten records, authorizing himself for the most part upon other histories whose greatest authorities are built upon the notable foundation of hearsay" (Sidney 2004: 14).

Much of the tension surrounding these issues stems from unresolved debates concerning the relation of the modern to the postmodern. Whereas Jameson explicitly distances his interest in the narrative structure of modernity from Jean-François Lyotard's postmodern declaration "of the end of grand narratives," I suggest we revisit Lyotard's work to challenge the methodological evasiveness of much of the work that has been produced under the rubric of the "new modernist" studies. Of particular value to any such effort is Lyotard's *Le Différend*, a text that, by confronting the work of Holocaust revisionists, points out the inescapable contingency and contestability of all efforts to narrate the past. As Lyotard maintains, the mere accumulation of factual evidence does nothing, in and of itself, to settle a dispute, particularly when the disagreements are byproducts of radically incommensurable beliefs. In a brutally pointed analysis of the scientistic style of Holocaust denial epitomized by Robert Faurisson, Lyotard shows that such adversaries can never be persuaded or rebutted by scholarly tactics of empirical evidence and syllogistic reasoning. Before a figure such as Faurisson would ever admit that a gas chamber was indeed a gas chamber, he would insist on hearing the testimony of "a victim of this gas chamber" (Lyotard 1988a: 4). As Lyotard thus brutally reminds us, there are disturbing instances in which a blunt appeal to empirical evidence will not suffice.

As with Foucault's concept of the archive, the contingency of testimonial evidence presents an insurmountable challenge to the notion that, by immersing ourselves in the materiality of the archive, we can somehow uncover (or, at least, approximate) the unquestionable, incontrovertible truth about the past. Although the repression of living memory is seldom as horrific as it is in the case of Holocaust denial, all efforts at historical recovery are undermined by the sheer quantity of testimony that, either through chance or intention, has never been actualized as a trace or an enunciation, and that, as a result, has never achieved the status of retrievable immanence. No matter what the quantity of material evidence, our suppositions about history are shadowed by a darkness that we can penetrate only by using assumptions grounded, not in legible, visible evidence, but, rather, in beliefs regarding the silent and invisible intimations of the unwritten and the unspoken. If we fail to rise to the hermeneutic challenge of what Agamben has provocatively identified as "the aporia of testimony" (Agamben 2002: 163)—that is, if we simply abandon the theoretical burden of epistemological indeterminacy in the name of the Enlightenment virtues of empirical certainty—we make it harder, not easier, to resist efforts to appropriate the historical record for politically destructive and regressive purposes. This does not mean that, in disputes regarding what is or is not true, theoretical forms of argumentation are necessarily any more effective than those that rely on appeals to the empirical data manifested in the archive. But it does mean that there is no unmediated, pre-theoretical way of circumventing the contingencies of interpretation and evaluation.

Any attempt to come to terms with these issues is haunted by the specter of de Man's influential efforts, over the course of the 1960s and 1970s, to resist the view that there could be meaningful commerce between the protocols of literary being and the contingencies of historical existence. De Man stands at a crucial point of intersection between modernism and theory. His most obvious tie to modernism in the broad sense comes through his readings of Yeats, a poet who, by blurring the boundary between late romanticism and high modernism, challenges the effort to periodize modernism. By the late 1950s, when de Man produced the sustained reading of Yeats that appears in his Harvard dissertation, there was already an active debate regarding whether or not Yeats was a modernist. De Man exhibits no interest in modernism as a periodizing category, let alone Yeats's relation to it. His focus instead is on issues that defy conventional approaches to literary history. Challenging the rhetoric of temporality that informs conventional narratives of literary modernity, de Man raises theoretical questions about the mimetic status of poetic language: questions that compel us to ponder the relation between romantic and modernist aesthetics, and that remind us of the degree to which the story of modernism must always be, out of narrative necessity, a theoretical story. Discerning in Yeats an "a priori commitment that maintains itself in the face of all attacks and denials" (de Man 1984: 146), de Man argues for the centrality of Yeats's "stylistic evolution" (de Man 1984: 148), which embodies a logic that cannot be plotted in correlation with the development of thematic issues and concerns.

Despite the unfortunate wording of the critique of positivistic history with which he closes "Literary History and Literary Modernity," there is much value in the warning that he provides about the use of the term modernity "as a device for historical periodization": a use that entails an "unawareness that history and modernity may well be even more incompatible than literature and modernity" (de Man 1983: 142). It is also worth remembering that, running counter to the enabling premises of modernist studies, de Man does not accord a privileged position to modernism as a movement in art, music, or literature. In "Lyric and Modernity," he skeptically alludes to the historians' "dream" of achieving "a reconciliation of memory with action," and describes as an instance of this "dream" the manner in which "Hans Robert Jauss and his group" exhibit "no qualms about dating the origins of modernism with historical accuracy" (de Man 1983: 183). As de Man explains, the Jaussians operate on the basis of the "assumption that the movement of lyric poetry away from representation is a historical process that dates back to Baudelaire as well as being the very movement of modernity" (de Man 1983: 183). De Man's view of historical process powerfully rejects such moments of diachronic lucidity. These reflections on history, modernity, and de Man return us to the status of modernist studies as a disciplinary formation. If there are, as de Man suggests, no fixed historical limits to the relation between literature and modernity, is it not reasonable to argue that all literary studies should be regarded as a subset of modernist studies? Or is it instead more reasonable to argue that modernist studies are based on an illusory notion of historical rupture and progression, and that modernism is therefore nothing more than a false object of disciplinary desire? For that matter, given de Man's own immersion in the postsymbolist contact zone between lyric and modernity, might we read his work as an articulation of concerns that qualify as late modernist, or possibly even as high modernist? In a broader sense, why is it widely assumed that stories about reading are somehow less historical than stories about someone's day-to-day experience of public and/or private life? And why has it come to be widely assumed that theory is somehow an extrinsic imposition on those narratives of modernity that have come to be named as instances of modernism? Such questions can never be answered by a trip to the archive. Such questions call for theory.

Notes

1 The two notable exceptions are a 1983 article by Alex Zwerdling on Virginia Woolf and a 1984 article by Andrew Ross on T. S. Eliot's *The Waste Land*. Zwerdling's

emphasis on empirical facts, rather than Ross's emphasis on problems of modernist subjectivity, eventually dominated the historical turn in modernist studies.

2 This trend is apparent in Helen Sword's *Ghostwriting Modernism*. Jean-Michel Rabaté, while acknowledging the undeniable merits of Sword's commitment to modernist historiography, points out the limitations of her wish that, somehow, "one could simply provide the 'hard' facts of archives and avoid the deconstructive tactics which lead to a generalized 'hauntology'" (Rabaté 2003: 216).

3 North (1999) provides a particularly elegant example of this tendency. The focus on thick historical description is carried to a far greater extreme in Filreis (1994). Notable in such work is the almost complete absence of the theoretical dimension that informs, for example, the work of Marc Angenot, whose diachronically based explorations of social discourse are always grounded in a rigorously detailed engagement with broader debates in philosophy, linguistics, and sociology. For an exemplary illustration of Angenot's methods, see his Angenot (1989).

4 Since Foucauldian conceptions of the archive thrive on gaps, fissures, and discontinuities, it is not surprising that the New Historicism arose in relation to the Renaissance rather than Modernism. The principle at work is anticipated in Foucault's suggestion that "it emerges in fragments, regions, and levels, more fully, no doubt, and with greater sharpness, the greater the time that separates us from it" (Foucault 1972: 130).

Bibliography

Agamben, G. (2002) *Remnants of Auschwitz: The Witness and the Archive*, trans. D. Heller-Roazen, New York: Zone Books.

Angenot, M. (1989) *1889: Un état du discours social*, Longueuil, Quebec: Le Préambule.

de Man, P. (1979) *Allegories of Reading: Figural Language in Rousseau, Nietzsche, Rilke, and Proust*, New Haven: Yale University Press.

—— (1983) *Blindness and Insight*, revised edn, Minneapolis: University of Minnesota Press.

—— (1984) *Rhetoric of Romanticism*, New York: Columbia University Press.

—— (c. 1986) *The Resistance to Theory*, Minneapolis: University of Minnesota Press.

Filreis, A. (1994) *Modernism from Right to Left: Wallace Stevens, the Thirties and Literary Radicalism*, Cambridge and New York: Cambridge University Press.

Fineman, J. (1989) "The History of the Anecdote: Fiction and Fiction," in H. Veeser (ed.) *The New Historicism*, New York: Routledge, 49–76.

Foucault, M. (1972) *The Archaeology of Knowledge and The Discourse on Language*, trans. A. M. Sheridan Smith, New York: Pantheon Books.

Greenblatt, S. (1980) *Renaissance Self-Fashioning: From More to Shakespeare*, Chicago: University of Chicago Press.

Horwitz, H. (1988) "'I Can't Remember': Skepticism, Synthetic Histories, Critical Action," *South Atlantic Quarterly* 87(4): 787–819.

Howard, J. E. (1986) "The New Historicism in Renaissance Studies," *English Literary Renaissance* 16: 13–43.

Jameson, F (1981) *The Political Unconscious*, Ithaca, NY: Cornell University Press.

—— (1984) "Wallace Stevens," *New Orleans Review* 11(1) (Spring 1984): 10–19.

—— (1991) *Postmodernism, or, The Cultural Logic of Late Capitalism*, Durham, NC: Duke University Press.

—— (2002) *A Singular Modernity: Essay on the Ontology of the Present*, London: Verso.

Lentricchia, F. (1989) "Foucault's Legacy: A New Historicism?" in H. Veeser (ed.) *The New Historicism*, New York: Routledge, 231–42.

Liu, A. (1989) "The Power of Formalism: The New Historicism," *ELH (English Literary History)* 58: 721–71.

Lyotard, J.-F. (1988a) *The Differend: Phrases in Dispute*, trans. G. Van Den Abbeele, Minneapolis: University of Minnesota Press.

—— (1988b) *The Postmodern Condition: A Report on Knowledge*, Minneapolis: University of Minnesota Press.

Marcus, J. (1989) "The Asylums of Antaeus: Women, War, and Madness—Is there a Feminist Fetishism?" in H. Veeser (ed.) *The New Historicism*, London and New York: Routledge, 132–51.

Morrison, P. (1996) *Poetics of Fascism: Ezra Pound, T. S. Eliot, Paul de Man*, New York: Oxford University Press.

North, M. (1999) *Reading 1922: A Return to the Scene of the Modern*, New York: Oxford University Press.

Porter, C. (1988) "Are We Being Historical Yet?" *South Atlantic Quarterly* 87(4): 743–86.

Rabaté, J.-M. (2003) "Review of Helen Sword's *Ghostwriting Modernism*," *Modernism/Modernity* 10(1): 214–16.

Rainey, Lawrence (1991) *Ezra Pound and the Monument of Culture: Text, History, and the Malatesta Cantos*, Chicago: University of Chicago Press.

—— (1999) *Institutions of Modernism: Literary Elites and Public Culture*, New Haven: Yale University Press.

Ross, A. (1984) "*The Waste Land* and the Fantasy of Interpretation," *Representations* 8 (Autumn): 134–58.

Sidney, Sir P. (2004) *Sidney's* The Defence of Poesy *and Selected Renaissance Literary Criticism*, ed. G. Alexander, Harmondsworth, UK: Penguin.

Smith, B. H. (2005) *Scandalous Knowledge: Science, Truth, and the Human*, Edinburgh: Edinburgh University Press.

Sword, H. (2002) *Ghostwriting Modernism*, Ithaca, NY: Cornell University Press.

Veeser, H. Aram, (ed.) (1989) *The New Historicism*, New York and London: Routledge.

White, H. (1987) *The Content of the Form: Narrative Discourse and Historical Representation*, Baltimore: Johns Hopkins University Press.

—— (1989) "New Historicism: A Comment," in H. Veeser (ed.) *The New Historicism*, New York: Routledge, 293–302.

Zwerdling, A. (1983) "Anger and Conciliation in Woolf's Feminism," *Representations* 3 (Summer): 68–89.

Modernism and the moment of defeat

Response to Andrew John Miller

Scott McCracken

To encounter modernist studies today can be compared with the experience of walking into the 2006 exhibition at the Victoria and Albert Museum, 'Modernism: Designing a New World'. The visitor stepped off the street into a modernist utopia, where everything from the art on the wall to the Bauhaus fitted kitchen sink belied the reality of the interwar period, when modernist forms were a minority taste, even when they did seep gradually, from the end of the 1920s, into everyday life as book covers or posters on the underground. The last twenty years have seen a comparable spectacle in modernist scholarship: the growth of the Modernist Studies Association; the establishment of its journal, *Modernism/Modernity*; and countless titles with the words, modern, modernism or modernity in their titles.

Such spaces, aesthetic and scholarly, have always been part of the appeal of different modernisms. To bring them together in one space, at the MSA or the V&A, is partly to fulfil their dream, but it is also to lose some of the critical distance required to achieve an historical understanding. Just as the V&A offered a partial picture, contemporary modernist studies can be accused of a certain narrowness. Its examples are too often drawn from Anglo-American literature. There is too little work on the visual arts or music and little to remind us of the widespread scepticism modernist forms provoked in the twentieth century. Modernist studies differs markedly from its more staid and cautious cousin, Victorian studies, which has, over a somewhat longer period, consolidated a productive interdisciplinarity, where text and image, literary and historical and even economic studies co-exist. History and theory are in constant dialogue in Victorian studies. In modernist studies, the conversation falters.

Andrew Miller suggests that the problem lies in theory: that the turn to the archive is the sign of a retreat from the big epistemological questions, which have been replaced with dense descriptions of the relics of the past. I would argue that the real problem is not one of methodology. It is to be found in history itself. The nineteenth century, while far from over in its effects, can at least be contemplated from a distance. The twentieth century has barely ended; its historiography remains in doubt, without the comfortable markers and boundaries of earlier periods. No wonder then that modernism was relatively untouched by the playfulness of new historicism (when new historicism was *new*), there were few or no historical verities to play with. Even Eric Hobsbawm's magnificent *The Age of Extremes: The Short Twentieth Century*, likely to remain the benchmark for all future attempts to chart the century's contours, covers only 1914–91.

The unfinished twentieth century means an unfinished relationship with modernism. Contra Miller, then, I contend that the most urgent theoretical issue for modernist studies today is the historiography of the twentieth century, a problem that is as much political as it is theoretical or historical. For while many of the theoretical currents of the last century, like modernism itself, had their genesis in revolution, the current situation for the Left is, as Perry Anderson has commented, in his editorial to the relaunched *New Left Review*, one of defeat. As Anderson points out, despite all the socialist experiments of the twentieth century, capitalism is rampant and there appear to be no checks on the rise of global inequalities in wealth. As a consequence, the scholars are working within (although often also weakly against) historical narratives imposed by the consequences of that defeat. The de Man controversy is significant, not because of what it might or might not tell us about poststructuralism, as Miller maintains, but because it reveals the battles of the twentieth century that have not yet been laid to rest. The dominant narrative now is neo-conservative and it is likely to remain so for some time, despite that position's current setbacks, because of the lack of a popular Left alternative. A version of Fukuyama's, now recanted, 'end of history', the neo-conservative version of the twentieth century does not argue so much that the triumph of the market and capitalist democracy were inevitable, but that it represents the victory of good over a series of evils by men and women, Winston Churchill, Ronald Reagan, Margaret Thatcher and George W. Bush, who were prepared to stand up to Nazism, the Soviet Union and 'Islamic Fascism' respectively. The twentieth century is flattened out, its diverse ideologies are judged as 'with us' or 'against us', a process that suggests two possible responses.

The first is to say: 'Well, it's complicated … ' Complexity has, in fact, been a stock response of the Left to its own narratives of triumphalism and progress. Walter Benjamin critiqued the social democratic version of progress in 'On the Concept of History'; and it was crude, one-dimensional versions of Leninism that were the target of the new social movements that formed around issues of gender, sexuality and race after 1968. Where complexity has threatened to harden into essentialized identities, so that history once again flattens out into being for or against a transcendent structure, the academy has insisted on yet more complexity. Indeed, getting more complicated became, at the high point of theory, the only way to score academic points. It's a strategy that has paid dividends, but has also had costs. It is questionable how far its benefits can be turned to advantage in the current conjuncture.

The alternative is Anderson's position, that: 'The only starting-point for a realistic Left today is a lucid registration of historical defeat. Capital has comprehensively beaten back all threats to its rule, the bases of whose power … were persistently underestimated by the socialist movement' (Anderson 2000). The historical perspective his position affords is set out in a series of comparisons between the end of the century and the political circumstances in which *New Left Review* was (re)started in the early 1960s. Anderson differs from most commentators in that his recognition of defeat does not cause him to dismiss the alternatives to capitalism the twentieth century presented. If not always palatable, they were at least, like the Soviet Union, 'dynamic' realities. His arguments have been taken up by a few,[1] but have had little resonance in the new modernist studies. In the 1980s, Anderson argued for the 'proximity of social revolution' as a defining condition for the emergence of modernism. For him, 1917 was the splash and modernism one of its ripples. Neither the October revolution nor its defeat register now.

But registering defeat need not be defeatist. Thinking through the concept of defeat, learning its lessons, can be productive. First, because registering defeat acknowledges that there has been a conflict; and if there was a conflict then there were alternative outcomes. History's victors write out not just their victims, but also the possible futures they represented. Those futures do not disappear. Second, because to register a conflict is to question today's widespread historico-political amnesia. Such amnesia is nothing new. Earlier periods of quiescence have experienced it. In 1868, when, for almost two decades European radicals had been subdued, Marx wrote of Eugène Ténot's study of the coup d'état of 1851 (*Paris en décembre 1851, étude historique sur le coup d'état*):

> The enormous sensation created by the book in Paris, and in France as a whole proves a very interesting FACT namely that the generation that has grown up under Badinguet [Napoleon III] knew nothing at all about the history of the regime under which it is living.
>
> (Marx and Engels 1988: letter dated 14 December 1868)

To which Engels replied,

> It is a necessary result of every victorious reaction that the causes of the revolution and especially of the counter revolution should pass into oblivion: in Germany the younger generation knows absolutely nothing about [18] 48 ... history comes to a complete stop at the end of '47.
>
> (Marx and Engels 1988: letter dated 18 December 1868)

In periods of defeat like our own, alternative histories are consigned to oblivion – later, Marx writes that Ténot's 1851 study of the provinces shows that 'Had the Parisians held out a couple of days longer, the *Empire* would have been *foutu*. The [republican] movement among the rural population was much bigger than we knew' (Marx and Engels 1988: letter dated 19 December 1868). Normalization of *what is* becomes necessary ideological work. Anderson points to Francis Fukuyama, Zbigniew Brzezinski, Samuel Huntington, Thomas Friedman as compelling historians 'of where the world is going, or [where it] has stopped', who insist that any other present than what exists is absurd, or outdated, hopelessly idealist or downright dangerous. Marx's reception of Ténot suggests an alternative historical method. A return to the decisive moment of defeat reveals the alternative outcomes concealed in the past. Using the same method would produce a different historiography of the twentieth century. It suggests we need to go back to the decisive moments of the twentieth century and learn the lessons of defeat.

What would such a methodology mean for modernist studies? Hardly a celebration, it would mean a return to the moments of loss, failure, and defeat that lie at the heart of some of the great modernist works. The antithesis of 'trauma studies', which seeks to see such moments from the point of view of those who experienced them, such a methodology would seek instead to understand history not, to paraphrase Brecht, as a natural disaster, but as the outcome of human agency. It would mean a renewal of theories of antagonism and conflict: a recognition that complexity has interests and patterns, which it is possible to interpret. For the present conjuncture, the most revealing moments of the twentieth century are likely to be the moments when the multiple futures imagined in modernism – nationalist, Fabian, feminist, anarchist, communist, socialist – were defeated. The 1930s emerges then as a crucial decade, Brecht's 'Svendborg' poems are one response to the experience of 1933; but a reappraisal of the 1920s is also due. The decade of high modernism can be reread as a series of defeats. Taking Britain alone, we might note the impact of the 1914–18 war, the failure of the first Labour government, the collapse of the General Strike and the Depression, the first three of which are revisited in Storm Jameson's unflinching trilogy, *Mirror in Darkness*, written in the early 1930s and thus also in the context of the Depression and the rise of Fascism.[2] Her novels show the extent to which historicizing the present was an important part of the struggle. It is something we need to do now, in the manner best exemplified by Philip Roth's recent novels.

In the interwar period, the years between the General Strike and the Nazis' seizure of power are perhaps the most important, marking the transition between utopian and political aesthetics. A proper analysis of such moments would historicize modernism in relation to the battle over the enlightenment that raged throughout the twentieth century and would be to recognize that where we are now is not where we will always be, that many other historical outcomes were possible and, to utilize Ernst Bloch's concept, remain possible in the not-yet-become.

In 1920, Dorothy Richardson wrote to Edward Garnett, 'I can under influence be wrought up to a white heat of pure Bolshevik rage; but left to myself I can be either Bolshevik or a diamond grabbing imperialist or anything or nothing by turns' (Richardson 1995: 39). Such political debates were the context in which modernism was forged, opening up the possibility of art that sought a radical transformation, new ways of seeing. Richardson's 'anything or nothing' combines with a refusal to be bound by one ideology, but it cannot be understood except in relation to the political alternatives offered by the early twentieth century. We now need not a return to high theory, but a return to history that recognizes these competing claims and gives some account of their defeat, a defeat that it would be foolish to think of as permanent.

Notes

1 See Bewes and Gilbert (2000: 1–19).
2 *Company Parade* (1933), *Love in Winter* (1935), *None Turn Back* (1936).

Bibliography

Anderson, P. (2000) 'Editorial', *New Left Review*, 1 (January–February): 5–24. Online: www.newleftreview.org/?view = 2092 (accessed 27 January 2008).

Bewes, T. and Gilbert, J. (2000) 'Politics after Defeat', in T. Bewes and J. Gilbert (eds) *Cultural Capitalism: Politics after New Labour*, London: Lawrence and Wishart, 1–19.

Hobsbawm, E. (1994) *The Age of Extremes: The Short Twentieth Century, 1914-1991*, London: Michael Joseph.

Marx, K. and Engels, F. (1988) *Collected Works*, Vol. 43, London: Lawrence and Wishart.

Richardson, D. (1995) 'Letter to Edward Garnett, 7 February 1920', in G. G. Fromm (ed.) *Windows on Modernism: Selected Letters of Dorothy Richardson*, Athens and London: University of Georgia Press, 39.

Part III

Forum

Introduction

This section of *Modernism and Theory* differs from the previous two in that there are no responses to the essays. Instead, the essays stand as individual responses to the insistent question behind this volume: how are modernist studies to proceed in light of modernism and theory's significance to each other? These essays thus indicate future directions for modernist studies and echo some of the concerns and insights in Parts I and II: the relationship between art and philosophy; time, ethics, and the event; the body, the sublime, the everyday, and capitalist globalization; kitsch, surrealism, and the avant-garde; novelty and the current state of modernist studies; and finally theory itself. The result is a powerful summing up and a forceful set of statements about terms that will remain central to modernist studies for the foreseeable future. One might even read this last part of *Modernism and Theory* as the first installment in a future lexicon, a *Keywords* for modernist studies in the twenty-first century. As a consequence of the terminological focus here, there is little call for the kind of elaboration of terms provided in the introductions to Parts I and II. The contributors here have spontaneously made defining their terms their primary focus. In doing so, they have perhaps gone to the very heart of this book's intention: not to remake modernist studies in a theoretical vein, or theory in a modernist vein, but to redefine the terms themselves so that their apparent opposition manifests as continuity. In this regard, they help to illuminate *Modernism and Theory*'s fundamentally dialectical intent: to overcome a manifest antinomy in favor of an expanded viewpoint that acknowledges profound continuities between the estranged members of critique's family tree.

9 Aesthetics

Charles Altieri

An age of criticism is not an age of writing, nor an age of reading: it is an age of criticism. People still read, still write—and well; but for many of them it is the act of criticism which has become the representative or Archetypal act of the intellectual.

(Jarrell 2001 [1953]: 66)

Forgive me for beginning on a personal note. But feeling old in this profession seems to impose the personal, especially when making general remarks. The problem is how not to rest in lament or nostalgia when reflecting on the state of literary studies. Therefore my first thought was to do what I could to combat the various forms of "materialist" studies now dominant. But if I could say something new about that topic, a big "if," the odds are good that it would go unheard. I need a different path. I must propose some model for future work that is compatible with the prevailing ideologies but divergent from them. The not so young will realize the magnitude of this task.

The only way to do that is to milk the personal for what it's worth, then attempt a self-correction that can point to a path for future work. Recalling what first excited me as possibilities for professional study when I was leaving graduate school in the late 1960s, I argue that the excitement younger critics find in the cultural criticism now dominating modernist studies is substantially the same, with one major difference. Ambitious critical work shaped by innovations in the late 1960s tried to show that writers produced imaginings necessary for the culture. Today's theories minimize authorial agency, showing how texts read historically illuminate their cultural contexts. This is not a small difference. But stressing it tempts us to overlook the elements common to the two models. Negatively, both insist that close reading could not suffice because criticism has to contextualize its materials and show how it addresses pressing cultural problems. Positively, this ambition leads to what I will call allegorical projects: to elucidate the text's cultural role, critics must provide a larger story into which the details fit. The links among details are quite different— especially insofar as they stressed or minimized the achievements of authors as thinkers and makers. Yet we should not ignore the shared model of satisfaction in developing the larger stories and in feeling that criticism directly addresses profound cultural needs. This shared model of satisfaction is one important reason critics could readily switch allegiances, e.g. from deconstruction to materialism.

After forty years of "advanced" criticism largely shaped by allegorical models, it is time to ask what those practices cost and whether there are alternative ways of honoring our concerns to make criticism relevant to our culture. To the extent that these critical stances depend on allegorical frameworks to realize their cultural ambitions, they often generalize too quickly from the particular art object to make claims about its possible force in relation to cultural values.[1] These generalizations seem compelled to minimize the intensities, sympathies, and identifications the art makes possible. So, my positive argument is that much critical work remains to be done from a primarily aesthetic perspective, emphasizing the affective force of particular objects. That work will *also* have to be framed in general terms, but the framing will be less a story the works share than an abstract need to address their particularity.

The stakes in this shift are substantial. Clearly, there are significant social benefits in developing agents capable of wide and deep concrete admirations, sympathies, and delights so that society develops richer alternatives to academic culture's dominant Enlightenment epistemic ideals. These ideals assume that the only socially important thinking is structured by disciplines, enabling them to secure knowledge claims and propose models for solving problems and conflicts. Instead, we can concentrate on how particulars engage our capacities to respond to and reflect upon affective dimensions of experience; criticism should emphasize how the manner of a work's engaging the world affords a different kind of matter.[2] The value of criticism need not depend on individual works' participation in a general story or struggle concerning how society forms its beliefs. Our criticism matters socially because it sustains and affords reflection on the many ways we live by other than epistemic values. Critics can promise to make readers aware of their powers and investments as affective beings, and can promise that their work will challenge them to respond more fully to particular texts' ability to come alive for the imagination. This kind of work won't thematize social issues, but it will make citizens more aware of their capacities for self-enjoyment and for sympathy with how people are governed by cares, attachments, and projections of more satisfying lives. We have seen enough of ideas and arguments: we should try other routes to reducing violence and reconciling differences.

Two documents from the late 1960s illustrate how sophisticated criticism becomes allegorical and how the major critics in the 1960s set ambitions that still govern how critics imagine their tasks. These two texts have different emphases and political commitments, but both stress how European philosophy can illuminate modernist writings' resistance to the nihilism that infected cultural life early in the twentieth century. The major impact of J. Hillis Miller's *Poets of Reality* (1965) was its demonstration that one could honor literary texts' complexity and imaginativeness without the exhaustive close reading or thematics of paradox in which we were trained. One could treat writers as thinkers, and their texts as aspects of dialectical processes realizing that thinking's potential. Miller told a compelling story of how modernist writing, especially modernist poetry, developed a "journey beyond nihilism toward a poetry of reality" (1965: 1). Strikingly, Miller's language still convincingly rises to the level of the crisis he posited, but only by composing an elaborate allegory: "When God and the creation become objects of consciousness, man becomes a nihilist. Nihilism is the nothingness of consciousness when consciousness becomes the foundation of everything" (1965: 3). Technology's triumph is the ultimate mark of this consciousness; the culture comes to depend on its products rather than on what is given by the world. Yet, Miller shows, some modern writers have the courage and intelligence to make the "nihilism latent in our culture ... appear as nihilism" (1965: 5). It then becomes possible "to go beyond it by understanding it" (Miller 1965: 5). Writers can turn from the recesses of "subjectivism" to abandon "the independence of the ego" (Miller 1965: 7). By learning to "walk barefoot in reality" (as Wallace Stevens put it), they could accept a world that is a surface of co-presences rather than the traditional divide between appearance and depth: "This space is the realm of the twentieth century poem," a "space in which things, the mind, and words coincide in the closest intimacy" (Miller 1965: 8).

Irving Howe's tone is strikingly different—it's not that of an academic to other academics—as is his broader perspective on modernist writing. But the allegorical core of his account of modernism turns to the same challenge posed by the writers' sense of nihilism pervading modern social life. Howe begins the introduction to *Literary Modernism* (1967) with his characteristically keen attention to what writers feel as cultural imperatives:

> Modern writers find that they begin to work at a moment when the culture is marked by a prevalent style of perception and feeling; and their modernity consists in a revolt against this prevalent style, an unyielding rage against the official order.
>
> (Howe 1967: 13)

Then he lists a series of reasons for that rage that all emphasize a sense of spiritual crisis forcing literature to play roles once reserved for theology and philosophy. For Howe, as for Lionel Trilling, modernism's characteristic shift is from the quest for truth to "writing as the purification of a sincerity at least capable of accurately portraying an individual's suffering and desires for change, whatever the objective conditions might bear" (Howe 1967: 19): "There is a hunger to break past the bourgeois proprieties and self-containment of culture toward a form of absolute personal speech, a literature deprived of ceremony and stripped to revelation" (Howe 1967: 16). For Miller, idealizing personal speech would only exacerbate the subjectivism of the age. But as Howe warms to his topic he increasingly echoes Miller's concerns. He treats modernism as rooted in Romanticism but seeking alternatives to its transcendental hopes (Howe 1967: 21–2). Therefore modernity confronts an "extreme sense of historical impasse, the assumption that something about the experience of our ages is unique, a catastrophe without precedent" (Howe 1967: 15). The catastrophe is most pronounced in the dynamic that emphasizes personal speech: for modern culture, "the object perceived seems always on the verge of being swallowed up by the perceiving agent, and the act of perception in danger of being exalted to the substance of reality" (Howe 1967: 14). Then Howe can address what happens in modernist poetry:

> For the Symbolist poet, the archetypal figure in modernism, there is no question, however, of *describing* such an experience: for him the moment of illumination occurs only through the action of the poem, only through its thrust as a particular form. Nor is there any question of relating it to the experience of a life time, for it is unique, transient, available only in the matter—perhaps more important, only in the moment of the poem. The poet does not transmit as much as he engages in a revelation.
>
> (Howe 1967: 27)

One feels Howe's distaste for symbolism. Unlike Miller, he does not believe in the efficacy of such revelation, but he is bound as a literary historian to accommodate himself to the poets' offer of hope. Howe seems almost convinced by Trilling's famous lament of his students' lack of discomfort with modernist demands on the spirit; his own unhappiness with the model testifies to his authenticity in allying himself with it.

The most striking aspect of rereading Miller and Howe is how intently their philosophical allegorizing takes on an edifying, even preacherly, urgency. So it doesn't seem a large leap to argue that cultural criticism shares with Miller and Howe the sense that culture is in a parlous state and the role of the critic is to address its blindness, self-satisfaction, and insensitivity to what makes desirable change possible. There is in common the language of exposing crisis, the sense that literature should directly address the causes of culture's suffering (although the 1960s did not see that the literature might be one of these causes), and above all an allegorical thinking that divides fields of inquiry into what matters for addressing a cultural plight and mere literature. The modernist writing that mattered seemed to have to engage the increasing objectification in which empiricist or capitalist thinking divided subject from object and threatened nihilism. This meant stressing those powers of art that offered direct or indirect engagements with that condition. Of chief relevance were versions of negativity like irony or withdrawal into abstraction, and sufficiently complex and dense structures to be taken seriously as modes of non-discursive thinking allied with the kinds of philosophy that opposed the empiricist causes of nihilism.

For the 1960s this picture enabled a vision of the artist as hero. For our new century the critic must play the hero: only the critic can elucidate the author's negativity, or impose negativity on authors' lapses into self-projection or utopianism. Our allegorical stage sets literary examples in social contexts, then allows these contexts to provide critical terms for resisting seduction by imaginary states, all to show what that seduction masks. That contemporary criticism seeks universalizing tales is most explicit in Fredric Jameson's claims about totalization. But critics who oppose Jameson, most eloquently Judith Butler, tend to develop their own universalizing tales of how only a species of otherness can save modernism from its fantasies of mastery. Criticism becomes the discipline able to produce a historical consciousness that illuminates how that otherness has been evaded by capital's normalizing force.

Whatever one's critical orientation, however, it seems impossible to deny that Miller and Howe are right about two things: (1) modernism staged itself as responding to world-historical crisis, so that criticism would be thin if it did not try to take seriously the terms of that crisis, at least provisionally; (2) that crisis demanded of writers that they reject, in form and content, the basic roles society had scripted for them. Significant writing could not be content to delight and instruct. It had to try to convince audiences of their spiritual crisis, and it had to reject descriptive tasks so that it could perform work that would enact how minds might experience the powers of language to articulate fresh ways of engaging the world.

However, those justified ambitions created a serious problem for criticism. How could critics respond to that general sense of crisis and still establish the particular stakes various writers wagered? How could they dramatize the writer's seriousness without emphasizing how they too confronted nihilism and its correlates like commodification? On the other hand, how could they capture the distinctiveness of individual texts if they required for each instance the same story of how each writer developed his or her methodological version of stepping "barefoot into reality"? The most ambitious critics would have to engage what I call "ontological projects" (later to become social projects), and emphasize the meta-dimensions that allied texts with one another. There could be little attention to the writers' many efforts to elaborate other projects or simply set their imaginations to work at finding release from such crushing seriousness. How many philosophical or cultural critics descending from Miller or Howe attend to the anti-allegorical Dada poems in *Spring and All,* or the intricacies of Eliot's "La Figlia Che Piange," or Pound's visionary *Cantos,* or the range from delight to attunement to fatality that Stevens wrests from his fascination with the imagination? Much more critical energy is devoted to the ideal of the poem creating a reality than to how poems actually compose realities. And criticism still founders when it tries to specify how these texts establish terms for close readerly attention to texts that could insist on its differences from philosophical reflection.

If my criticisms are valid for treatments of those poets who are habitually dragged out in discussions of the struggle against nihilism, imagine how the problems get exacerbated in relation to poets like Crane, Frost, Moore, H. D., Hughes, Cullen, and especially Stein (who could not abide talk of nihilism). The concern for philosophical generalization that shaped the modernist canon in the 1960s occludes a significant range of feelings, emotions, and reflections that these writers compose in their work. Not only does excluding these particular states impoverish "reality," it also vitiates the struggle against nihilism. For nihilism may be far less vulnerable to abstractions than it is to the proliferation of the complex embodied pleasures in existence provided by art. Critiques of nihilism that never mention sympathy and delight, or privilege lyric ecstasies like Pound's early *Cantos,* seem peculiarly obtuse to the practical aspects of cultural crisis. (Their earnestness might even provide good reason to take up nihilistic attitudes.)

To change this situation we have to assume that while major writers certainly are thinkers, they often concentrate on how the resources of a given medium might allow them to treat this thinking as ineluctably embodied in particular structures. The primary crisis for a maker is how to make this particular investment of time pay off by charging this particular object with what will compel an audience's attention. Writers do not lose their sense of cultural crisis, but there are good reasons to worry that addressing only such a general concern will not produce sufficient care for differentiating objects. And it will not make for much range in subjective investments. Perhaps the best response to nihilism is not to try to make the "nihilism latent in our culture ... appear as nihilism" or even compose a "space in which things, the mind, and words coincide in the closest intimacy" (Miller 1965: 5, 8). Instead, we should take pleasure in the thinking that makes objects and rhythms awaken the senses, diction startle the mind, and interpretation startle with wisdom and sympathy. A primary task now for modernist criticism is to attend to the variety of affective situations enabled by modernist culture. Some of these will demand cultural criticism, but others will show how to delight in what modernity makes possible. It is high time to work out how theory might go about facilitating the appreciation of that variety.

As a step in that direction, I will show how important it is to distinguish between Heideggerian phenomenological ontology and a looser, more practical phenomenology that teases out stakes for consciousness as it fosters intricate relationships with intentional objects. Heideggerian thinking is doomed to subordinate particulars to talk about "being" and then to talk about being in terms of generalized entities like "consciousness" or "language" or "spirit" or, increasingly, just "otherness." Cultural criticism came to power in justified resistance to that level of abstraction and that distance from quotidian practices. This cultural criticism is very good at talking about social relations and analyzing the material effects of art objects as they relate to readers and institutions. But it does not have the resources to handle one of those quotidian practices—making art objects that focus on what can be exemplary in concrete manners of action. Because most cultural criticism is committed to social realism, at least on the level of what it takes as effective reality, it cannot deal with the arts as intentional structures defining possibilities or potentials. It must collapse that potential into generalized interpretations of a work's significance or else focus its effects on actual readers, or perhaps on the careers of actual authors. At both poles criticism misses not only the distinctive reality art brings to the world as possibility, but also the nature of the site where art can claim a distinctive philosophical role.

For art's thinking is not bound to the aboutness of empirical or even generalizing propositions. Art's thinking begins in hypotheticals: what would thinking and feeling be like if the artist makes these assumptions or acts in this manner? Then it quickly leaps to offering a hypothetical about this hypothetical, an "as if" about an "as if." Having constructed the hypothetical and pushed it toward realization in several dimensions, art invites the audience to grapple with provisional processes of identification, or to refuse or to modify identification. Art does not offer argumentative paths for thinking so much as affective engagements with a concrete embodiment of particular states the artist deems worth investing in. Audiences are invited to use these as exemplars for directing their attention, caring for what they encounter, or determining what is worthy of emotional investment.

I am not arguing for a formalism or a return to philosophically informed close-readings. Instead I propose a different way to imagine how poets articulate particular modes of thinking that are important for their culture's struggles against nihilism and against commodity fetishism (i.e., nihilism in practice). Philosophy confronts nihilism by argument or by Wittgensteinian and Heideggerian modes of thinking that appear inseparable from processes that treat aspects of the world as if they were laden with value. But the arts best realize values when they appeal to our judgments of manner, of how the work makes specific gestures that command interest and project exemplary qualities. Art is thinking, but thinking as a way of making something happen in how objects guide our engagement with the world.

We can test the value of this way of honoring the philosophical engagements of modernist writing by turning to two quite well-known modernist poems. The first is typically read as an allegory about nihilism in modern culture; the second is rarely attended to by critics because it does not allegorize, but remains one of the most complex expressions of feeling among modernist lyrics. My first example is the first stanza of Eliot's *The Waste Land*. It is certainly not a passage about delight or ecstasy, and even its sympathy is painfully analytic: "I was frightened. He said, Marie, / Marie, hold on tight" (ll. 15–16). Yet I attend to it because the best way to indicate the powers of an affective reading is to establish what that reading brings out that allegorical and philosophical readings miss. There are few passages in modern poetry more fundamental to abstract literary accounts of modernist nihilism. But there are also few passages where attending to the allegorical matter so drastically impoverishes the affective intensities produced by how the experience is rendered.

Typical allegorizing accounts of Eliot's poem tend to emphasize the opening two sentences from this first stanza ("April is the cruellest month … "; "Dull roots kept us warm … "). But these critical accounts rarely ask why Eliot might feel the need for the supplementary sentences that make up the rest of the paragraph. They add nothing to the allegorical situation, so they seem mere gestures toward honoring the role of the concrete image. Yet if we read for how the *manner* of this sequence affords a distinctive *matter*, we track an extraordinarily evocative range of shifts in feeling that ultimately justify and ground how the poem will proceed.

Notice first the sound and sweep of the long sibilant eighth line that provides a turn against winter: "Summer surprised us, coming over the Starnbergersee." The "us" speaking in the previous sentence seems to be coming to life and preparing for the assertions of first-person agency in the following lines. The poem moves from an oppressive generalized view of the cultural situation to human possibilities that specific human voices seem to afford. One might even say that the four lines comprising the third sentence are a muted bourgeois version of the scene with the hyacinth girl. There is the same strong sense of innocence combined with remembered delight in particular situations, although there is no ecstasy and no drastic drop off to despair here. These bourgeois voices seem not to have felt April as the cruelest month and are at home in the quotidian: "we stopped in the colonnade / And went on in the sunlight, into the Hofgarten" (ll. 9–10). Yet what power they have is incomplete and fleeting, largely because if the audience identifies with this initial speaker, it will be difficult to protect against the need or the aggression of other voices. For example, the Lithuanian's assertive voice expresses not only exile but also a sharp sense of difference from the other more comfortable voice: "Bin gar keine Russin, stamm' aus Litauen, echt deutsch" (l. 12). Then that distancing effect extends to Marie's voice, partially because of its upper-class qualities, and partially because this voice seems not quite to mean what it says. Now a manifest dis-ease comes through. We hear a neediness and even an incipient hysteria that Marie's memories and descriptions cannot conceal. So when Marie interacts with a male companion, the scene gets strangely doubled. "Hold on tight" has a much more general scope than the speaker recognizes. And Marie's version of freedom is like a mask projected to cover the mention of fear that becomes more pervasive the more she tries to present something like a normal life (for her class).

These are observations about the dramatic forces at play. Eliot wants us also to feel some of the more general aspects of his rendering of the situation. It seems as if the poem turns to particular subjects to mollify the severity of the impersonal and generalizing allegorical voice speaking the first two sentences. But these personal voices cannot face the spiritual anxiety behind the impersonal voice. (Marie may speak the closing lines or perhaps not—the important point is that what she articulates attracts other possible voices.) As Marie's voice (or what it surrogates) becomes increasingly distant and theatrical, we find a gulf between the desire for self-possession and an incipient panic demanding the kind of impersonal analysis that opens the poem. As Marie turns to the comfort of a male savior, it is difficult not to think of that analysis taking Lacanian form. Marie desperately demands that such a figure will turn her uneasy fluid feelings into strong, explicit affirmative emotions.

At the same time, the expansive lines about summer give way to increasingly jagged syntax and monosyllabic diction that emblematizes the individual speakers' inability to find words they can fully inhabit. The personal and the impersonal begin to live one another's lives and die one another's deaths: "In the mountains, there you feel free. / I read, much of the night, and go south in the winter" (ll. 17–18). The effort at knowledge leads to an effort at sympathy, which in turn makes careful readers understand better the need for that first allegorizing voice. Yet their states of awareness deepen a sense of secular subjectivity that will never conform to what impersonality has to offer. By the end of the first stanza we learn to feel the need for what the poem pursues, even as we come to understand better why that pursuit will generate little more than an intensified madness. We feel why subjects need something larger than themselves, and we confront the burden of defensive projections that make it impossible to recognize that a "third" may already be with them. We feel what it will take the entire poem to understand.

My second passage is William Carlos Williams' elegy for his grandmother, "Dedication for a Plot of Ground," a second poem about burial that sets a very different spiritual agenda. Its commitment to intense particularity adamantly refuses allegory and therefore does not easily accord with the generalizing philosophical bent critics want as exemplary of modernism. Here the poetry resides in how the insistent particular predications compose a powerful amalgam of feelings much too subtle for any public discourse. The poem combines delight with grief as closely as the imagination can, while also beggaring the labels "delight" and "grief" in contrast to what is concretely happening in the language: "Emily Dickinson Wellcome / who was born in England; married; / lost her husband and with / her five year old son / sailed for New York" (ll. 4–8).

Williams initially privileges the artist's agency by emphatically defining a particular place then quickly shifting to Emily's power to overwhelm this sense of place. That sense then gives way to predicating details that increasingly call out for the kind of attention the poem gives. We see that Emily can only be known by the impression made upon one who has felt the cumulative effect of the details he now conveys to others: "defended / herself against thieves, / storm, sun, fire, / against flies, against girls / that came smelling about," and so on (ll. 25–9). This is a life that takes on substance through blunt, abrupt narrative colloquially heaping up details and refusing lyric adornment. There are so many significant details to Emily's life that interpreting or garnishing them would be silly excess, and perhaps a sign of their disavowal. So Williams establishes her strength of character in one stunning supple sentence that contains the variety of direct predicative statements elicited by her memory, as if only the abstract form of the sentence could synthesize this identity. The feeling produced prevents the poem from slowing down and having to provide an interpretive hierarchy of details. The single sentence refuses even to present contrasts that would weaken or substitute for the sense of constant expanding modification—a sense which might lead us to appreciate why society needs and fears strong characters (e.g. the repetition of "against" with virtually no contrasting "for").

I speak as if the predication's energy suffices to establish a substance for the elegy. But the poem also emphasizes important differences in tone and perspective as Emily gets older and more accustomed to the life of combat these details require. Once she loses her daughter and seizes the two boys from her son, the poem gravitates toward her own perspective. With the mention of fighting for the sons and of defending herself against thieves, then resisting the girls who "came smelling about," the poem seems no longer content to record the facts. Its verbs take on qualities that at least embody her sense of the struggles dominating her life. As we open ourselves to her perspective, the poem also develops a more abstract aspect of identification: "against the weakness of her own hands, / against the growing strength of / the boys ... / ... / against her own mind" (ll. 32–6). Repetitions of "against" become almost anaphoric because that term captures the elemental force of Emily's life. Williams finds a linguistic emblem allowing his expansiveness to merge with the source of the subject's intensities.

Nor is his inventiveness exhausted. At the stanza's end he quickly abandons Emily's subjectivity to complete his picture of it. She could not know that she even struggles against her own mind, but the poet sees this as the price of identifying oneself with constant resistance. The second stanza brilliantly shifts from the anaphoric profusion of "against" to a series of main verbs, one to a line. This returns us to Emily's basic drives, but now at a later stage in her life. Refusing to accept defeat, she "blackguard[s]" her son into buying her a plot of land (l. 39). The verbs' sequencing captures Emily's satisfaction in inhabiting her land after so many years of owning only negation: "grubbed … domineered … blackguarded … lived … attained" (ll. 37–41). These verbs enact her most intimate pleasure, and they allow the poet to share her sense of having made a home to enable them. More important yet, this level of intimacy makes her "final loneliness" an ultimate achievement, as if this state were the culminating wisdom born of her sense of struggle. Attaining this level of consciousness prepares her for death and makes it something other than a disaster.

The only one who risks disaster at the end of this elegy is "you," the sudden presence of what we see now is its audience. And what a great "you" it is. The speaker has so taken on Emily's spirit that he assumes the worst and sets himself against even the possibility that he may not need to struggle against all those involved in her story. No wonder he stresses the auditor's carcass, the parallel to the dead body that he has been trying to revivify: "If you can bring nothing to this place / But your carcass, keep out" (ll. 42–3). His awareness of an audience also makes the poet stress his role as a teacher. Williams probably does not want an allegory about pouring one's heart out to teach canonical texts to carcasses, but that identification is hard for me to resist. After all, his task is to show the gulf between the body in the grave and what the imagination can make of the life it still possesses for him, if he can preserve a sense of its particularity. This, one might say, is how one combats nihilism. But to the credit of this poem, unlike "Spring and All", this allegory is at best faintly in the background.

What would it take to have the "you" bring more than his carcass? Minimally it would take respect for the life Emily lived. But respect is too public an emotion and not bound sufficiently to the details. Ideally, respect would be tempered in one direction by amusement at how her voice comes through the poet's sense of her struggles and, in the other direction, by a healthy dose of fear that one might have to handle an Emily in one's own life. The poem also holds out the possibility of a more general and more profound identification—not so much with the life she lived as with what she may have learned from that life about preparing for death. "You" might bring an understanding of what is involved in attaining that final loneliness, where one can fully embrace being a carcass and project the sense of relatedness that makes possible.

If this "you" is allegorically inclined, and at the same time suspicious of allegorical claims about nature or about responses to nihilism, he or she might extend this final challenge in the poem to include the demands a modern poetry can make. "You" might reflect on how this poem manages without allegory to produce an appreciation of how this woman could forge a substantial character out of her suffering, how the poet's effort at unadorned naming gives imaginative access to that character, and how the audience is tempted to turn away from the defensive orientation that wants to avoid facing both Emily's intense possession of her place in life and her "final loneliness."

Notes

1 What follows is a version of the argument made popular by Cary Nelson that the shaping of the modernist canon blinded us to a wide range of significant writing. I propose, however, that the blindness came not from aestheticism but from particular allegories intensifying a selective use of aesthetic criteria—hence the link with cultural criticism that uses much the same allegorizing for other purposes (e.g. Jameson's tales of symptomatic cultural practices). I differ from Nelson in wanting to preserve a primarily aesthetic framework that encourages an emphasis on canonical or potentially canonical writers rather than opening the field to writing that matters for its political and social filiations. I am contrasting one prevailing aesthetic language with other possible aesthetic frameworks that promise adjustments in the canon and incentives to return to close reading, albeit in relation primarily to affective rather than conceptual values.

2 I spell this out in *Particulars of Rapture* (Altieri 2004).

Bibliography

Altieri, C. (2004) *Particulars of Rapture*, Ithaca, NY: Cornell University Press.

Eliot, T. S. (1970) *T. S Eliot: Collected Poems 1909–1962*, New York: Harcourt Brace, Jovanovich.

Howe, I. (1967) "Introduction: The Idea of the Modern," in I. Howe (ed.) *Literary Modernism*, New York: Fawcett, 11–40.

Jarrell, R. (2001 [1953]) *Poetry and the Age*, Gainesville: University Press of Florida.

Miller, J. H. (1965) *Poets of Reality*, Cambridge: Harvard University Press.

Nelson, C. (1989) *Repression and Recovery*, Madison: Wisconsin University Press.

Perloff, M. (1999) *Poetics of Indeterminacy*, Evanston, IL: Northwestern University Press.

Williams, W. C. (1968) *The Collected Poems of William Carlos Williams*, ed. A. Walton Litz and C. MacGowan, New York: New Directions.

10 Ethics

Melba Cuddy-Keane

In *The Question of Ethics: Nietzsche, Foucault and Heidegger*, Charles E. Scott explains the ethical predicament of our contemporary world:

> All values that have in their history the ideas of ultimate order and the ontological privilege of meaning are experienced as questionable. Thought that has been formed in this heritage is equally questionable. Yet we live by values and thought that are also questionable. How are we to live in their questionableness?
>
> (Scott 1990: 10)

The paradox Scott identifies goes to the heart of the ethical predicament in a pluralist frame. Respect for alterity leads readily to perceptions of culturally relative, interchangeable and, in consequence, non-compelling attributions of value. Ethics, in contrast, is predicated on some notion of compulsion, some concept of obligation, some demand for response in the way we live.

As Scott's phrasing indicates, however, despite radical skepticism about truth claims, fundamental assumptions about value inescapably inform our lives. Even theories of alterity that overtly critique and reject essentialism, for example, still take what we might call a minimalist normative leap, assuming a universal obligation to oppose the exclusion and oppression of marginalized voices and to work for the eventual achievement of equal rights. Widespread agreement about such assumptions makes human rights discourse one of the more promising areas for collective ethical action today. Yet in a world without absolutes regarding specific behaviors, as Geoffrey Harpham points out, the underdetermination of such minimal agreement immediately runs into problems with the overdetermination of multiple ethical possibilities. In a pluralist frame, ethical choice, as Harpham states, is "never a matter of selecting the right over the wrong, the good over the evil," or even the principled over the unprincipled act; the painful predicament is that "ethical choice is always a choice between ethics" (Harpham 1995: 396).

The discourse of ethical choice must therefore grant access to compelling alternatives, so that ethical choice is made visible without hiding the questionableness of the choice that is made.[1] The viability of alternative ethical systems, however, is something that theory is arguably ill-equipped to convey. Presenting perhaps an extreme limit case, Scott argues that the discourse of thought, however much it attempts to question its own principles, is unable to provide "the play of other-to-thought in thought"; "the unthinkable is covered over by thought" and "that covering is itself an ethical problem" (Scott 1990: 11). Literary works of course also solicit the reader to move cognitively inside the frame of a text's mode of thinking, but a greater provisionality, a more pervasive functioning within the conditional "as it were," more generally obtains. Arguing literature's contribution to ethics, Martha Nussbaum delineates the advantage of literature's particularism over the universalism of theory, opposing literature's contingently generalizable against categorical imperatives or universal essentialisms. Following Scott's line of questioning, however, takes us to the further advantage of literature's discursive indeterminacy, an advantage proceeding not merely from literature's inability to contain and delimit meanings but, more radically, from its welcoming that very lack. Trapped by the difficulty of capturing the other-to-argument in argument, Scott's prose itself testifies to the challenge of writing a theoretical statement about ethics that self-reflexively questions its own discursive mode. In contrast, literature's ready capacity for self-questioning takes us past the usual subordination of literature to philosophical theory, to access ethics through the way that a literary text thinks. And while all literature arguably participates in this multivalent inflection, modernist literature, in this respect, may well have some special claim.

Discursive disruption is clearly what Derek Attridge has in mind when he relates the ethical dimension in the works of J. M. Coetzee to Coetzee's extensions and revitalizations of modernist form. As Attridge states,

> My argument, briefly, is that what often gets called (and condemned as) the self-reflexiveness of modernist writing, its foregrounding of its own linguistic, figurative, and generic operations, its willed interference with the transparency of discourse, is, in its effects if not always in its intentions, allied to a new apprehension of the claims of otherness, of that which cannot be expressed in the discourse available to us.
>
> (Attridge 2004: 4)

Furthermore, Attridge identifies, in modernist practices, a "responsiveness to the demands of otherness" (2004: 5) that at the same time preserves an element of the unknowable, not by inscribing the other's "essential ineffability," but by imposing constraints on our inevitably universalizing tendencies through the "very productivity and proliferation" of modernist discourse itself (2004: 4). Modernism, that is, achieves such constraints through the "permanent possibility of irony" and the "resistance to closure" inherent in modernist form:

> Modernism's foregrounding of language and other discursive and generic codes through its formal strategies is not merely a self-reflexive diversion but a recognition ... that literature's distinctive power and potential ethical force

reside in a testing and unsettling of deeply held assumptions of transparency, instrumentality, and direct referentiality, [thus opening] a space for the apprehension of otherness which those assumptions had silently excluded.

(Attridge 2004: 930)

In this respect, Attridge's notion of constraint resembles the "voluntary self-binding" that Dorothy Hale emphasizes in her discussion of narrative ethics, and which she finds enacted, in exemplary fashion, in the novels of Henry James. Where Attridge differs from Hale, however, concerns an aspect that arises in the course of Hale's discussion but that she ultimately gives less stress: beyond the "negative" ethics of disclaiming epistemological certainty, the "positive" ethics of the obligation to act. Under the conditions of cognitive pluralism, the ethical subject is simultaneously bound "not to know" and also, even if problematically and paradoxically, bound "to do." If the ethical *modern* subject takes its point of departure from Hamlet's problem—how to act in an ethically uncertain and ambiguous world—the ethical *modernist* subject must take a further step, actually preserving uncertainty and ambiguity in order to act in ethical ways. Modernist ethics meets the question of how to live ethically in a questionable world with a paradoxical conjunction of metaphysical uncertainty and individual answerability.

To make such a claim, however, posits a certain reading of modernism, a reading that depends on our reading practices and what we as readers select for attention in modernist texts. Much of the criticism of the late twentieth century approached modernism as the art of formalism, understood as wholeness and unity, leading critics and theorists of *post*modernism to consider modernism an essentialist and totalizing form. It is worthwhile remembering, however, that such assumptions about modernism's closure did not prevail in the mid-century, especially in constructions of modernist narratives, which were frequently read against the putative closure of Victorian forms. Alan Warren Friedman, to cite an example from the 1960s, contrasted the closed form and resolution of the Victorian novel with the open form, endlessness, and flux of experience encountered in modernist narrative; James Gindin, to take an example from the early 1970s, set the centrally coherent focus and the formal, moral, or theological absolutes of Victorian fiction against modernism's "inconclusive" or "partially conclusive endings," denial of absolutes, and focus on process as opposed to truth (Gindin 1971: 6). The difference in view derives in part from the difference in context: modernism reveals different sides relative to the use of postmodernism and Victorianism as comparative frames. But the difference also reflects the degree to which critics emphasize rhetorical reading and engage with the indeterminacy of modernist form.

Most current narrative studies of ethics approach the text not in a Leavisite manner, for the moral vision it passionately espouses, but for the way the text stages ethical dilemmas and debates.[2] Furthermore, such analysis extends beyond the action in the storyworld to include the dynamics of representation and reception as ethical acts. Ethical analysis becomes attentive on three levels, which Adam Zachary Newton specifies with the following terms: "narrational ethics," or the ethical ramifications of story-telling as a communicative act; "representational ethics," or the way fictional characters are used to instantiate supra-fictional ethical problems; and "hermeneutic ethics," or the way we as readers assume ethically charged positions, as we interpret, evaluate, welcome, or reject the texts that we read. Narrative is always an encounter: a conveying, a something conveyed, and a receiving; and encounters are, inescapably, ethically charged. Encounters in modernism occur in a context of radical doubt, with, however, this further complexity to absorb: modernist texts situate ethical dilemmas in a frame of questionableness even when, or *necessarily* when, the text itself expresses a preference for one or another stance. Answerability requires ethical response, yet the questionableness of that response must be preserved to avoid doing violence to alternative ethical routes. The necessity of choice and its equally necessary uncertainty play thoroughly entangled roles. The examples that follow come from modernist narratives, and specifically from narratives that overtly signal their ethical concerns; equally important to my readings, however, are the modes through which ethical choice is represented and ethical reading is in turn solicited from us. My first two examples show how choice and questionableness are doubly inscribed, first through an intrusive narrator, and second, in delayed revelation at the level of plot. My second two examples continue such narrative investigation but foreground two prominent themes: the "virtuous lie" (our ethical responsibility to others) and "unvirtuous possession" (our ethical responsibilities not only to others but also to things) in a morally ambiguous world.

In modernism, even intrusive narrators can destabilize ethical views, as evidenced in a brief but paradigmatic scene from E. M. Forster's *Howards End* (1910). On her deathbed, Mrs Wilcox scribbles a note, unsigned and in pencil, leaving Howards End, the house she inherited from her family, the Howards, to Margaret Schlegel, a relatively recent friend. Mr Wilcox and the Wilcox children debate their responsibility to the "letter," and what, as its recipients, they should ethically do. Accepting the writing as genuine and untroubled by its non-legal nature, Mr Wilcox nevertheless judges against the rationality of the request and they burn the little piece of paper in the fire.

Theoretically, the request sets up a tension between competing ethical systems—a deontological ethics, asserting a universal obligation to respect the last wish of a loved one, against a logical and consequentialist ethics, assessing the rational intentionality behind the request and weighing the comparative benefits of acceding or not to its wish. The Wilcoxes unwaveringly follow the second mode; and then the narrator, as self-designated "commentator," steps in to judge. Speaking first as the "practical moralist," the narrator justifies the Wilcoxes's decision; even shifting from instrumental to intuitive ground, the narrator still "acquits" them for taking the sensible course. Suddenly, however, a dissenting word enacts a characteristically modernist "turn": "He who strives to look deeper may acquit them—almost" (Forster 2000: 85). "Almost" signals the narrator's *subjective* preference for yet another mode of ethical response—not deontological obligation, but open receptivity to a singular human voice. For the Wilcoxes, the narrator adds tellingly, did ignore "a personal appeal." Oppositional ethics thus obtains at the level of principles (a teleological and utilitarian ethics versus a human claim) and epistemology (rational versus emotive/intuitive) as well. In choosing ethical reasoning, the Wilcoxes have shut their ears to a human voice. Ethical justifications are thus companioned with a sense of ethical loss.

In tonal implication, the narrator sides with the personal over the rational, yet even that persuasive preference does not authorize the "rightness" of fulfilling Mrs Wilcox's wish. The turn hinges on a fragile "almost," and when the narrator images the Wilcoxes as "sailors of Ulysses voyag[ing] past the Sirens," his skepticism falls equally on end-oriented determination and impulsive emotional response (Forster 2000: 87). If the novel's epigraph—"only connect ... "—gestures toward resolution through combination, even that ideal is rendered problematic when there is but one house to give. There is no absolute answer; every choice is infiltrated by what it lacks. Nonetheless, a latent injunction inheres in the added detail that Ulysses' sailors "stopped one another's ears with wool";[3] Ulysses himself, we are indirectly reminded, listened to the Siren's song, though he had himself securely bound to the mast. The implicit indictment of the Wilcoxes is thus not for their course of action but for their failure to grasp the dilemma informing their choice. In a world of competing ethics, the ethical position is one that apprehends and acknowledges alternative views. Finally, if this injunction is conveyed through narrational ethics, it pertains to hermeneutic ethics as well. We have been discussing a scene of reading, of interpreting, and responding to marks on a page, so that the ethical problematic in reading Mrs Wilcox's letter translates by implication to the question of how we read Forster's text. We are bound to pursue a direction; we are equally bound not to stop up our ears with wool. Thinking, and thinking other to our thinking, is both thematized in the novel's action and implicit in the narrative's form.

My reason for choosing *Howards End* rather than Forster's *A Passage to India* (1924) as my first example is to demonstrate ethical questioning at work even in what seems to be, on its surface, one of modernism's more straightforward texts. In Forster's later novel, ethical viewpoints are more numerous and more profoundly disturbing; tensions and questions less easy to bypass or ignore. This is not to say that, in Forster's texts, ethical views aren't asserted: both the map of Africa carved up like whale's blubber in the Wilcox office and the British presence in India appear as unequivocally wrong. But declaring the ethically right is more difficult—a point furthered by subjecting the reading experience to reversing or wobbling views. And if such rhetorical reversal is subtly performed by Forster's narrator, it is overtly staged in a scene of delayed revelation in Joseph Conrad's *Lord Jim* (1900).[4]

In *Lord Jim*, ethical dilemmas abound: in the character-plot, Jim's life alone raises the problematics of instinctual response versus duty, mercy versus responsibility, and love versus loyalty to a code, with the further entangled difficulty of separating respect for the code of another culture from devotion to the personal code Jim upholds for himself. In the narrator-plot, Marlow's involvement stages the ethical complexities of witnessing, interpreting, judging, and trying to help another human being, raising hairline distinctions between humanitarian concern, empathic identification, critical self-reflexivity, and self-serving exploitative use. The point I isolate here, however, is an a-chronological hiccup in the "reading-plot" and its hermeneutic effect. Conrad holds back a crucial piece of evidence from his readers: the events subsequent to Jim's impulsive leap into a lifeboat from a damaged, listing, and suddenly dangerously heaving ship. The effect, I argue, is to replicate Jim's experience in the reading experience, heaving the narrative ground on which we have stood.

Of the many questions surrounding Jim's action, none is more crucial than this: what degree of guilt attaches to a chief mate who jumps with the skipper and crew, abandoning the passengers, from a fatally damaged ship? Guilt itself is not questioned, but *relative* guilt determines the possibilities for atonement, even whether atonement can be made. The first six chapters set up two competing ethical frameworks: one shared by the authorial narrator and the internalized thoughts of Jim during the inquiry, in which "a sinister violence of intention" (Conrad 2000: 43), "something invisible, a directing spirit of perdition" (Conrad 2000: 60), exposes the human actor's helplessness against the universe's annihilating force; the other governed by the humanly conceived and axiomatic claims of "duty" requiring that a captain and his officers be the last to leave a sinking ship. Human and cosmic visions vie for allegiance, inexorably separated by the incommensurability of the hollow factual discourse of a judicial inquiry and the peculiar inexplicable horror accruing around the tale. Into this tension of opposites, Chapter 7 drops a new fact. The striking delay in disclosure obtains not at the level of representational ethics, since it is knowledge both Marlow and Jim already possess, although Marlow throws out this detail—*which for him seems to place the matter in a different light*—to gauge its impact on Jim.[5] The factual withholding is from readers, and thus explicitly hermeneutic in intent. Our misapprehension is indeed reinforced in the preceding paragraph, which refers to "the steamer *Patna* sunk at sea" (Conrad 2000: 101–2); then, casually, subtly, but devastatingly, Marlow interjects the truth: the ship did *not* sink; it was later discovered, with its cargo of living passengers, abandoned but still afloat. Retrospectively, the revelation clarifies Marlow's preceding reference to the "unforeseen conclusion of the tale," which drives him to wonder if Jim "felt the ground cut from under his feet" (Conrad 2000: 102). The narrative turn, I suggest, calls on our willingness to allow the text to destabilize us—to pull, in effect, the narrative *ethical* ground out from under our feet.

Belatedly, knowledge redefines the ethical choice involved: the alternative to Jim's leap was not (as he believed) the unsupportable scene of mass drowning but the inconceivable (to him) possibility that all would survive; rather than nothing to be done, there had been everything to do. The shift obtains not only at the representational level, in terms of what Jim thought and what he later found out; hermeneutically, readers *experience* a similar jolt. As the shock becomes a delayed decoding of Marlow's own fascinated horror, however, the reversal aligns us less with Jim than with Marlow's double vision of Jim's tale. For instead of discovering "truth," we are plunged into mutually contradictory views: an ethics of intention that judges an action by the conscience or good will of the person performing the act, and what they knew and perceived at the time, versus an ethics of result, or a consequentialist ethics, that holds a person responsible for the act's effects. As the chapter proceeds, we must enter the frame of subjective perception that Jim struggles so hard to convey and yet always see, starkly imaged, the poignant reminder of an alternate reality whose implications, despite Marlow's seemingly cruel insistence, Jim seems not fully to grasp.[6] Reading itself thus proceeds with a fundamental instability now at its core: we must follow, in its full human implications, the trajectory of one particular voyage, without stopping our ears to other claims.

I turn briefly, in my next two examples, to suggest the way such narrative destabilization bears on the representation of ethical themes. Lies and possession are fundamental ethical issues, confronting us with a putative violence to the Other, which Emmanuel Levinas identifies as the central problem in the self's relation to the world. For Levinas, our primary ethical obligation is to the "face" of the Other, which he conceives rather like a world-membrane where our fingers end. All conjecture is thematization of the membrane, a turning of its quidditas (whatness) into figuration—and therein lies Levinas's objection to art. The following examples both instantiate and interrogate Levinas's critique of conjecture, through, respectively, the attempt, in the virtuous lie, to avoid doing violence to the other, and the inescapable possessive violence enacted in language itself.

Henry James's *The Ambassadors* (1903) focalizes its narrative through its main character Lambert Strether, although the voice of a "narrator-focalizer" emerges as well, establishing an ironic distance from Strether that leads us, at the same time as we sympathize, to regard him with amused, skeptical, or critical views. Always shadowy presences, however, the ironic indicators disappear in the final scene, leaving us—rather as we are in the shift to the diary mode at the end of James Joyce's *A Portrait of the Artist as a Young Man* (1916)—to continue our judgments on our own. While Strether's final decision has itself been a subject of much critical discussion, my focus here is with the way he communicates that decision with a virtuous lie.

Strether confronts the difficult situation of no longer desiring the world his dear friend Maria Gostrey has to offer, but telling her in a way fully considerate of her feelings, a way that allows her, we might say, to save face. For Strether, Maria epitomizes a life of "selection" guided by "beauty and knowledge," the values that occasioned his first revolution in ethical understanding, but which a further and more catastrophic revolution has caused him now to regard with diminished appeal: "It was awkward, even stupid, not to seem to prize such things; yet none the less so far as they made his opportunity they made it only for a moment" (James 1994: 346). But how can he do what seems right for himself, without committing the wrong of treating Maria in a brutal way? He struggles for words, then finds he has "got it at last": to take up Maria's implicit offer of marriage would be to gain from the situation, and Strether must justify his interference in the lives of others with disinterested motives; he must, in the end, take nothing for himself, "to be right." His words, echoed by Maria, place his action in the ethical sphere, but for the reader, the echo is deeper, taking us back to an earlier virtuous "lie" played out by Mme de Vionnet—a charade enacted, in that instance, to offer *Strether* temporary protection from his exposed naivety, to allow *him*, in effect, to save face. Shattered in many ways by his own acquisition of delayed information, Strether nevertheless believes in Mme de Vionnet's ability to make something good out of false appearance; he can "trust her to make deception right"—a phrase that ambiguously means to right the false impression, but also to make acting a fiction the right thing to do (James 1994: 320). Strether's "lie" to Maria Gostrey—not false to his motivation but false to the role in it that she plays—thus repeats the virtuous deception that Marie de Vionnet had performed for him.

Narrative echoes thus offer a textual pattern, but narrative guidance for reading them disappears. Less suddenly and more subtly than in *Lord Jim*, the narrative ground is just as surely pulled from under our feet. Mainly dramatized rather than narrated, the closing conversation makes it impossible to locate a narrator's voice. We are given one slight indication of Maria's perspicacity— "Honest and fine, she couldn't greatly pretend she didn't see it" (James 1994: 347)—but it is unclear whether it is the narrator or Strether who testifies to Maria's comprehension, and ambiguous what "it" she perceives. Narrational ethics infuses both representational and hermeneutical ethics with a radical freedom, refusing to provide any assurance that Strether's act, or even his assessment of the situation, have been "right." Like Marlow's lie to the Intended at the end of *Heart of Darkness* (1902), James's ending leaves open the possible violence done to the alternative scenario in which truth might have been openly told. Yet in each instance the attempt speaks to our answerability to the human relation, asserting the ethics of making, not the right decision, but the best decision that is, for each individual, possible, in an uncertain void.

When ethical choice means the seemingly "better" or "best" as opposed to the "right," however, it also signifies the choice of a seemingly lesser wrong. The aspect of ethical impossibility thus factored into any alternative informs the anguish at the centre of Willa Cather's *The Professor's House* (1925). In this novel, the embedded narrative within the frame narrative concerns the discovery of a long-deserted pueblo in New Mexico, whose fate raises many of the ethical issues debated in museum studies today. For Tom Outland, the young man who first comes upon it, it involves a further impossible choice: between loyalty to the cultural integrity of artifacts that would mean disloyalty to a friend, and between loyalty to friendship that would mean accepting or tolerating the conversion of historical artifacts into possessions that can be sold. The ethical problematic is further compounded by the possibility that Tom's loyalty to the artifacts derives from personal attachment, not true regard for the people whose heritage they bespeak.

In the frame narrative, Tom's predicament is both echoed and escalated in the ethical dilemmas confronting Godfrey St Peter, the Professor of the titular house. Living in the materialist American culture of the 1920s, Godfrey becomes increasingly opposed to the social value accorded the acquisition of goods; but a house bought with prize money for academic work presents more complex issues, incriminating the concept of intellectual property itself. Ideas can be circulated like objects for gain; knowledge itself is a form of acquisition, appropriating the lives and the objects that it concerns. The university in this novel may seem surprisingly familiar, with its increasing expectation of applied research "to give the taxpayers what they wanted" and its corresponding deprecation of "research work of an uncommercial nature" (Cather 1990: 121), which only Godfrey and one other faculty member defend. Yet not only have Godfrey's prize-winning gains derived from his historical volumes on *Spanish Adventurers in North America*, making his work a secondary stage in colonial expansionism: the problem of assigning "rightful" commercial gains from Tom's patented research begins to infect any notion that academic research can be "pure." Seeking some form that escapes the element of personal aggrandizement, Godfrey abandons historical metanarratives for the work of annotating and writing an introduction for Tom's diary, then turns to Tom's diary itself as the better form still: factual recordings, "used to present the objects under consideration, not the young explorer's emotion," imply that "minute description," or perhaps just a pencil sketch, may be the one form of ethical representation left (Cather 1990: 238). Yet the challenge to his identity drains the Professor's strength. Losing the power of agency, since agency itself is corrupt,[7] his predicament poses the final question of whether *not preventing* one's death, in abandonment of agency, is ethically any different from suicide as an act.

In confronting the acquisition inherent in the act of writing, Cather's own writing both thinks and thinks against itself. In raising the inescapable contamination of intellectual "property," the novel both becomes self-reflexive and demands self-reflexive reading too. And we are asked here not merely to conceive other than our own ideas, but to interrogate the production of ideas themselves. Our reading practice is thus placed fully under question, yet with the paradox that we can only engage the question when and if we continue to read. We must both continue in a fallible process and yet be answerable for what we do.

Tom Outland's ethical predicament leads him to feel he will "be called to account when [he] least expect[s] it" (Cather 1990: 229)—the feeling, perhaps, that prompts him to fight in the First World War. For Godfrey St Peter, the crisis leads less to resolution than to a way through an impasse, demanding his surrender of desire and ideals to the frail but universal connection implicit in inescapable death. Through the seamstress Augusta's stoic yet unwavering commitment to watch by the sick and the dying, Godfrey arrives at a sense of "obligation ... instinctive, escaping definition, but real" (Cather 1990: 256–7), finding some basis for living by feeling "the ground under his feet" (Cather 1990: 258). The image might seem to counter the shaken narrative ground of *Lord Jim*, yet Cather's novel, too, ends on an ambiguous note. Stabilization comes for Godfrey at the cost of "having let something go"; it entails the loss of "something very precious, that he could not consciously have relinquished, probably" (Cather 1990: 258). The sentence wobbles in its certainty, wobbles in terms of whether it is focalized through Godfrey's or the narrator's view, wobbles certainly in any unambiguous endorsement of the Professor's choice. The lives of Tom Outland and Godfrey St Peter leave us with a difficult tangle of loss and gain; ethical stance is exposed as a choice of the subjectively preferable, always to be haunted by the alternative course.

Although individual works, no matter how numerous, can never stand in for cultural thought, my examples speak to something distinctively modernist in their multi-layered ethical approach. At a fundamental level, they endorse what we might call a weak or a minimalist deontological imperative, holding us accountable to other people, living or dead, and even to objects, in all their spoken and unspoken claims. At the same time, narrative turns, reversals, and indeterminacies forestall any assurance of ultimate resolutions or answers, offering in their place the response-able action of what is still impure and fallible choice. Such pluralism and ambiguity, however, result not in weak relativity but in a new contextual imperative, applicable to the storyworld and reading world alike: an obligation to respond to each particular context, to each situation's demands and needs.

The modernist text, in these ways, achieves in enactment what much current ethical theory urges in theory: a dwelling in between questionableness and answerability, between the uncertain and the "ought," perhaps between—in the sense of bringing together—Victorian ethical responsibility and postmodernist free play. We must continue to draw on theory, both for its insights and for the critical purchase it offers from a position outside the literary text. Yet we should remember that theoretical understanding is implicit in action as well as in statement, and that theory and literature display crucial and ethical differences in the way that their discourses work. Ultimately, if ethical pluralism depends on a paradoxical saying and unsaying, it may be the modernist text that best models an ethical praxis, inscribing the quest to live ethically while still holding ethically open the questions of a questionable world.

Notes

1 I do not imply that choices are necessarily rational, conscious, and voluntary. Mr Wilcox and Strether in my examples tend toward this type of decision-making, yet the actions of Lord Jim and Godfrey St Peter are over-determined by instinctual and unconscious motivations. Choice is evident in an event which then becomes available for an ethical analysis of alternatives.

2 The criticism of F. R. Leavis (1895–1978) highlighted a canonical "Great Tradition" distinguished by moral intensity and commitment to universal human values. The evident problems embedded in selectivity, with its normative construction of "good," were in part responsible for the turn *away* from ethical reading in subsequent years.

3 In the *Odyssey*, the sailors plug their ears with wax.

4 For a much fuller discussion of narrative ethics in *Lord Jim*, see Newton's Chapter 3 (1995: 73–124).

5 Marlow reiterates this point in Chapter 12: "And there were no dead" (Conrad 2000: 141).

6 Jim is able to perceive "what might have happened" as a missed opportunity (Conrad 2000: 102–3); whether or not he is able to grasp the existence of alternative ethical systems is, I suggest, an issue adumbrated, but not resolved, at the end.

7 The problem is raised both facetiously and tellingly in Fielding's remark in *A Passage to India*: "I take up some other fellow's air, don't I, when I breathe?" (Forster 2000: 102). Reprehensible if meant to excuse the British presence in India, the question, in a world of scarcity, troubles the very basis of our lives.

Bibliography

Attridge, D. (2004) *J. M. Coetzee and the Ethics of Reading: Literature in the Event*, Chicago: University of Chicago Press.

Cather, W. (1990) *The Professor's House*, New York: Vintage.

Conrad, J. (2000) *Lord Jim*, ed. C. Watts, Peterborough: Broadview.

Forster, E. M. (2000) *Howards End*, with notes and intr. by D. Lodge, London: Penguin.

—— (2005) *A Passage to India*, ed. O. Stallybrass, with intr. by P. Mishra, London: Penguin.

Friedman, A. W. (1966) *The Turn of the Novel*, Oxford: Oxford University Press.

Gindin, J. (1971) *Harvest of a Quiet Eye: The Novel of Compassion*, Bloomington: Indiana University Press.

Hale, D. J. (2007) "Fiction as Restriction: Self-Binding in New Ethical Theories of the Novel," *Narrative* 15 (May): 187–206.

Harpham, G. G. (1995) "Ethics," in F. Lentricchia and T. McLaughlin (eds) *Critical Terms for Literary Study*, second edn, Chicago: University of Chicago Press, 387–405.

James, H. (1994) *The Ambassadors*, second edn, ed. S. P. Rosenbaum, New York: Norton.

Levinas, E. (1969) *Totality and Infinity: An Essay on Exteriority*, trans. A. Lingis, Pittsburgh: Duquesne University Press.

Newton, A. Z. (1995) *Narrative Ethics*, Cambridge, MA: Harvard University Press.

Nussbaum, M. C. (1990) *Love's Knowledge: Essays on Philosophy and Literature*, New York: Oxford University Press.

—— (1995) *Poetic Justice: The Literary Imagination and Public Life*, Boston: Beacon Press.

Parker, D. (1994) *Ethics, Theory, and the Novel*, Cambridge: Cambridge University Press.

Scott, C. E. (1990) *The Question of Ethics: Nietzsche, Foucault, Heidegger*, Bloomington: Indiana University Press.

11 Green

Bonnie Kime Scott

You'd never know it from the attitudes and theories of many modernist authors and later critics, but modernism takes an abiding interest in nature, human interdependencies with it, and even in its preservation: think of the odor of lilies in Marcel Proust's *A la recherche du temps perdu*; the walk on the beach in T. S. Eliot's "Prufrock," the gardens by the sea in H. D.'s poetry; the liminal, Celtic imagination that haunts Yeats's poetry; the innumerable trees and rivers in James Joyce's *Finnegans Wake*; the birds, butterflies, and watery worlds encountered throughout Virginia Woolf's novels, essays and stories; or the green world of Zora Neale Hurston's *Their Eyes Were Watching God*. We hear instead about urban modernity, scientific epistemologies, mechanical, technical, and experimental forms. First circulating in the 1870s, "ecology" derived from the Greek for "house" (*oikos*), and took on from the first a feminine association apparently foreign to modernism's predominantly masculine values. Theoretical turns toward gender and materialist analysis, and a heightened concern for the environment in an era of global warming, however, warrant another look.

I begin with early authorities who offered little prospect for a nature-friendly form of modernism: theorizing provided for futurism and vorticism, including Ezra Pound's insistence on modernist *techne*. In the androcentric modernist theory associated with "the men of 1914," there is a further rationale that nature, because it is feminine, should be mastered. Lewis, credited with conceptualizing "the men of 1914," shares with Hulme a preference for classicism over nature-friendly romanticism. Hulme's metaphor for artistic control is a springy piece of steel that can be bent precisely by the artist's fingers. The goal is "to bend the steel out of its own curve and into the exact curve which you want. Something different to what it would assume naturally" (Hulme 1986: 183–4). His process renounces nature in design: his favored texture, "dry hardness" in "Romanticism and Criticism" (1986: 48), suggests that the best organism is a dead one. Lewis structures gender and art on vertical, hierarchical planes. He assigns masculinity/art to surface articulation, and femininity/nature to the chaotic depths of being. Lewis's *Tarr* groups "woman and the sexual sphere" with "jellyfish diffuseness" (Lewis 1926: 334) that is the antithesis of Hulme's "dry hardness," implying common origins in base, primordial ooze, where the feminine is contained; art must rise above. The proliferation of girders and gears, and bits of metal bent to specification in "Timon of Athens" also relates to Hulme's flexible steel template for art. Ecofeminists offer various starting points for masculine domination of nature, including the scientific revolution's substitution of a mechanical for an organic metaphor for nature (Merchant 1979: xviii) and the rational tradition, dating back to the Greeks (Plumwood 2002).

Lewis's construction of gender allows him to designate as feminine homosexual men like Marcel Proust and Lytton Strachey. Disapproving of Woolf's essays, particularly as they relate to a "more masculine" James Joyce, Lewis ensconces Woolf as the presiding figure in an enfeebled feminine artistic realm: "an introverted matriarch, brooding over a subterraneous 'stream of consciousness'—a feminine phenomenon after all" (Lewis 1934: 138). In "A Retrospect," Pound intensifies the subjective aspect of imagism, centering more upon maker/perceiver than the natural object, with his "Image" presenting "an intellectual and emotional complex in an instant of time" ("complex" read in the "technical sense employed by the newer psychologists") (Pound 1986: 60).

Pound resisted many of the recent versions of modernism, as he tried to bring his version of modernism to *The Freewoman* and *Poetry*, and discouraged Amy Lowell's influence on imagism. Consider Harriet Monroe's investment in American landscapes, and cultivation of this interest in *Poetry* magazine, against Pound's advice, and her urging of the Senate to prevent construction of the Hatch Hetchy reservoir, which devastated a scenic valley in Yosemite. Lowell's correspondence with D. H. Lawrence reveals their mutual interest in flowers, which each brought to erotically expressive modernist forms, outside imagism's mainstream.

In her own version of imagism, H. D. makes a complex of natural materials, emerging from a depressed, still condition, and developing their own energies, as when she takes the rose from the rock in "Garden." This complex poem seems to require that the poet stir: that she break through stone and heat to produce the flower, the fruit of her art. Likewise, the waves and evergreen fir whirl together in "Oread" to produce exaltation in nature. Eurydice, pulled by Orpheus toward the flowers she has sorely missed, first loses them to his arrogance, then arrives at a better alternative in "the flowers of [her]self," that both contrast and emerge from the black rocks of hell. She determines that hell must "open like a red rose/For the dead to pass" before she will be lost (Doolittle 1983: 55). H. D. moves from dialogue with nature and its gods to commanding the self to work with nature in a motivational form of art. Writing of "Hymen," H. D.'s sister poet, Marianne Moore, ponders the masculine "tendency to match one's intellectual and emotional vigor with the violence of nature" (Moore 1990: 352). She finds in "the absence of subterfuge, cowardice, and the ambition to dominate by brute force" in H. D.'s work "heroics which do not confuse transcendence with domination and which in their indestructibleness, are the core of tranquility and intellectual equilibrium" (Moore 1990: 352). H. D.'s case demonstrates the connection between nature and the dark places of psychology, heralded by Woolf as one of the major concerns of modernist writing. She works in collaboration with, rather than domination of, the natural world, partaking of its forces in a combination of ritualistic attending, resisting, and yielding. Had I time, I would go on to consider the connections established in H. D.'s "Notes on Thought and Vision," where she imagines non-traditional mind–body connections and immerses herself in a fluid world that is both embryonic and oceanic—a concept I shall return to.

Modernist women writers reveal a different sense of the classical world, and of the capacity of myth. Following Jane Harrison, H. D. and Woolf exemplarily pursue the classics into alternate scenarios. Harrison paves the way for ecofeminism's focus upon original myths of earth-goddesses. Harrison interestingly adds to the modernist debates about classicism and romanticism because, as Marianna Torgovnick has argued, she offers a different kind of classicism, one well known in her day, but neglected in canonized accounts (Torgovnick 1990: 138–41). In *Prologomena to a Study of Greek Religion*, Harrison reaches back to early Greek tradition, and through archaeological artifacts, finds evidence of goddess (Great Mother) worship, matrilinity, and the predominance of rites over myths. While Apollo's rational control was the classical norm for "the men of 1914," Harrison, like Nietzsche, restores the companion values of Dionysus: ecstasy and proximity to nature. Originally the son or consort of the Great Mother, rather than the son of Zeus, Dionysus is a liminal figure, reaching back from masculine myths to earlier feminine rites, involved with natural objects and settings. Like these modernists, ecofeminists also achieve a different form for the classics through the concept of "Gaia," a term derived from an early Greek earth mother, but extended into the holistic concept of the entire earth as a living organism. This too is present, though insufficiently acknowledged, in modernism.

Challenged to identify the significance of Joyce's *Ulysses* to modernist literature, T. S. Eliot turned to its androcentric mythic superstructure, which he argued paralleled modern life. Hélène Cixous's "The Laugh of Medusa" and "Castration or Decapitation" were revolutionary texts, forever changing the way feminists viewed mythology, the subject, and Freudian family romance. French Feminism, as articulated by Cixous, Luce Irigaray, and Julia Kristeva, also took unabashed pleasure in the female body and the very liquid metaphors that had been eschewed by Lewis and other male modernists. Derrida's metaphor of dissemination, and the rhizomatic forms privileged by Deleuze and Guittari, suggest that nature re-entered theory in the era of deconstruction, shared by French Feminism. Theory of *écriture féminine* and the semiotic invited more feminine readings of Joyce.[1]

There is also an under-acknowledged modernist fascination with non-human life, particularly animals and trees, that overlaps an interest in the primitive world, locus of vital sexual and spiritual energies, and access to ancestors. Following Picasso, modernists co-opted ritual masks and other art forms that allowed humans to put on animal and vegetative forms. Joyce's Leopold Bloom challenges the species barrier by trying to think like his cat in *Ulysses*, as Woolf does in taking on the perspective of hungry birds in *The Waves*. Animals including the kingfisher, salmon, panther, and cow interrupt modernist order with alternate messages and language, calling out from a different, less rational world. Modernists like Hemingway who demonstrate an understanding of the hunted creature's environmental situation, thereby join company with one group of environmentalists.

Woolf was among the modernists who satirized the natural history buff and the Victorian trophy hunter. Like T. S. Eliot and D. H. Lawrence, she was introduced as a child to the collecting, classifying culture of natural history. Little wonder that Prufrock is anxious about being pinned in a specimen box, or that Woolf satirizes her child band of moth collectors both in her diary, and in the child collectors in *To the Lighthouse* and *The Waves*.

Holism is also firmly planted in the modernist era. Environmental feminist Josephine Donovan notes that first-wave feminists (which, after the gendering of modernism, we now include among the modernists) "articulated a critique of the atomistic individualism and rationalism of the liberal tradition. They did so by proposing a vision that emphasized collectivity, emotional bonding, and an organic (or holistic) concept of life" (Donovan 1993: 173). This bears comparison to the "oceanic," which Marianna Torgovnick describes as "a dissolution of boundaries between subject and object and between all conceived and conceivable polarities" (Torgovnick 1990: 18). The oceanic describes a "feeling of totality, oneness and unity" expressed by Kate in Lawrence's *The Plumed Serpent* (1951: 165), as she yields to a masculine primitive dance. Torgovnick suggests that the organic threatened Freud's ego-based psychology. She finds that Freud's solution, expressed in *Civilization and its Discontents*, was to attach the "oceanic feeling" to the early phase of the infant at its mother's breast (Torgovnick 1990: 206–7), and to suggest that this primitive stage of development was absorbed into later phases, not preserved. Freud's move demonstrates a typical form of masculine conceptual control. Post-Freudians take interest in a number of gender-related theories he may have prematurely cast off. Encouraged by Kristeva and others, we may detect patterns of oscillation rather than masculine, linear progression as more typical of life patterns.

The holism that appears in both deep ecology and ecofeminism offers another way of assessing unity versus fragmentation in modernist texts. Many of Woolf's most brilliant natural images occur in collages of modernist fragments—bits and pieces, or a rapid series of apprehensions. These are often the conceptions of characters in crisis or survivors of trauma, and provide alarms concerning the sustainability of culture and the environment. In some cases a character has the hope of regaining balance and sustaining tenuous existence. Septimus Smith's hallucinations in *Mrs Dalloway*; Rhoda's work with abstract shapes, water, and flowers in *The Waves*; Cam's mental collages in *To the Lighthouse*; Sara in *The Years*; and Isa in *Between the Acts*—all fall into this category. Cam is represented by the leaf turning in the hollow of the wave at the close of *To the Lighthouse*. It involves gesture, performance, recollecting, going on. Yielding as she is, the conceiver of this collage is sustained by creating her own complex images of nature. There is hope that, by returning to the primordial, the semiotic, or material, as many of Woolf's characters do, a different cycle of human nature may arise.

We might also want to meditate on various strands of theory and issues of their accessibility. Ecology has as one of its antecedents natural history as it flourished in the nineteenth century. Natural history was not accessible to all: the leisure to appreciate the natural world, money to travel, imperial assignments to remote places, and being in the West where natural history originated were clear advantages. But women and even working-class people could participate, and there was an attached educational mission that aimed at extending knowledge as far as possible. The rise of science brought forth a new emphasis upon theory and specialization, prizing them over observation and collection. The turn toward science also brought greater exclusivity, as it became necessary to be credentialed in professional organizations and qualified as members of institutions of higher education. This is paralleled in the institutionalization of English studies, with its turn toward theory, starting in the modernist period, and culminating in the difficult theories that prevailed through the 1980s. Ecology is a scientific hybrid, an interdisciplinary venture brought to the sciences in an era of increasingly isolated disciplinary formation. Its linguistic centering of the concept of the "home," and its investment in the "feminine" aspects long associated with nature mean that it offers a different theoretical venture: one that is vital to our understanding of the modernist past, and planning for a culture that invests itself in nature.

Note

1 See for example my *James Joyce* (Scott 1987: 111–21).

Bibliography

Breton, M. J. (1998) *Women Pioneers for the Environment*, Boston: Northeastern University Press.

Donovan, J. (1993) "Animal Rights and Feminist Theory," in G. Gaard (ed.) *Ecofeminism: Women, Animals, Nature*, Philadelphia: Temple University Press.

Faulkner, P. (1986) *A Modernist Reader: Modernism in England 1910–1930*, London: B. T. Batsford.

H. D. (Doolittle, Hilda) (1983) *H. D.: Collected Poems 1912–1944*, New York: New Directions.

—— (1990) "Notes on Thought and Vision," in B. K. Scott (ed.) *The Gender of Modernism*, Bloomington: Indiana University Press, 93–109.

Harrison, J. (1955) *Prologomena to a Study of Greek Religion*, New York: Meridian.

Hulme, T. E. (1986) "From Romanticism and Classicism," in P. Faulkner (ed.) *A Modernist Reader*, London: B. T. Batsford, 47–52.

Lawrence, D. H. (1951) *The Plumed Serpent*, New York: Vintage.

Lawrence, D. H. and Lowell, A. (1986) *The Letters of D. H. Lawrence and Amy Lowell, 1914–1925*, C. Healey and K. Cushman (eds), Santa Barbara: Black Sparrow Press.

Lewis, W. (1926) *Tarr*, New York: Knopf.

—— (1934) *Men Without Art*, London: Cassell.

Merchant, C. (1979) *The Death of Nature: Women, Ecology, and the Scientific Revolution: A Feminist Reappraisal of the Scientific Revolution*, San Francisco: Harper and Row.

Moore, M. (1990) "Hymen," in B. K. Scott (ed.) *The Gender of Modernism*. Bloomington: Indiana University Press, 350–1.

Plumwood, V. (2002) *Environmental Culture: The Ecological Crisis of Reason*, London: Routledge.

Pound, E. (1986) "A Retrospect," in P. Faulkner (ed.) *A Modernist Reader*, London: B. T. Batsford, 59–71.

Scott, B. K. (1987) *James Joyce*, Brighton: Harvester.

—— (ed.) (1990) *The Gender of Modernism*, Bloomington: Indiana University Press.

Torgovnick, M. (1990) *Gone Primitive: Savage Intellects, Modern Lives*, Chicago: University of Chicago Press.

—— (1996) "Discovering Jane Harrison," in C. M. Kaplan and A. B. Simpson (eds) *Seeing Double: Revisioning Edwardian and Modernist Literature*, New York: St Martin's Press.

Woolf, V. (2005) *To the Lighthouse*. Orlando: Harcourt.

12 Avant-garde

Jane Goldman

'Modernism' is always already a theoretical term with a material history, deriving its current usage from the cold war definitions of Clement Greenberg *et al.* Since then it has been applied to aesthetic modes associated with a period whose dates are always under critical negotiation, and whose heterogeneous modes refuse the homogenizing impetus of this flabby term. Modernism, it should be emphasized, 'comprises numerous, diverse and contesting, theories and practices which first flourished in a period that knew little of the term as it has now come to be understood' (Kolocotroni *et al.* 1998: xvii). Since the 'historical turn' in literary studies, there has been a growing interest in the stakes of historicizing modernist texts. Yet modern literary theory was importantly forged in modernist enterprises. 'Modernity' and the 'modern' refer to both historical eras and certain modes of inhabiting a perpetual present, certain notions of the perpetually new. History is the nightmare from which modernist writing seeks to awake; as such, modernist writing symptomatizes its contexts; at the same time, in making it new, modernist writing proposes a productive site of change, rupture or escape from such contexts. As recent contextualizing and historicizing criticism recognizes, such an agenda requires sophisticated methodologies. To historicize and contextualize such aesthetics is no simple matter.

The more simplistic materialist turns in modernist studies that seek to dispense with theory are doomed to fail because they elide the material history of 'modernism' and internalize its limited capacity to address the aesthetics and contexts of the art and the arbitrary period they examine. On the other hand, the recent returns to theory and (new) aestheticism would be impoverished by ignoring the fruits of historical, materialist, and archival criticism. Acknowledging the precise cultural referencing of modernist texts only enriches our readings of their stylized play.

The current revival of interest in 'avant-garde' symptomatizes the redundancy of 'modernism'; a revised theory of the avant-garde yields both critical precision and a more robust theoretical apparatus for any critical project exploring the historical materialism of 'modernism'. The self-conscious and aesthetic modes of the manifesto become crucial here. 'Avant-garde' is supple enough too to be productively applied to readings of 'realist' as well as 'modernist' aesthetics. Before addressing modernism and the avant-garde, I want to reflect on recent experiences of teaching modernism and on my recent research.

'Ur Sonata' blues

As I reluctantly turn down the volume of the opening salvos ('Fümms bö wö tää zää Uu') of Kurt Schwitters' experimental 'Ur Sonata', I ask my students for their responses (Schwitters 1993: 52). 'What's "modernist" about it?' I ask. More and more frequently comes back a forlorn litany: 'alienation', 'fragmentation', 'mechanization', 'industrialization', 'futility', 'horror'. Or, I ask them to sample the pleasures of Blaise Cendrars' and Sonia Delaunay's simultanist work, *Prose on the Trans-Siberian Railway*; or I might get one or two of them to read aloud some energetic incantation of Gertrude Stein's, a random sampling of Molly Bloom's soliloquy, or, following the example of Suzanne Bellamy, I get them to perform in two groups simultaneously the two paragraphs of Virginia Woolf's 'Blue & Green'. As their rhythmical, often joyous, chanting subsides, again I ask: 'What's "modernist" about it?' Again, comes the litany of woe: 'alienation', 'fragmentation', 'mechanization', 'industrialization', 'futility', 'horror'. When did modernism become so miserable? Admittedly, there may occasionally be slightly less miserable mutterings about self-reflexive aesthetics, and the sterile, autonomous work of art as 'refuge', but never a word about the exhilaration of the new, resistance, transgression or dissidence, never mind the pleasures of the text. But these students are responding not so much to 'modernism' as to a received caricature of 'modernity'; their readings of modernist aesthetics are infected by the irony and cynicism of a postmodernism they can only dimly define. I suspect Adorno is to blame. Access to some fruits of the reactionary aspects of the historical turn's scholarship may prove fatal, at this point, to any interest in the historical and political interventions of modernism, to its understanding of these works' cultural work, and to appreciating the potency of their continuing, transformational capacities. Applying the reactionary model of history, favoured by *some* modernist writers, to *all* modernist writing confirms the stereotype of miserable modernism: 'In opposition to progressive notions, the Modernists found much more reality in cyclic views of the past … The Modernists themselves viewed the time in which they lived as one of chaos and confusion' (Williams 2002: 2, 3). Whereas 'modernism' and 'modernity' may encourage us to read 'modernist' texts as representatively autonomous, in an autonomous sphere of art 'avant-garde' allows for a broader and more sophisticated understanding of the capacities of (autonomous) art's ability to undo the boundaries between art and life, and to trace how art and history interpenetrate.

Contextualizing Woolf, editing Woolf

My interest in contextualizing Woolf began with my first book, *The Feminist Aesthetics of Virginia Woolf: Modernism, Post-Impressionism and the Politics of the Visual* (1998), where I read Woolf's colour and light tropes through both Bloomsbury formalism and suffragist aesthetics. This process undermined more orthodox readings of her putatively high-modernist aesthetics in *To the Lighthouse* and *The Waves*, but it also affirmed for me the Janus-like qualities of her writing, captured in her term: 'granite and rainbow'. She combines the 'granite-like solidity' of truth, materiality and fact with the abstract, 'rainbow-like intangibility' of 'personality' (Woolf 1986–94, vol. 4: 473). Woolf was as committed to fact as to imagination. *A Room of One's Own*, for example, identifies new ways of writing and reading signifiers of women as simultaneously material, historical referent and textual, rhetorical figures:

> What one must do to bring her to life was to think poetically and prosaically at one and the same moment, thus keeping in touch with fact – that she is Mrs Martin, aged thirty-six, dressed in blue, wearing a black hat and brown shoes; but not losing sight of fiction either – that she is a vessel in which all sorts of spirits and forces are coursing and flashing perpetually.
>
> (Woolf 1929: 56–7)

Any endeavour to trace the historical and contextual significances for Woolf's work must begin with the bifurcation in her writing. On one hand, her texts explore the material and historical foundation of literary production; on the other, her writing seeks to break free from all such limitations, illustrated in her attempts to create a new language purged of historical and political concerns, and propounded in her model of androgynous writing. Skilled readers of Woolf must carefully attend, then, to textuality as much as context. Contextualizing Woolf is not simply a historical turn. It entails a simultaneous return to theoretical and critical contexts, in which the processes of historicizing and contextualizing are always already placed. Identifying Woolf's precise citations of the feminist politics of her time requires historicist, archival skills, but the impetus even to look for, and take seriously, these citations in the first place, and then to try to assess precisely how Woolf's writing engages them, comes from feminist literary theory.

More recently, I have become an editor of Woolf's writing, a project that has propelled me towards the archive as never before. The task of annotation requires me to attempt the empirical act of glossing her teeming cultural and historical referents. But this cannot be done in all innocence of theory. It is the stated aim of the forthcoming *Cambridge University Press Edition of the Writings of Virginia Woolf* that 'it will be more thoroughly annotated, with regard to historical, factual, cultural and literary allusions, than any previous edition has had the scope for, paying long overdue respect to the astonishing density and breadth of intellectual referencing in Woolf's work'.[1] Whereas the learned literary and cultural references of Eliot, Pound, and Joyce have long since been thoroughly annotated, Woolf's deceptively fluent writing has not yet been properly attended to. Not so long ago, for instance, critics simply presumed Woolf's lack of education rather than acknowledge her satirical characterization of Mrs Dalloway's mistaken assignation of Clytemnestra to the *Antigone* in *The Voyage Out*. But Woolf's translation of *Agamemnon*, languishing in the archives, is clear evidence to the contrary. Woolf's post-war reputation as an etiolated, naïve aesthete, or as the high priestess of high-modernist style, prevented generations of critics from noticing the precision and density of her material references. The historical reality of her champagne bottles opened with corkscrews in *Between the Acts*, for example, has only recently been acknowledged, where previously they were patronizingly seen as an unworldly error. If the recent historical turn encourages us to explore Woolf's precise references to material culture, it also forces us to rethink our theoretical approach to her modernism and sense of modernity. Yet the accumulation of historical, cultural, and intertextual glosses may also encourage a perverse repositioning of Woolf's (and modernism's) texts as 'realist', as if such referentiality were not a staple of modernist aesthetics.

Take, for example, the opening lines of *Mrs Dalloway*, where the reader is alerted to radically distanced sense(s) of place (social, political, geographical) by Mrs Dalloway's insistence that 'she would buy the flowers herself', taking on her servant's work: 'for Lucy had her work cut out for her. The doors would be taken off their hinges; Rumpelmayer's men were coming.' Taking the doors off is preparation for the party, the novel's crowning scene, but it simultaneously heralds the unhinging of the novel's own narrative portals. A standard modernist reading of this passage would emphasize the narrative function of the image as a threshold between the present and the past, and would accommodate the intertext with a line from Walt Whitman as a moment of self-conscious textuality. Woolf's line rehearses the expansive gesture of *Leaves of Grass*: 'unscrew the locks from the doors! / Unscrew the doors themselves from their jambs!' Here, Whitman celebrates himself in terms of free-roaming sensuality and sexuality and follows his injunction to remove the barriers of social hierarchy as well as sexual propriety with a declaration of solidarity: 'whoever degrades another degrades me, / And whatever is done or said returns at last to me' (Whitman 1973: 52). Doors unhinged for Mrs Dalloway's party unhinge *Mrs Dalloway* itself, opening a portal to Whitman's progressive unhinging in Manhattan. But a standard historical gloss of the name of the catering firm whose men will pass through Mrs Dalloway's unhinged doors would point up two possible historical referents to catering companies of that name in London and Paris whose premises Woolf visited.[2]

Acknowledging these different orders of information concerning the unhinged doors leaves the reader on the threshold between modernism and modernity. How are we to theorize the various unhingeings performed by Woolf's writing? How are we adequately to historicize them? Whereas the exhausted terms 'modernity', 'modernism', and 'postmodernism' tend to leave us on one side of the threshold or the other, the more broadly redefined term 'avant-garde' productively gets us swinging on the hinges without falling off on either side.

Thoughts on the avant-garde and modernism

Over two decades ago, Andreas Huyssen rightly argued for the recovery of 'a sense of the cultural politics of the historical avantgarde' (Huyssen 1988: 4), but his argument was responding to the risky theoretical neglect of postmodernism's relationship to mass culture. 'Too many discussions of postmodernism', he complains, 'fail entirely to address this problem, thereby losing, in a certain sense, their very object and getting bogged down in the futile attempt to define the post-modern in terms of style alone' (Huyssen 1988: viii). Analysis of the historical avant-garde's relationship to mass culture, including the 'perhaps deluded dream of an avantgardist mass culture' would furnish a resolution to this theoretical impasse (Huyssen 1988: x). He urges taking up 'the historical avantgarde's insistence on the cultural transformation of everyday life and from there … develop[ing] strategies for today's cultural and political context' (Huyssen 1988: 7). Modernist studies has since attended to such calls, but in doing so, it sometimes fails to provide the precise theoretical framing that helps make sense of our findings and to map out the nuances and variations in the historical avant-garde. While 'modernism' is so firmly entrenched in our scholarly discourse that it would be folly to avoid it altogether, we must nevertheless open up its study more fully to the powerful theoretical and historicizing capacities in a more informed usage of 'avant-garde'.

It is worth rehearsing the spectrum of definitions of 'avant-garde', a term whose discourse distinctly precedes the modernist period.[3] Originally a military term designating the advanced guard,

> avant garde [emerged] in the third decade of the nineteenth century, not in debate about art as such, but in the early socialist tradition as left-wing intellectuals and politicians tried to think through concepts of progress and freedom in emerging modern societies.
>
> (Wood in Edwards 1999: 187)

'Avant-garde,' Matei Calinescu points out, 'has an old history in French. As a term of warfare it dates back to the Middle Ages, and it developed a figurative meaning at least as early as the Renaissance.' But it was not used as a metaphor for 'expressing a self-consciously advanced position in politics, literature and art … with any consistency before the nineteenth century' (Calinescu 1987: 97). Art came to be seen in this period 'as a kind of "advance guard" for social progress as a whole' (Wood in Edwards 1999: 187). Henri de Saint-Simon, who first used the term in relation to art, rallied artists in 1825 to 'unite' and 'serve as the avant-garde: for amongst all the arms at our disposal, the power of the Arts is the swiftest and most expeditious' in spreading 'new ideas amongst men' (Saint-Simon in Edwards 1999: 187). Clearly, this definition of 'avant-garde' could be applied to realist aesthetics; and at one point it was actually opposed to the late nineteenth-century aestheticism that many understand to have its legacy in modernist aesthetics (see Wood 1999: 187). As Calinescu concludes, the avant-garde 'was little more than a radicalized and strongly utopianized version of modernity', in that, historically, it 'started by dramatizing certain constitutive elements of the idea of modernity and making them into cornerstones of revolutionary ethos' (Calinescu 1987: 95).

In the period after World War II, Anglophone art criticism began to foreground 'modernist' as the epithet for the autonomous, 'experimental' art of the early twentieth century, a rhetorical manoeuvre exemplified in the work of Clement

Greenberg. At this point, 'avant-garde' became interchangeable, even synonymous, with 'modernist'. 'It is one of those odd twists of history,' Wood observes, 'that the dominant understanding of "avant-garde" in the years after 1945 should in effect have come to signify the opposite of what was originally intended' (Wood in Edwards 1999: 187). This is the result of 'the way art itself evolved in modern western bourgeois societies. These societies have experienced what is widely understood as a "separation of the spheres"' (Wood in Edwards 1999: 187). This volte-face came about in part because of the way 'modern art has evolved a set of procedures, and references, techniques and assumptions, which add up to something like its own characteristic "language"' under this social and historical process of separation of spheres (Wood in Edwards 1999: 187). The volte-face occurs when 'avant-garde' becomes synonymous with an aesthetic mode, understood as a new language, and enshrined as a theory of the aesthetic, the point where the 'notion of being "in advance" came to denote not so much modern art's relationship to society at large, as certain kinds of art's relationship to other, more conventional kinds of art' (Wood in Edwards 1999: 187). Wood identifies the 1960s as the moment when 'this modernist understanding of the idea of an artistic "avant-garde" came under challenge'; the rise of postmodernism is the impetus for the 'importance of art's active and explicit relationship to the wider culture beyond art' to be 'once more ... widely canvassed' (Wood in Edwards 1999: 187). As a result,

> the appellation 'avant-garde' has been withdrawn by many writers and critics from those 'autonomous' art movements with which it was for long identified ... The idea of an avant-garde has been returned to those practices which explicitly sought to overcome the separation of art from life, the separation of aesthetics from politics.
>
> (Wood in Edwards 1999: 187)

On this reading, postmodernism has returned us to a clearer position: 'avant-garde' is to be withdrawn from Greenbergian 'modernism' and more accurately applied to those practitioners, like photomontagist John Heartfield and satirist George Grosz, who sought to liquidate art itself 'as an activity that is split off from the praxis of life' (Bürger 1984: 22). But this is a reductive gesture and a missed opportunity. It is more fruitful to attend to the theories of the avant-garde engaged by the artists and writers retrospectively designated as 'modernist'. Bürger's theory of the avant-garde has recently been revisited by critics who recognize the need to both revise his definition and apply it more widely to the historical avant-garde as well as to the post-war works Bürger identifies as neo-avant-garde (see Murphy 1999 and Scheunemann 2000). They further argue that Bürger's analysis of the historical avant-garde's aims may, itself, be mistaken. This interest in revising 'avant-garde' and in broadening its application is not only most productive, but also accommodates the historical turn without sacrificing modernism's theoretical force.

Whereas avant-garde aesthetics might be considered at the least transgressive, if not dissident, modernist aesthetics are at most transgressive. Avant-garde texts may be read as interrupting, disrupting, and even *transforming* contexts, rather than escaping them (see Bürger 1984; Eysteinnson 1990). To be avant-garde may mean to be at the cutting edge of art, forging new aesthetics, breaking with aesthetic tradition while celebrating a release into aesthetic oblivion. Here avant-garde has become synonymous with its earlier antonym, *l'art pour l'art*. This is the definition of 'avant-garde' that many definitions of modernism seem to coincide with (see Bradbury and MacFarlane 1976). But the concept of the avant-garde is also rooted in the attempts of various movements to liquidate art itself 'as an activity that is split off from the praxis of life' (Bürger 1984: 22).

This is a radically dissident aesthetics deployed to break rather than merely transgress aesthetic, social, cultural, and political boundaries. Military shock tactics reappear in avant-garde performances where passive aesthetic enjoyment is dashed by transgressive violence, like the attacks on the public advocated by the Futurists: 'go out into the street, launch assaults from theatres and introduce the fisticuff into the artistic battle' (Goldberg 1979: 12). Poetry, according to Filippo Marinetti's 'Manifesto of Futuris' (1913), 'must be conceived as a violent attack' (Kolocotroni *et al.* 1998: 251); it must in fact '*glorify war*' (ibid.). Tristan Tzara's 'Dada Manifesto, 1918' rules that 'every page should explode' (Kolocotroni *et al.* 1998: 277). He gives a lyrical account of the revolutionary moment when the boundaries between art and life are smashed:

> a unique fraternity comes into existence at the intense moment when beauty and life itself, brought into high tension on a wire, ascend towards a flash-point; the blue tremor linked to the ground by our magnetized gaze which covers the peak with snow. The miracle. I open my heart to creation.
>
> (Tzara, 'A Note on Art', cited in Kolocotroni *et al.* 1998: 280)

Berlin Dadaists, who joined the anti-Weimar revolution, declared themselves the 'Dadaist Headquarters of World Revolution' (Richter 1965: 126).

It is difficult to tell sometimes where political activism shades into performance art. Think of the Wobblie troubadour, Joe Hill, who wrote many of the incendiary lyrics in *The Little Red Songbook*. Before his judicial murder by the State of Utah in 1915 (he had been framed for murder), Hill requested to have his ashes mailed to every state except Utah, not wishing to be caught dead there. The Joe Hill Memorial Committee duly obeyed, and were delighted when some of the packages burst open, disrupting the mail (Kornbluh 1964: 157), this accident adding further dada to Hill's avant-garde agenda. Hill's last message to his comrades was: 'Don't mourn – Organize!', imperatives to match the 'make it new' of avant-garde aesthetics. Hill recommended in *Solidarity* (December, 1911) that

> if a person can put a few cold, common-sense facts into a song and dress them (the facts) up in a cloak of humor to take the dryness out of them, he will succeed in reaching a great number of workers who are too unintelligent or too indifferent to read a pamphlet or an editorial on economic science.
>
> (Hill cited in Kornbluh 1964: 11)

Perhaps this manifesto item is merely a prosaic version of Horace's dictum that poetry should both instruct and delight. (In fact the 'dress' and 'facts' of Hill's famous songs are more sophisticated than he makes out; see, for example, Van Wienen 1997.) They have certainly penetrated Western culture with their rich imagery. 'Pie in the sky', for example, is from his most famous song 'The Preacher and the Slave'; and the eponymous 'Mr Block' is the *Ur* 'blockhead', a semi-reified industrial worker loyal to the bosses, with his own subversive cartoon strip, and possibly also an ancestor of Bob Dylan's 'Mr Jones'.

Proponents of art-for-art's-sake, however, abhor the misuse of art for political effect: propaganda pollutes the purity of aestheticism. To smuggle in teaching, political doctrine, or ideology is perhaps unavoidable, and not merely a matter of outward dress versus content. But the achievement of 'modernist' art is nevertheless to initiate and develop avant-garde transformational languages. 'There is a language of sculpture, of painting, of poetry', acknowledges Benjamin:

> Just as the language of poetry is partly, if not solely, founded on the name language of man, it is very conceivable that the language of sculpture or painting is founded on certain kinds of thing-languages, that in them we find a translation of the language of things into an infinitely higher language, which may still be of the same sphere. We are concerned here with name-less, nonacoustic languages, languages issuing from matter; here we should recall the material community of things in their communication.
>
> (Benjamin 1996: 73)

Avant-garde language translates from multiple such sources into another trans-formational language, if not 'into an infinitely higher language'. Benjamin recognizes that 'Language communicates the linguistic being of things', and the art of this period often draws on every kind of language, visual and verbal, in its attempts to forge a new language. Just as 'All language communicates itself' (Benjamin 1996: 63), so the avant-garde, in a sense, communicates itself. Benjamin also alerts us to the idea that poetry is a higher form of everyday language, just as the visual arts transform the material of the everyday world, itself a kind of language. Theories of the avant-garde are much better equipped to attend to the languages of art and of things, and to negotiate the hinges between them.

Kraus memorably invokes avant-garde practices, and the interpenetration of visual, musical, and verbal aesthetics in his rage against the decline of German language, and the related decline in the understanding of enriching, literary, language, which he saw as concurrent with the rise of right-wing politics in the Weimar period:

> Literature is beyond help. The farther it removes itself from comprehensi-bility, the more importunately do people claim their material. The best thing would be to keep literature secret from the people until there is a law that prohibits people from using language, permitting them to use only sign language in urgent cases. But by the time such a law comes into

being, they will probably have learned to answer the aria 'How's business?' with a still life.

(Kraus 1986: 64)

Kraus points up the differences between literary language and the language of the everyday, at the same time acknowledging their interpenetration. He depicts the gestures typical of avant-garde activism, 'smearing one another with paint, or throwing plaster at one another' (Kraus 1986: 64), displacing the language of the everyday; but his closing observation on the absorption of art by capitalist business is simultaneously an avant-garde gesture and a warning to the avant-garde of its ultimate containment by the forces it seeks to transform. Yet the historical, transformational languages of the avant-garde, commodified and culturally enshrined, nevertheless may potentially disclose forces for continuing resistance and change.

Avant-garde movements not only dealt in an (anti-) aesthetic of violent intervention, but they also, on occasion, incurred violence. Futurist and Dadaist exhibitions and performances frequently incurred violent attacks, whether from outraged audiences or police. Bürger maintains that the 'attack of the historical avant-garde on art as an institution has failed, and art has not been integrated into the praxis of life, art as an institution continues to survive as something separate from the praxis of life' (Bürger 1984: 57). Art, in this post-avant-garde era, 'can either resign itself to its autonomous status or "organize happenings" to break through that status' (ibid.). Such happenings, however, cannot achieve the kind of political and social revolution that Bürger has identified as the true aim of avant-garde. 'All art that is not against its time is for it,' Kraus declared in 1912: 'Such art can make the time pass, but it cannot conquer it … Art can come only from denial. Only from anguished protest. Never from calm compliance' (Szasz 1977: 158).

Denial, of course, may have many different inflections, depending upon context. George Grosz, the Berlin Dadaist, is marked in Nazi SS files of 1939 as 'one of the most evil representatives of degenerate art who worked in a manner which was hostile to Germany' (cited in Lewis 1991: 231); but after he had fled to New York, he dropped his revolutionary style of satirical caricature. Yet Grosz, while not as extreme or desperate as he was in the context of German culture, and while also attempting an optimistic American outlook (Lewis 1991: 236), nevertheless continued to shun conformity, as is suggested by his November 1932 editorial in *Americana*: 'We are Americans who believe that our civilization exudes a miasmic stench and that we had better prepare to give it a decent but rapid burial. We are the laughing morticians of the present' (cited in Martin 1984: 215).

Huyssen warns against the critical inclination to exclude all but the most extreme tendencies of Dada as authentically avant-garde, in the sense of political engagement:

> While only Dada Berlin integrated its artistic activities with the working-class struggles in the Weimar Republic, it would be reductive to deny Dada

Zurich or Dada Paris any political importance and to decree their project was 'only aesthetic', 'only cultural'. Such an interpretation falls victim to the same reified dichotomy of culture and politics which the historical avantgarde had tried to explode.

(Huyssen 1988: 11)

The logic of this argument extends beyond Dada, as demonstrated by the work of more recent scholars of the avant-garde and neo-avant-garde. This means, for one thing, rethinking Bürger's dominant theory of the avant-garde. Dietrich Scheunemann, in his influential departure from Bürger, for example, argues against 'projecting the sublation of art into life', and calls for attempts to 'promote the advance of literary technique, with a view to strengthening literature's capability to penetrate contemporary life and make contemporary experience discernible' (Scheunemann 2000: 41). The focus on 'technique' is not necessarily a retreat into style, but a recognition of the shifting cultural and political space that is 'montage'. Montage opens the space where the technological meets the aesthetic, to produce 'new, epic possibilities' (Benjamin 1996: 301) (Scheunemann 2000: 41). Scheunemann amplifies Bürger's observation that montage 'may be considered the fundamental principle of avant-gardiste art', that is, a '"fitted" (*montierte*) work' that 'calls attention to the fact that it is made up of reality fragments; it breaks through the appearance (*Schein*) of totality' (Scheunemann 2000: 72). Bürger recognizes the paradox of a work of art itself realizing the destruction of 'art as an institution' (Bürger 1984: 72); and Scheunemann is, likewise, alert to the paradox of advocating any one technique or 'single formula' as 'a reliable guide to the variety of avant-gardist [*sic*] concepts and productions' (Scheunemann 2000: 41). But Scheunemann rightly understands that the project of following all the diverse responses to the challenge posed by technological advances 'not only allows for precise and substantive qualification of the very formation of the avant-garde, but also for exploring and contradictions of its further development and the variety and heterogeneity of its manifestations' (Scheunemann 2000: 41). The hinge-like quality of montage, in interpenetrating art and reality, accounts for its historical dominance as an avant-garde technique. Scheunemann urges us to map both developments of montage and departures from it.

By the 1930s there is already available, then, a tradition and a transformational language of 'the new', familiar enough to be satirized and yet supple enough to be stretched into new locutions – aesthetic, cultural, political, and historical. The historical avant-garde's assault on the institution of Art transforms all aesthetic and interpretative practices. Any appraisal of the period must take account of the position(ing) of specific artists, writers, movements, works, and texts in relation to it. The historical turn in modernism is the moment to acknowledge the exhaustion of 'modernism' as a theoretical term, and to address the pressing issues of modernism and history through a return to theories of the avant-garde. We need to rethink our readings of the impasse Bürger has dealt us. There is a blind spot at the heart of Bürger's model, namely his fundamental ambiguity with regard to the category of aesthetic autonomy. For surely the possibility of reconceptualizing social practice is itself predicated upon the privilege of attaining a certain independence from the real (rather than being merged with it) and upon a sense of critical distance from the object to be criticized.

(Murphy 1999: 27)

We also need to rethink the scale of transformation achieved by avant-garde art. Wholesale transformation is one extreme end of the spectrum of transgression to dissidence. In reading modernism through the extreme positionings of the historical avant-garde and simultaneously broadening the application of 'avant-garde' to work beyond Bürger's historical avant-garde, we can attend to the transformative and interpenetrative capacities of modernist aesthetics, and we can continue to pursue the mutually enriching twin impetuses in modernism and modernist criticism – both to historicize and to theorize, and thereby acknowledge both textuality and context.

Notes

1 Unpublished general editorial statement.
2 See Goldman (2006: 69–71).
3 See Goldman (2004: 7–9, 11–16, 18, 20).

Bibliography

Barrett, E. (1997) 'Unmasking Lesbian Passion: The Inverted World of *Mrs Dalloway*', *Virginia Woolf: Lesbian Readings*, ed. E. Barrett and P. Cramer, New York: New York University Press.

Benjamin, W. (1996) 'On Language as Such and On the Language of Man', *Selected Writings: Volume 1: 1913–1926*, ed. M. Bullock and M. W. Jennings, Cambridge, MA, and London: Belknap Press.

Bennett, A. (1917) *Books and Portraits: Being Comments on a Past Epoch 1908–1911*, London: Chatto and Windus.

Bradbury, M. and MacFarlane, J. (1976) *Modernism 1890–1930*, Harmondsworth: Penguin.

Bradshaw, D. (2002) '"Vanished, Like Leaves": The Military, Elegy and Italy in *Mrs Dalloway*', *Woolf Studies Annual* 8: 107–26.

Bürger, B. (1984) *Theory of the Avant-Garde*, trans. M. Shaw, Minneapolis: University of Minnesota Press.

Calinescu, M. (1987) *Five Faces of Modernity: Modernism, Avant-Garde, Decadence, Kitsch, Postmodernism*, Durham: Duke University Press.

Edwards, S. (ed.) (1999) *Art and Its Histories: A Reader*, New Haven and London: Yale University Press.

Eysteinnson, Astradur (1990) *The Concept of Modernism*, Ithaca, NY: Cornell University Press.

Friedman, S. S. (2001) 'Definitional Excursions: The Meanings of Modern/Modernity/Modernism', *Modernism/Modernity* 8(3): 493–513.

Goldberg, R. (1979) *Performance: Live Art 1909 to the Present*, London: Thames and Hudson.

Goldman, J. (1998) *The Feminist Aesthetics of Virginia Woolf: Modernism, Post-Impressionism and the Politics of the Visual*, Cambridge: Cambridge University Press.

—— (2004) *Modernism, 1910–1945: Image to Apocalypse*, Basingstoke: Palgrave.

—— (2006) '1925, London, New York, Paris: Metropolitan Modernisms – Parallax and Palimpsest', in B. McHale and R. Stevenson (eds) *The Edinburgh Companion to Twentieth-Century Literatures in English*, Edinburgh: Edinburgh University Press.

Green, B. (1997) *Spectacular Confessions: Autobiography, Performative Activism, and the Sites of Suffrage, 1905–1938*, Basingstoke: Macmillan.

Greenberg, C. (1961; revised edn 1965) 'Modernist Painting', in Frascina and Harrison (eds) *Modernist Art and Modernism: A Critical Anthology*, New Haven: Yale University Press.

—— (1973) *Art and Culture*, London: Thames and Hudson.

Huyssen, A. (1988) *After the Great Divide: Modernism, Mass Culture and Postmodernism*, Basingstoke: Macmillan.

Kolocotroni, V., Goldman, J. and Taxidou, O. (eds) (1998) *Modernism: an Anthology of Sources and Documents*, Edinburgh and Chicago: Edinburgh University Press and University of Chicago Press.

Kornbluh, J. L. (ed.) (1964) *Rebel Voices: An I. W. W. Anthology*, Ann Arbor: University of Michigan Press.

Kraus, K. (1986) *Half-Truths and One-and-a-Half Truths: Selected Aphorisms*, trans. H. Zohn, Manchester: Carcanet.

Lewis, B. I. (1991) *George Grosz: Art and Politics in the Weimar Republic*, Princeton: Princeton University Press.

Martin, J. (1984) *Nathanael West: The Art of His Life*, New York: Carroll and Graf.

Melly, G. (1978) *Owning Up*, Harmondsworth: Penguin.

Murphy, R. (1999) *Theorizing the Avant-Garde: Modernism, Expressionism, and the Problems of Postmodernity*, Cambridge: Cambridge University Press.

Richter, H. (1965) *Dada: Art and Anti-Art*, London: Thames and Hudson.

Scheunemann, D. (ed.) (2000) *European Avant-Garde: New Perspectives*, Amsterdam: Rodopi.

Schwitters, K. (1993) *PPPPPP: Poems Performance Pieces Proses Plays Poetics*, ed. and trans. J. Rothenberg and P. Joris, Philadelphia: Temple University Press.

Szasz, T. (1977) *Karl Kraus and the Soul-Doctors: A Pioneer Critic and His Criticism of Psychiatry and Psychoanalysis*, London: Routledge and Kegan Paul.

Van Wienen, M. W. (1997) *Partisans and Poets: The Political Work of American Poetry in the Great War*, Cambridge: Cambridge University Press.

Whitman, W. (1973) *Leaves of Grass*, ed. S. Bradley and H. W. Blodgett, New York: Norton.

Williams, L. B. (2002) *Modernism and the Ideology of History: Literature, Politics, and the Past*, Cambridge: Cambridge University Press.

Wood, P. (ed.) (1999) *The Challenge of the Avant-Garde*, Newhaven: Yale University Press.

Woolf, V. (1929) *A Room of One's Own*, London: Hogarth.

—— (1986–94) *The Essays of Virginia Woolf*, Vols 1–4, ed. A. McNeillie, London: Hogarth.

—— (2000) *Mrs Dalloway*, ed. D. Bradshaw, Oxford: Oxford University Press.

13 Theory

Susan Stanford Friedman

I am struck by the sense of irony—perhaps even injustice—out of which this volume arose. In his initial call for essays in 2005, Stephen Ross issued an eloquent *apologia* for theory as constitutive for modernist studies, puzzling at the "two-fold irony" that the ever-expanding boundaries of modernism evident in the new modernist studies have "come at the expense of a key area of inquiry that is both intimately linked to modernism and largely responsible for the rejuvenation of modernist studies: critical theory." I couldn't agree more with the foundational premise of this volume: that "critical theory" is fundamentally continuous with modernism and not a radical break from it, as the misleading but common terms "post-modern theory" or "postmodernism" suggest. But I want to probe the implications and possible limitations of Ross's assertion in his call that "the massive rejuvenation of modernist studies was enabled precisely by theory's confrontation with the predominant notions of the literary, canon formation, disciplinary formations, high and low culture, progress, civilization, and imperialism."

Ross's initial proposition that "critical theory" or "theory"—the first term slides imperceptibly into the second—is "largely responsible for" the rejuvenation of modernist studies is a big claim. It is softened somewhat in his impressive introduction, but nonetheless remains in his assertion that the "occlusion of theory" from the new modernist studies "ignores theory's essential role in clearing the ground for a new approach to modernism". What intellectual and political genealogies does this claim presume? Has "theory" performed the *only* "confrontation with the predominant notions of the literary, canon formation, disciplinary formations" that paved the way for the new understanding of modernism? What do we mean by "theory," anyway? If "theory" is to get credit for dismantling the "old" and constituting the "new" modernist studies, then we ought to understand what "theory" means and presumably what it excludes: in short, what is "not theory" and does the opposition of theory/not theory have its own definitional politics based on the logic of inclusion/exclusion by which definition typically operates? The metonymic slide between "critical theory" and "theory" provides a starting point that links the diachronic and synchronic questions I have posed.

In a narrow sense, "critical theory" invokes Critical Theory, associated with the Frankfurt School. As Ross points out, Critical Theory develops alongside modernism, going back to the founding of the Institute for Social Research in 1929 and including the work of such preeminent theorists of modernity and modernism as Walter Benjamin and Theodor Adorno. Anthologized in the influential *Aesthetics and Politics* (1977), Benjamin and Adorno in particular remain centers of exciting new work in modernist studies, which assumes Critical Theory to be both contemporaneous with modernism and a resonant framework for reading it.

In a broader sense, however, "critical theory" has a less certain meaning. Sometimes, it refers to the philosophical and psychoanalytic theories of significance and the symbolic order associated with varieties of poststructuralism emanating from France since the 1960s. At other times, "critical theory" includes any theory that is critical of the social order, as James Bohman notes: "any philosophical approach with similar practical aims [as Frankfurt School Critical Theory] could be called a 'critical theory,' including feminism, critical race theory, and some forms of post-colonial criticism" (Bohman 2005).[1]

While Critical Theory is widely understood as part of modernism, "critical theory" or just "theory" often is not. The slippage from "critical theory" to "theory" as well as the definitional boundaries of "theory" comes into play here. Does "critical theory" or "theory" refer to "high theory," implying an analogy with "high modernism," a phrase that itself slips between *avant-garde* modernism and "establishment" modernism? If so, theory invokes poststructuralism, most centrally of the French variety. This theory continues early twentieth-century modernism into other discursive systems: philosophical, linguistic, historical/political.

In the US academy, poststructuralism had its heyday in the 1980s, its proponents often occupying positions of privilege and prestige even as their work was resisted, mocked, and barely understood by those steeped in the complex *oeuvre* of Derrida, Lacan, Foucault, Kristeva, Barthes, Cixous, Irigaray, Deleuze and Guattari, and the relevant philosophical traditions. During the 1980s, modernist scholars often turned to poststructuralism for frameworks, concepts, and strategies for reading modernists from earlier in the century that anticipated later poststructuralist thought. An uncanny symbiosis between figures like Joyce and Derrida, Woolf and Kristeva, Stein and Barthes, Barnes and Foucault, H. D. and Irigaray pervaded many studies of modernism (including my own). High modernism and high theory stepped out together like beautifully paired, high-strutting steeds pulling the carriage of criticism, seemingly leaving the clodhopping methods of literary history, author studies, archival studies, and so forth behind.

Ross's *apologia* suggests that the newly expansive modernist studies has forgotten the role that poststructuralism played in the critique of knowledge that reinvented scholarship, particularly in the humanities and the American academy. For some, poststructuralism has become a toolbox of reading strategies to be drawn upon whenever a deconstructive hammer or a Lacanian screwdriver seems handy. Such fragmentary uses ignore the varied philosophical frameworks of poststructuralism, reducing a coherent body of theory into partial and selective strategies that can wrench the components out of their larger frameworks, displacing them into other, possibly incompatible frameworks. To protest such redeployment of poststructuralism sounds perfectly reasonable, and yet I fear that it is sometimes based on a desire that ought to be (but isn't in practice) incompatible with poststructuralist theory: namely, the desire to control and keep "pure" the subsequent uses of theory, to keep theory within the parameters of what Francois Roustang called "dire mastery" in his discussion of Lacan and Lacanians. Rather than genealogies of discipleship, I prefer to track the circulation, transplantation, adaptation, and indigenization of theory as it moves from one location to another. I remain much influenced by Edward Said's "Traveling Theory" (1983) and "Traveling Theory Reconsidered" (1994), which emphasize the need to understand how theories change as they are used in different places and for different purposes. As Said reflects, the transplanted theory often becomes more transgressive and powerful, not diluted, in its new environs.

Translating "high theory" into other critical languages, however, is not my only concern with this volume's premises about the relation of theory to modernism. I have two others: first, the genealogy of critique that has enabled the new modernist studies; and second, the meaning of theory itself in the context of contemporary literary studies in general, and modernist studies in particular. Rather than see critical or poststructuralist theory as a single stream of ideas solely responsible for opening up the modernist canon, I regard it as one among many theoretical streams that ran parallel to each other, sometimes confronted each other, and eventually joined into a sea-change in modernist studies. Even before the theory of the Frankfurt School or of French poststructuralism had much impact on modernist studies in the United States, the rise in the 1970s of feminist literary theory, lesbian/gay theory, race studies, and multicultural and class theory blew open the established canons of literary studies in general. The hegemony of French "high theory" in the United States *follows*, not precedes, the radical critique of prevailing notions of the literary and the canon, and of the methodologies and institutions of literary studies. The recoveries of many modernist women writers in the 1970s as well as new attention to women's role in modernist cultural production represented the ground of critique that opened modernist studies to ideas from France in the 1980s. Similarly, the rise of African-American Studies in the 1970s and its spread into the multiculturalisms of the 1980s enabled consideration of movements like the Harlem Renaissance as part of modernism. Crediting "theory" as sole enabler of the new modernist studies forgets a history of critique rooted in the political movements of the 1960s—Civil Rights, feminist, anti-war, gay/lesbian, and so forth. No doubt Marxism, influential in the Frankfurt School, also played a role in the movements of the 1960s and their aftermath. But the Frankfurt School itself is not the origin of radical critique in the US; rather, it is one of the streams of critique that developed in that particular moment. As continental theory transplanted into the US academy, its deconstructions of systems of signification found a strong foothold in many disciplines and interdisciplines, in part because earlier theories and movements had challenged the prevailing objectivist and exclusivist epistemologies that had ignored, marginalized, or otherwise ideologically represented whole populations, cultures, and issues. Lumping these earlier politically based theories with "critical theory" swallows up what were distinctive theoretical strands under a general rubric that still frequently signifies poststructuralist or Frankfurt School theory.

The case of postcolonial studies is somewhat different, and here I see the histories of Critical Theory and poststructuralism much more entangled with the rise of postcolonial studies, now one of the most exciting areas in the new modernist studies. As translator of *Of Grammatology*, Gayatri Chakravorty Spivak symptomatizes how postcolonial theory is tied to the intellectual traditions of both the Frankfurt School and poststructuralist theory. Even in this case, though, I would suggest not that theory enabled postcolonial studies, but that they enabled each other.

My second concern is to resist the metonymic slide from critical or post-structuralist theory to theory itself. During what Wallace Martin has called "the epoch of theory" in the 1980s, the sentence "I do theory" commonly designated a specialization whereby self-definition as a literary theorist meant not an expertise in theory in general, but rather knowledge of specific French theories. "Doing theory" was typically ahistorical and decontextualizing in approach. But the production and use of this theory *has* a geohistory (an intersecting space and time) however much it might be suppressed. In "Theory Today," Jacques Lezra provocatively suggested that "the era of 'high theory'" in the US, "which runs roughly from 1967 to 1988," represents the anti-nationalist/internationalist response of a generation of intellectuals "in the US literary scene" who resisted the logic of the Cold War by looking "to a post-national Europe for their intellectual models" (Lezra 2006: 2). Today, Lezra points out, the conditions that produced the "heyday of 'high theory'" have dissipated; instead, the twenty-first century is producing new kinds of theory, with a "thematic focus on matters of ethnicity, transculturation, globalization" (Lezra 2006: 2). He asks us to remember that the word "theory" shifted in meaning in the late sixteenth century from signifying "spectacle" or "a form of contemplation" to denoting, "as the OED has it, a 'systematic statement of rules or principles to be followed'" (Lezra 2006: 2).

We need to think more broadly about the meaning of "theory," refusing to equate one set of theories with the act of theorizing itself. In my view, "theory" signifies a mode of thought, a synchronic form of cognition that reaches for the generalizable rather than the particular. It is a system of thought that has explanatory power for many particularities located in different times and spaces. Not a "systematic statement of rules or principles," theory is also not inherently "critical"—it can be hegemonic as well as oppositional (or some combination thereof), and it can serve radically different politics. It is the opposite of what Clifford Geertz has called the "thick description" of "local knowledge," a methodology that seeks out particularity and resists the comparative or generalizable. Theory is transdisciplinary, though it is often articulated in and through particular disciplines. It resists the tendency of local knowledge to claim exceptionalism or uniqueness. Often containing the traces of its disciplinary production, theory takes many forms: philosophical, paradigmatic, modeling, aphoristic, narrative, figural, prophetic, etc.[2] As much as it might invite the transparent application of its systematic mode of knowing, it too has a materiality and form that opens to close reading for its internal contradictions, absences, multiplicities, and vast potentialities. Just as local knowledge has its limitations, theory too has its excesses: totalization, homogenization, decontextualization, deterritorialization, dehistoricization. Both modes of knowing—theorization and localization—have limitations; combined, each counters the excesses of the other. Neither exists very effectively without the other.

Understanding "theory" in this broader sense fosters a different approach to the entanglements of theory and modernist studies. It prevents the slippage from "theory" to "critical theory" to "poststructuralist" or Continental theory that is often unacknowledged. Most importantly it allows us to see the widespread use in the new modernist studies of what is often called "cultural theory." Cultural theory exists alongside the continuing resonances of critical and poststructural theory. Lezra's observation that the current emphasis in literary studies is "a focus on matters of ethnicity, transculturation, globalization" is both astute and slightly misleading. On the one hand, he notes the growing importance of cultural theory in literary studies; on the other hand, he does not name it as such, calling it instead a *"thematic* focus." The phenomenon he addresses reflects the shift from one kind of theoretical dominance to another. Cultural theory has in many ways supplanted poststructuralism as the main theoretical discourse to which many literary scholars turn for interdisciplinary and geohistorical engagements.

This shift has been a long time coming, at least in the United States. In a provisional and non-linear genealogy, the roots of the rise of cultural theory go back to the historical conditions Lezra alluded to, *and* to the confluence of several developments in literary studies: globalizing literary studies; interdisciplinarity (especially uses of anthropology, geography, media and popular culture studies, sociology, and science); the impact of fields like women's studies, race and ethnic studies, gay/lesbian/bisexual and queer studies, postcolonial, diasporic, and transnational studies, and disability studies; the spread of New Historicism from Early Modern Studies; and British Cultural Studies and its transatlantic fusion with New Historicism in the 1990s and the critical interdisciplines named above.[3]

The interest in "ethnicity, transculturation, globalization" that Lezra mentions engages with, uses, and sometimes produces cultural theory in many ways. Interestingly, the new dominance of cultural theory has not meant the complete abandonment of French theory. First, some poststructuralists still writing by the twenty-first century—Derrida and Cixous, for example—themselves became engaged with cultural theory, especially issues of nation, transculturalism, and transnationalism. Second, some of the theorists allied with poststructuralism during its heyday have been bridge figures to the present, continuing to be influential because their work substantively engaged geohistorically with questions of culture—preeminently, Foucault, Althusser, and Deleuze and Guattari. Third, other theorists whose work has been a form of cultural theory from the beginning—such as Pierre Bourdieu, Michel de Certeau, and Henri Lefebvre— have become at least as important, if not more so, as major sources of theory used widely in literary studies, including modernist studies. Their concepts of the *habitus* and the cultural field of production, circulation, and consumption (Bourdieu), culture as everyday practice (Certeau), and social spatiality (Lefebvre), for example, pervade current modernist studies. In a sense, Critical Theory—particularly that of Benjamin and Adorno—is now read through the lens of cultural theory as a form of cultural theory itself. The time is ripe, perhaps, to revisit both Critical Theory and poststructuralism either as particular forms of cultural theory or for their contributions to cultural theory.

It's one thing to assert that cultural theory is currently ascendant in literary studies. It is another to define what cultural theory is and how it might differ from other forms of theory such as social theory, critical theory, and poststructuralist theory. The borders between different kinds of theory are extremely porous, producing endless hybrid combinations, and the work of individual theorists often self-consciously blends disparate theoretical traditions. Distinctive emphases in different kinds of theory do exist, however, and it is a mistake to ignore the tendencies toward slippage whereby one kind of theory comes to stand for theory itself. Sound bites for different theory might look something like this: poststructuralist theory examines the significance of language and signifying systems in the symbolic order; critical theory offers political critique of ideology and political orders; social theory focuses on societal formations, stratifications, and distributions of power; feminist, race, and sexual theory address identity formations, axes of difference, and intersectionality; and cultural theory generalizes about cultural products and practices. Such shorthands, while useful, also demonstrate how impossible it is to maintain pure distinctions among types of theory. How, for example, can cultural theory address cultural products and practices without looking at signifying systems or social stratifications? Or ideology, race, and gender? As Rita Felski writes, "To study culture is to study everything that signifies … The structure of social life cannot be separated from layerings of symbolic meaning in which they are embedded" (Felski 2000: 56). The blend of cultural, social, and linguistic theories is everywhere evident. Nonetheless, each type of theory has a distinctive emphasis and contribution.

A second, and arguably more important, problem in defining cultural theory is the instability of the term "culture" itself. The meaning of "culture" is in flux and often interrogated in cultural theory itself. Cultural theory has all the heterogeneity of the competing concepts of "culture." Moreover, cultural theory often carries the marks of the disciplines out of which the theorists predominantly work. "Culture" for anthropologists and literary scholars signifies different objects and different methodologies of study. Increasingly, however, cultural theory is transdisciplinary, drawing on and often combining disciplines in the humanities and social sciences. Reflecting late twentieth-century globalism, spatial modes of theorization are especially pervasive. Cultural theory abounds in the rhetoric of location, landscape, network, conjuncture, linkage, intersection, mobility, displacement, and dislocation.

Cultural theory forms particularly at the intersection of culture with a capital "C" and culture with a little "c"—that is, culture as aesthetic productions of "high culture" and culture as the *ethnos*, the normative values, narratives, rituals, and practices of everyday life. The first grows out of the nineteenth-century meaning of culture as "the best which has been thought and said in the world"

(Arnold 1981: 6). The second also grows out of nineteenth-century thought in the founding of anthropology: "Culture, or Civilization, taken in its wide eth-nographic sense, is that complex whole which includes knowledge, belief, art, morals, law, custom, and any other capabilities and habits acquired by man as a member of society" (Tylor cited in Stocking 1982: 73). As Stuart Hall points out, these early and competing notions of culture have evolved considerably (Hall 1997: 2). Cultural theory in particular works across the supposed divide between "high" and "low" culture, examining popular culture, mass culture, and "little" traditions alongside the more prestigious forms of aesthetic production. It also works in the borderlands between culture as product and culture as a "set of practices" (Hall 1997: 2). Like poststructuralism, cultural theory often addresses signifying systems and codes as constitutive of culture; like social and critical theory, cultural theory often examines culture in the context of power relations, oppression, and forms of collusion, subversion, and resistance.

As Felski points out, the new import of cultural theory for modernist studies is linked to revisiting the issue of modernity: "Modernity is back with a vengeance. People are reflecting anew on the protean meanings of the modern, on its ambiguous legacies and current realities" (Felski 2000: 55). This attention to the "modern" blends the multiple meanings of "culture" in modernist studies, often bringing together the aesthetic achievements of "high modernism" and the cul-tural practices of everyday life, of popular and mass culture, of material culture, and of the "little traditions" of marginalized peoples. The theoretical interest in cultural practices instead of just cultural products has also brought new approa-ches to the study of "high culture," ones that assume the aesthetic object to be part of the cultural field or sphere (to invoke Bourdieu and Camboni) and thus a representational system involving both production and reception. Additionally, the new modernist studies has moved beyond the culture capitals of a few great European and American cities to a newly global and transnational scale, taking up the networks and cultural flows between the traditional centers of modernism and the colonies and former colonies; treating other parts of the world as centers of modernity and aesthetic production in their own right; and exploring the interrelationship of non-Western modernities and modernisms with one another. Comparative modernism has become increasingly global in perspective, challenging the older Eurocentric models.

Cultural theory pervades the new modernist studies, not to the exclusion of poststructuralist and critical theory, but often alongside them. A snapshot of selected work I first heard at Modernist Studies Association conferences since 1999 demonstrates the centrality and scope of cultural theory. Victoria Rosner's *Modernism and the Architecture of Private Life*, winner of the 2006 MSA Prize, exam-ines the relation between psychic life and private life in British modernism through the lens of interior design and spatiality. Felski's "New Cultural Theories of Modernity" issues an open call to modernist studies to use the new cultural theory of modernity. Mark Wollaeger's "Woolf, Postcards, and the Elision of Race" blends anthropology, material culture, and postcolonial studies in a reading of Woolf's *The Voyage Out* centered on ethnographic postcards sent home by travelers in the colonies. Laura Doyle and Laura Winkiel's *Geomodernism: Race, Modernism, Modernity* examines modernities and modernisms centered outside the West, defined in and through colonial relations. Giovanna Covi's *Modernist Women Race Nation: Networking Women 1890–1950, Circum-Atlantic Connections* uses theories of the cultural sphere, nation, race, and gender to examine the production and reception of women's transnational modernism. *Modernism/Modernity*'s 2006 special issue of Modernism and Transnationalism, edited by Cassandra Laity, is bookended with essays by postcolonial cultural theorists, Simon Gikandi and Sonita Sarker. However much this work draws on poststructuralist or critical theory, it is unthinkable without substantial use of cultural theory.

In spite of my insistence on the distinctiveness and significance of cultural theory for modernist studies, I would like to end with a plea for the depriviledging of any one kind of theory—whether poststructuralist, critical, or cultural—in modernist studies. We can note special affinities between modernism and different kinds of theories—for example, the way that the radical ruptures of representational poetics and practices that underlay early twentieth-century Anglo-American and European modernisms are linked to later poststructuralist theories of language; the equally radical shatterings of gender and racial barriers in the modernisms of the New Woman and the New Negro are linked to the later feminist and race theory of the post-1970 revolutions of knowledge. But we should avoid letting any one kind of theory stand in for the act of theorization itself or for the plurality of theoretical approaches, each one of which has vital and distinctive contributions to make to understanding the play between modernism and theory.

Notes

1 See also Lois Tyson's *Critical Theory Today* (2006) and *The Routledge Companion to Critical Theory* (Maples and Wake 2006), where "critical theory" incorporates any theory critical of hegemony.
2 On theory in the form of narrative, metaphor, or parable, see, e.g., Christian (1990: 38) and Nfah-Abbenyi (1997: 20).
3 For the differences between British and American Cultural Studies, see for example During (1999) and Grossberg *et al.* (1992).

Bibliography

Arnold, M. (1981) *Culture and Anarchy*, ed. J. D. Wilson, Cambridge: Cambridge University Press.
Bloch, E., Adorno, T. W., Benjamin, W., Brecht, B. and Lukács, G. (1977) *Aesthetics and Politics*, ed. and trans. R. Taylor, afterword by F. Jameson, New York: Verso.
Bohman, J. (2005) "Critical Theory," *Stanford Encyclopedia of Philosophy*. Online at http://plato.stanford.edu/entries/critical-theory/ (accessed 28 January 2008).
Bourdieu, P. (1980) *The Logic of Practice*, trans. R. Nice, Stanford: Stanford University Press.
—— (1993) *The Field of Cultural Production*, New York: Columbia University Press.
Camboni, M. (2004) "Networking Women: A Research Project and a Relational Model of the Cultural Sphere," in M. Camboni (ed.) *Networking Women: Subjects, Places, Links— Europe–America: Towards a Re-Writing of Cultural History, 1890–1939*, Roma: Edizioni de storia e letteratura, 1–26.

—— (2005) "Networking as a Cultural Model and Circum-Atlantic Networking Women," in G. Covi (ed.), *Modernism Women Race Nation: Networking Women 1890–1950, Circum-Atlantic Connections*, London: Mango Publishing, 11–31.

de Certeau, M. (1984) *The Practice of Everyday Life*, trans. S. Rendall, Berkeley: University of California Press.

Christian, B. (1990) "The Race for Theory," *The Nature and Context of Minority Discourse*, ed. A. R. JanMohamed and D. Lloyd, Oxford: Oxford University Press, 37–49.

Covi, G. (ed.) (2005) *Modernism Women Race Nation: Networking Women 1890–1950, Circum-Atlantic Connections*, London: Mango Publishing.

Doyle, L. and Winkiel, L. (eds) (2005) *Geomodernisms: Race, Modernism, Modernity*, Bloomington: Indiana University Press.

During, S. (ed.) (1999) *Cultural Studies Reader*, second edn, London: Routledge.

Felski, R. (2000) "New Cultural Theories of Modernity," *Doing Time: Feminist Theory and Postmodern Culture*, New York: New York University Press, 55–76.

Geertz, C. (1973) *The Interpretation of Cultures*, New York: Basic Books.

—— (1983) *Local Knowledge: Further Essays in Interpretive Anthropology*, New York: Basic Books.

Grossberg, L., Nelson, C., and Treichler, P. (eds) (1992) *Cultural Studies*, London: Routledge.

Hall, S. (1997) "Introduction," in S. Hall (ed.) *Representation: Cultural Representations and Signifying Practices*, London: Sage, 1–11.

Laity, C. (ed.) (2006) *Modernism/Modernity*, Special Issue on Modernism and Transnationalisms, 13(3) (September).

Laity, C. and Gish, N. K. (eds) (2004) *Gender, Desire, and Sexuality in T. S. Eliot*, Cambridge: Cambridge University Press.

Lefebvre, H. (1996) *The Production of Space*, trans. D. Nicholson-Smith, Oxford: Blackwell.

Lezra, J. "Theory Today," paper presented at Symposium on Theory To-Day, University of Wisconsin–Madison, February 2006.

McCabe, S. (2005) *Cinematic Modernism: Modernist Poetry and Film*, Cambridge: Cambridge University Press.

Maples, S. and Wake, P. (2006) *The Routledge Companion to Critical Theory*, London: Routledge.

Martin, W. "In Theory's Wake," (2006) *Comparative Literature* 58(3) (Summer): 241–55.

Miller, N. K. (1986) "Arachnologies: The Woman, the Text, and the Critic," in N. K. Miller (ed.) *The Poetics of Gender*, New York: Columbia University Press, 270–95.

Nfah-Abbenyi, J. M. (1997) *Gender in African Women's Writing: Identity, Sexuality, and Difference*, Bloomington: Indiana University Press.

Rosner, V. (2005) *Modernism and the Architecture of Private Life*, New York: Columbia University Press.

Roustang, F. (1982) *Dire Mastery: Discipleship from Freud to Lacan*, trans. N. Lukacher, Baltimore: Johns Hopkins University Press.

Said, E. W. (1978) *Orientalism*, New York: Vintage.

—— (1983) "Traveling Theory," in *The World, the Text, and the Critic*, Cambridge: Harvard University Press, 226–47.

—— (1994) "Traveling Theory Reconsidered," in *Reflections on Exile and Other Essays* (2002), Cambridge: Harvard University Press, 436–52.

Stocking, G. W. Jr (1982) *Race, Culture, and Evolution: Essays in the History of Anthropology*, revised edn, Chicago: University of Chicago Press.

Tyson, L. (2006) *Critical Theory Today*, second edn, London: Routledge.

Wollaeger, M. (2001) "Woolf, Picture Postcards, and the Elision of Race: Colonizing Women in *The Voyage Out*," *Modernism/Modernity* 8(1) (January): 43–75.

Afterword

Fredric Jameson

This confrontation of two historical phenomena—modernism and theory—astonishingly revives both: positioned after the end of modernism, it also reflects the rumors about the death of theory, rumors fueled by Lyotard's prophecy about the "end of grand narratives," as well as by the seeming disappearance of the grand theory of Marxism, along with a professionalization of the disciplines that has led cultural studies, film studies, literary studies themselves back into more respectably empirical research (along with the flight of the historians from "philosophies of history" and the regression of the philosophers into their archival sub-fields like epistemology and ethics).

Yet it would seem to be enough to pronounce the obituary on both modernism and theory alike for both to rise up from their alleged resting places and to regain a vitality that claims our interest. How can this be so, particularly when one of these phenomena—modernism—is certainly over in any historical sense, its monuments receding into the past (I do not think the same is true of theory, but like everything else it has its life in history)?

The project here was, as I understand it, that "blasting open of the continuum of history" evoked by Benjamin for a politics that gave new life to those discontinuous moments of the past with which it had elective affinities: the age of Robespierre revived by Lenin. This was always a meeting place between two historical situations, however distant from each other in the "homogeneous time" of calendars and chronologies. Nor was it only the present that gave new life to the past: as witness Marx's equally famous remarks about revolutionary nostalgia: "Luther donning the mask of the Apostle Paul." The past thus gives life to the present as well, nor is this a mutual enlivenment which only characterizes revolution as such. It derives, I think, from the fact that the historical affinities have to do, not so much with the actors themselves (Robespierre and Lenin, Luther and the Apostle Paul), nor with the movements, or even with their success or failure. The affinities are between the historical situations themselves, provided you grasp situation as a way in which the heterogeneous elements of a "context" are unified into a dilemma or a contradiction, a problem or a question, to which an answer or solution is imperiously demanded. The military analogy is the best one: the commander, looking out over an uneven landscape—marshland, a few hills, a few roads, bad weather—suddenly, in a practiced *coup d'oeil*, pulls it together in a strategic configuration, in which he sees either his own or the enemy's chances. The was indeed Proust's notion of artistic innovation as such, in which the *coup d'oeil* of the artist grasps the aesthetic situation confronting him *as a situation* and suddenly sees what is to be done, grasps the nature of the intervention he is called on to make.

This is then the deeper meaning of Benjamin's figure: the present revives the urgency of the historical situation, until then slumbering neglected in the history manuals, and the past allows the protagonists in the present to grasp their own moment in terms of a situation in which they are able to intervene. And this is why it does Rorty no service to consult his feeble sermon on cultural patriotism in order to extract so stereotypical a misunderstanding of historical interpretation as this: "viewing [the text] as the product of a mechanism of cultural production" (Rorty 1996: 13). On the contrary, it is a reinvention of the historical situation alone that allows us to grasp the text as a vibrant historical act, and not as a document in the archives. And this is why even those texts which seemed to have become documents in a now distant past, like the one-time masterpieces of the modern, suddenly come alive as living acts and forms of praxis—aesthetic, social, political, psychoanalytic, even ontological—which imperiously solicit our attention. (It is also why Neil Levi thinks I am at least in part still a modernist.)

The confrontations here are of a very different type than one might have staged with an older literary theory, which was essentially method-oriented, and which saw at least in certain privileged texts the occasion for a demonstration and for a confirmation of certain aesthetic ideas and values. For now and today the participants are able to follow Deleuze's great principle that both art and philosophy think, only they think in different languages, the one with concepts, the other with its own specific materials. The philosopher produces a new concept, while the painter produces a new color, or if you prefer a new brushstroke, a new layer of oil paint. But the work of both is a work with categories, is a form of thinking and of experimentation with new thinking—a principle which obliges us to revise the very notion of comparison as such.

It can no longer for one thing consist in enumerating similarities and analogies, or even parallels. It is, to be sure, very useful indeed to find that Deleuze's concept of the "body without organs" replays Artaud; or that the inner conflicts of the surrealists both repeat Kant and anticipate contemporary theoretical debates. The very retreat from theory itself is according to Stephen Ross yet one more spiral in the persistent (theoretical) critique of critiques that have themselves become hegemonic: the figure is reminiscent of Adorno and Horkheimer's vision of the widening gyres of Enlightenment positivism (in *Dialectic of Enlightenment*).

The authors have no trouble demonstrating Deleuze's association of artists and philosophers: the great ebb and flow of Lawrence's vital and earthly forces (true affects these, which rebuke any one-sided view of this writer as sexist or authoritarian) is as energizing and exhilaratingly theoretical as anything in Deleuze and Guattari. Meanwhile, Virginia Woolf (who seems to be the presiding figure in this collection) is shown to be herself a subtle "philosopher" of time and temporality, closer to Husserl or Heidegger than to Bergson, and richly meriting her equally central place in Ricoeur's *Time and Narrative*. But may I take this occasion to deplore the rather provincial anglophone limits of the aesthetic references here, mostly representative of English modernism, just as most of the theoretical references turn to the continent?

The other face of the Deleuze principle would logically be, indeed, the reception of philosophers as artists. This is perhaps easiest to do with Adorno, who actually was a composer, and whose thinking (as Gelikman shows) always resisted the pure or the unmixed, whether in philosophy or in art itself (his defense of Beckett's minimalism is put in perspective by his admiration for Alban Berg's "impure" music—Adrian's last composition in *Doktor Faustus* gives us a vivid sense of these maximalist experiments). So it is that, in a way, Adorno resists pure philosophy itself, and in particular aesthetics: the partisans of the "autonomy of the aesthetic" have to be rebuked by sociology, just as the more vulgar contextualists need to be confronted by aesthetic specificity itself. Adorno's *Aesthetic Theory* is thus not really an aesthetics (you can read it as the deconstruction of all philosophical aesthetics as such, the demonstration of their impossibility): rather, it offers the view of artistic production from the inside, its "ideas" express the contradictions of the work itself, its blockages, failures, lines of flight. This is the sense in which we may consider Adorno an artist as well, rather than a philosopher.

Much the same might be said of Deleuze, whose "concepts"—the smooth and the striated, desiring machines, codes versus axiomatics—can just as easily be taken as the production of new colors—"*Luft aus anderen Planeten*," Stefan George called them—rather than new ideas. Is this to say that Deleuze is a theorist rather than a philosopher?

The distinction—called for by Shiach here, but never answered—is a fateful one, and can only be exacerbated by the appearance of Henri Lefebvre. It is a welcome appearance indeed, and marks a long-postponed engagement with this philosopher of modernity, whose celebration of possibility rebukes the long and gloomy tradition of *Kulturpessimismus* and who goes a long way towards restoring those non-English references—Baudelaire, Rimbaud—on whose absence we have already commented. Lefebvre also opens a path to cultural studies and to the admission of questions of the media, mass culture, and the public sphere, which cannot be said to impinge on the attention of canonical thinkers like Adorno and Deleuze.

On the other hand, he is clearly much more conventionally a technical philosopher than either one, despite his association with the Situationists. Modern art is for him so many exhibits in the argument. Nor can one make for him the claim of philosopher-as-artist I have advanced above for Deleuze and Adorno. Lefebvre will, however, remain a basic ally in any attempt to restore a longer historical view of modernism as a movement and as a period (even if both those terms remain contested).

But he also stands allegorically as the emissary of Space in a debate still largely dominated by Time: and thereby hangs another tale. For Lefebvre's work on modernity is driven by his virtual invention of the concept of everyday life;

and crowned in turn by his work on the urban and his philosophical theorization of space itself. Meanwhile the opposition between temporality and space has been seen as one of the great dividing lines between modern and postmodern: and it is characteristic that the theorists here still prefer to think of *Mrs Dalloway* as a book about time rather than a book about the city.

The thematics of temporality then engender the further discussions here about modernism's fetish of the new and whether it needs to be reinvented or laid to rest; about narrative as a temporal process; and finally about periodization as such, which was of course always the deeper nagging thorn—the battle between "philosophies of history" and *explication de texte*, macro- versus micro-analyses, *grands récits* or the linguistic games of the individual poems. Few are so willing to dismiss the former as Altieri, who, identifying the conventional mediation between the two levels as allegory, then proceeds to offer us some allegories of feeling in his own readings. My sense is that there is a sensitivity about periodization in English departments that is conditioned by the non-paradigmatic trajectory of English modernism (if there really is such a thing) as well as by the wholly episodic eruptions of the modern in American literature (until it imports modernist theory).

Yet we must insist on a fundamental and structural gap between the macro-concepts of any periodizing history (or philosophy of history) and the detailed field work on any individual text. This gap is a contradiction: it cannot be "solved" or "resolved" by any conceptual synthesis; it must always be starkly acknowledged and remain itself the provisional starting point for any working procedure. "Allegory" is far from being the only mediation possible here, and if it is useful at all it is because the very structure of allegory (as opposed to that of the symbol) insisted in advance on its own inadequacy and its own imminent break-down.

It also has the advantage of being in effect a postmodern concept: distinguished from traditional allegories which are based on personification, its postmodern form excludes categories of the subject. But, to be sure, postmodernity is here notable for its absence from these debates, so that the discussion of the modern—by avoiding what sets historical limits to it—always appears to return to the question of whether we can "return" to it, reinvent it, or revive it. And this is, I believe, also the secret of the other absence which has been deplored, but only in passing: namely the distinction between philosophy and theory. For the latter opposition harbors the former one: philosophy is assumed to be modern, while theory is postmodern. In that case, we have been reading our philosophers as theorists fully as much as they have been reading their modernists as postmodern writers. Deleuze is perhaps only the most scandalous example of such rewriting, defended as such with a truly postmodern shamelessness.

I have myself defended the position that our reading of the past and of past writers is not an individual contact between two people or even two historical sensibilities, but rather the momentary convergence of two distinct moments of history (or even modes of production) which pass judgment on each other in a kind of dialectical modification of Benjamin's "blasting open of the continuum of history." It seems to me perfectly justified to rewrite Virginia Woolf as a post-modernist, provided we acknowledge the objective existence in her work of themes and features which were secondary or subordinate in the modernist period and for modernist readings, and which are now reconstructed as the dominant ones. The reconstruction is a critical and an interpretive act (indeed, a historical one), but it also has its objective basis and is not a matter of caprice and private inclination (save insofar as these are also objective). Still, it would be good to keep something of the violence and the passion of Benjamin's formula: as long as the debate about modernism is vibrant, for so long also modernism itself remains alive.

Bibliography

Rorty, R. (1996) "The Inspirational Value of Great Works of Literature," *Raritan* 1: 8-17.

Index

1848 68–69

Abelard and Heloise *see* Heloise and Abelard

abject, the 53, 167

abolitionism 4, 5

aboriginal people 134

Absolute, the 146–48, 149

Adorno, Theodor Wiesengrund 2, 5, 6, 66, 113–15, 118, 121–22, 138, 142, 145, 156–75, 180, 226, 238, 242, 248–49; and Horkheimer, Max, *Dialectic of Enlightenment* 6, 171, 248

aesthetic ideology 66, 120

aestheticism 166, 207, 225, 229, 232

aesthetics 2, 9, 14, 29, 33, 52, 66, 68–69, 71–72, 76–77, 80–81, 84, 86, 101–3, 109, 116–18, 121, 123, 130, 132, 140–57, 159–68, 170–75, 187, 193, 197–99, 207, 225–27, 230–35, 242, 248–50; realist 230

Aesthetics and Politics 238

affect 19, 198, 202–3

African-American Studies 9, 239

Agamben, Giorgio 2, 19–21, 86–94, 97, 100, 103–4, 109, 113, 179, 186; *The Time That Remains* 92

Agamemnon 227

Albright, Daniel 145

alienation 69, 71, 83, 118, 175, 226

allegory 160, 197–206, 250

Althusser, Louis 10, 113, 140, 143, 150, 154, 176, 178, 241

Altieri, Charles 14, 250; *Particulars of Rapture* 207

Americana 233

Amis, Kingsley 123

amour fou 51, 57, 62, 63

anarchism 4, 193

ancien régime 4

Anderson, Perry 122, 191–92

Angelus Novus 125

Angenot, Marc 188

Ansell-Pearson, Keith 46

answerability 210–11, 215, 217

Antigone 227

anxiety 118, 120, 160, 163, 204

anxiety of influence 169; see also Bloom, Harold *The Anxiety of Influence*

Apocalypse 23, 27, 37, 236

Aquinas 173

Aragon 70, 71

archive 1, 12, 14–15, 151, 179, 183, 186–88, 190, 227

Aristotelian 166, 182

Armstrong, Tim 37

art 2, 6, 13, 19–20, 23–24, 31–36, 38, 41, 47, 61, 65–67, 71–73, 75–76, 80–82, 102, 106, 115, 118–23, 131, 137–38, 140–49, 156, 158–74, 187, 190, 193, 195, 200–203, 214, 219, 225–26, 229–35, 248–49; history of, 141; work of 142, 144–45, 161, 163–65, 167, 234

art for art's sake 231–32

Art Monthly Review 159

Artaud, Antonin 23–24, 40–46, 49, 248

artist as athlete 29, 31, 35

artwork 33, 73, 156–57, 159, 162–65, 167–68, 172–73

Attridge, Derek 209–10

authenticity 120, 127, 175, 177, 200

authoritarianism 15, 117, 121, 278

automatic writing 51, 62, 157, 169

automatism 26

avant-garde 8, 14, 15, 66, 71, 73, 77, 117, 123, 137–38, 140, 143, 146–47, 149, 151, 153, 174–75, 195, 225–26, 228–35, 238; aesthetics 230

Badinguet (Napoleon III) 192
Badiou, Alain 50, 58, 1154 119–22
Bakhtin, Mikhail 2
Baldwin, James 13
Balzac, Honoré de 107, 135
Barker, Howard 123
Barnes, Djuna 7, 238
Barthes, Roland 11, 38, 51–52, 57–58,
    84, 99–100, 104–5, 238; *Camera Lucida*
    58; *Mythologies* 84; *The Pleasure of Text*
    51, 105; *Roland Barthes by Roland Barthes*
    51
Bataille, Georges 2, 12, 19–20, 49–64, 80,
    84, 159; *Documents* 50; *informe* 51, 57;
    Summa Atheologica 53
Baudelaire, Charles 65, 67–71, 78, 80,
    82, 84, 107, 157–58, 160, 168–69, 187,
    249; *Les Fleurs du Mal* 159, 160; *Le*
    Spleen de Paris 168
Baudrillard, Jean 10
Bauhaus 190
Beardsley, Monroe C. 8
beautiful, the 20, 52, 57
Becher, Bernd 80
Becher, Hilla 80
Becket, Fiona 28, 35, 37; *D.H. Lawrence:*
    The Thinker as Poet 37
Beckett, Samuel 6, 12–13, 24, 77, 117,
    122–23, 249
Bell, Michael 37
Bellamy, Suzanne 226
Benjamin, Walter 2, 6, 19–21, 68, 78,
    80–81, 84, 86–97, 100, 102–10, 113,
    117–18, 121–22, 125–26, 171, 176,
    191, 232, 238, 242, 247–48, 250–51;
    The Arcades Project 78; *Charles Baudelaire:*
    A Lyric Poet in the Era of High Capitalism
    78
Berg, Alban 249; *Doktor Faustus*, 249
Bergson, Henri 2, 25, 37, 248
Berliner Ensemble 83, 84
Bettelheim, Bruno 45
Blanchot, Maurice 65, 76–77, 171;
    L'entretien infini 77; *The Infinite Conversation*
    77
Blavatsky, Madame 25
Bloch, Ernst 121, 149, 162, 193
Bloom, Harold 3, 8, 169; *The Anxiety of*
    Influence 3
body, the 10, 19–21, 25, 29, 38, 40–48,
    51, 57, 75, 195; the human 51;
    schizophrenic 44
Boer war 6
Bohman, James 238

Bonaparte, Napoleon 4
Borges, Jorge Luis 12
Bourdieu, Pierre 241, 243
Bourgeois Publishers 37
Braque, Georges 137
Brecht, Bertolt 65, 67, 72–73, 83–84,
    118–19, 121–23 125, 145, 193; *Der*
    kaukasische Kreidekreis 83; *Leben des Galilei*
    83; *Mutter Courage* 83
Breton, Andre 2, 7, 19–20, 49–58, 60–64,
    66, 70–71, 157; *Nadja* 50, 58, 61–63;
    La Révolution surréaliste 50–51; *Le*
    Surréalisme au service de la révolution 50; *see*
    also Surrealism
Brook Farm 4
Brown, Wendy 108
Bryden, Mary 28, 37
Brzezinski, Zbigniew 192
Bürger, Peter 174–75, 230, 233–35
Burgess, Anthony 123
Burke, Edmund 20, 21
Burke, Kenneth 109
Burroughs, William S. 24
Burrow, Trigant 37
Bush, George W. 191
Butler, Judith 10, 11, 200

Caillois, Roger 49
Calinescu, Matei 229
Camboni, Marina 243
Campbell, Tony 74
canon 1, 57, 84, 118, 201, 207, 237, 239
Cantor, Georg 119
capital, late 146–48
capitalism 4, 7, 19, 27, 66–67, 72, 75–76,
    115, 122, 129, 134–37, 139, 153, 182,
    191–92; pre-130, 134
capitalist modernity 129, 130
Carroll, Lewis 40, 42–43
Carter, Angela 123
Cather, Willa 216; *The Professor's House*
    215
Caughie, Pamela: *Virginia Woolf and*
    Postmodernism 100–101, 110
Cavell, Stanley 142
Caws, Mary Ann 71
Celtic Revival 136
Cendrars, Blaise 226
Certeau, Michel de 241
Cezanne, Paul 161
chaos 7, 32–36
Chaplin, Charlie 5, 65, 72, 83
Char, René 70, 78
Churchill, Winston 191

Chinese cultural revolution 119
Chronicle of Higher Education 99
city, the 74, 75, 250
civilisation 1, 9, 29
Cixous, Helene 10, 11, 221, 238, 241
Clark, T. J. 80, 138, 159
class 2, 10, 53, 113, 128, 131, 133, 139,
   146, 204, 223, 239
classical modernism 117–18, 123
classicism 129, 219, 221
close reading 197–98, 203, 207, 240
COBRA (COpenhagen, BRussels,
   Amsterdam) 76
Coetzee, J. M. 209
Cohen, Margaret 50
Cold War 146, 174, 240
Colebrook, Claire 66, 77
colonial 6, 216, 238, 244
commodification 201
commodity fetishism 203
communism 6, 193
composition, plane of 33, 35, 41
concepts 28, 33, 35, 40, 141, 248
Congo 6
Conrad, Joseph 6, 7, 9, 12–13, 115, 178,
   212–13; *Heart of Darkness* 215; *Lord Jim*
   115, 212, 215–16, 217; *Nostromo* 132
consciousness 5, 12, 20, 25–27, 35, 61,
   72–73, 76, 105, 109, 119, 123, 160,
   162, 199, 202
consequentialist ethics 211, 214
Constant, Benjamin 75, 83
Cooper, David 24
corporatism 5
cosmopolitanism 5, 129
cosmos 35–36
Covi, Giovanna: *Modernist Women Race
   Nation: Networking Women 1890–1950,
   Circum-Atlantic Connections* 244
Crane, Hart 201
critical race theory 238
critical theory 108, 141, 185, 237–38,
   239–44
critique 2, 3, 5–15, 23, 27, 29, 31, 40, 52,
   65–67, 69, 73, 75, 77, 82–83, 107–8,
   114, 131, 153–56, 162, 164, 168, 182,
   185, 187, 195, 239, 248, 278
Crosby, Harry: *Chariot of the Sun* 34
Cuddy-Keane, Melba 14
Cullen, Countee 201
cultural capital 173
cultural crisis 201–2
cultural criticism 197, 200–202, 207
cultural history 132

cultural life 198
cultural materialism 178–79, 183, 185
cultural patriotism 248
cultural poetics 178–79
cultural production 82, 113, 137, 147,
   185, 239, 248
cultural sphere, the 244
Cultural Studies 83–84, 241, 244, 247,
   249
cultural theory 241–44
cultural thought 217
culture 1, 8, 11, 26, 80, 82–83, 89, 102,
   108, 118, 121, 127, 131, 134, 137–40,
   143, 146, 149–50, 155, 168, 180, 197,
   199–200, 202, 222–23, 230, 232, 237,
   241–43; high 1, 9, 153, 242–43

Dada 71, 73, 76–77, 201, 231, 233, 234
Dalí, Salvador 70, 78
Dante Alighieri 135
de Certeau, Michel 20, 241
de Duve, Theirry 142, 173–75; *Pictorial
   Nominalism* 175
de Man, Paul 3, 9, 113, 140, 154, 177,
   179–81, 186–87, 191; affair 181
death 32, 43, 51, 62, 73, 76, 83, 89, 96,
   159, 206, 216
Debord, Guy 20, 66, 73, 74, 77; *Critique of
   Separation* 77; *Oeuvres cinématographiques
   completes: 1952–1978* 77
decadence 5, 67
deconstruction 10, 178, 181, 197, 221,
   249
deep ecology 222
defamiliarization 66, 72, 75, 82, 83; *see
   also* estrangement
degenerate art 233
degeneration 6, 139
DeKoven, Marianne 101
Delaunay, Sonia: *Prose on the Trans-Siberian
   Railway* 226
Deleuze, Fanny 23
Deleuze, Gilles 2, 10, 12, 19, 20, 23–50,
   54–58, 60, 62–64, 221, 238, 241, 248,
   249–50; body without organs 24, 25,
   40, 44, 248; *Dialogues* (with Claire
   Parnet) 29–31, 37; *Dialogues II* (with
   Claire Parnet) 30; *Eros et les chiens* 27,
   37; *Essays Critical and Clinical* 48; *The
   Logic of Sense* 41, 42, 46; with Felix
   Guattari *Anti-Oedipus* 37, 39, 4; *A
   Thousand Plateaus* 23, 29–31, 37; *What is
   Philosophy?* 24, 29, 31, 32, 34, 35, 37,
   41, 47

Depression, the Great 193
Derrida, Jacques 2, 10–12, 19–20, 49–50,
    53–54, 56–58, 60, 62–64, 100, 104–5
    176, 178, 221, 238, 241; *Archive Fever*
    12; *Of Grammatology* 240
Descombes, Vincent 57, 169
desire 19, 63, 105
desiring-production 42
deterritorialization 241
dialectic 24, 29, 52–53, 55, 63, 69, 76,
    82, 117–18, 127, 143–46, 153, 158,
    164, 166; negative 156, 171
dialectics 67, 71, 83, 132
Didion, Joan 135
différance 63
dirty little secret 27, 30, 37, 38, 40
disability studies 241
disciplines 32, 140, 198, 240, 242, 247
dissociation of sensibility 155
Donovan, Josephine 222
Doyle, Laura 244; with Laura Winkiel
    Geomodernism: Race, Modernism, Modernity
    244
dualist 54
Duchamp, Marcel 173–75; *The White Box*
    175
Duns Scotus 173
Dylan, Bob 232

early modern *see* Renaissance
Early Modern Studies 241
Eco, Umberto 173
eco-criticism 14
ecofeminism 220–22
ecology 89, 219, 222
economics 69
écriture féminine 221
Eder, Edith and David 37
egalitarianism 5
ego, the 27, 47, 199
Eliot, Thomas Stearns 1, 2, 7–9, 12, 128,
    132, 135, 137, 139, 146, 155, 172, 201,
    203–4, 219, 221–22, 227; *Art and
    Culture* 139; *The Waste Land* 8, 132, 203
elitism 9, 185
Elliott, Jane 99
Eluard, Paul 56, 70, 71
emergency, state of 87, 88, 95, 97
Levinas, Emmanuel 214
Empire 122, 192
empiricism 4, 29–30, 181, 200
Encore magazine 83
Encyclopaedia Universalis 42
end time 86, 87

Engels, Friedrich 192
Enlightenment, the 1, 3–13, 101, 130,
    186, 193, 198, 248; counter-, 8
environment, the 63, 219, 222
epic theater 72, 119
epistemology 9, 123, 212, 247
essentialism 208
estrangement 81, 82, 84, 122; *see also*
    defamiliarization
Esty, Jed: *A Shrinking Island* 122
ethical 1, 6, 9, 13, 37, 95, 129, 208–9,
    211–17; theory 217; turn 119
ethics 9, 14, 21, 86, 97, 114, 117, 119,
    195, 208–10, 212–13, 247;
    deontological 211; hermeneutical,
    211–12, 215; narrational 210, 212,
    215, 217; oppositional 211; of truths
    119; utilitarian 211
ethnic studies 241
ethnicity 13, 240, 241
Euro-centrism 7
event, the 72, 113–16, 119–22, 125, 127,
    195; fidelity to 114, 119–22, 125
everyday life 77, 190, 229, 242–43, 249
everyday, the 19–20, 65–77, 80–84, 109,
    123, 174, 195, 232–33, 241
exception, state of 20, 21, 88, 93, 98
exceptionality 91–92, 97
existentialism 2, 80
Expressionism 118

Fabian 193
Fanon, Frantz 10
fascism 7, 27, 134, 180–81, 191, 193
fascist 9, 38, 84
Faulkner, William 13
Faurisson, Robert 186
Felski, Rita 20, 66, 77, 242–43
femininity 86
feminism 2, 4, 9–10, 38, 81, 99–102,
    107–9, 113, 176–77, 193, 222, 227,
    238–39, 242, 244
feminist theory 107
film studies 247
Filreis, Alan 188
Fineman, Joel 184
Flaubert, Gustave 65, 107, 158, 163,
    165–66; *Madame Bovary* 165–66, 168
Ford, Ford Madox (Hueffer) 7, 9
Ford, Henry 5
form 2, 9, 13–14, 33, 34, 36, 42, 51, 61,
    66–67, 69, 70, 72, 76, 82–84, 91, 104,
    107, 115, 121, 131, 138, 140–43, 147,
    163–66, 168–69, 173–74, 201, 209, 212

formal innovation 158, 172
formalism 2, 81, 137–38, 140, 148, 153, 158, 167, 169, 171, 174, 203, 210, 226
Forster, E. M. 7, 9, 13, 211–12; *Howards End* 211–12; *A Passage to India* 212, 217
Foster, Hal 50
Foucault, Michel 2, 10, 12, 38, 50, 58, 176, 179, 184, 186, 188, 238, 241
Frankin, André 73
Frankfurt School 100, 237–40
Frankfurter Zeitung 81
Freewoman, The 220
French Communist Party 69
French Revolution 4, 5, 119
Freud, Sigmund 24, 25, 26, 37, 40, 47, 50, 57, 81, 82, 176, 221–22; *Civilization and its Discontents* 222
Fried, Michael 159
Friedman, Alan Warren 210
Friedman, Susan Stanford 14, 136, 237
Friedman, Thomas 192
Frost, Robert 201
Frow, John 67
Fukuyama, Francis 191–92
Futurism 117–18, 120–21, 231, 233

Galileo Galilei 119
Gardiner, Michael 66, 77
Garnett, Edward 193
Geertz, Clifford 181, 240
Gelas, B. and H. Micolet: *Deleuze et les écrivains* 36
Gelikman, Oleg 115, 156, 171–72, 174–75, 249
gender 1, 2, 7, 10, 131, 191, 219–20, 222, 242, 244
General Strike 193
Genette, Gerard: *Narrative Discourse* 105
geopolitics 128
George, Stefan 249
Gide, Andre 12
Giedion, Sigfried 80–81
gift, the 129, 132, 136
Gikandi, Simon 244
Gindin, James 210
Ginsberg, Allen 38
Ginzburg, Carlo 81
global warming 64, 219
globalization 1, 12, 98, 178, 195, 240–41
God 46, 53, 93, 199
Godard, Jean-Luc 122
Goldman, Jane 14; *The Feminist Aesthetics of Virginia Woolf: Modernism, Post-Impressionism and the Politics of the Visual* 226

government 69, 134
Greenberg, Clement 117, 137–40, 143–44, 146–49, 153–54, 169, 225, 230
Greenblatt, Stephen 178–79, 181, 184
Grosz, George 230, 233
Guattari, Felix 10, 19–20, 23–32, 34–38, 40–43, 45–47, 50, 54–56, 58, 221, 238, 241, 248; with Gilles Deleuze *A Thousand Plateaus* 23, 29–31, 37; *What is Philosophy?* 24, 29, 31, 32, 34, 35, 37, 41, 47
Guilluame, Gustave 93
Guterman, Norbert 67

H. D. (Hilda Doolittle) 129, 201, 219–21, 238
Hale, Dorothy 210; *What Women Want: An Interpretation of the Feminist Movement* 109
Hall, Stuart 243
Hallward, Peter 58
Hamlet 127, 210
Hardy, Thomas 38
Harlem Renaissance 239
Harold Rosenberg 172
Harpham, Geoffrey 208
Harrison, Jane: *Prologomena to a Study of Greek Religion* 221
Haydn, Franz Joseph 119
Hayles, N. Katherine 10
Heartfield, John 230
Hegel, Georg Wilhelm Friedrich 2, 5, 15, 50, 52–55, 57, 76, 93, 143–44, 278; Hegelian dialectics 70; *Phenomenology of Spirit* 5
Heidegger, Martin 2, 37, 50, 57, 77, 176, 179–80, 202–3, 248
Heisenberg, Werner 11
Heller, Agnes 77
Heloise and Abelard 119
Hemingway, Ernest 221
Heracleitos 25
hermeneutics 42, 49, 142, 161, 177, 179, 186, 213
Hess, Rémi 67, 73
hetero-normativity 7, 9
hierarchy 5, 8, 26, 141, 228
Highmore, Ben 20, 66, 77–78
Hill, Joe 231–32; *The Little Red Songbook* 231
historical materialism 109
historical turn 99, 188, 225–28, 230, 234
historicism 1, 15, 104, 107–8, 127, 143, 163, 167, 171, 176–79, 181, 183, 185, 227, 241

history 3, 4, 9, 20–21, 34, 51, 57, 65,
    67–71, 74, 87–88, 91–92, 97, 99–105,
    107–9, 114, 117, 121–22, 125, 128–30,
    134, 142, 149, 155, 159, 163, 166–68,
    174, 177–78, 182, 186–87, 190–91,
    193, 226, 229–30, 234, 247, 250
history of ideas 184
Hobsbawm, Eric 124, 191; *The Age of
    Extremes: The Short Twentieth Century* 191
Hölderlin, Friedrich 24
Holocaust 6, 185–86
homophobia 9
homosexuals 6, 11
hooks, bell 10
Horkheimer, Max 5, 6, 14, 142, 248; and
    Adorno, T. W., *Dialectic of Enlightenment*
    6, 171, 248
Horwitz, Howard 185
Howard, Jean E. 180
Howe, Irving 199–201; *Literary Modernism*
    199
Hughes, Langston 13, 201
Hugnet, Georges 78
Hulme, T. E. 219
human rights 208
humanism 4, 10–11, 130
Huntington, Samuel 192
Hurston, Zora Neale *Their Eyes Were
    Watching God*, 219
Husserl, Edmund 2, 50, 57, 176, 248
Huyssen, Andreas 14–15, 147, 228, 233;
    After the Great Divide, 15
Hyppolite, Jean 50

id, the, 47
idealism, 26, 29, 31, 51, 54, 66, 57, 71,
    144, 147, 158, 164–65, 167, 192
identity, 8
identity politics, 11
ideology, 2, 5, 7–11, 66, 75–76, 106, 115,
    120, 123, 125, 130–32, 135, 141, 143,
    146, 148, 154, 157, 161–62, 165, 168,
    192–93, 232, 242
ideology critique, 10, 177, 180
Imagism, 181, 220
imitation, 138, 140–41
immanence, 35, 41, 55–56, 58, 162, 178,
    184, 186; plane of 19, 21, 33, 35, 41,
    56
imperialism, 1, 4, 5, 7, 9, 115, 122, 129–30,
    134, 136, 139, 146, 193, 222, 237
impersonality, 8, 128, 204
Impressionism, 80–81; Impressionists,
    159, 161

incest, 25, 27
Independent Group, 83, 84
indigenous, 11, 122
individual, the, 62, 71, 122
individualism, 5, 27, 28, 123, 222
industrialization, 4, 7, 226
Institute for Social Research, 238
interhistoricizing, 100, 107, 109
Internationale Situationniste, 73, 74
Ionesco, Eugene, 77
Ireland, 130
Irigaray, Luce, 10, 11, 221, 238
Ishiguro, Kazuo, 123

James, Henry 9, 12, 211; *The Ambassadors*
    214
James, William 2, 25, 37
Jameson, Fredric 3, 12, 14, 41, 43–44,
    104, 106, 109–10, 113–15, 117–28,
    130–35, 140–41, 146–48, 154, 178,
    179, 182–85, 200, 207; *Archaeologies of
    the Future* 130; *Brecht and Method* 118; *The
    Political Unconscious* 110, 178, 183–84; *A
    Singular Modernity* 117–18, 125–26, 179
Jameson, Storm 193; *Company Parade* 194;
    Love in Winter 194; *Mirror in Darkness*
    194; *None Turn Back* 194
Jauss, Hans Robert 187
jazz 180
Jews 6
John of Patmos 24, 28, 37
Johnson, B. S. 123
Johnson, James Weldon 13
Joyce, James 1, 9, 12–13, 15, 30, 37, 65,
    72, 118–20, 122, 129, 132, 135, 172,
    214, 219–21, 227, 238; *Finnegans Wake*
    219; *A Portrait of the Artist as a Young Man*
    214; *Ulysses* 37, 65, 120, 172, 221
Jungian 25, 37
justice 8, 21, 90, 131; divine 90

Kafka, Franz 12, 23–24, 48, 122
Kandinsky, Vasily 145, 163
Kant, Immanuel 2, 20, 21, 52, 56, 58, 60,
    61, 62, 143, 154, 248; *Critique of
    Judgment* 60
Kerouac, Jack 38
Kierkegaard, Soren 2
Kinkead-Weeks, M. 37
Kitsch 137–38, 140, 146–47, 149–51, 153,
    168, 195
Klee, Paul 125
Kluge, Alexander 122
Knapp, Stephen 184

Kracauer, Sigfried 82
Kraus, Karl 232–33
Krauss, Rosalind 50, 175
Kristeva, Julia 10–12, 221–22, 238

Lacoue-Labarthe, Phillipe 144
L'Ouverture, Toussaint 4
La Nouvelle Revue Française 77
Labour government 193
Lacan, Jacques 2, 10–12, 15, 44, 176, 204, 238–39
Lacoue-Labarthe, Philippe 144, 154, 170
Laing, R. D. 24
Laity, Cassandra 244
Lamartine, Alphonse de 61
Latour, Bruno 108, 110; *We Have Never Been Modern* 110
Lautréamont, Comte de (Isidore Lucien Ducasse) 68
law, the 88, 92–93
Lawrence, David Herbert 1, 2, 7, 9, 12–13, 19–20, 23–32, 34–38, 40–41, 47, 220, 222, 248; *Fantasia of the Unconscious* 25, 35, 37, 40, 47; *Phoenix* 26, 37, 40; *Aaron's Rod* 29, 37, 38, 40; *Psychoanalysis and the Unconscious* 25, 40; *Studies in Classic American Literature* 23, 29, 30, 31, 37; *The Man who Died* 38; *The Plumed Serpent* 40, 222; *Women in Love* 37
Le Corbusier (Charles-Édouard Jeanneret-Gris) 145
Leavis, F. R. 7, 210, 217
Lecercle, Jean-Jacques 37
Lefebvre, Henri 12, 19–20, 65–73, 75–78, 82–84, 241, 249; *Introduction to Modernity* 65, 68, 77, 83; *Critique of Everyday Life Volume III*, 66, 77; *Everyday Life in the Modern World* 65, 67; *The Critique of Everyday Life Volume II* 77; *The Critique of Everyday Life* 65, 70; *Rhythmanalysis: Space, Time, and Everyday Life*, 66
Left, the 131–32, 134, 191
LeGuin, Ursula 135
Leiris, Michel 49
Lenin, V. I. 247
Leninism 121, 140, 150, 191
Les Champs magnétiques 157
Lessing, Gottfried 145
Levi, Neil 113, 117, 127, 248
Levinas, Emanuel 214
Lévi-Strauss, Claude 184
Lewis, Wyndham 7, 12, 117, 127, 178, 219–21; *Tarr*, 132, 229

Lezra, Jacques 240, 241
liberal 7, 10, 75, 77, 101, 121, 127, 129–30, 134, 222
Lindner,Richard: *Boy with Machine* 46
line of flight 23, 29, 30, 31, 249
linguistic turn 99, 101, 105
literary, the 1, 2, 28, 29, 42, 68, 117, 144, 237, 239
literary studies 176, 180–81, 183, 187, 197, 225, 239, 241–42, 247
literature 1, 19–21, 23–24, 29–31, 38, 40, 47, 67–68, 70, 80–82, 89, 100, 102, 104, 107, 119–20, 135, 146, 166, 172, 187, 190, 199–200, 209, 217, 229, 234
Littlewood, Joan 83
Liu, Alan 184
Low, Barbara 37
Lowell, Amy 220
Lowry, Malcolm 38
Loy, Mina 108
Lukács, Georg 10, 140
Luther, Martin, 94, 247
Lyon, Janet 4
Lyotard, Jean-Francois 37, 50, 52, 58, 113, 176, 185, 247; *Le Différend* 185; *The Postmodern Condition* 52

MacKay, Claude 13
make it new 5, 115, 127, 130, 156, 231
Mallarmé, Stephane 24, 68, 159–61, 169
Malraux Andre, 159
Manet, Eduardo 80, 84, 158–61, 169; *Déjeuner sur l'herbe* 159; *Olympia* 159
manifesto 1, 4, 7, 50, 117, 225, 231–32
Mannheim, Karl 176
Mao, Douglas 1, 136
Marcus Aurelius 81
Marcus, Jane 177
Marcuse, Herbert 76, 162
margins 1, 57, 80
Marinetti, F. T. 6–7, 29, 117, 231
Marker, Chris 122
Martin, Wallace 240
Marx, Karl 5, 57, 69, 70, 139–41, 147–50, 154, 183, 192, 247
Marxism 2, 4, 7, 10, 71, 76, 113, 128, 130–31, 140, 143, 150, 163, 178–79, 184, 239, 247
Masoch, Leopold von Sacher-42
mass culture 7, 147, 153, 228–29, 243, 249
material, the 33, 53, 62, 63, 169
material culture 228, 243
materialism 197

materialist dialectic 143, 150
Mauron, Charles 37
May, Todd 58
McNichol, Stella 86
Melville, Herman 24, 27, 29, 31; *Oomoo*
　31; *Moby Dick 31; Typee* 31
messianic time *see* time, messianic
messianism 19, 21, 87, 89–90, 91–93,
　96–97, 103
Metaphysical Poets 155
Michaels, Walter Benn 184
Miller, Henry 24, 38, 200–202
Miller, J. Hillis 198–201; *Poets of Reality*
　198
mimesis 138–40, 142, 144–45, 147, 163,
　165, 167, 171, 186
mind 19–21, 25–26, 46, 51, 60–61, 68,
　71, 101, 124, 174, 199, 202, 221
misprision 3, 4, 8, 11
modern art 158–59, 161, 230, 249
modern culture 199, 203
modern poetry 203, 206
modern, the 3, 6, 7, 26–28, 40, 60, 65–69,
　71, 76, 80–81, 102, 107, 118, 128, 132,
　134, 149, 156–57, 159–60, 162, 175,
　180, 185, 225, 243, 248, 250
modernism 1–3, 5–9, 11–15, 19–21, 30,
　43, 49, 67–68, 80–84, 86, 93, 97, 100,
　102–4, 107–8, 113–23, 126–35, 137,
　140–42, 143–51, 153–63, 166–69,
　172–74, 176, 178–83, 188–90, 190–93,
　197, 199–201, 205, 209–12, 219–22,
　225–26, 228–31, 234–35, 237–39,
　243–44, 247, 249–51; high 2, 12, 117,
　118, 174, 180, 186–87, 193, 227, 238,
　243; ideology of 8, 117, 122; late 8,
　117, 120, 123, 135, 146, 147
Modernism/Modernity 190, 244
modernisms 1, 12, 114, 127–28, 132,
　135, 190, 243–44
modernist 6, 8–10, 13–14, 23, 26, 28–29,
　37, 41, 43, 66, 80–83, 86, 100–102,
　107, 113–14, 117–25, 127–28, 130,
　133, 135–36, 139–40, 142, 145–47,
　150, 153–54, 156–59, 161–63, 165–68,
　171–72, 174, 180, 185–88, 198–203,
　207, 209–11, 217, 219–22, 225–26,
　229–30, 232, 238, 248, 251; aesthetics
　66, 226, 228–29, 235; art 138, 140,
　147; 154, 157, 162–63, 168, 175;
　poetry 139, 198, 200; theory 250
modernist studies 1, 3, 4, 12, 14–15, 114,
　142, 176–79, 182–83, 185, 187–88,
　190–91, 193, 195, 197, 225, 229,

237–39, 241–44; *see also* new
　modernisms *and* new modernist studies
Modernist Studies Association 190, 243
modernities 114, 134, 182, 243–44
modernity 1–3, 5–7, 9, 12, 52, 80, 82, 86,
　93, 100, 105, 107, 110, 113–14, 117–18,
　120, 122, 130, 140, 142–44, 149, 156,
　160–61, 176, 179–80, 182–83, 185–87,
　190, 199, 202, 219, 225–26, 228–29,
　238, 243, 249
modernity, critique of 6, 7
modernization 122, 148
Moi, Toril 99, 101; *Sexual/Textual Politics*
　101
Monaco, Beatrice 37
monism, 54, 97
Monroe, Harriet 220
montage 81, 122, 234
Moore, Marianne 201, 220
Morhange, Pierre 67
Mosley, Nicholas 123–26; *Imago Bird* 124;
　Judith 10, 124; *Catastrophe Practice* 123–25;
　Hopeful Monsters 123–25; *Serpent* 124,
　126
multiculturalism 131, 239
myth 5, 11, 90, 92, 129, 157, 221

Nabokov, Vladimir 119, 123
Nancy, Jean-Luc 144, 148, 154, 170
Napoleon III *see* Badinguet
narcissism 30
narrative 3, 5, 6, 8, 11–13, 81, 100–101,
　103, 105, 108, 114, 125, 128–30, 166,
　176, 187, 211, 250
narrative theory 105
nation 13, 241, 244
nationalism 5, 30, 193
natural, the 64
natural history 165, 222–23
nature 5, 60–62, 110, 115, 165–67, 171,
　175, 206, 219–23
Nazi 6, 88, 97, 179, 180, 193, 233
Nazism 15, 191, 278
negative theology 53
negativity 71, 132, 148, 151, 169, 200
Nelson, Cary 207
neo-classicism 171
neo-conservative 191
neurosis 30, 38
new, the 4, 43, 67, 82, 86, 99–100,
　113–16, 121, 129, 149, 154, 156–62,
　169, 171–74, 196, 226, 234, 250; cult
　of 172
New Babylon 75

New Criticism 2, 7, 185
New Historicism 2, 14, 176–77, 179, 183–84, 188, 190, 241
New Left Review 191–92
new modernisms 2, 12, 15, 142, 183, 185
new modernist studies 1, 2, 107, 181, 192, 237, 239–41, 243; *see also* modernist studies
New Negro 244
New Orleans Review 178
New Woman 107, 244
Newton, Adam Zachary 209
Nietzsche, Friedrich 2, 23, 25, 28, 37, 38, 44, 53, 57, 163, 169, 221
Nieuwenhuys, Constant 67, 72
nihilism 198–203, 206
Nin, Anais 38
Nizan, Paul 67
nominalism 113–16, 162, 172–75, 184–85
North, Michael 15, 188
Norton Anthology of Theory and Criticism 11
nouveau roman 77
Nussbaum, Martha 209

occult 25–26, 36, 71, 165
Odyssey, the 217
oedipal 27
Oedipus 23–25, 27–29, 38, 50
Oedipus complex 24, 25, 28
ontology 123, 202
Osborne, Peter 149
Oster, Daniel 51
other, the 209, 214
otherness 32, 35, 130, 167, 200, 202

Paolozzi, Eduardo 80
Parnet, Claire 23, 29, 30
Paul, Saint 23, 37, 93–94, 97, 247; Pauline Christianity 120
Paulhan, Jean 49
people of colour 1, 11
periodization 3, 113–16, 118, 120–21, 125–28, 132, 149, 180, 182–83, 185, 187, 250
perversion 26, 38, 81, 120
pharmakon 63
phenomenology 2, 77, 80, 202
philosophy 1, 10, 19–21, 23–25, 30, 32–33, 35–38, 40–41, 52, 62–63, 65, 69, 80, 89, 113, 115–16, 118, 140–42, 144–45, 154–55, 163, 183, 188, 195, 199–200, 202, 248–50; European 198
Picabia, Francis 80
Picasso, Pablo 119, 221

Piccone, Paul 148
Plato 38, 76
Platonic 63, 173
Platonism 164
PMLA 99
poetry 29, 34, 53, 56, 159, 187, 219–20, 232
political correctness 11
political unconscious 128, 130, 132
political, the 21, 66–67, 69, 71, 84
politics 9, 10, 69, 89, 95, 101, 108, 119, 127–28, 130–31, 134, 155, 227, 229, 232, 240, 247
Politzer, Georges 67
Pollock, Griselda 108
popular culture 241, 243
Porter, Carolyn 183
positivism 53, 55, 142, 163, 248; anti-179
postcolonialism 2, 9, 10, 13, 178, 182, 240–41, 243, 244
postmodernism 3, 8, 15, 19, 49, 52, 101–2, 108–9, 113–15, 117–23, 127–28, 132, 135, 147, 174, 177–78, 179–82, 185, 210, 217, 226, 228–30, 237, 250–51
postmodernity 2, 120, 182, 250
post-national 10, 240
poststructuralism 2, 49, 50, 99, 101–2, 104, 107–9, 180–81 191, 238–44
Poulet, Georges 68
Pound, Ezra 1, 6–9, 12, 115, 118, 121, 125, 129–30, 145, 149, 172, 181, 201, 219–20, 227; *Cantos*, 201
pragmatism 77
primitivisms 129
progressivism 5, 7, 21, 129–30
Proust, Marcel 23–24, 30, 38, 62, 106–7, 219–20, 248; *A la recherche du temps perdu* 219
pseudo-Longinus 20
psyche, the 87
psychoanalysis 2, 10, 19, 23–26, 29, 41, 43, 80
psychologism 115
psychology 26–27, 82, 86, 220, 222
public sphere 249

queer theory 2, 10, 239, 241
Quin, Ann 123

Rabaté, Jean-Michel 188
race 1, 10, 13, 28, 43, 129, 131, 191, 239, 241–42, 244
racism 1, 7, 9, 180

Rainey 15, 179, 181; *Ezra Pound and the Monument of Culture* 181; *Institutions of Modernism* 181
Rancière, Jacques 142, 145, 150
rationalism 96, 222
rationalist 6
rationalization 67, 76
Ray, Man 78
Raymond Williams 83
readymade 82, 173–75
Reagan, Ronald 191
Real, the 3, 10, 43, 51, 73, 109, 146
realism 9
reason 1, 4–5, 7–9, 11–12, 20, 41–42, 46, 52–53, 55–56, 60–62, 64, 165, 212
reference, plane of 33, 41
Reich, Wilhelm 24
relativism 11, 185
religion 7, 148
Renaissance, the 2, 161, 173, 276, 180–81, 188, 229
representational ethics 211, 213, 215
Representations 176
repression 25, 47, 131, 186
revolt 63
revolution 4, 5, 63, 125, 150, 233, 247
rhythmanalysis 75, 76
Richardson, Dorothy 7, 193
Ricoeur, Paul: *Time and Narrative* 249
Rimbaud, Arthur 24, 65, 66, 68, 249
Robbe-Grillet, Alain 77
Robespierre, Maximilien 247
Romanticism 9, 61, 76, 120, 158, 167, 170, 186–87, 199, 219, 221
Romantics 135
Rorty, Richard 121–22, 248; *Achieving Our Country* 121
Rosenberg, Beth Carole 102
Rosner, Victoria: *Modernism and the Architecture of Private Life* 243
Ross, Stephen 99, 237, 248
Roth, Philip 193
Roustang, Francois 239

sacred, the 62, 69
Sadler, Simon 73
Said, Edward 12, 239
Saint-Simon, Henri de 229
Sarker, Sonita 244
Sartre, Jean-Paul 2
Saussurean 178
Schelling, Friedrich 61
Scheunemann, Dietrich 230, 234
Schiller, Friedrich 66

schizoanalysis 24, 27–28, 38
schizophrenia 41–48, 50; *see also* body, schizophrenic
Schmitt, Carl *Political Theology* 20, 88
Schoenberg, Arnold 119–21, 145, 163
Scholastics, the 173
Schopenhauer, Arthur 2
Schwitters, Kurt 226
science 1, 19, 24, 32–33, 35–36, 38, 40–41, 75, 119, 133, 143, 223, 241
Scott, Charles E. 208–9; *The Question of Ethics: Nietzsche, Foucault and Heidegger* 208
Scudéry, Mademoiselle de: *La Carte de Tendre* 74; *Clélie* 74
Sedgwick, Eve Kosofsky 11
Self, Will 123
self, the 173
self-consciousness 118, 123–25, 138, 179, 181, 184
semiotic 10, 221–22
Semitism, anti-9, 177
serialism 119
sex 1, 2, 7, 10, 19, 23–28, 38, 43, 135, 219, 221, 228, 242
sexism 7, 9
sexuality 10, 23–28, 53, 81, 191, 228
Sherirngham, Michael: *Everyday Life: Theories and Practices from Surrealism to the Present* 78
Sherry, Vincent 95
Shiach, Morag 249
Shields, Rob 71
Shklovsky, Viktor 20, 82
Sidney, Sir Philip: *Defence of Poesy* 185
Simmel, Georg 81
simultanism 226
Situationist International 66–67, 72–77, 83, 249
slavery 1, 4
Smith, Barbara Herrnstein 182
snobbery 9
social, the 4, 62, 64, 71, 75, 77, 162
social realism 202
social theory 242
social totality 151
socialism 7, 134, 138–39, 146–47, 193, 229
Socrates 38
Solidarity 231
Soupault, Philippe 56, 157
sovereign 20, 71, 88–89, 91–92, 94, 97
sovereignty 1, 13, 89, 92, 95, 103, 134, 174

space 249
Spender, Stephen 172, 174
Spinoza, Baruch de 23–24, 30, 40
spiritual, the 143, 164, 168
spiritualism 1, 5
Spivak, Gayatri Chakravorty 240
Stein, Gertrude 7, 108, 120, 122, 201, 226
Sterne, Lawrence 82; *Tristram Shandy* 82, 114
Stevens, Wallace 2, 178, 199, 201
Strachey, Lytton 220
Stravinsky, Igor 120
stream of consciousness 37, 124, 220
structuralism 2, 10, 30, 60, 178
style 9, 24, 27, 101, 118–19, 123, 127, 148, 159, 163, 227, 229, 234
style indirect libre 166
subject, the 9, 32, 47, 101, 118–19, 121–22, 124, 144, 158, 162, 173, 175, 185, 204–5, 210, 221, 250
subjectivism 199
subjectivity 2, 10, 56, 122, 127, 135, 158, 188, 204
sublime, the 19–21, 34, 52, 56–57, 60–64, 114, 148, 195; sublime, dynamic 20, 56; mathematical 20, 56
suffragist 226
supernatural, the 69
superstition 1, 7
Surrealism 20, 49–50, 52–54, 56–58, 60, 65–67, 70–71, 73, 76–78, 83, 157, 195; Second Manifesto of Surrealism 50; *see also* Breton, Andre
sustainability 64, 222
Sword, Helen: *Ghostwriting Modernism* 188
symbolism 26, 31, 200

Tanguy, Yves 78
Taylor, Frederick Winslow 5
technique 2, 3, 9, 26, 66, 81, 138, 141, 234
Tel Quel 58, 155; *Théorie d'ensemble* 155
temporality 20, 100, 105, 122, 140, 149, 153, 186, 248, 250
Ténot, Eugène: *Paris en décembre 1851, Etude historique sur le coup d'état* 192
textuality 100, 105, 227–28, 235
Thatcher, Margaret 191
Theatre of Catastrophe 123
Theatre Workshop 83
theology 53, 89, 117, 199
theory 1–3, 6, 8–15, 19, 21, 28, 46, 49–50, 52, 61, 73, 80–81, 86, 97,

99–104, 110, 113–17, 121, 127, 132, 135, 140–44, 147–50, 153–56, 161–62, 164, 166, 168–69, 175–88, 190–91, 195, 202, 209, 217, 221–23, 225, 227–28, 230, 234, 237–41, 245–49, 250; anti-126, 181; high 99, 193, 238–39
time 13, 19–21, 75, 89, 92–96, 100, 103–8, 149–50, 195, 248–50; of art 160; historical 125; interceptional 97–98, 103, 106, 113; messianic 20, 21, 92–93, 97, 103, 114
timeliness 100, 113–17, 125, 127–28
Tin Pan Alley 137, 139, 146
Tolstoy, Leo 81, 82
Toomer, Jean 13
Torgovnick, Mariana 221–22
totality 56–57, 61, 72, 81, 132, 135, 140–41, 144, 148, 161–62, 164, 179, 184, 234
totalization 241
tradition, the 6, 82, 153, 157–59, 161–62
transcendence 53, 55–56, 58, 66, 69, 70–71
transculturalism 241
transculturation 240–41
transnationalism 1, 241, 243–44
trauma studies 193
Trebitsch, Michel 73
Trilling, Lionel 199
truth 10, 31–32, 63, 89, 92–93, 115, 123, 162–63, 172, 177, 179–80, 186, 199, 210, 213, 215
Tzara, Tristan 70–71, 231

unconscious 23, 25–28, 42–43, 47, 53, 81, 217
uneven development 67, 133–34, 141, 155
untimeliness 100, 108, 113
urbanism 74, 75, 76
utopia 4–6, 21, 29, 63, 66–67, 69, 71, 75, 114, 118, 125, 127–28, 130–36, 190, 193, 200
utopianism 69, 125, 130, 200

Valéry, Paul 68, 158, 169
Veeser, H. Aram 177; *The New Historicism* 176, 179, 183–84
Victorian studies 190
Victorianism 210
Victorians 135
violence 21, 52, 91, 95, 127, 130, 198, 211, 214–15, 231, 233, 251; divine 21, 90–92, 96, 114; mythic 21, 90–91

vitalism 19, 20, 26
vorticism 117, 219

Wagner, Richard 162, 172
Walden 4
Walkowitz, Rebecca 1
Warburg, Aby 159
Weber, Max 5, 176
Weismann, August 46
Wells, H. G. 132
West, the 223, 244
White, Hayden 177
Whitman, Walt: *Leaves of Grass*, 228
Williams, William Carlos 205–6;
   "Dedication for a Plot of Ground"
   Emily, 205–7; *Spring and All* 201, 206
Wimsatt, W. K. 8
Winkiel, Laura with Laura Doyle:
   Geomodernism: Race, Modernism, Modernity
   244
Wittgenstein, Ludwig 2, 110, 176, 203
Wolfson, Louis 45; *Le schizo et les langues* 48
Wollaeger, Mark 243
women 1, 11, 26, 28, 38, 40, 107, 134,
   177, 191, 221, 223, 227, 239, 244
women writers 86, 107
women's studies 241

Woolf, Virginia 1, 2, 6–7, 9, 12–13,
   19–21, 65, 86–90, 92–93, 95–98,
   100–109, 113, 119, 132, 219–22,
   226–28, 238, 243, 248, 251; *Between the
   Acts* 102, 109, 222, 228; *Mrs. Dalloway*
   86, 89, 93, 95, 100, 103, 105, 108, 120,
   222, 250; *A Room of One's Own* 227; *Mrs
   Dalloway* 227–28; *Mrs. Dalloway's Party*
   87; Bradshaw, Dr. 90, 92, 95; Clarissa
   Dalloway 92, 94, 96–97, 104, 106;
   Conversion 95; Septimus Smith 89,
   90–93, 96, 222; *The Voyage Out* 227,
   243; *The Waves* 221–22, 226; *Writings of
   Virginia Woolf* 227; *The Years* 222; *To the
   Lighthouse* 222, 226
Wordsworth, William 4, 5, 61
World Trade Center 108
World War II 6, 71

Yeats, W. B. 7, 9, 13, 129–30, 186–87,
   219

Zarathustra 38
Žižek, Slavoj 9, 10, 12, 15, 49, 50, 57,
   278
Zwerdling, Alex 95